THE DISCOVERY

OF

THE SCIENCE OF MAN

THE WOMANHOOD OF GOD

THE WOMANHOOD OF GOD

Volume One

The
Discovery
of the
Science of Man

The Life of
Mary Baker Eddy
(1821-1888)

Doris Grekel

Healing
UNLIMITED

1999

The picture appearing on the front cover is of a granite pyramid marker placed at the site of Mary Baker Eddy's childhood home in Bow, New Hampshire. This marker was commissioned by the Masons (Mrs. Eddy's first husband, George Glover, was a Mason.), who recognized in Mary Baker Eddy the fulfillment of prophecy concerning God's second witness. (See Zechariah 4:11-14 and Revelation 11:3). The beautiful marker made out of a solid piece of granite—the largest ever quarried in New Hampshire—was designed as an exact replica of what was to be the capstone for the Great Pyramid in Giza. This unique symbol was dynamited by the Board of Directors of the Mother Church in the 1960's and buried in an undisclosed location.

The inscriptions on the stone are: North — from *No and Yes* 38:13; East — from Isaiah 28:16; West — (translation) The New Order of the Ages; South — from a letter by Mrs. Eddy to Rufus Baker, her cousin.

The rear cover picture of Mrs. Eddy is a portrait taken about 1883.

Cover design by David L. Keyston

And though the Lord give you the bread of adversity, and the water of affliction, yet shall not thy teachers be removed into a corner any more, but thine eyes shall see thy teachers. *Isaiah 30:20*

First Trade Edition
©1999 Doris Grekel *All rights reserved.*

Published by
Healing Unlimited (800) 962-1464
2100 Third Avenue, Suite 1901, Seattle, WA 98121
Email: heal@ChristianScience.org
http://www.ChristianScience.org

Publisher's Cataloging-in-Publication
(Provided by Quality Books, Inc.)

Grekel, Doris.
    The discovery of the science of man : the life
of Mary Baker Eddy (1821-1888) / Doris Grekel.
    p. cm. -- (The womanhood of God ; v. 1)
    Includes bibliographical references and index.
    ISBN: 1-893107-23-X

    1. Eddy, Mary Baker, 1821-1910. 2. Christian
Scientists--United States--Bibliography.   I. Title.
II. Series: Grekel, Doris. Womanhood of God ; v. 1.

BX6995.G73   289.5'092 [B]
                    QBI99-1051

Printed in the United States of America.

CONTENTS

THE DISCOVERY

PREFACE

O N the twenty-sixth of November in 1897, Mrs. Eddy wrote in a letter to Julia Field-King, "People seem to understand C.S. in the exact ratio that they know me and vice versa. It sometimes astonishes me to see the invariableness of this rule." In March of 1907 when Joseph Pulitzer of the *New York World* was spearheading an attack and a lawsuit against the Revelator to this age, she said to a student, "The papers are writing up my history; the history of my ancestry; writing lies. My history is a holy one."

For many years the author has been seeking to know Mrs. Eddy and to learn her holy history. Though she feels she has little more than begun on this vast search, it has been rewarding beyond expectations. This research has convinced her that an understanding of the trials and triumphs of Mary Baker Eddy is essential for those who "would enter by the door."

The publication of these pages is a small, partial payment toward the great debt we owe to the Discoverer of the Science of Man.

DORIS and MORRIS GREKEL

JESUS RAISING

JAIRUS DAUGHTER

The frontispiece for Science and Health for many editions beginning with the second edition in 1878.

"Damsel, I say unto thee, arise."—Mark v.41

CHRISTMAS EVE
The fourth picture in *Christ and Christmas* first published in 1893.

THE DISCOVERY
OF THE SCIENCE OF MAN

CHAPTER I

A REMARKABLE BEGINNING

In tender mercy, Spirit sped
A loyal ray
To rouse the living, wake the dead,
And point the Way—
Christ and Christmas

1817

E ARLY in the nineteenth century there was a man sent from God whose name was Henry David Thoreau. He was not that Second Coming of the Christ that Henry David Christians were expecting, but he came to bear Thoreau born witness to a life divine entirely apart from mor- July 12, 1817 tal existence. His was the voice of one crying in the wilderness saying, "Can a man feed and clothe himself gloriously, who keeps only the truth steadily before him? who calls in no evil to his aid?"

There abode in the same country (which was the New England section of the United States of America) in the nearby state of New Hampshire, a devout woman of Puritan ancestry named Abigail Ambrose Baker. Her husband, Mark Baker, was an upright man and just. The ancestors of both husband and wife were Israelites, though they knew it not. As were all the white Christian people who settled and founded New England, they were truly the lost sheep of the house of Israel.

Abigail had borne five handsome children,—Samuel, Albert, George, Abigail, and Martha,—and she was a dutiful and devoted wife and mother. But in the spring of 1821 her

1

thoughts were troubled. According to mortal law she was beyond years for child-bearing; yet, like Sarah, wife of Abraham, she was expecting a child. Could this be the child of God instead of Mark and Abigail Baker?

One morning while climbing the narrow stairs to the attic where the wool was kept for spinning, she was suddenly filled *Abigail's exaltation* with a sense of light, power, and dominion. The attic room became radiant with glory, and the devout thought of this saintly woman was reassured. But the religious training and the concepts of that day conflicted with her exaltation, so that it, too, troubled her. She confided in a neighbor, Sarah Gault, and these two women prayed together repeatedly and earnestly. Even though fearing that it might be blasphemous, Abigail could not keep from the thought that this child was holy and consecrated and set apart for wondrous achievements.

On the sixteenth day of July the days were accomplished *Birth of Mary Baker July 16, 1821* that she should be delivered, and she brought forth her sixth child, a beautiful daughter; and they called her name Mary Morse Baker.

Baby Mary was the special charge of her aged grandmother, albeit she was beloved by all the family including numerous aunts, uncles, and cousins on neighboring farmsteads. Though this sweet, adorable child was loved by all, Abigail and Mark knew that she was unlike other children, even her own brothers and sisters.

When she was tiny, still sleeping in a trundle bed in her parents' room, she would call to her father who was reading in *Second sight* the parlor: "Father, I know what you are doing. You are reading the newspaper." Mark would answer, "Hush, child, go to sleep." Then Mary would reply, "I'll read it to you." And from the trundle bed in the dark bedroom she would tell him what he was reading, although she could not pronounce the long words.

At one time the oldest boy, Samuel, severely injured his leg while chopping wood with an axe. After several days in bed, the wound refused to heal, and the family had begun to despair for the boy's life. Mark picked up little Mary, approached the bed, turned aside the covers and gently placed Mary's hand over the wound, holding it there for some little time. From that moment Sam's leg rapidly grew well, although Mary suffered with fever for several days afterward.

A somewhat similar accident occurred to her brother George Sullivan. George fell out of an apple tree onto a broken bottle, gashing his thigh deeply. A surgeon was summoned to put in some stitches. The boy was screaming with agony. The father picked up little Mary and carried her into the room backward so that she could not see the wound when he placed her hand on it,—and the pain ceased.

Why were the peculiar circumstances of Jesus' childhood not included in the gospels? Probably because they were not understood or were disbelieved, for undoubtedly his childhood was as unusual as Mary Baker's.   Mary's playmate
She would see another little Mary playing with her,—another self; and they were so happy together. Her playmate was beyond the comprehension of mortal mind. A sentence from *Miscellaneous Writings* will help the Christian Scientist to understand this circumstance: "The noblest work of God is man in the image of his Maker; the last infirmity of evil is so-called man...elbowing the concepts of his own creating."

Abigail's love for and devotion to the Scriptures was markedly manifested in the child Mary who was so impressed by the Scriptural narrative of Daniel's praying   Seven daily prayers
three times each day that she decided to pray to God seven times each day. The little tot implemented her decision by retiring to the woodshed that her devotions might be uninterrupted. What is more, she marked on the wall of the shed each time with a piece of chalk to be sure that she did not fail in fulfilling her obligation. The world has never known such a child.

Mary had a characteristic of giving to others. She would give her playthings to poor children, and sometimes even her dresses until her mother had to threaten her with punishment if she did not stop giving away her belongings.

The child Mary was called of God in a most remarkable way. In about her eighth year her name was called distinctly three times in an ascending scale, in a voice like that   Mary's calling
of her mother. Mary went to her mother very much as the child Samuel went to Eli, saying, "Here am I; for thou didst call me." And Abigail's answer was the same as

3

Eli's,—"I called thee not." This happened repeatedly over a period of many months until the mother grew anxious and the child discouraged.

Abigail pondered the Biblical account of Hannah's child, Samuel, whom she gave to the Lord. The voice that called him three times in the temple was not unlike the voice calling Mary. Eli, the priest of Israel, heard not the voice that called Samuel, but he "perceived that the Lord had called the child." In the poet's words:

Samuel's calling

> Hushed was the evening hymn,
>   The temple courts were dark,
> The lamp was burning dim,
>   Before the sacred ark
> When suddenly a Voice divine
>   Rang through the silence of the shrine.
>
> The old man, meek and mild,
>   The priest of Israel, slept;
> His watch the temple child,
>   The little Samuel kept;
> And what from Eli's sense was sealed,
>   The Lord to Hannah's son revealed.

When a visiting cousin heard the voice call, "Mary," Abigail was able to instruct her child as Eli instructed Samuel. That night she bade her daughter answer the next time she was called, "Speak, Lord, for thy servant heareth." The call came; but Mary was afraid and did not answer. Afterward she wept.

The little girl prayed to be forgiven and resolved to answer the next time. The voice did call again, and she did answer in Samuel's words, "Speak, Lord, for thy servant heareth." Many, many years later Mary disclosed to a student in her home what transpired after her response. Her body was lifted lightly from the bed to a height of about one foot, then gently returned; the unusual phenomenon being repeated three times. Little wonder that she wrote in later years, "Many peculiar circumstances and events connected with my childhood throng the chambers of memory."

Mary answers

A less remarkable occurrence involved the family dog, Ben. When the family was assembled in the sitting room, Ben was made to understand that he must always lie under the table. But he would sometimes disregard this injunction and come out to sit before the fire with the family.

Mary did not want the dog scolded. When she saw that he was in for trouble because of his presence in the room, she would address him mentally but silently, "Ben, go under the table and lie down," and immed- iately the dog would rise and walk under the table and lie down. She learned that without speaking a word aloud, the dog would obey her mental instructions. This particular occurrence was repeated many times during her childhood.

The family dog, Ben

How did Mary know when the dog's transgression would be tolerated and when he was about to be scolded? In later years she wrote to a student:

> I can discern in the human mind, thought, motives, and purpose:...It is as impossible to prevent this native per- ception as to open the door of a room and then prevent a man who is not blind from looking into the room and seeing all it contains....this phenomenon appeared in my childhood; it is associated with my earliest memories.

What a wonderous woman! Mediums and spiritualists tried to claim her for their own because of her wonderful and un- usual powers so far above those of the average individual. But her desire was to understand and explain extraordinary phenomena. And her devotion was to God and Christianity.

Spiritualism enjoyed great popularity in the 1860's right after the Civil War, and Mary did not shun the spiritualists; however, if they could not comprehend her explanations nor accept her Christly dedication, she had to part company with them. She had a divine commission for all humanity.

CHAPTER II

TWELVE—A CULMINATION

Immediately after the tribulation of those days shall the sun be darkened, and the moon shall not give her light, and the stars shall fall from heaven.

Jesus

1833

MRS. Eddy wrote: "my religious experience seemed to culminate at twelve years of age." At the age of twelve Jesus was found questioning the doctors in the temple. Mary Baker, too, began questioning the doctrines taught by the church.

One day when she was twelve years old she asked her mother whether she thought that eternal punishment really was true.
Questioning at age twelve

Abigail was a loving, forgiving mother who had taught her children to repent for naughtiness and say, "I am sorry and will not do so again." But to doubt the church doctrine was considered heresy, so she sighed deeply when she answered, "Mary, I suppose it is."

"What if we repent and tell God 'we are sorry and will not do so again,'" said Mary. "Will God punish us? Then He is not as good as my mother and He will find me a hard case."

Mary found this a hard question to resolve. She had been a devout, obedient child, well-taught by both father and
Predestination a hard problem

mother. Occasionally during her childhood her father endeavored to force Mary to conform to his stern will, but the gentle mother would intercede and deter him by saying, "Mark, you must not antagonize Mary. You know she is always right." Her desire to be right was conflicting with the erroneous doctrine of predestination, or unconditional election, which she had been taught, and her thought was

sorely troubled; nor was she able to dismiss it as other young-
sters might. As a consequence she became ill and was stricken
with fever. The family physician was summoned; but little did
he know that her critical illness was due to the crisis in her
religious experience.

Her father was sincere in endeavoring to save his youngest
daughter from heresy, but his relentess theology and merciless
Jehovah made his words harsh. They fell like blows on the
stricken child. But her religious experience was culminating.
To culminate means to reach the highest point of altitude.

The gentle mother told Mary to lean on God's love and turn
to Him in prayer. Mary knew not the import of this occasion,
but in turning unreservedly to God for guidance   Christ
she was healed so quickly of the fever that the   healing
physician marvelled. And she was freed forever from Calvin's
"horrible decree" of predestination.

Abigail witnessed the Christ healing and rejoiced. And there
were signs in the heaven that pointed to this progressive development. When the disciples went to Jesus asking for a sign
of Christ's Coming, he said that there would be great tribulation, the sun would be darkened, the moon would not give
light, "and the stars shall fall from heaven."

North America experienced a Dark Day on May 19,1780 in
which it was midnight darkness at noonday. Though the moon
had been full the night before, the following   The Dark
night it gave no light. Mr. Teeney of Exeter,   Day of
New Hampshire wrote, "The darkness of the   1780
following evening was probably as gross as has ever been observed since the Almighty fiat gave birth to light." A German
astronomer recorded: "The Dark Day of North America was
one of those wonderful phenomena of nature which will always
be read with interest but which philosophy is at a loss to
explain."

And now, in 1833, the stars fell from heaven. This phenomenon of shooting stars pointed to Boston, though Mary knew
not that her future lay in that city. It was com- Shooting stars
puted that on the morning of November 13, 1833 of November 13,
no fewer than two hundred forty thousand   1833
meteors were at the same time visible above the horizon of
Boston. A professor of astronomy at Yale University wrote:

"The morning of November 13th, 1833 was rendered memorable by an exhibition of the phenomenon called shooting stars which was probably more extensive and magnificent than any here-to-fore recorded.... probably no celestial phenomenon has ever occurred in this country since its first settlement which was viewed with such admiration and delight by one class of spectators, and with so much astonishment and fear by another. During the three hours of its continuance, the day of judgment was believed to be waiting only for the sunrise."

In her autobiography, *Retrospection and Introspection,* which she published in 1891, Mary included a chapter titled "Theological Reminiscence" in which she wrote briefly of her experience at the age of twelve. But she depicted it more graphically two years later when she presented the story of her life in poetry and paintings.

In a casual perusal of *Christ and Christmas,* the second picture might be mistaken for Jesus' raising of the twelve year *Jesus raising* old daughter of Jairus. That event was illus-*Jairus'* trated as the frontispiece for Science and Health *daughter* from the second edition through the twentieth, with the caption, "Damsel, I say unto thee, arise—Mark V:41." This drawing follows Luke's description, "And he put them all out, and took her by the hand," for only the two figures, Jesus and the maid, in first century attire, appear in the scene. This picture was reproduced in a window of the Mother Church in 1894. It is interesting to contrast the depiction of this first century event with the scene in *Christ and Christmas,* which first appeared in 1893.

The figures of Jesus and the father in "Christ Healing" are both clad in garments of an earlier era, but the mother and *Christ healing* daughter are in nineteenth century attire. The *Mary Baker* coffin, too, is definitely a portrayal of the era of Mary Baker, not of Jairus' daughter. When this picture is seen as portraying Mary's culminating religious experience in 1833, it is interesting to analyze it according to some of the instructions Mrs. Eddy gave to her artist at the easel. Corresponding to the three degrees on pages 115-116 of Science and Health, blackest in each picture is *First Degree:* Depravity—PHYSICAL. Gray is *Second Degree:* Evil beliefs disappearing —MORAL. White is *Third Degree:* Understanding—

SPIRITUAL.

Jesus is dressed in white and is directly under the light from the seven-pointed star, though the black robe on his shoulders could indicate the cross. Mother and daughter are both dressed in white, but they are in the gray of the second degree. The mother's eyes are opened, and she sees the healing, but she is just outside the white light of understanding. The father is totally in the dark and dressed in black. Abigail was glad when she saw the Christ healing: Mark was astonished. Mary is being raised from a very black coffin, and her eyes are just beginning to open.

Hands indicate power,—the right hand the dominant power, the left hand a secondary power. Jesus' dominant power is healing in the gray, second degree. His left hand is in the light pointing to the Principle, or source of the light. Abigail's hands are clasped in the gray. The father's right hand is out of sight; his left hand is tentatively reaching out from the black into the gray. Mary's right hand is resting. Her left hand is being drawn toward the light.

Though the Science of her being is lying dormant as depicted by the resting right hand, a secondary power that is being drawn toward the light is apparent in a poem Poem written Mary composed when she was twelve years old. at age twelve A revised version is in her published *Poems,* but the original, as follows, is from her girlhood notebook.

RESOLUTIONS FOR THE MORNING

I'll rise in the morn and drink in the dew,
    From flowers that bloom in the vale—
So mildly dispensing their charms ever new,
    Over hillocks, and flowery dales.

I'll gaze on the orb in yon eastern sky,
    For loftier thoughts 'twill invite!
His beams can enlighten the spiritual eye,
    And inspire my pen as I write.

I'll form resolutions with strength from on high,
    Such physical laws to obey,
As reason with appetite, pleasures deny,
    That *health* may my efforts repay.

I'll go to the altar of God and pray,
    That the reconciled smiles of his son
May illumine my path through the wearisome day,
    And *cheer* me with *hope* when 'tis done.

I'll grateful remember the blessings I've shared,
    And make this my daily request:
Increase Thou my faith, my vision enlarge,
    Clothe me with the garment of peace.

I'll earnestly seek for deliverance from
    Indulgence in sinful mirth:
From *thoughtlessness*, vanity, all that is wrong,
    With *ambition,* that binds me to earth.

And O, I'll remember my *dear absent* friends,
    Though distance may part us the while,
I'll breathe forth a prayer for their *spiritual* gain,
    That goodness, may sorrow beguile.

To these resolutions should I but prove true
    Through faith, free from spiritual pride,
I'll love to acknowledge my days *must be few*
    For they'll waft me away to my God.

In her illustrated poem Mrs. Eddy has recorded for the world the importance of her experience at twelve years of age. Study and analysis begin to reveal that everyone reaches a culminating point at the age of twelve. It seems that the child is under God's protection for the first twelve years,—his world is God's universe. Then he meets the world according to the tree of knowledge which usurps the place of the tree of Life. If parents understood this, they would carefully supervise every aspect of their child's education for

> Twelve, a culmination

the first twelve years, so that his culminating experience could be one of courage built upon righteousness backed by wisdom and intelligence. Then the teen years, instead of being trials to parent and child alike, would be a period in which the progressiveness and resoluteness of youth could overthrow the false decrees of the world even as Mary Baker overcame the false decree of predestination and eternal punishment for herself and for the world forever.

CHRIST HEALING

From *Christ and Christmas* first published in 1893.

CHAPTER III

YOUTH AND EDUCATION

*I will instruct thee and teach thee in the way which thou
shalt go; I will guide thee with mine eye.*

Psalm of David

1830's

M ARY was not robust. From earliest childhood her
sensitiveness to all about her affected her physical
well-being. When quite a child she adopted the Graham system to cure dyspepsia and for many years ate only bread and
vegetables and drank nothing except water, but to little avail.
One of her most critical biographers wrote: "The real story of
Mary Baker's youth was the story of her health." The third
stanza of her youthful "Resolutions for the Morning" tends to
substantiate this conclusion:

I'll form resolutions with strength from on high,
   Such physical laws to obey,
As reason with appetite, pleasures deny
   That *health* may my efforts repay.

But her obedience to physical laws, her self-denial, even
though aided with strength from on high, did not reward her
with the health she so desired.

The fourth picture in *Christ and Christmas,* the Christmas
Eve scene, could depict this phase of Mary's experience. The
"Christmas   young girl in the wheelchair in the foreground is
Eve"   pensive,—looking away from the merriment.
Physical suffering turns us toward Spirit; and there is no indication of Spirit at all in this picture. The seven-pointed star
and the white light it radiates are absent: there is no light of
understanding. The Christmas tree dominates the scene and is
far too large. Is not this as it would appear to the heavenly

12

homesick? Do not the Christmas tree and material gift giving dominate the Christmas festivities?

Look again at the youthful invalid. Is she not receiving tender, loving care? But it is strictly human care and attention. She is dressed in black,—third degree, de-   Adam's pravity, physical. The man (father?) is dressed   Christmas in black. The woman (mother?) is dressed in gray,—second degree, evil beliefs disappearing, moral. But where is the light of the Christ so sorely needed by the invalid? The song of the angels might reach her, but no one is listening for *spiritual* songs in the hubbub of merrymaking.

Another New England poet who suffered much from ill-health also turned away from the Christmas Eve scene to thoughts spiritual. John Greenleaf Whittier's   Whittier's poem would appeal to the physical sufferer   Christmas seeking release and longing for the Christ in   poem Christmas.

> Let every creature hail the morn
>   On which the holy child was born,
> And know, through God's exceeding grace,
>   Release from things of time and place.
>
> I listen, from no mortal tongue,
>   To hear the song the angels sung,
> And wait within myself to know
>   The Christmas lilies bud and blow.
>
> The outward symbols disappear
>   From him whose inward sight is clear,
> And small must be the choice of days
>   To him who fills them all with praise.
>
> Keep while ye need it, brother mine,
>   With honest zeal your Christmas sign,
> But judge not him who every morn
>   Feels in his heart the Lord Christ born.

Despite the physical suffering and her longing and striving for health, Mary's childhood was a happy one centering around the homestead in Bow.

Her formal education began in the summer of 1826 when she accompanied her older sisters for the first time to Bow School Number Three which was a mile from the Bakers' home. Her father had drawn the plans for the building of this school several years earlier and was continuously active on the school committee which was responsible for Bow's seven schools.

Mary learned quickly and easily, though her attendance at school was very irregular due to ill-health. However, the home was as much a classroom as was the school, for both parents read well and as much as a busy farm life would allow. The conversations were kept pleasing and profitable for everyone, which often included a boarding district schoolteacher or traveling clergyman in this hospitable family circle. Mrs. Eddy wrote in her autobiography, "My childhood home I remember as one with the open hand. The needy were ever welcome, and to the clergy were accorded special household privileges."

Mark was very much in favor of higher education and was pleased when Albert decided to study law. The lad helped to
Albert teaches school
finance his education by teaching several terms at district schools, his first being in 1826 when he taught School Number Eighteen in Concord for a salary of $3.35 a month.

In the winter term of 1830 when Mary was eight years old, there was an opening at Bow School Number Three, and the Baker girls were delighted when it was learned that Albert was to be the new schoolmaster. From his vantage point as teacher he discovered a depth of scholarship in Mary equal to his own, thus cementing a bond between them. This was Albert's last term of teaching before leaving for Dartmouth, but he continued assisting Mary with her formal education by tutoring her during his vacations from college.

The family circle was dwindling. Samuel had entered business in Boston several years earlier; Albert was away at
Albert's graduation 1834
college, and in 1832 Abigail left the home circle to attend Pembroke Academy as Albert had done before her. The year after Albert's graduation from Dartmouth in 1834 there were even greater changes

14

in store for the Bakers.

Early in 1835 Grandmother Baker died at the age of ninety-one. Mark had cared for his mother. Being the youngest son, he had stayed at home to help his father on the   Letter to
farm, and he had expected his youngest son to George Sullivan
do the same. But George left the farm in the September, 1835
summer of 1835. On the seventh of September Mary wrote to him:

> Yet though in the enjoyment of these blessings, you in-
> formed us there was one thing wanting to fill up the
> measure of your happiness,—to know that Father was
> reconciled to your leaving us. I think from what we have
> heard him say in the family, and tell others, he was sensible
> as well as all of us, the exchange was necessary for your
> health.... she (Mother) wishes me to give her love to you,
> and as for Father, he will write by Mr. Cutchins if he sees
> him, if not, by the Mail, and give you the result of his re-
> searches at Sanbornton as he is now there with Mother to
> look at a farm.

By the end of the year the Bakers were making arrangements to move to their new farm just one mile from the town of San-bornton Bridge. The older girls were delighted, but Mary and her mother found the parting from home and   Poem to
friends very difficult, and were ill as a conse- Andrew Gault
quence. The Gault family had been dear friends and neighbors as long as Mary could remember, and to the older Gault boy, Andrew, she composed a parting verse.

> Hard is the task to take a final leave
> Of friends whom we shall see, ah never,
> With unaccustomed grief my bosom heaves
> And burns with latent fire forever.
>
> A vernal feeling thrills my very breast
> And scarce the accustomed word is spoken
> We firmer grasp the hand still loath to part
> And wish that grasp might never be broken.

> But go—those finer feelings riven
> Which through my bosom shot
> And with thee take this flower of Heaven
> The flower forget-me-not.

Abigail did not soon recover from her illness, but the move was completed in January of 1836. Three beautiful, gracious young ladies made a very favorable impression on the town of Sanbornton, and their new home was very soon a social center. Albert spent the summer of 1836 at home with the family while Abigail was teaching the village school and living in town. At the end of August Albert wrote to George:

Albert's letter
to George
August, 1836

> Mary has attended school all summer....Martha commences going next week, when Abigail's school closes. ...Father is as happy as a clam....He lives in the neighborhood of two Sanctuaries—a matter of the greatest moment—two Academies.

All New Hampshire towns had their district schools, but very many did not have an academy for advanced education. Sanbornton had two, and the Baker home was between Sanbornton Academy on the south and Woodman-Sanbornton Academy farther to the north. Mary, who had just turned fifteen, had attended the local district school for the summer term, but seventeen year old Martha was looking forward to the fall term at the academy.

A little later when Mary was attending the academy, an incident occurred which was long remembered in Sanbornton. A man who had escaped from the asylum for the insane at Concord invaded the schoolyard brandishing a club. The children ran indoors,—all except Mary who advanced toward him. From the windows they saw him wield the club above his head, but she walked straight up to the man, took his disengaged hand, and led him quietly to the gate. He reappeared the following Sunday, entered the church, and stood beside Mary during the hymn singing, afterward allowing himself to be taken into custody without resistance. Mary so loved the world that her life was an exemplification of Saint John's words, "perfect love casteth out fear."

Mary quiets
the lunatic

In *Retrospection and Introspection* Mrs. Eddy writes, "It was my fair fortune to be often taught by some grand old divines." One of those distinguished Christian Mary's teacher clergymen was the Rev. Enoch Corser who Rev. Enoch moved to Sanbornton Bridge from nearby Corser Loudon in 1837 very shortly after the Baker's move. Mr. Corser was a scholar with several years of teaching and tutoring experience, and the community lost no time in engaging him as principal-teacher for Sanbornton Academy. Mark Baker was elected to the board as a trustee at the same time, serving in different positions, including president, for the next eight years.

The Bakers and Corsers became good friends, and the clergyman soon recognized Mary's ability. He stated to his son, Bartlett, "I never before had a pupil with such Bartlett depth and independence of thought. She has Corser's some great future, mark that. She is an in- statement tellectual and spiritual genius." Bartlett did mark his father's words and gave them to the world.

Mary pursued a course of writing and began contributing to local newspapers at the age of sixteen, encouraged by more than one of her teachers. In later years she realized that the true blessing in her early education lay in the character and nobility of her teachers which they imparted along with the academics. She wrote in Science and Health, "The pure and uplifting thoughts of the teacher, constantly imparted to pupils, will reach higher than the heavens of astronomy;" and again in *Retrospection and Introspection,* "After my discovery of Christian Science, most of the knowledge I had gleaned from schoolbooks vanished like a dream.

"Learning was so illumined that grammar was eclipsed. Etymology was divine history, voicing the idea of God in man's origin and signification. Syntax was spiritual order and unity. Prosody, the song of angels, and no earthly or inglorious theme."

CHAPTER IV

THE BEGINNING OF SORROWS

Mine eyes are ever toward the Lord; for he shall pluck my feet out of the net. Turn thee unto me, and have mercy upon me; for I am desolate and afflicted.

Psalm of David

1837

MARY'S older sister, Abigail, married Alexander Hamilton Tilton in the summer of 1837, which united

Abigail's marriage July, 1837

two of the finest families in Sanbornton Bridge. The Bakers were doubly pleased, because shortly after Abby's marriage George returned home and entered into a partnership with Tilton. This was the beginning of the Tilton Woolen Mills which soon became the town's leading industry and eventually caused the town to be renamed Tilton.

The two young businessmen helped Mark Baker with his investments, and he, too, prospered. But before the second

Death of Albert Baker October, 1841

daughter was married in 1842, tragedy struck. Three of the Baker children, Mary, Martha, and Albert, had suffered much from ill-health. In the summer of 1841 Albert was again suffering from illness which proved fatal a few weeks later,—on the seventeenth of October. His death interrupted a brilliant career and was a great loss to the state of New Hampshire, but a greater loss to his family. The year before his demise he had written to Mary and Martha:

If you knew how much satisfaction I take in reading your letters, you would write oftener—though I never wrote. If there is a brother in this world, who is happy in the love of

his sisters, it is I. Indeed it is to me the oasis in the desert of
life—the only spot upon which I rest with *entire* safety. I
know there is *honesty* and *sincerity* in a sister's love.

And now Mary's life seemed a desert without an oasis. She
loved all her brothers and sisters dearly, but there had long
been a special bond between Mary and Albert.

The following year Mary's dear friend, Augusta Holmes,
married Samuel Swasey and moved to Haverhill, New Hampshire. Scarcely a month later her sister Martha married Luther
Pilsbury and moved to Concord. To the former Mary wrote,
"Really, Augusta, you cannot tell how 'doubly lone' I feel
since you and Martha have gone. I have tried to forget sis, but
Phoenix-like her image is constantly rising up before me from
some desolate vestige." But another year brought the promise
of married bliss to Mary.

More than ten years earlier brother Samuel had married
Eliza Ann Glover, the sister of his young business partner,
George Washington Glover. In the intervening years George
had moved to Charleston, South Carolina, and had become
exceptionally prosperous as a building contractor. On a visit
back home he had renewed old acquaintances which included
the Baker family. The youngest Baker he had met as a child
was now a strikingly beautiful, mature young woman. Their
admiration was mutual, and he and Mary began a correspondence.

Mark and Abigail were not happy at the prospect of having
Mary move so far away, but they were resigned to it by the
time the young couple had set the date for the   Marriage to
wedding. So in the parlor of her parents' home   George Glover
which was crowded with friends and relatives,   December, 1843
Mary was wedded to George Washington Glover on the tenth
day of December in 1843. In later years she wrote, "I married
young the one I loved."

By the end of December George Glover had brought his
bride home to Charleston in the sunny southland. Before the
end of January something of great moment had   Beginning
taken place in Mary's experience. Perhaps it   The Great Step
was, that within her own consciousness she   January, 1844
assumed the responsibility of motherhood which was destined

19

to expand to embrace the whole world. As is so often the case, the import of that moment was seen by no one, including herself. But it was foretold in an imperishable record.

In our "Bible in stone," The Great Pyramid, there is a passage called "The Grand Gallery" which corresponds to the Christian Era. The time line worked out by mathematicians and astronomers places its beginning at the time of the resurrection of Jesus of Nazareth. At the other end of The Grand Gallery there is what is known to pyramidologists as "The Great Step." Exceedingly accurate mathematical calculations place the beginning of The Great Step at midnight, January 25-26, 1844.

Mary had begun The Great Step, but she knew it not. She entered into her new life in South Carolina, and although she missed New England and her childhood home, she was missed much more as is evident in a letter from her mother.

Letter from Abigail Baker May 6, 1844

> My ever dear Child,
>
> Will you not be glad to hear again from your aged mother...Dear Child, your memory is dearer to *me* than gold. Everything reminds me of you. Language cannot express my feelings. My sight is almost failed with weeping. And when shall I see you and Dear George? I think not very soon, but I rejoice to hear from you so often. Don't write too much for fear it hurts you. How is your health, and how is your back? Can you lie down and rise again without a groan?...Do you remember our Twilight meeting? It is a precious time to me, for there I feel like meeting with you, and sometimes I fear I worship Mary instead of the great Jehovah...."

The mental meeting each day at twilight speaks of the strong bond between Mary and her sainted mother.

Abigail was to see her youngest daughter far sooner than anyone expected. Little more than a month after this letter was written, her new son-in-law was stricken with yellow fever while the young couple was on a business trip to Wilmington, North Carolina, and nine days later George Glover expired,—the attending physician stating that it was nothing but his wife's prayers that kept him alive that long.

Death of George Glover June 27, 1844

Mrs. Glover thought in poetry more than in prose and her journal entry at this time was "Thoughts at a Grave."

> Spread o'er the turf
> The spirit's fetterless
> And free to range the golden streets of Heaven
> A higher boon than earth to it was given
> Tenant of loathsome clay
> From sin how blest to be away . . .
> Ye stricken ones who sorrow o'er the sod
> No love of thine outweighs the love of God.
> It is for thee
> Meek at this mystery
> Of Heaven's dark fiat calmly to submit. . .
> Linger not here. . .
> Go forth and to thy duty once again. . .
> Say unto youth, say to the hoary head!
> Prove faithful to the living as the dead.

George Glover's masonic brethren opened their hearts and their homes to his bereaved widow which helped her through those first few days and weeks. She was ever grateful for their kindnesses which extended even to escorting her to her parents' home in New England. What a bittersweet reunion with her family! But her thoughts turned always to God as expressed in "The Widow's Prayer" which she wrote at this time:

> For trials past I would not grieve,
>   But count my mercies o'er;
> And teach the heart Thou hast bereaved
>   Thy goodness to adore.
> Thou gavest me friends, in my distress,
>   Like manna from above;
> Thy mercy ever I'll confess,
>   And own a Father's love.

Her brief marriage seemed almost like a beautiful dream with a sad ending. Though she was back in Sanbornton Bridge her thoughts were not, as she penned "Wind of the South."

21

Ye scenes my heart still loves to own,
Ye scenes which thrill deep notes of woe,
Departed joys, blest friendships flown!
Sad in the south wind murmur low.

Yet stay! ah! whither wouldst thou roam,
Gay restless essence, bounding free?
Bliss to my bosom were the boon
Of wings to wander back to thee.

Yes, balmy breeze, when evening glows
O, pitying come and kiss my cheek,—
But no, thy sighing would disclose—
Thee hither from the *grave* I seek.

Oh say do worms dare revel round
The *casket* where no gems can rust?
Hath loveliness a level found,
Beneath the cold and common dust?

The following September, on the twelfth of the month, Mary gave birth to a healthy son; but everyone feared for the

Birth of
Mary's son
September, 1844

mother's life. Mahala Sanborn, who had been domestic servant and family nurse for the Bakers for many years, was Mary's special nurse for the next several months; while the baby, who had been named George Washington Glover II after his father, was given over to the care of a Mrs. Morrison who had recently lost one of her infant twins.

In time, when Mary's health was sufficiently recovered, baby George was brought home, but his care fell largely to Mahala and Abigail. Much as Mary yearned to be a perfect mother, the story of her womanhood was the same as that of her youth,—one of health, or the lack of it.

George, though a sturdy baby, was a difficult one whose lusty screams filled the house. The fact that he could not be

Letter to
Martha Rand
March, 1848

comforted may have been a reflection of Mary's own state of consciousness. Her gay laughter and light spirit, which had always been characteristic in spite of her physical suffering, were ofttimes clouded by an underlying melancholy which persisted for many years. In a letter to her friend, Martha Rand, she wrote:

> Now dearest Mathy...I have half determined this very moment to throw aside my pen and wait to weep. But then what availeth this mood...'tis like looking down through transparent waters of the sea of life, checkered with sunshine and shade—into the mighty deep, in which our happier days have sunk, and where they are lying still visible like golden sands; and half in hope grasp after them again, then draw back the hand filled only with briny tears!

One day a young man stopped by to visit his friends the Bakers. Georgy was howling inconsolably, and with Mary's permission the young man took him from her arms into the next room. She heard him say to the child, "I know what you want; you want a father, you want your papa. I am going to be your father, little man. I'll be your papa." This impressed both Mary and the baby, for he quieted down and was somewhat calmer in the future. But George's future was as uncertain as was that of his mother.

In her grief Mary had given no thought to her husband's property, and it was lost to her. Thus, the problem that confronted her now was support for herself and son.

In 1845 Sanbornton Academy was replaced by the New Hampshire Conference Seminary. The following year the principal, Rev. Richard Rust, prevailed upon Mrs. Glover to substitute for his leading teacher during the latter's absence of several weeks. He *America's first kindergarten* paid Mrs. Glover a fine compliment on her work and encouraged her to continue teaching. Mary's independence of thought, combined with her parental responsibilities, caused her to think in terms of education for the very young. With the help of her sister, Abigail, she secured a building, had it painted and equipped, and opened what was probably America's first kindergarten. Her ideas were revolutionary for that time, and her school attracted considerable attention. The word kindergarten was not then in the American vocabulary, and encyclopedias now say that the first kindergartens in America were begun in the 1860's. But Mrs. Glover pioneered the concept nearly twenty years earlier with her successful "Infants School" in 1846.

Mary's health did not allow her to continue teaching for any length of time; and the care of George fell largely to Mahala

"Immortality of the Soul" May, 1847

Sanborn who had him with her often in her father's home and blacksmith shop. As a source of income Mary turned more to her writing. Mary Glover's article, "The Immortality of the Soul," appeared in the May, 1847 issue of *The Covenant*. The following excerpts give an indication of the trend of her thought.

> Who does not sometimes conjecture what will be his condition and employment in eternity? Will the mind be continually augmenting its stock of knowledge, and advancing toward complete perfection? It cannot be otherwise.
>
> We shall there apprehend fully the relations and dependencies incomprehensible to understandings encircled by clay. The boundless ocean of truth will be fathomed and investigated by those, whom, like Newton, a residence here scarcely acquainted with a few pebbles in its trackless shore. The result of all experiments will then be satisfactory, since they will accord with the deductions of enlarged and enlightened reason.
>
> Most authors have but dimly shadowed forth their own imaginings, and much of what they intended is involved in obscurity. This makes an approach to the regions of science and literature so extremely difficult; there this obstacle will be removed. No veil will hide from our observation the beauties, lovely, inimitable, of wisdom and philosophy; all their charms will there be displayed.
>
> The imperfection of language will be no hindrance to the acquisition of ideas, as it will no longer be necessary as a medium of thought and communication. Intelligence, refined, etherealized, will converse directly with material objects, if, indeed, matter be existent. All will be accessible, permanent, eternal!

At the age of twenty-five we find Mrs. Glover using the term science as something most desirable to be sought after,— nearly two decades before her great discovery of the Science of

Man. Here, too, she is doubting the permanence or perfectability of matter.

*   *   *

Mary and John Bartlett had been friends since childhood, but she was not considering him as a husband. About the time that John departed for his final term at Harvard   Letter to Law School, Mary wrote to her sister, Martha,   Martha "I feel as if I must begin something this summer,   March, 1848 if my health is sufficient. I am weary working my way through life from the middle to the end. . . . I shall not marry anyone I know at present—the future however may do better by me in this respect." John, it seems, had other ideas.

In August of 1848 Mary traveled to Cambridge to attend John Bartlett's graduation from Harvard. He had made a brilliant record at law school and had the promise of a fine future. Family and friends were expecting the young couple to marry; and Mary was changing her mind, for her mother wrote of the situation to George, "I think her mind is fully established." But John was not yet established and did not yet have the means to provide a home for a wife and son.

The battle for health was nothing new to Mary. She had never been free from it for any length of time, but in the spring of 1849 she seemed to be losing the fight. Her parents sent her to Warner, New Hampshire for two months under the care of Dr. Parsons Whidden. Abigail reported to George that "the Dr. says she could not live long as she was."

She seems to have found some relief, for by the end of summer she was engaged to marry John H. Bartlett. He was going to the fabulous California of 1849 to establish a law practice in Sacramento. She had chosen a new course for her future, but the coming weeks and months would be filled with days of waiting.

Not so for the rest of the Bakers. Mark was building a fine new house in town. Though Abigail was not feeling well, she was preparing for a wedding; for George, who   Marriage of had left Sanbornton Bridge two years earlier,   George Baker was coming home to marry Martha Rand. The   November, 1849 wedding took place on the fourth of November, and George left with his bride immediately for Baltimore, little knowing the sad news he would receive from Mary before the month's end.

November 22, 1849

My Dear Bro:

This morning looks on us bereft of a Mother! Yes, that angel on earth is now in Heaven! I have prayed for support to write this letter, but I find it impossible to tell you the particulars at this time. She failed rapidly from the time you saw her, but her last struggles were most severe, her physician spoke of it as owing to so strong a constitution. Oh! George, what is left of earth to *me!* But oh, my Mother! She has *suffered long with me;* let me then be willing she should now *rejoice,* and I bear on till I follow her. I cannot write more. My grief overpowers me. Write to me.

Your affec' Sister,
Mary

Died last night at half-past seven o'clock; will be buried next Saturday. I wish you could be here.

Abigail Baker was indeed an "angel on earth." She was one of those rare individuals who was loved by everyone. Even Mrs. Eddy's bitterest critics have had no word to say in condemnation of Abigail Ambrose Baker. This was the greatest loss that Mary had yet sustained, and from her pen came "To My Mother in Heaven." Two of the seven stanzas read:

> Death of
> Mary's mother
> November, 1849

> The wild winds trace, the stars which light
> Their shining lamps on high,
> Point to thy rest, thy being bright,
> Thy home beyond the sky!
> And all with mournful memories blent,
> No hopes of earth restore—
> Oh, winds and stars may wander by,
> *Thy* footsteps are no more!

> I bless thee, Mother, precious guide,
> For my most sacred share

> In all the secrets of thy heart,
> Thy sorrow and thy prayer;
> Supporting faith be mine below
> Life's parting words to greet;
> Thy mantling virtues o'er me throw
> Till child and Mother meet!

Her griefs and heartaches were with her in Sanbornton, but Mary's hopes for the future, if she could muster any, lay in Sacramento with John Bartlett. But the news that she received from California in December was not from John, but about him. On the eleventh of the month John H. Bartlett had died in Sacramento.

Death of John Bartlett December, 1849

With the obituary she wrote for the *New Hampshire Patriot*, Mrs. Glover included these words: "The young man was engaged to the daughter of an aged friend. The daughter survived both mother and lover. The mother dying first, in two weeks he followed." This was accompanied by a poem entitled. "The Meeting of the Two Spirits," in which the mother asks the young man,

> Bear'st thou no tidings from my loved of earth,
> The desolate whose stricken joys have dearth...
> What of my child?

Life was desolate for Mary, but this was not the end of her sorrows. Little did she know that this very poem, revised, would apply again in her experience. But desolation has its reward. In later years she was able to write, "It is well to know, dear reader, that our material, mortal history is but the record of dreams, not of man's real existence, and the dream has no place in the Science of being."

CHAPTER V

SORROWS MULTIPLIED

The troubles of my heart are enlarged: O bring thou me out of my distresses. Look upon mine affliction and my pain; and forgive all my sins.
                                        Psalm of David

1850

THE move into the new house in town was a sad one indeed for Mary and her father. The house was not a home without Abigail. And the hired girl could not begin to replace Mahala Sanborn, who had married and was moving to North Groton forty miles away. All Mary had left in this world was five-year-old Georgy, and he was a sore trial to his grandfather. She wrote despairingly to her brother a few months later:

> Last year, a little later than this I went into that cold, damp house with Father, helped cleanse and set it in order and lived alone with a little girl and him all winter; in the spring he told me if George was not sent away he would send him to the Poor House (after abusing him as he did through the winter).

Mark's remarks were not from financial necessity but from frustration, for his life was not easy at this juncture. He bore the responsibility for Mary and her son, but George was a difficult, boisterous youngster, and Abigail's gentle persuasion was no longer present. In October of 1850 word came from the West where Martha's husband had gone for greater fortune, that he, Luther Pilsbury, had died very suddenly on a Mississippi River steamboat. Now the grief-stricken Martha and her two daughters, Ellen and Mary, were added to the household. It was another bittersweet reunion. But this arrangement did not continue for long.

28

Of the adults in this gloomy, solemn band only **Mark was** happy at Thanksgiving of 1850, for he was to marry **Mrs. Eliz-** abeth Patterson Duncan of Candia, New Hamp- Mark Baker's shire on the fifth of December. Mrs. Duncan   marriage was a genial, well-to-do widow from a promi- December, 1850 nent family, and it was a happy union for all concerned, save Mary. No one could replace her loved Mother, and, at first, the marriage seemed a sacrilege to her.

Martha and her daughters went to stay with her husband's family, and Abigail opened her spacious home to Mary. But no one wanted little George! That is, no one but Mahala San- born Cheney. Either the family could not tolerate George's boisterousness, or they felt that his presence was detrimental to Mary's delicate health. It was probably for both reasons that George was not welcome in Aunt Abigail's house nor in that of his Grandfather Baker next door.

It is also probable that Abigail and her father arranged, without Mary's knowledge, to pay Mahala and her husband for George's board before convincing Mary that he   Letter to should go to North Groton to live with them.   Glovers What a blow that was! Mary had no home for   April, 1851 herself and son and neither the means nor the health to provide one. She had no alternative but to yield to the plan. George was sent to visit his uncle and aunt, Mr. and Mrs. Andrew J. Glover, in Concord while the Cheneys were getting settled in their new home, and only a very little of the anguish Mary felt in her heart crept into her letter to her brother-in-law and his wife.

Sanbornton Bridge, April 22

My dear Bro and Sis,

Mrs. Cheney came here last Thurs. and will return next week on Saturday. You can send my dear child when you please, the latter part of the week, as she is very anxious to have him when she goes home. She is very fond of children and Georgy in particular, but her health is very poor, this I regret. She told me their school (which is about one quarter of a mile distant) will commence in a few weeks, and I am anxious to have him attend. But Oh! how I miss him already! There seems nothing left me now to enjoy. I often stand by my window when the shades of evening close o'er me and gaze on yonder sacred spot where sleeps my peaceful Mother and invoke her blessing and counsel, while I almost envy her repose. But I must not write on this subject for words are impotent things to utter the feelings of a Mother's heart.

Won't you send me a line by him or come yourselves? I want very much to know how you have succeeded with him and if he has been a good boy (some naughty things of course) there is no child whom we expect mature in every respect, but take Georgy with the aggregate, is he not a pretty good and very dear boy? You can speak to the conductor to take care of him and his little baggage and Mr. Tilton is always at the depot so he will see to him there. Will dear little Sully be sorry to have him leave? How is Fath and Moth's health? Give much love to them from me and accept the same yourselves. Kiss the little one for me and tell him aunty remembers those roguish eyes.

In much haste yours—
Affectionately,
Mary

Mary often kept her mental meeting at twilight with her Mother,—the one person in the world with whom she had had spiritual rapport. The words her mother had penned a few years earlier applied to Mary now: i.e., "your memory is dearer to me than gold. Language cannot express my feelings. My sight is almost failed with weeping." How she longed for her mother's counsel in this present trial! She knelt by George's bedside and prayed for relief the long night before he was sent away. The next day, after he was gone she wrote "Mother's Darling" in her journal, "Written on the 9th day of May on parting with my babe."

George sent to Cheney's May 9, 1851

Go little voyager, o'er life's rough sea—
Born in a tempest! choose thy pilot God,
The Bible, let thy chart forever be—
Anchor and helm its promises afford.

Could monarch's diadem or lordly crown
Or oriental treasures purchase thee?
Ah! 'twere a mockery, 'twere a paltry sum
Coined for so bright a gem as little G.

A Father's love! my heart, be still or break,
  Not to thy infant hours in joy made known,
And thou mayest live to learn thy hapless fate,
  Reft of thy parent stock, frail, sick, and lone.

Then wilt thou share thy Mother's voiceless woe
  Too keen for utterance, too deep for tears!
Yet God forbid, thy guileless heart should know
  The early blight of unprotected years....

Thy smile through tears, as sunshine o'er the sea,
  Awoke new beauty in the surge's roll!
Oh, life is dead, bereft of all, with thee,—
  Star of my earthly hope, babe of my soul!

Mary's grief was truly "too keen for utterance, too deep for
tears." With George gone she had nothing to live for. Little
wonder that her physical problems intensified and she suffered
a serious relapse. The physical agony she endured, confined
often to her bed, reflected the anguish in her heart. Her loving
family saw not the connection between her loss and her suffering and felt they had done the right thing in sending her child
away.

It seemed that Mary could not recover. Everyone, including
her father, stepmother, and the doctor did all they could for
her, but the burden fell heaviest on Abigail.   Martha's
By midsummer Martha had come to help both   letter
her sisters as recorded in her letter of August 10   August, 1851
to her brother and his wife, George and Martha:

> ...I am quite worn out and sick, and have come up to
> Father's to try rest with a little medicine....But have we not
> the assurance, and can I ever doubt it, that "as thy day so
> shall thy strength be." May mine continue that I may con-
> tribute to dear Mary's comfort while she may live, if she can-
> not recover, and afford Abby the assistance she so much
> needs.

Martha bought a house for herself and children to make the
move to Sanbornton Bridge permanent; but much of her time

was spent nursing Mary. The weeks dragged into months and the new year saw no improvement in Mary's condition. Martha wrote despairingly to Martha Rand Baker, George's wife, on the fourth of January in 1852:

> Found her very sick, from one of her most severe attacks of dispepsia, liver-complaint and nervous disease. It would be impossible to point out the changes, or trace the progress of disease down to the present time, or describe the hopes and fears, doubts and expectations that have affected us respecting the result, during this long period of continued suffering having been all the time confined to the room and bed, except when possibly able to be helped into a carriage to ride. And what can I say of her now? How tell you, that after so long and inconceivable suffering, though still living, and perhaps doomed to yet longer and greater affliction by an all-wise but inscrutable Providence, yet there is scarcely a ray of hope left us of her recovery. Her strength gradually fails, and all the powers of life seem yielding to the force of disease. O, Martha! it would move the sternest soul, and make mortality shrink, to witness the agony she often endures...

But from this seemingly hopeless condition Mary did recover, and in time she was enjoying working in the garden, visiting her father and step-mother next door or their dear friends, the Clements, across the street. The Clements were as literary as the Bakers and Tiltons, so they enjoyed the exchange of both books and conversation.

Mary kept her anguish in her heart and for her hours of solitude. To her friends and relatives she was the same cheerful, sweet, witty Mary of gentle disposition. Sarah Clement, who had attended Mrs. Glover's Infant School the years it continued, was now eleven years old and a constant visitor in the house across the street. In later years she was angered by the press' malicious attacks on Mrs. Eddy and refuted their false claims of this period in her reminiscences.

Recollections of Sarah Clement Kimball

> I saw her daily in those years of my childhood. The Tilton house was directly across the street from our house and Mrs.

Eddy was a frequent visitor, while I ran over to her house any time of the day, hanging about, as children will, sometimes unobserved, but always observing. Mrs. Eddy was never too absorbed in what she was doing to be gracious and interested in my childish conversation. Tall, slender, and exceedingly graceful, she was altogether one of the most beautiful women I have ever seen....My uncle...said that as a boy he used to sit in church without thinking of the service, his thoughts being busy contemplating Mrs. Glover's beauty. She was always neatly, but simply dressed. Mrs. Tilton was inclined to be the dressy member of the family....

Mrs. Eddy had a happy disposition; she was always cheerful. I never saw her when she was the least depressed, and I have seen her at all times and on all occasions. She read a great deal and used to borrow books from our library. Her laugh was very sweet and I often used to hear her talking to my mother and laughing. She had a nice sense of humor....I was quite a pet of Mrs. Eddy's and sometimes when I went over she would read to me. I remember her reading Longfellow's 'Hyperion,' a little German tale, especially....

Toward night I would see her working in the garden. She always wore gloves with the finger tips cut off. I used to run across the road and hang over the gate and discuss things.... People often ask me if she was an educated woman. She and her whole family were refined and very bright, intellectual people of their day. Mrs. Eddy herself was better educated at that time despite its limited opportunities than half the girls nowadays. Not many girls of today can translate the *Iliad,* and she did....

[Mrs. Tilton] was also a handsome woman, but extremely determined and very fiery when angry....Mrs. Tilton was a leader in everything.

* * *

It is probable that Mrs. Glover first met Dr. Daniel Patterson socially as he was related to her stepmother; but by the end of 1852 she was consulting him pro- Dentistry by fessionally for the care of her teeth. He was a Dr. Patterson 1852 fine, progressive dentist, who evidently extracted some of Mary's teeth, for she wrote him on the twelfth of December, "I would like to retain as long as possible all I have *left!* feeling the chagrin of my present mouth, most essentially. Never knowing before the loss of teeth I was ignorant of *all* the difficulties I find attend it."

Daniel Patterson was attracted to the beautiful young widow from the first, but the attraction was not altogether one-sided. Daniel was tall, handsome, well-dressed, and very genial. He had attained a degree of competence and success in dentistry, frequently traveling through rural areas to practise his profession. And he had recently located more permanently by opening an office in Franklin, three miles from Sanbornton Bridge. When he proposed marriage in March of 1853, Mary's objection was on religious grounds. She wrote him after a sleepless night, "I have a fixed feeling that to yield my *religion* to yours, *I could not;* other things compared to this are but a grain to the universe."

Daniel was persistent, but Mary's family objected to the union. Mark, it seems, had heard "dark things" about this

Letter from Dr. Patterson April, 1853

itinerant dentist. So a second time Mary said no. In response Daniel wrote,

Franklin Monday Morn Apr 11
1853

Dear Mary,

It seems that I have lost you at last. That you have made *your* final decision against me— and refuse to see me again, and there is nothing left for me to do but submit to your decree—

I thought I would at first vindicate my Moral character, and prepared a letter for your Father's perusal— but on more mature deliberation, and knowing that *you* had become dissatisfied with my Disposition and wished— yes had already irrevocably dismissed me, I concluded to withhold all I had written...

With this farewell letter, Daniel included a touching poem:

> Like a linkless chain enthraling
> Like the sleepless dreams that mock,

Like the frigid ice drops falling,
From the surf-surrounded rock:

Such the drear and sickening feeling
That has caused this heart to know,
Stabbed me deeper by concealing
From the world its humbling woe—

Once it fondly, fondly, called thee
All that fancy deemed divine
Then it honored and esteemed thee
As an idol and a shrine!

Yet when my lone life is over,
Should thine own be lengthened long
Thou mayst then *alone* discover
By thy feelings all my own.

The first two stanzas applied more to Mary's past experiences than to Daniel's present state, but his persistence was affecting Mary's resistance. Marriage to him held out the promise of a home for herself and Georgy. The letter he had withheld (temporarily) may have softened her father's attitude:

Franklin Apl 10— 1853

Mary M. Glover

Much to my surprise, I learn that your family object to our union, on grounds new, and strange to me—

You say they have heard "Dark things."

Of what they *are* I am ignorant—But of the Source I am not ignorant. They must have been probing (not a Heavenly—"Angel"—blest—"Bethesda" the sure Panacea of all the sufferings of Humanity, but) some low cesspool of foul Slanderous *Suspicion*—down which Lucifer plunged his hydra head and dividing hoof...

I will take your father to all the places where I have made a stand and he may make enquiries, in relation to my conduct, of any reliable persons; I will take him to my native town, and introduce him to Clergymen, and businessmen of character and standing in society, who have long known, and dealt with me some of the members of the Congregational Church who are in no way connected by blood or interest with me, but who have known me from infancy. I should like to take him up to Hill and introduce him to Esq. Sumner in whose family I have boarded most of the time spent in that place. He is a prominent member of the Congregational Church and a man of property and standing in society. I will also take him to Lowell, and introduce him to those well acquainted with me there, and so all of the places where I have visited, if he will take the trouble to go I will bear his expenses, or I will give him any number of reliable names whom he may address on the matter...

The first reactions of both Mary and her family should have been heeded. Perhaps being dissuaded and learning by experience enabled Mrs. Eddy to write in Science and Health, "The first impression, made on a mind which is attracted or repelled according to personal merit or demerit, is a good detective of individual character." But Daniel was personable, likeable, and persuasive, so before the end of April he and Mrs. Glover were engaged to be married.

In her autobiography Mrs. Eddy has little more to say than "My second marriage was very unfortunate," but this unfortunate union continued for thirteen long years.

MAHALA SANBORN CHENEY   RUSSELL CHENEY

CHAPTER VI

THE PATTERSON YEARS

And there appeared a great wonder in heaven; a woman clothed with the sun.

Revelation

1853

B EFORE the date set for the wedding Mary again became ill. On the twenty-ninth of April she wrote to Daniel:

> I am sick—Wed. afternoon my illness increased...My only relief is to take *Morphine* which I so much disapprove....My sufferings are at times extreme. I do want to see you. I know not what this attack may result in, but one thing I pray, that it may be divine will that I am not to languish out months on a sickbed; nevertheless, "not my will but Thine be done."

A few days later she had found relief in a manner that she did not disapprove. A cousin, Dr. Alpheus Morrill, had counseled her as to the use of homeopathic medicine   Relief from which was becoming very popular in America,   homeopathy and she felt that she was recovering. Daniel was dabbling in homeopathy and had the utmost confidence that he would be able to cure Mary of the diseases which had plagued her life.

So on the twenty-first of June, still suffering from ill-health, Mary was united in marriage to Daniel Patterson in a simple ceremony in her father's home. The Pattersons   Marriage to settled in Franklin and soon bought a house.   Dr. Patterson Daniel exchanged his horse for a cow, indicating   June, 1853 an established rather than an itinerant dental practice. But he was not willing that George should come to live with them.

Mary's health did not improve, and she, rather than Daniel,

37

became the student and practitioner of homeopathy. She practically memorized Jahr, from *Aconitum* to *Zincum oxydatum* and had a good deal of success in curing others. She has related some of her experiences in Science and Health. As for herself, although she still suffered, homeopathy relieved her of the necessity for drugs. In an interview with a newspaper correspondent in 1901 she said, "I was a sickly child. I was dosed with drugs until they had no effect on me. The doctors said I would live if the drugs could be made to act on me. Then homeopathy came like blessed relief to me."

After her discovery of Christian Science, in the early years of her metaphysical practice she had this to say:

From *Aconitum* to *Zincum oxydatum* all through the two hundred and sixty remedies of the Jahr—I could give the general symptoms, characteristic peculiarities, and moral symptoms to which each medicine was applied, and this helped me as a pharmacist, for when I shook the paper or the bottle that contained the drug thirty times in preparing it, and retained but one drop of the original tincture, to one hundred drops of prepared alcohol thirty times, I was thinking thirty times of what that remedy ought to cure; the result was I got more metaphysics than physics into the dose; hence the potency of the higher attenuations, and their increasing efficacy as matter disappeared, and mind went into the medicine. I would attenuate *Aconitum* until it was no longer aconite, but sugar of milk; and this self-same sugar named aconite, would at once allay febrile symptoms, reduce the pulse, and promote powerful perspirations. . . .

The highest attenuation I ever reached in homeopathy was not to medicate the sugar of milk, and with this harmless dose I cured an inveterate case of dropsy. This was my last material medicine. I then took a step forward, not from matter to mind, but from mind to Mind, for I had learned that homeopathy was the stepping-stone to metaphysics, if only homeopathy would say there is nothing in a name, and mind is more potent than milk coagulated.

Here is a figure; I never thought of it before; the infancy of metaphysical healing was at a period of milk, when the poison was going out of remedies, and mind was coming into them.

In her later writings she said, "homeopathy is the last link in material medicine. The next step is Mind-medicine." And, "Metaphysics, as taught in Christian Science, is the next stately step beyond homeopathy."

Mrs. Patterson's practice of homeopathic medicine had only its beginning in Franklin, for they were there less than two years. It is probable that her longing for her son induced Daniel to move to North Groton. He enjoyed consulting with his affluent, socially prominent relatives in Sanbornton Bridge, and most likely had their understanding and cooperation where Mary and George Glover were concerned. At any rate Martha Pilsbury held the mortgage on the home which Daniel purchased in North Groton. The new homestead included a sawmill which Daniel intended to operate as the small town could not support a dentist full time. For this supplementary work he also acquired one hundred acres of timberland.

Move to North Groton March, 1855

The biggest disappointment was George. He had had very little schooling, and his lack of academic education was a blow to his mother,—the most scholarly of the studious Bakers. To his stepfather he was as great a trial as he had been to his grandfather. Before long Daniel forbade him in the house. Myra Smith, who worked for Mrs. Patterson in North Groton, recalled in later years:

Reminiscences of Elmira Smith Wilson

> Mrs. Patterson came there with the Dr. to be near her child, and so that she could teach him, but this she was not permitted to do as the Dr. did not like children and would not allow him to come to the house. The boy was not liked by the other children at school and the Cheneys did not make him go. My Brother was working for Mr. Cheney and while there he and the boy slept together. My Brother did not like him because he was rough and would not mind anyone. Mrs. Patterson grieved and worried, because she could not see her child and told the Dr. that she had given up her folks and had come off up there with him and that she must see her boy and teach him, but Patterson would not let him come near, and without her knowing it one day the Cheneys moved away, out west and took the boy with them and before they left

my Father had a hard fight to get the money from him, that
he owed to him for my Brothers years work.

It is only fair to state that after George Glover's death his
daughter said that as he grew up he wanted to go to school but
Cheney insisted that he work on the farm instead. This however, was probably in Minnesota rather than North Groton.

George was not Daniel's only concern. He was improvident
and was not able to pay Martha the interest due on the mort-
Martha's letter gage, which in turn caused her financial
to George Baker problems. On the twenty-seventh of April she
April, 1856 wrote to her brother for advice:

> Dr. Patterson is unable to pay me a dollar of interest this
> spring So I have to call on Mr. Tilton to pay all my debts
> and they are pretty heavy. What shall I do, foreclose at once?
> I suppose I can do this as he has broken his obligation by not
> paying annual interest. Mary has been sick several months
> and I expect they are brought to *absolute want!*

The Tiltons, too, were experiencing economic difficulties, for
their mill had burned to the ground in December of 1855.
George Glover The next few years were not easy for them fi-
taken West nancially while they were rebuilding. But it has
April, 1856 been assumed that Daniel appealed to Mary's
family in Sanbornton Bridge for help, and that they provided
the funds for the Cheney's move to the West. Everyone except
Mary seems to have known about it. She wrote in *Retrospection and Introspection:*

> ...A plot was consumated for keeping us apart. The family
> to whose care he was committed very soon removed to what
> was then regarded as the Far West.
> After his removal a letter was read to my little son, inform-
> ing him that his mother was dead and buried. Without my
> knowledge a guardian was appointed him, and I was then in-
> formed that my son was lost.

Her concerned family thought that Mary suffered from seeing her son, but how little they understood the mental anguish
Martha's and physical suffering that would result from
letter this final separation. When Abigail went to
June, 1857 North Groton to visit Mary the following spring,

her report distressed everyone. Martha Pilsbury wrote to George's wife, Martha Rand Baker, on the sixth of June:

> ...Abi's visit to Mary has been constantly before my mind. I long to hear the particulars in a letter from her. I hope it will not make dear Abi worse, though such a picture of suffering and misery is enough to break a sister's heart. But Mary! poor child—Alas what words can express her condition. Everything is nought compared to that. One year and a half confined to her bed, and perhaps now there is not even a hope that she will ever be able to rise again, though how long life may last, God alone knows.

The want of health was Mary's one concern. Only those who have experienced severe physical suffering know the true value and meaning of health and the spiritual longing such suffering induces. Little wonder Mary would write in Science and Health:

> Did the careless doctor, the nurse, the cook, and the brusque business visitor sympathetically know the thorns they plant in the pillow of the sick and the heavenly homesick looking away from earth,—Oh, did they know!—this knowledge would do much more towards healing the sick and preparing their helpers for the "midnight call," than all cries of "Lord, Lord!"

Yet her spirit was not quenched by her bodily suffering. In the spring of 1857 she pasted into her scrapbook a poem entitled "Consolations," which included the following stanza, beside which she wrote, "Mine, April 5th, 1857."

> My childhood knew misfortune of a strange and weary kind,
> And I have always worn a chain, though not upon my mind,
> And I render thanks to thee, oh God! from my prison, that I
> live
> Unshorn of that best privilege which thou alone canst give!
> I mean a soul to apprehend the beauty that is spread
> Above me and around me and beneath my feeble tread...
> And though bereft of freedom in the body, I can fly
> As high as Heaven on wings of thought, like an eagle to the
> sky.

Her thought did fly like an eagle to heaven, hungering and thirsting after spiritual reality. But her increased spirituality tended to increase the gap between Mary and those around her. She was sincerely interested in other people, but oh, so alone! These lines marked in a poem she pasted into her scrapbook give an indication of her aloneness:

> The poet sadly sighed,
> "Expect no song of pride,
> Lady, from me, no glad and bright revealings.
>
> . . .
>
> "I occupy alone,
> An intellectual throne,
> My shrinking subjects will not let me love them:
>
> "Even my kindred, learn
> In trembling awe to turn
> From the kind gaze of him who towers above them."

Because of her intellectual and spiritual superiority she was criticized and sometimes disliked by some of the rural rustics,

Reminiscence of Mrs. Sarah G. Chard

but those true discerners of character, the children, loved her and sought her company. After world fame found Mrs. Eddy, many were the reminiscences of those who had been children when she was Mrs. Patterson in North Groton, and they were all fond recollections similar to Sarah Chard's:

> She was very fond of children. My little sister, Nettie, and I used to go and play in her house and Mother used to leave us with Mrs. Patterson for half a day sometimes when she went to the village. . . . Days when Mrs. Patterson was not up around she used to lay on a couch which had a head board that could be raised or lowered. When she was laying down she used to tell us to take the string and pull her up. The string would fall back. Then she would lie and laugh at us and tell us to try it again. . . . Days when she was able to sit up she would take my sister on her lap and I would stand beside her and she would talk to us. I don't remember what she told us but I guess it must have been good. We always wanted to come back.

Not only small children, but the teen-age young people loved her. These she tutored in their academic studies,—particularly young Daniel Kidder from the neighboring farm. As an elderly man, when he recalled the following, his eyes filled with tears:

Reminiscence of Daniel Kidder

> She was a fine looking woman. Intellectual and stately in appearance. She kept her house in the most perfect order. She wrote for the magazines of the day, mostly poetry. This was a source of much interest and pleasure to me. Mrs. Patterson took a great interest in the education of the young then living near her. She was a great help to me in my studies at that time. I remember her as a sincere friend.

The Pattersons' house was on a noisy creek in the White Mountains and was a delightful summer home, but the winters there were long and harsh and bleak. Mary's hours were made even longer by loneliness, for Daniel was often away for days at a time. She had occasional days when she felt she might recover, but they were few, and her days of weakness and suffering were many. One day Myra Smith broke her bottle of homeopathic pellets when accidentally knocking them to the floor. Mrs. Patterson told her not to mind, because they were no good anyway. Her faith and hope in homeopathy had dwindled, for though she often helped others she found no lasting improvement for herself. Her Bible was her only refuge and solace.

At this dark period of earthly experience Mary turned unreservedly to God and vowed a vow, as had Jacob. She gave the promise to God that, if He restored her health, she would devote her future years to helping sick and suffering humanity. There truly

Mary's vow to God c.1859

"appeared a great wonder in heaven; a woman clothed with the sun." Jesus had foreseen the emergence of woman and prophesied to John of this event before the end of the first century, but it was nearly eighteen hundred years before such a woman appeared. Long after 1866, Mrs. Eddy put her initials to the statement of the above mentioned vow with the further statement that she had kept it faithfully.

It was seven more years till the time of her great discovery, but her ministry to suffering humanity truly dates from the

time of her vow to God. From the nearby village
of Rumney Mrs. Smith brought her daughter
whom she feared was blind. In Mrs. Eddy's own
words:

Spiritual healing in the 50's

> In the fifties, Mrs. Smith of Rumney, N.H., came to me
> with her infant, whose eyes were diseased, a mass of inflam-
> mation, neither pupil nor iris discernible. I gave the infant no
> drugs—held her in my arms for a few moments while lifting
> my thoughts to God, then returned the babe to her mother
> healed. In grateful memory thereof Mrs. Smith named her
> babe "Mary," and embroidered a petticoat for me. I have
> carefully preserved that garment to this day. [1902]

Mary's life soon began to change for the better, albeit very
deep waters preceded the new conditions. Improvident Daniel
had mortgaged everything,—even his wife's personal belongings (including her dictionary), and still had
not paid Martha a cent. Probably all the family
felt that Daniel might do better elsewhere,
and that it would be better for Mary to move to a new location and for Martha to have her money. In her notebook on
the twentieth of September Mary wrote, "On this day my
sister sells our homestead." A neighbor noted in his diary that
Dr. Patterson had had an auction on that date. A month later
the same neighbor recorded, "Dr. Patterson sold out today,"
probably referring to some of his other holdings.

Mortgage foreclosed September, 1859

No reason is given for Daniel's procrastination, but he was
still occupying the house the following February when he was
assaulted while splitting wood by two men, a
father and son, Joseph and Charles Wheet.
When Mary rushed upon the scene from her
sickbed, the younger Wheet had felled and
stunned Daniel with the axe. With unwonted strength she
seized the young man and prevented his dealing the death
blow. When help arrived she had to be carried back to her
bed. The newspaper account entitled "Female Bravery,"
described how she had saved her husband's life. She had also
prevented the Wheets from being murderers, although they
were not grateful at the time.

Wheets attack Patterson February, 1860

Abigail came on the nineteenth of March to drive Mary to a boardinghouse in Rumney six miles distant. As soon as they departed, the Wheets took possession of the Pat- Move to tersons' property. Mary wept bitterly all the Rumney slow journey, but rather typically, Daniel was March, 1860 absent.

The depths of despair which Mary had experienced during the Groton years caused her to write in retrospect: "God had been graciously preparing me during many years for the reception of this final revelation of the absolute divine Principle of scientific mental healing." And for her hundreds of thousands of children that she is awakening to the glory of being she wrote, "Remember, thou canst be brought into no condition, be it ever so severe, where Love has not been before thee and where its tender lesson is not awaiting thee. Therefore despair not, nor murmur, for that which seeketh to save, to heal, and to deliver, will guide thee, if thou seekest this guidance."

DR. DANIEL PATTERSON

CHAPTER VII

THE CIVIL WAR

But now they desire a better country, that is, an heavenly:
wherefore God is not ashamed to be called their God: for he
hath prepared for them a city.

Paul

1860

A FTER a short time in Rumney Daniel managed
somehow to acquire a house in a lovely setting above the
village. Mary's health was slightly improved, but her mental
health was much improved. The deep despair she had been
through was behind her, and she resumed her writing which
had nearly come to a standstill in North Groton. She could
see the trials she had endured as a strengthening and purifying
process. She wrote in her notebook "The Heart's Unrest" in
which she views the buffeting storms as "the teachings of
wisdom and love."

> Yet through the rough billows and pitiless storms
>   The Pilot acquires his art,
> And thus our dear Savior by conflict forms
>   The meek and enduring heart.
> These, these are the teachings of wisdom and love,
>   So lean on thy Father's breast,
> 'Tis the fold for the lambkin, the cote of the dove,
>   Where the love of thy heart *can rest.*

The trials that form "the meek and enduring heart" also
develop a strength that is beyond the comprehension of the
world. It is a spiritual strength that is able, despite appearances, to say to error, "Thus far and no farther." In her
"Ode to Adversity," written in Rumney, Mary refused to repeat the despair of the Groton years:

Am I to conflicts new to be inured?
No! I have long the utmost wrongs endured
And drawn fresh energies from sharpest blows
Thus from rude hammer strokes or burning heat
With each successive change, refined, complete
The gold is purged of dross and brightly glows.

1860 was a year of political turmoil over the issue of States' Rights. The industrialized North was endeavoring to dictate to the agricultural South; tempers flared and feelings ran high, while the heads of state in Washington, D.C. endeavored to steer a safe course midst such stormy waters. Southrons saw it as an infringement on their American independence, and conservatives both North and South were seeking for a peaceful, just solution. When the radical Republicans gained the presidential election in the fall, the South lost all hope, and on the twentieth of December South Carolina seceded from the Union.

Mary Patterson was never conservative on any issue. She had been for the abolition of slavery when she lived in South Carolina, and she rushed now, with her pen, to the defense of the Union.

Southerners were fighting for their independence, and they had able leadership. Little wonder the first several battles were defeats for the Union even though the North was superior both numerically and in resources. Great Britain and France were looking favorably on the Confederacy of Southern States.

In the summer of 1861 General Benjamin Butler wrote a lengthy letter to the Secretary of War which was published in the press.

Mrs. Patterson "addressed a letter to Gen. B. F. Butler" who was a native son of New Hampshire "begging him in behalf of God's behests to our nation, of its people and the women in New Hampshire to take a firm step toward liberating slaves in our land as a sure protest for stopping the war,...The measures he adopted were accomplished." But before President Lincoln began drafting the Emancipation Proclamation, Mary Patterson had a pleasant surprise.

Early in October a letter arrived addressed to Mrs. Patterson. It was in the handwriting of one David Hall, but the

letter was from her son, George. George Washington Glover II,
who did not get along well with his foster fa-

Letter from
George Glover
October, 1861

ther, Russell Cheney, had left home and joined
the army, giving his age as a year older than the
sixteen he had been at the time. David Hall was in his regiment and acted as amanuensis for many of the boys who wanted to write home but were illiterate. Hall had been responsible for locating George's mother for him. Mary shed tears of joy upon receipt of the letter and was proud that her son was serving the Union.

A letter written by Dr. Patterson a few days after the news
from George shows that Mary's health was

Letter to
P.P. Quimby
October, 1861

still a major concern.

Rumney, N.H. Oct. 14, 1861

Dr. Quimby,
Dear Sir: I have heard that you intended to come to Concord, N.H. this fall to stop a while for the benefit of the suffering portion of our race: do you intend, and if so, how soon? My wife has been an invalid for a number of years; is not able to sit up but a little, and we wish to have the benefit of your wonderful power in her case. If you are soon coming to Concord I shall carry her up to you, and if you are not coming there we may try to carry her to Portland if you remain there.

Please write me at your earliest convenience and oblige,

Yours truly,
Dr. D. Patterson

Mary was interested in the circular that Daniel received from Dr. Quimby, but she leaned more toward Dr. Vail's Hydropathic Institute in Hill, N.H., and Hill was also much closer to home than was Portland, Maine.

Daniel had never been able to settle down to home life for long at a time, and with all the excitement of war he was
chafing to be off again. Shortly after the first

Daniel
in Prison

of the year he received an appointment from
Governor Berry of New Hampshire to go to the
South and disburse funds to Southerners loyal to the Union. In

March he was in Washington enjoying his position and the social life, but his mission was cut short. Early in April Mary received a letter from Daniel dated April 2:

> Dear Wife,
>   You will be amazed to learn that I am in prison in the Confederate States prison, but it is so, I was taken one week ago today. . . .But God alone can tell what will become of my poor sick wife with none to care for her. . .

Daniel had blundered into Confederate territory while sightseeing. He asked her to contact their representative in Congress on his behalf, which she did immediately. But a communication from Daniel the following month was most discouraging:

> May 19, 1862
>
> Dear Wife
>   . . .I am now about 900 miles from home and Heaven only knows when I shall be any nearer. I did expect McLellan would cut off the southern roads and take and release us in Richmond as he easily could have done but his eternal tardiness has blasted that hope and we are fixed for the war beyond a possibility of an earlier release. . . .I hope you hear good news from George often and that he will soon be discharged and go and take care of you as I can do nothing for you or even for myself. . . .

Mary wrote to Franklin Pierce seeking help for Daniel, to Dr. Quimby seeking help for herself, and "To A Bird Flying Southward," a poem for publication:

> Alas! sweet bird, of fond ones reft,
> Alone in Northern climes thus left,
> To seek in vain through airy space
> Some fellow warbler's resting place;
> And find upon the hoarse wind's song—
> No welcome note is borne along.
>
> Then wildly through the skies of blue,
> To spread thy wings of dappled hue,
> As if forsooth this frozen zone
> Could yield one joy for bliss that's flown;

While sunward as thine eager flight
That glance is fixed on visions bright.

And grief may nestle in that breast,
Some vulture may have robbed its rest
But guileless as thou art, sweet thing,
With melting melody thou'lt sing;
The vulture's scream your nerves unstrung,
But, birdie, 'twas a woman's tongue.

I, too, would join thy sky-bound flight,
To orange groves and mellow light,
And soar from earth to loftier doom,
And light on flowers with sweet perfume,
And wake a genial, happy lay—
Where hearts are kind and earth so gay.

Oh! to the *captive's* call I'd sing
A song of hope—and *freedom* bring—
An olive leaf I'd quick let fall,
And lift our country's blackened pall;
Then homeward seek my frigid zone,
More chilling to the heart *alone.*

Lone as a solitary star,
Lone as a vacant sepulchure,
Yet not alone! my Father's call—
Who marks the sparrow in her fall—
Attunes my ear to joys elate,
The joys I'll sing at Heaven's gate.

In her letter to Dr. Quimby she queried, *"Can* you, *will* you
visit me at once?" She also stated, "I was getting well this
spring, but my dear husband was taken prisoner of war by the
Southerners and the shock overcame me and brought on a relapse;...My disease is chronic and I have been unable to turn
myself or be moved by any but my husband for one year at
a time. I am just on the verge of such sufferings again. Do come
and save me."

Mary was seeking, seeking true healing. The regular schools

had failed to afford her more than temporary relief. Dr. Quimby had enjoyed some favorable publicity, and though many healthy people considered him a charlatan, many sufferers turned to him with renewed hope. Mary so longed for someone who could give her hope; but Dr. Quimby did not come. He was very busy in Portland; so Mary went instead to Dr. Vail's Hydropathic Institute in Hill, New Hampshire, thus terminating her sojourn in Rumney.

While the discoverer of the Science of being was experiencing numerous trials, such tribulation was also being heaped upon that portion of the earth that was preparing a place for her. Unlike any other nation in history, the United States of America began with a Constitution guaranteeing freedom, justice, and equality to the individual, and with the greatest gift of God to humanity, the Christian religion. Woman could not bring forth the child that was to rule all nations until the earth was ready for it and had prepared the place. Such a nation had appeared as thirteen states united and had asserted its protection of further advancement and progress, in writing, in the First Amendment to the Constitution: "Congress shall make no law respecting an establishment of religion, or prohibiting the free exercise thereof; or abridging the freedom of speech, or of the press; or the right of the people peaceably to assemble..."

Could this free nation stand and maintain its place in the earth? In 1862 Southerners thought the issue was States' Rights. Some citizens of the North thought the great issue of their day was slavery, but it was not! The great issue at stake was the survival of the Republic of the United States of America, the place the earth had prepared for the woman's discovery.

George Washington, the Father of the United States, turned often to Divine Providence, for all else had failed to sustain him during the hard and desolate winter of 1777-78 at Valley Forge. The War for Independence seemed a hopeless cause during those dark days of tribulation; but Washington was granted relief in the form of a vision, following which, it was interpreted to him in these words: "Son of the Republic, what you have seen is thus interpreted: *Three great perils will come upon the Republic. The most fearful is the second,* passing which the whole world united shall not prevail against her. Let every child of the Republic learn to live for his God, his land and union."

His description of the perils leaves no doubt that he was involved in the first. The second was as follows:

> Before me, spread out in one vast plain, lay all the countries of the world: Europe, Asia, Africa and America. I saw rolling and tossing between Europe and America, the billows of the Atlantic Ocean...Again I heard the mysterious voice say, "Son of the Republic, the end of the century cometh, look and learn." At this the dark, shadowy angel turned his face southward, and from Africa I saw an ill-omened spectre approach our land. It flitted slowly and heavily over every town and city of the latter. The inhabitants presently set themselves in battle array against each other.
>
> As I continued looking, I saw a bright angel, on whose brow rested a crown of light on which was traced the word "Union," bearing the American flag, which he placed between the divided nation and said, "Remember ye are brethren." Instantly the inhabitants, casting from them their weapons, became friends once more, and united around the National Standard.

One of the few people who saw the vital issue in 1862 was the president of the United States, Abraham Lincoln. He said, "My paramount object in this struggle is to save the Union. If I could save the Union without freeing any slaves I would do it; and if I could save it by freeing all the slaves I would do it; and if I could save it by freeing some and leaving others alone, I would also do that. I shall do less whenever I shall believe what I am doing hurts the cause, and I shall do more whenever I shall believe doing more helps the cause."

By midsummer Lincoln had drafted a plan for freeing some of the slaves and leaving others alone. On the twenty-second of September he issued a preliminary proclamation stating that in one hundred days he would free the slaves in any State "the people whereof shall then be in rebellion against the United States." In pursuance thereof the Emancipation Proclamation was issued January 1, 1863.

The effects were far reaching. From that point on the issue

became slavery in the popular mind. Anti-slavery sentiment ran strong in both France and Britain and thus precluded the possibility of their assisting the Confederacy. This marked the beginning of the end of the war which terminated when General Lee surrendered to General Grant at Appomattox on the ninth of April, 1865.

"The rights of man were vindicated in a single section and on the lowest plane of human life, when African slavery was abolished in our land. That was only prophetic of further steps towards the banishment of a world-wide slavery, found on higher planes of existence and under more subtle and depraving forms." So wrote Mrs. Eddy. But in 1862 Mrs. Patterson was almost constantly seeking freedom from the pains and suffering of the body.

MRS. MARY BAKER PATTERSON
From a tintype given to Sarah G. Crosby in 1864.

CHAPTER VIII

THE QUIMBY YEARS

The serpent beguiled me and I did eat.

Genesis

1862

T HERE were numerous articles in the New England
newspapers in the early 1860's regarding the marvelous
cures of Dr. P. P. Quimby of Portland, Maine. One New
Hampshire editor had written:

> ...there is a good deal said about Dr. Quimby of Portland,
> and it may not be considered amiss to mention the case of a
> young lady of this town who has been greatly benefited by
> him.
> For nearly three years she has been an invalid—a great
> part of the time confined to her bed, and never left the room
> unless carried out by her friends. A few weeks since she heard
> of Dr. Quimby and resolved to visit him. She did so, and after
> remaining under his care four days she returned home free
> from all pain and disease, and is now rapidly regaining health
> and strength.
> ...The increasing respect and confidence of the public in
> his success, suggests the day of miracles and brings up a
> question as absurd as that of two thousand years ago, "Can
> any good come out of Nazareth?" Can actual disease be
> cured by a humbug? Dr. Quimby effects his cures without
> the aid of medicine or outward applications, and his practice
> embraces cases like the above, where all ordinary treatment
> has failed to relieve. . . . Not fearing to investigate the opera-
> tion of the mind, he penetrates the region where nothing but

magicians, sorcerers, witchcraft and spiritualists have ventured, and going far beyond them in his experiments, he arrives at the principle of regulating happiness.

It may have been this very article that had prompted Daniel to write to Quimby the previous fall, and this article or another had confirmed Mary's feeling that miracles of   Letter to healing were possible today even as they had   Dr. Quimby been by the Sea of Galilee. She had chosen a   August, 1862 more conventional treatment, but she had not forgotten the claims of miraculous cures in seemingly hopeless cases. And once again her condition seemed utterly hopeless. She wrote to Dr. Quimby in despair:

Hill, Aug. 1862.

Dr. P. P. Quimby,

Dear Sir: I am constrained to write you, feeling as I do the great mistake I made in not trying to reach you when I had more strength. I have been at this Water Cure between 2 and 3 months, and when I came could walk ½ a mile, now I can sit up but a few minutes at one time. Suppose I have faith sufficient to start for you, do you think I can reach you without sinking from the effects of the journey? I am so excitable I think I could keep alive till I reached you but then would there be foundation sufficient for you to restore me is the question. I should rather die with my friends at S. Bridge, hence I shall go to you to *live* or to them to *die* very soon. Please answer this *yourself.*

Truly yours,
Mary M. Patterson

*   *   *

Phineas Parkhurst Quimby was born in Lebanon, New Hampshire February 16, 1802. When he was two years old his family moved to Belfast, Maine where he grew up. As a boy he had very little education and at an early age was apprenticed to a clock maker, at which profession he did well, for he was patient and exacting. He was small of stature and had a keen, enquiring mind. When mesmerism was first introduced into New England he studied it on his own and soon discovered that he had a remarkable ability in that area. Before long he was giving lectures and demonstrations and soon gave up his clock-making to devote full time to mesmerism. In time his rare humanity caused him to devote his ability to relieve the suffering. He developed advanced views on the subject of magnetic healing and felt that he had left mesmerism for this nobler profession. By 1862 he maintained a large suite of rooms at the International Hotel in Portland where he both lived and carried on his work.

Dr. Quimby responded to Mrs. Patterson's letter encouragingly, so she enlisted the aid of her older brother Samuel and his wife Mary Ann who lived in Boston to assist her in making the trip. It was strictly an act of kindness on their part, for Mrs. Baker wrote later, "Both my husband and myself made careful inquiries in regard to Mr. Quimby's system of treatment while Mrs. Eddy was under his care, and we considered his methods to be the essence of quackery." Nevertheless, to Mary it was a last hope, so the considerate sister-in-law gave of her time and aid to help the feeble invalid who once again was unable to dress or even to stand without assistance. Thus on the tenth of October this party of three arrived in Portland,—one with expectant hope, the other two with dubious misgivings.

Mary Patterson was, at the time she arrived at the International Hotel, very much as the woman who only touched the hem of Jesus' robe and was healed; for from the moment she met Dr. Quimby it could be said of her, too, "Woman, thy faith hath made thee whole." She found almost immediate relief from her physical suffering, but she found even more than that. She found sympathetic understanding for the first time since the loss of her mother thirteen years earlier. Many years later Mrs. Eddy wrote of Dr. Quimby, "On his rare humanity and sympathy one could write a sonnet."

For many, many years Mary had been seeking a scientific cause and cure for disease, and she now thought that she had found it in the advanced views of Phineas Quimby. However, he was learning more from her than she was from him, which he readily acknowledged. She was not only the most remarkable woman he had ever met, but the most remarkable woman the world has ever seen. Although not a religious man, Quimby was honest and good, and he saw Mary Patterson's mission more clearly than she then did when he made the statement: "I see now what you mean, and I see that I am John, and that you are Jesus."

The parallel offended Mary's religious sense, but Quimby was very close to right. Many years later she was compelled to deny Quimby even as Jesus had denied John the Baptist, saying, "he that is least in the kingdom of heaven is greater than John." Quimby's mental healing was strictly the use of the human mind combined with physical manipulation. Science and Health now says of those who promote such practice, "They regard the human mind as a healing agent, whereas this mind is not a factor in the Principle of Christian Science." And it asks those Scientists who cling to a personal sense of mind in matter, "When will the ages understand the Ego, and realize only one God, one Mind or intelligence?" But in 1862 neither Mrs. Patterson nor Dr. Quimby understood his method of healing.

Another of Dr. Quimby's patients the latter part of 1862 was Emma Morgan whom he treated for severe neuralgia. Her father, W. P. Morgan, offered Quimby "one thousand dollars to explain his method of treating disease; to which the doctor replied—*I cannot; I do not understand it myself.*'" The spiritual Mrs. Patterson had advanced views of her own on mental therapeutics, and she and Dr. Quimby spent many hours discussing the subject and sharing their views and experiences.

Mary was never lukewarm on any subject, and in the fall of 1862 P. P. Quimby was her savior. He had wrought wonders, and her praise was lavish. She stayed in Portland after Samuel and Mary Ann returned to Boston, moving into Mrs. Martha Hunter's boarding house where other Quimby patients were living. One of the latter was Mr. Julius Dresser whom she first met at the Hydropathic Institute in Hill. He had noted her arrival on October 10, and wrote in his diary a week later:

> The most peculiar person I have seen of late is Mrs. Patterson, the authoress, who came last Friday, a week ago today, from Vail's Water Cure in Hill, N.H., where Melville, Fanny Bass, and I were; and is now under Dr. Quimby, and boarding also, at Mrs. Hunter's. She was only able to get

here, and no one else thought she could live to travel so far, but today, she, with Mrs. Hunter and sister, Nettie and I went up into the dome of the "New City Building" up seven flights of stairs, or 182 steps. So much for Dr. Quimby's doings.

Mary spent every moment extolling the doctor's praises and endeavoring to fit his cures into her evolving theory of God, man, and the universe on a scientific basis. During their long conversations he asked her to look over his notes which were descriptions of his patients and their disease, and to put them in grammatical form. When correcting she added some of her own ideas at his request. He adopted some of her terminology including the term science which he had not used previously.

Mrs. Patterson was aware that she had no clear understanding of her miraculous recovery. She knew a great discovery was involved and thought erroneously that Quimby rather than herself was the discoverer. On the seventh of November she wrote a letter to the *Portland Courier* which read in part:

Letter to
Courier
November, 1862

> ...I can see dimly at first, and only as trees walking, the great principle which underlies Dr. Quimby's faith and works; and just in proportion to my right perception of truth is my recovery. ...That this is a science capable of demonstration, becomes clear to the minds of those patients who reason upon the process of their cure. ...At present I am too much in error to elucidate the truth, and can touch only the keynote for the master hand to make the harmony. May it be in essays instead of notes! say I. After all, this is a very spiritual doctrine; but the eternal years of God are with it, and it must stand firm as the rock of ages. And to many a poor sufferer may it be found, as by me, "the shadow of a great rock in a weary land."

The only patient Quimby had who reasoned upon the process of his cures was Mrs. Patterson, and she was wishing that he had essays she could read for enlightenment rather than notes which needed elucidation. The spirituality was in Mrs. Patterson's theory rather than Dr. Quimby's doctrine, but it was many years before she understood this, plus the fact that

Quimby's practice was a benevolent form of mesmerism. When she did understand it, she wrote:

> The material body manifests only what mortal mind believes,... We say that one human mind can influence another and in this way affect the body, but we rarely remember that we govern our own bodies. ... The operator would make his subjects believe that they cannot act voluntarily and handle themselves as they should. If they yield to this influence, it is because their belief is not better instructed by spiritual understanding.

At this time her belief was "not better instructed by spiritual understanding," and she yielded completely to Quimby's influence; but she had touched the keynote of the Science of Man and the master hand would make the harmony of being clear to her; but that master hand was infinite Mind,—not a mortal man.

From the time of Mary's recovery her thought had been to secure Daniel's release from prison and to this end she sought the aid of Daniel's brother John in nearby Saco, Maine, and of Governor Berry of New Hampshire,—both of whom responded. But before embarking on her planned trip to Washington, she learned that Daniel had escaped from prison and was safe. By mid-December he had joined her in Portland and shortly thereafter they returned to Sanbornton Bridge.

Mary had gone a step beyond homeopathy into the mental realm from the day she first met Dr. Quimby. From him she had learned the power of positive thinking to produce health and the power of negative thinking to produce disease. His humanitarianism had won her heart, and she was a staunch disciple endeavoring to practise her interpretation of his theory both on herself and others. But she needed his mental "visits" as did many of his patients when they were away from his magnetic personal presence, as her letter of January 12 indicates:

Letter to P. P. Quimby January, 1863

Sanbornton Bridge
Jan. 12, '63

Dr. P. P. Quimby
Dear Sir: Yours of recent date was received with pleasure.

My felon finger must account for bad penmanship in answering it. Yesterday I took care of a woman in fits, and in the spasm she grasped my finger, which has made it somewhat troublesome today. Your angel visit here removed all my stomach pain, the particulars of which were very remarkable and sometime I will narrate them to you.

I am to all who once knew me a living wonder, and a living monument of your power: five or six of my friends are going to visit you. My sister, Mrs. Tilton, will not find it convenient to leave at present. I am at this time with her, and company from Boston will detain her at present. She wishes me to accompany her son to Portland to see you and probably he will visit you soon. . . .

I eat, drink and am merry; have no laws to fetter my spirit now, though I am quite as much of an escaped prisoner as my dear husband was.

Many thanks for your kind wishes for my future. I mean not again to look mournfully into the past, but wisely to improve the present, and go forth to meet the future with a woman's courage. I somewhat expect my husband will take up arms to serve our nation's rights, he yearns to do it, and I shall try to acquiesce. . . .

The Dr. wishes to be kindly remembered,

Yours ever,
Mary M. Patterson

Daniel Patterson was yearning for adventure, and not at all eager to assume responsiblity. Mary was longing for a home of her own, but Daniel seemed perfectly contented to accept the largess of their relatives. By the end of January her old ailments were returning and she again wrote the doctor for help, stating, "Yet if 'twere not for *visiting* I could manage myself; but not being at *home* I have no *tranquility* wherewith to aid myself."

March found Mary still in Sanbornton Bridge writing to a friend in Portland, "I will try to send my Philosophy by Mrs. Tilton when she accompanies her son to the International" [Hotel in Portland] . Daniel was still dallying,—wandering about New England speaking here and there, wherever he could find listeners, about his prison experience. He neither enlisted in the service nor showed any inclination toward resuming his profession.

With no house to call her own Mary was beginning to feel tempest tossed,—a constant visitor in the homes of others. She seemed unable to maintain the health she thought she had found, so for lack of home and health she returned to Portland in the summer of 1863. That fall and winter she was still a visitor, this time with one or another of Daniel's relatives in Saco when she was not in Portland.

When she *was* in Portland, she spent almost every afternoon in long conversations with Dr. Quimby and every evening at her boarding house writing, writing, often far into the night. Some of her writing was for the local press, but most of it was on the subject nearest her heart,—spiritual healing. Those manuscripts were left with Dr. Quimby and were the source of much trouble years after her great discovery.

Dr. Quimby and Mrs. Patterson had much in common, for they both had natural qualities that spiritualists attributed to mediums such as second sight and the ability *Man and Woman* to read people's minds; but both had rejected   by Quimby spiritualism as being false and often fraudulent. They both had integrity and honesty and were dedicated to serving mankind. But Mrs. Patterson had a spirituality which Quimby did not possess. He was well aware of this fact and readily acknowledged her spirituality and its import for the progress of the human race. Had he lived, one has little doubt that he would have become an adherent of Christian Science and a devout follower of Mrs. Eddy after reading his article "Man and Woman."

> Man, like the earth, is throwing off a vapor, and that contains his knowledge. Out of this vapor comes a more perfect identity of living matter, more rarified than the former, and consequently in danger of being devoured by it. The latter life is less gross, therefore more spiritual, so that what it loses in physical strength it receives from a higher power approaching God or Science. This Science is the wisdom of God that controlls the intellect. As the earth is composed of different kinds of soil, so man varies from the lowest grade of animal intelligence to that higher state of consciousness

which can receive Science.... The spiritual rib that rises
from man is more perfect matter or soil, called woman....
I do not mean that woman means every female. Nor do I
pretend to say that man means everything of the animal. But
that the mind of the female contains more of that superior
substance required to receive the higher development of
God's wisdom. For this element is pure love...

...The male creation feeds on the lower order of life. It
makes the higher order a sort of pet for a while, the natural
man sports and plays with the female. While the purer part of
his nature is sympathizing with its own love in a higher soil
or life, the animal life is prowling around to devour the little
pleasure that is striving to grow in this barren soil. This keeps
science down, for it is not known to the natural man. But
put this science into the life or soil of the female, and then
she is safe from the animal life, and it puts her in possession
of a Science that the natural man knows nothing of. It separates her from matter and brings her into that spiritual state
that rises from all animal life with a knowledge of its character. Like a chemist she then stands among all kinds of matter,
which are under her control, and which she has the power of
changing. Then she becomes a teacher of that Science which
puts man in possession of a wisdom that can subject all
animal life to his own control, and separate the wisdom of
this world from the wisdom of God. Then woman becomes a
teacher of the young, and man stands to woman as a servant
to his Lord, ready to investigate all phenomena by Science....

As the soil of California is rich enough to produce gold, so
the soul or life of the female is rich enough to produce the
wisdom of God. It does not follow that the life of woman is the
only soil capable of producing Science, but it contains more
spiritual wisdom than is found in man. This is as it should
be, and if it could be admitted by man, so that woman could
have her place in the life of man, the world would in a short
time be rid of the scourges....

Quimby saw that Mrs. Patterson gave a spiritual interpretation to his theories he had never dreamed of. He also saw
that this spirituality carried over to her practice of his theories,

for she relied wholly on mind and never manipulated patients as he did.

It may have been the following case which caused him to write, "Like a chemist she then stands among all kinds of matter, which are under her control, and which she has the power of changing." A woman was taking her dying husband to his old home in Canada, but a doctor on the train advised moving him to the nearest hotel at the next station which was Portland. Mrs. Patterson was at the hotel when they arrived and shortly thereafter she heard that the husband had passed away. She went to the door of the bereaved wife, and when it was opened in response to her knock, "tried to comfort her. She said, 'Let us go and waken him.' They went, and she stood beside him for a few minutes and told his wife that he was waking, and that she must be close by so that he could see her when he opened his eyes which he shortly did. He said to his wife, 'Oh, Martha, it was so strange, to be at home and you not there,' and he spoke about meeting his parents and others of the family who died before." Mary had perceived undying life, and Martha had witnessed that Christ could raise the dead in the nineteenth century as in the first. Martha's husband was living when Mary Patterson left the hotel three days later.

*   *   *

Mrs. Sarah G. Crosby had journeyed from Albion, Maine to be treated by Dr. Quimby in the fall of 1863. In Portland she met Mrs. Patterson and there was an immediate affinity between the two women. They roomed in the same boarding house in the winter of 1863-64, and when Mrs. Crosby returned to her home it was with the promise that Mrs. Patterson would visit her very soon.

Before Mary had started for Albion she received a pleading letter from another of Dr. Quimby's patients, Miss Mary Ann Jarvis, to come to visit her in Warren, Maine. It was a call for help, so with the doctor's blessing she embarked upon her mission of mercy, arriving at Miss Jarvis' home late in March. *Visit to Warren, Maine March, 1864*

The house was a difficult one to be in, full of sickness and fears,—one of which was that Mrs. Patterson would not stay.

Letter to
Quimby
March, 1864 She did stay for two months and helped Miss Jarvis greatly, but at great expense to her own health. Quimby's method of first taking the patient's illnesses upon himself and then casting them off, was more detrimental to the enquiring spiritual thought of Mrs. Patterson than it was to the benevolent magnetic thought of the doctor. And, too, she was still a visitor in someone else's home. She wrote to Quimby on the thirty-first of March:

> ...I do not want to return to Portland to stop if I can avoid it. If I could have my husband with me and be at home, I would like it there: but! but! but! I like people of common sense, and common justice, or else I like to laugh where the joke comes in. I cannot be deceived in character—I have seen not a little of life in most conditions, and I cannot stoop to conditions. I will not bow to wealth for I cannot honor it as I do wisdom, and I despise an individual who does. I respect my "household God" and give it an identity, call it by no name, but always know it when I see it. It never appears in envy, or jealousy, but loves all good attainments in every one, pleased to acknowledge them better than riches, and exalting above all else their possessor.

No doubt it was Quimby's appreciation of womanhood in general and of Mrs. Patterson in particular that caused her to

Letter to
Quimby
April, 1864 take her courage in her hands and begin lecturing at this period of her experience, for speaking in public by women had always been all but forbidden by custom. Her adorable mother had never even offered audible prayer for her assembled family in her own home, though they had such every day; for a man was expected to be the head of the family and to do the speaking. It is not surprising that one of her first reviews, though praiseworthy of her appearance, intelligence, and presentation, also said, "This lady is not in the habit of public speaking, at least we should judge so from the tone of her voice which was too feminine to fill the hall." A lecture she delivered in Warren was the main topic of her letter of April 10 to Dr. Quimby. She said in part:

Some how I am "impressed" to write you as the spiritualists call it.

Last Wednesday at 12 M. I saw you in this parlor where I am now writing. You wore a hat and dress coat. I said to your Doctorship How do you do? whereupon you answered not again, but left, which I called dodging the question. "Well," I sighed, "am sorry I spoke," but really he need not have gone so suddenly. I was not intending to ask him to have staid to my lecture! But I did see you and was not thinking of you at that time. The lecture was thinly attended, but the precious few, were those whom a lady present (the manufacturer's wife) said were the uppertendam; only think of Yankee castes in *all* our *country villages.* I thoroughly wish we were understood as a people, the *true American idea*. . . .

One first reason of my thinking to lecture here at all, was the general opinion that I was a spiritualist. This came as I were told from one of your patient's reporting here that you were such. . . . I began like this . . . To correct any misconceived ideas on the subject we would first say—that a belief in spiritualism, as defined by rappings, trances, or any agency in healing the sick, coming from the dead, we wholly disclaim.

. . . Had a letter from the editor of the *"Independent"* to write for his widely circulated journal. But I am not strong enough to step out upon the waves yet. I fear at least wetting my feet. Wrote him I were not able. I long, long to be strong!

Dr. Quimby had used the word wisdom in endeavoring to explain his cures, and Mrs. Patterson had translated it to mean God in her philosophy. This synonym for Deity appears in her letter of April 24, as does reference to the second lecture she delivered in Warren:

Letter to
Quimby
April, 1864

Warren, Ap'l 24, 1864

Dear Dr.

I am a little bit lonesome, doing and suffering. Am wishing I was around the home-hearth with my child and husband amid the joys of liberty. . . . The cup which my Father—Wisdom hath prepared for me shall I not drink it? To our material sense 'tis even at times gall; but he that forsaketh not father and mother to follow me, is not worthy of me.

...Dr., I have a strange feeling of late that I ought to be *perfect* after the command of science, in order to know and do the right. So much as I need to attain before that, makes the job look difficult, but I shall try. When men and above all women, revile me, to forgive and pity. When I am misjudged because misunderstood, to feel: Wisdom forgive them for they know not what they do. ... All things shall work together for good to them who love wisdom. ... I can love only a good, honorable and brave career; no other can suit me. If I could use my pen as I long to do, and not sink under it: I would work after this *model* till it should appear a "thing of beauty which is a joy forever."

...I have changed my lecture to suit the occasion. This seems to me a spiritual need of this people. I like much the hearts of Warren folks, i.e., better than their heads. They are very respectful and kind to me. Would *you* have the courage to attend if here? *Sometimes* wisdom is known by her followers. ...

Mary truly outlined her own future in this letter, "to be *perfect* after the command of science," and to use her pen to "work after this *model* till it should appear a 'thing of beauty which is a joy forever.'" But her cup seemed a bitter one at this juncture. She had a semblance of health for the first time in her life, but not a spot on this earth to call her own. "The foxes have holes, and the birds of the air have nests; but the Son of man hath not where to lay his head." How dearly she learned what she later wrote in Science and Health, "Home is the dearest spot on earth."

She was still in Warren in May of 1864 planning to go on to visit the young widow in Albion, Sarah Crosby, when her plans were quickly changed by news from Daniel. She went instead to Lynn, Massachusetts, for he was opening a dental office there. But in Lynn she found neither a genial husband nor a happy home, so before the end of the summer she sought refuge in Albion. The visit meant much to her friend, for Mrs. Crosby recalled those days fondly after the lapse of nearly two score years. She wrote to Mrs Eddy in 1903:

...in fancy I often go back to the old farmhouse in Albion

as it was forty years ago with grandma Crosby the presiding spirit, ruling as with a rod, the rather too yielding *nominal* mistress of the household, the brood of noisy children frolicing from cellar to garret, the "hired girls" and "hired men" forming a little colony by themselves.

These form the background of a picture in which the central figures are two *lone women.* The one, fired with the prescience of a great mission, even in the depths of poverty, looking forth upon the world conscious of coming power;—the other, peering wistfully into a future that *seemed* full of shadows, yet with the aspirations of a young goddess.

Days and nights they sat in the little chamber of the *one,* or the nursery of the *other,* in such communion of soul as is seldom experienced by mortals; so full of tender love and sympathy for each other.

Mary's visit was the most stimulating and inspiring experience of Mrs. Crosby's life. A short time thereafter she took up the study of stenography and became one of the earliest female court reporters in New England which gave her independence and wealth.

During these weeks of companionship the topic nearest Mary's heart was true spiritual healing and correlatively the refutation of spiritualism which was gaining in popularity during the war years. As Mary had written to Dr. Quimby, she liked "to laugh where the joke comes in," and she thought one day to have a good laugh with her friend while proving her point regarding mediums. She suddenly simulated a trance, and in a low voice said that this was Albert Baker warning Mrs. Crosby— that in spite of his great love for his sister, and even though she loved Mrs. Crosby as much as she was capable of loving anyone, she might use their sacred confidences to further any ambitious purposes of her own. But there was no laughter where the joke came in. Mary had underestimated the credulity of her friend! From that moment Sarah Crosby believed (as Mary had said) that Albert Baker was her "guardian spirit." Little wonder in an early edition of Science and Health Mrs. Eddy wrote:

> We have explained to the class calling themselves Spiritualists, how their signs and wonders are wrought, and

have illustrated by doing them; but at the same time have said, This is not the work of spirits, and I am not a medium; and they have passed from our presence and said, behold the proof that she is a medium!

One day, after the weeks of her visit had turned to months, Daniel appeared in Albion. He was seemingly repentant for his infidelity, and Mary returned with him to Lynn. But his repentance was not genuine, for on the fourteenth of December in 1864 Sarah Crosby wrote Mary that she had received an amorous letter from Dr. Patterson. Nevertheless, Mary continued to try to hold her marriage together, while Daniel's behaviour grew more brazen and despicable.

Though not the helpless invalid she had been, Mary was still far from well and strong. In April she made another short trip to Portland to see Dr. Quimby. The following month the little doctor retired from his busy practice in Portland and returned to Belfast. In June, Dr. Patterson again left his wife for several months. His agreement to send her four dollars a week in his absence was kept for the first four weeks only. Alone and without funds, how she longed for human comfort and understanding.

Healing was ever in Mary's thought, for her health was so precarious. When she had tried to talk about spiritual healing with Daniel, he laughed at her. Mrs. Tilton had grown disinterested in mental healing when Quimby had failed to cure her son of alcoholism. To her father, Mark Baker, the topic was offensive, and he had said so in less than gentle terms. Quimby was the only one with whom she could discuss her unfolding ideas, so she had turned to him much as she had turned to her sympathetic mother in earlier years.

For three years her visits with the gentle doctor had been like an oasis in a weary world, but this relationship was not to last much longer. In October of 1865 Quimby had an experience which was new to him, in that he could not rid himself of the disease which he had taken on from a patient. He grew steadily worse and died three months later on the sixteenth of January, 1866.

Mary had had a brief interlude of sympathetic understanding in her acquaintance with Dr. Quimby, but she had no idea of the cost involved. Though she knew it not, she had seen the working of good mortal mind, and she was destined to experience its opposite,—the working of wicked mortal mind,—before many more years had passed. Perhaps both experiences were necessary for the Discoverer to find the Way and point it out clearly for all of her children on this earth.

PHINEAS PARKHURST QUIMBY

CHAPTER IX

THE GREAT DISCOVERY

And there appeared a great wonder in heaven; a woman
clothed with the sun, and the moon under her feet.

Revelation of John

February, 1866

THE door had scarcely closed on the Quimby years
when a new door opened in Mary's experience,—one
that was never to be shut. She had been as influenced by
animal magnetism as Eve had been by the same serpent in the
Garden of Eden, but her experience in February of 1866
marked the beginning of her awakening. It would be nine more
years before she was fully awake, but the incident that occured
on Thursday evening, February first, precipitated the falling
away of mesmerism and the revelation of her great discovery.

Daniel was again away on one of his jaunts, and his wife
was on her way with friends to a meeting of the Good Templars
Near fatal   when she fell on the ice and was severely injured.
accident   She was carried in an insensible condition into
February, 1866   a nearby residence, a doctor was called, and
friends stayed with her through the night. When she regained
consciousness the next morning, she insisted, against the
doctor's advice, on being taken to her home in Swampscott.
The physician made several visits and said on Saturday that
there was nothing more that he could do for her; and her friends
notified their minister.

In an interview in later years Mrs. Eddy said:

...the dear ones around me said, "If you can't live, tell us
something, do tell us something as you always do, of your

70

views,"...I said to them, "Why, I can't conceive in this vesti-
bule that there is death....It does not seem death to me;
life seems continuous, and my Father's face dearer than ever
before."...

The clergyman...entered and ...said, "You seem near
heaven. Do you realize that you cannot recover?" I said,
"They tell me so, but I cannot realize it," and he said to me,
"I must see you again; I am engaged now, but I will call in a
little time. I want to see you again living if I can."

He stepped out...I requested the others to leave the room
and they did. Then I rose from my bed perfectly sound; never
knew health before, always an invalid. I went downstairs...
The clergyman returned. He was so startled he did not know
whether to conclude it was me in the body or out. He said,
"What does this mean?" I said, "I do not know."

The doctor was sent for...He said, "How was this done?"
I said, "I cannot tell you in any wise whatever, except it
seemed to me all a thing or state of my mental consciousness. It didn't seem to belong to the body, or material condition. When I awakened to this sense of change I was there,
that is all I know."...he said, "This is impossible," and immediately I felt I was back again, and I staggered. He caught
me and set me in a chair and he said, "There, I will go out.
If you have done that much, you can again." ...When I found
myself back again I felt more discouraged than ever.

As I sat there it all seemed to come to me again with such a
light and such a presence, and I felt, "It is all the mind. These
are spiritual stages of consciousness," and rose right up again.
And then I felt I never could be conquered again.

Long after her discovery when Mrs. Eddy was teaching the
Divinity Course to a few of her students she told them:

When I first came to Christian Science I was lifted right
out of the belief of sickness into the belief of perfect health;
since then I am working out of that belief in health into the
Science of health, and it would have been easier if I had never
been in that belief, just as it is with one who sings by ear,
which is not the science of music; it would have been easier
to have commenced right in the first place than to have to
unlearn and learn over again.

She had much to unlearn from the Quimby years. Jesus had said of John, "Behold I send my messenger before thy face, which shall prepare the way before thee. . . . notwithstanding he that is least in the kingdom of heaven is greater than he." Jesus knew that John's work was entirely from a wrong basis, but Mrs. Patterson did not yet know this about Quimby's work.

Mary had suddenly found herself on the mountaintop. She did not know how she had gotten there, and she did not know how to stay there. Her contact with others tended to pull her down, so she wrote to Mr. Julius Dresser, one of Quimby's more intellectual patients, asking him to help her, and enclosing a eulogy she had written after Quimby's death.

Letter to Julius Dresser February, 1866

Mr. Dresser: Lynn, February 14, 1866

Sir: I enclose some lines of mine in memory of our much-loved friend, which perhaps *you* will not think overwrought in meaning: others *must* of course.

I am constantly wishing that *you* would step forward into the place he has vacated. I believe you would do a vast amount of good, and are more capable of occupying his place than any other I know of.

Two weeks ago I fell on the sidewalk, and struck my back on the ice, and was taken up for dead, came to consciousness amid a storm of vapours from cologne, chloroform, ether, camphor, etc., but to find myself the helpless cripple I was before I saw Dr. Quimby.

The physician attending said I had taken the last step I ever should, but in two days I got out of my bed *alone* and *will* walk; but yet I confess I am frightened, and out of that nervous heat my friends are forming, spite of me, the terrible spinal affection from which I have suffered so long and hopelessly. . . . Now can't *you* help me? I believe you can. I write this with this feeling: I think that I could help another in my condition if they had not placed their intelligence in matter. This I have not done, and yet I am slowly failing. Won't you write me if you will undertake for me if I can get to you?

Respectfully,
Mary M. Patterson

Mr. Dresser responded in the negative. Though his letter was kindly, he said in part:

> As to turning doctor myself, and undertaking to fill Dr. Quimby's place and carry on his work, it is not to be thought of for a minute. Can an infant do a strong man's work? Nor would I if I could. Dr. Quimby gave himself away to his patients.

Julius Dresser was the only Quimby patient aside from Mrs. Patterson who seemed to have any comprehension of the doctor's method. The Ware sisters, who were perhaps Quimby's most devoted followers had no success in healing. Emma Ware wrote in 1882: "I devoted myself exclusively to his instruction as long as he lived—but I never learned the art of healing."

Once again in her experience Mary had no place to turn but to God. Spirit had lifted her to the mountaintop, and Spirit would be her *only* instructor henceforth. Her instantaneous healing from the injury that neither surgery nor medicine could reach was the falling apple that led to her discovery. But her great discovery that *all* causation is Mind "and *every* effect a mental phenomenon" was not instantaneous. She had been seeking scientific healing for twenty years, and there were many more months of searching and pondering before she understood her own healing.

It was the latter part of 1866 before she arrived at the scientific certainty of how to be well herself and how to heal others. Even then she had not discarded Quimby's influence, so for many years thereafter she tended to date her discovery from her work in Warren, for it was there that she first had the peculiar feeling that she ought to be perfect after the command of Science. Seldom is a momentous occasion recognized at the time. But the distance of years gives a proper perspective until it is seen in all its import. So was it with Mrs. Patterson's healing in February of 1866. As the years increased it stood out more and more as the great turning point in her experience from which point she was directed by God and instructed by experience.

In 1881 she wrote a two and one-half page account of her healing in the third edition of Science and Health   Letter to
in which she said, "There were results connected   Caroline Frame

with our recovery at the time we have named that rendered it still more remarkable, which we have not given to the public." One of those results she revealed years later in a letter to a student, Caroline W. Frame:

> The first experience of mine in entering upon the discovery of Christian Science was the entire stoppage of the periods that are believed to be concurrent with the moon. Hence that saying of the Revelator of the spiritual idea, "The moon was under her feet." Often it seems to be *discouraging* to hear my female students talk of this period as if it was part of their life, normal and scientific.

Whether Caroline Frame was able to profit from this letter is not known, but it is known that other students have. When husbands and wives together have understood, embraced, and followed Mrs. Eddy's teaching on sex and marriage, the sublunary monthly period has immediately ceased.

Some further notes from the Divinity Course are as follows:

> In a booklet entitled *Fragment of a Lost Gospel,* published by the Oxford University Press, giving account of sayings of Jesus that are regarded as authentic by scholars, we find the following: "When Salome asked when those things about which she questioned should be made known, the Lord said, 'When ye trample upon the garment of shame, when the two become one and the male with the female, neither male nor female.'" The meaning being that Christ's kingdom on earth would not be manifested until man had returned to the state of innocence in which sexual ideas and relations had no place. "When Salome asked how long death would prevail, the Lord said, 'So long as ye women bear children, for I have come to destroy the works of the female'." Logia of Jesus, *Christian Science Journal* Vol. 25, "Jesus was asked, 'When shall the dominion of death cease?' Jesus saith, 'As long as (material) birth continues, for I came to destroy the works of birth.' See Matt. 5:17 and S.&H. 69."

This teaching on sex and marriage is basic to the scientific method of warfare as presented in the twelfth chapter of Revelation. It is a new song that mortals cannot learn without giving up their belief in mortality for an immortal basis, and the hundred and forty-four thousand who learn it are not only the redeemed of earth but the redeemers of the earth. These are they who are not defiled with sex, and who with mental anatomy, analyzing every thought, devote themselves constantly to self-purification until they be found with no guile and without fault before the throne of God.

MRS. MARY GLOVER.
From a tintype given to Lucy Wentworth
in 1870.

CHAPTER X

SIGNS IN THE HEAVENS

And then shall appear the sign of the Son of man in heaven.
Jesus

1866

SAINT John had foreseen the portrayal of the woman-hood of the spiritual idea when he recorded: "And there appeared a great wonder in heaven; a woman clothed with the sun, and the moon under her feet." The great wonder in heaven had appeared in the 1850's when Mary Patterson vowed a vow to God to devote her future years to helping sick and suffering humanity. And she was truly "clothed with the sun," — the sun symbolizing that her life was governed by Soul, by Truth, Life and Love.

Phineas P. Quimby was the first since her saintly mother to sense Mrs. Patterson's spirituality. Little wonder that it took sharp experiences before Mary learned that animal magnetism was the essence of his practice. Though Quimby's work was from a wrong basis, like John the Baptist he recognized the Christ idea when it came into his experience. He perceived the higher, spiritual, feminine thought and acknowledged it stammeringly when he said, "put this science into the life or soul of the female and then she is safe from the animal life, and it puts her in possession of a Science that the natural man knows nothing of. It separates her from matter...Like a chemist she then stands among all kinds of matter, which are under her control."

That is where Mrs. Patterson stood in February of 1866,— on a mountaintop with all matter under her control. She had yet to learn how she had gotten there, how to stay there, and how to teach others; but suddenly she was there. A great wonder had appeared in heaven, "a woman clothed with the sun, and *the moon under her feet."*

It was years before she could write, "The spiritual idea is clad with the radiance of spiritual Truth, and matter is put under her feet. . . . The moon is under her feet. This idea reveals the universe as secondary and tributary to Spirit." But when she reached this understanding, she could also look back and see the sign of the Son of man in heaven that Jesus had prophesied.

There is far more meaning to the aurora polaris than people of this twentieth century have ever dreamed. Admiral Richard E. Byrd did a great deal of exploring in the polar regions, and his statement of November, 1955, before embarking upon his last trip to the Antarctic is significant: "This is the most important expedition in the history of the world."

When Christian Scientists learn how to use the *key* to the Scriptures that our Leader has put into our hands, they will make marvelous discoveries and unlock mysteries that geographical explorers have only touched upon. When they begin to understand the aurora polaris, they will have learned much about origin. The spiritual is always the original.

George Kennan, who witnessed and recorded the Aurora Borealis of February, 1866, had no understanding of its import; but he sensed it when he wrote that the signs   Arctic Aurora in the heavens were grand enough to herald the   of February, destruction of a world: 1866

> On the 26th of February. . . there occurred one of the grandest displays of the Arctic Aurora which had been observed there for more than fifty years, and which exhibited such unusual and extra-ordinary brilliancy that even the natives were astonished. . . . Late in the evening. . . there burst suddenly upon our startled eyes the grandest exhibition of vivid dazzling light and color of which the mind can conceive. The whole universe seemed to be on fire. A broad arch of brilliant prismatic colors spanned the heavens from east to west like a gigantic rainbow, with a long fringe of crimson and yellow streamers stretching up from its convex edge to the very zenith. At short intervals of one or two seconds, wide, luminous bands, parallel with the arch, rose suddenly out of

the northern horizon and swept with a swift, steady majesty across the whole heavens, like long breakers of phosphorescent light rolling in from some limitless ocean of space.

Every portion of the vast arch was momentarily wavering, trembling, and changing color, and the brilliant streamers which fringed its edge swept back and forth in great curves, like the fiery sword of the angel at the gate of Eden. In a moment the vast auroral rainbow, with all its wavering streamers, began to move slowly up toward the zenith, and a second arch of equal brilliancy formed directly under it, shooting up another long serried row of slender colored lances toward the North Star, like a batallion of the celestial host presenting arms to its commanding angel. Every instant the display increased in unearthly grandeur. The luminous bands revolved swiftly, like the spokes of a great wheel of light across the heavens; the streamers hurried back and forth with swift, tremulous motion from the ends of the arches to the center, and now and then a great wave of crimson would surge up from the north and fairly deluge the whole sky with color, tinging the white snowy earth far and wide with its rosy reflection. But as the words of the prophecy, "And the heavens shall be turned to blood," formed themselves upon my lips, the crimson suddenly vanished, and a lightning flash of vivid orange startled us with its wide, all-pervading glare, which extended even to the southern horizon, as if the whole volume of the atmosphere had suddenly taken fire. I even held my breath a moment, as I listened for the tremendous crash of thunder which it seemed to me must follow this sudden burst of vivid light; but in heaven or earth there was not a sound to break the calm silence of night, save the hastily-muttered prayers of the frightened native at my side, as he crossed himself and kneeled down before the visible majesty of God. I could not imagine any possible addition which even Almighty power could make to the grandeur of the Aurora as it now appeared. The rapid alternations of crimson, blue, green, and yellow in the sky were reflected so vividly from the white surface of the snow, that the whole world seemed now steeped in blood, and then quivering in an atmosphere of pale, ghastly green, through which shone the unspeakable glories of the mighty crimson and yellow arches.

But the end was not yet. As we watched with upturned faces the swift ebb and flow of these great celestial tides of colored light, the last seal of the glorious revelation was suddenly broken, and both arches were simultaneously shivered into a thousand parallel perpendicular bars, every one of which displayed in regular order, from top to bottom, the seven primary colors of the solar spectrum. From horizon to horizon there now stretched two vast curving bridges of colored bars, across which we almost expected to see, passing and repassing, the bright inhabitants of another world. Amid cries of astonishment and exclamations of "God have mercy!" from the startled natives, these innumerable bars began to move, with a swift, dancing motion, back and forth along the whole extent of both arches, passing each other from side to side with such bewildering rapidity, that the eye was lost in the attempt to follow them. The whole concave of heaven seemed transformed into one great revolving kaleidoscope of shattered rainbows. Never had I even dreamed of such an aurora as this, and I am not ashamed to confess that its magnificence at that moment overawed and frightened me. The whole sky, from zenith to horizon, was "one molten, mantling sea of color and fire, crimson and purple, and scarlet and green, and colors for which there are no words in language and no ideas in the mind,—things which can only be conceived while they are visible." The "signs and portents" in the heavens were grand enough to herald the destruction of a world: flashes of rich quivering color, covering half the sky for an instant and then vanishing like summer lightning; brilliant green streamers shooting swiftly but silently up across the zenith; thousands of variegated bars sweeping past each other in two magnificent arches, and great luminous waves rolling in from the interplanetary spaces and breaking in long lines of radiant glory upon the shallow atmosphere of a darkened world.

With the separation of the two arches into component bars it reached its utmost magnificence, and from that time its supernatural beauty slowly but steadily faded. The first arch broke up, and soon after it the second; the flashes of color appeared less and less frequently; the luminous bands ceased to revolve across the zenith; and in an hour nothing remained in the dark starry heavens to remind us of the Aurora, except a few faint Magellan clouds of lumnious vapor.

The Arctic Aurora of February 26 is not the only sign that appeared in the heavens in 1866 to herald the end of the world,—i.e., the end of the world of matter and the beginning of the understanding that "man is not material, he is spiritual." The fact that the moon (matter) was under the feet of the Woman of the Apocalypse was signified in a manner that had never before occurred in the history of the world. "February, 1866, had no full moon. This remarkable feat of nature had never happened before."

HOUSE IN SWAMPSCOTT
Where Mrs. Eddy was living in the winter of 1866.

CHAPTER XI

THE PREGNANT YEARS

*Be in pain and labour to bring forth, O daughter of Zion,
like a woman in travail: for now shalt thou go forth out of the
city, and thou shalt dwell in the field, and thou shalt go even
to Babylon; there shalt thou be delivered; there the Lord
shall redeem thee from the hand of thine enemies.*

Micah

1866

THE spring and summer of 1866 were far from uneventful. The Pattersons moved to a room in Mr. Russell's
house in Lynn toward the end of March. Mrs. Patterson's
all-absorbing interest was scientific healing, and the Russells
became very hostile toward her and her views. Dr. Patterson
was disinterested as usual, and early in June he again deserted
his wife, this time eloping with the wife of a wealthy patient.
Lacking the $1.50 with which to pay the weekly room rent,
Mary was evicted by the bigoted Russells, and sought refuge
with elderly Quaker friends in Lynn, Thomas and Hannah
Phillips.

Their youngest son, fifteen year old Dorr, was suffering from
a painfully infected finger. Mrs. Patterson asked him if he
would like her to treat it for him, and he ac- Healing of
cepted eagerly. She asked his cooperation in not Dorr Phillips
looking at it or allowing others to do so, and also Summer, 1866
in dismissing it from his *thought* insofar as that was possible.
When he went to the nearby home of his married sister, Susan
Oliver, to spend the night, she wanted to inspect it and he
refused, explaining Mrs. Patterson's instructions. Next morning
they were both amazed to discover that there was not a vestige
of evidence of the painful felon that had kept him out of school

and in agony for several days.

But Mrs. Oliver was skeptical. Though she was fond of Mrs. Patterson, she doubted her theories. Her gentle father had no such doubts. He recognized Mary's spirituality and sensed her mission. In his mild way he rebuked his daughter's unbelief by saying, "Mary is a wonderful woman, Susie. You will find it out some day. I may not live to see it, but you will."

At this time Mary had no trace of her husband save his last letter in which he had written, "I hope some time to be worthy of so good a wife." Then toward the end of July a contrite Daniel appeared at the door, and once more Mary endeavored to pick up the shreds of an impossible marriage. They moved into a nearby boarding house owned by Mrs. Clark, but before the end of August Daniel had disappeared once again, this time to avoid arrest for his previous indiscretions. And once again Mary had to turn to friends for a sheltering roof.

She was always welcomed by the Phillipses and the Olivers and also by Mrs. Phillips' sister and her husband, Mr. and Mrs. Charles Winslow. The Winslows were people of considerable means and had a beautiful house on Ocean Street. They were devout Christians and their happiness was only marred by Mrs. Winslow's invalidism—she had not walked naturally for many years. Mrs. Patterson spent a good deal of time in one or another of the homes of these dear friends, and spoke much of spiritual healing.

One summer day in 1866 Mrs. Patterson was on the beach in Lynn when she saw a sad sight that needed healing. Mrs. James Norton of Lynn had taken her seven-year-old son George to Lynn Beach and left him there while she hitched the horse and went for water.

Healing of
George Norton
Summer, 1866

The child had club feet and had never walked. When the mother returned, she was stunned to see her boy walking hand in hand with a strange woman. Mrs. Norton and the stranger, Mrs. Patterson, looked into each other's eyes; then both wept and joined in thanks to God. The child was completely and permanently healed and lived a happy, useful life.

Mary's consuming interest was spiritual healing, and she was beginning to prove the truth of her hypotheses in practice;

Poem written
September, 1866

but she had no place to lay her head. Without home, without funds, she was a constant visitor in the homes of friends, and even the kindest were not much interested in her ideas. The dear Winslows had told her they thought it best if she would not discuss her revolutionary ideas. Without husband or family she was alone in the world as she depicted so graphically on the third of September in these words:

I'M SITTING ALONE

I'm sitting alone where the shadows fall
In somber groups at the vesper-call,
Where tear-dews of night seek the loving rose,
Her bosom to fill with mortal woes.

I'm waiting alone for the bridal hour
Of nymph and naiad from woodland bower;
Till vestal pearls that on leaflets lay,
Ravished with beauty the eye of day.

I'm watching alone o'er the starlit glow,
O'er the silv'ry moon and ocean flow;
And sketching in light the heaven of my youth—
Its starry hopes and its waves of truth.

I'm dreaming alone of its changeful sky—
What rainbows of rapture floated by!
Of a mother's love, that no words could speak
When parting the ringlets to kiss my cheek.

I'm thinking alone of a fair young bride,
The light of a home of love and pride;
How the glance of her husband's watchful eye
Turned to his star of idolatry.

I'm picturing alone a glad young face,
Upturned to his mother's in playful grace;
And the unsealed fountains of grief and joy
That gushed at the birth of that beautiful boy.

I'm weeping alone that the vision is fled,
The leaves all faded, the fruitage shed,

> And wishing this earth more gifts from above,
> Our reason made right and hearts all love.

Late in the summer she found a peaceful refuge with friends in Swampscott, Mrs. Mary Ellis and her son Fred, the village schoolmaster. Here she began writing in earnest on the theme nearest her heart. She would write all day in her chamber, and in the evenings read the pages to the Ellises for their comments and criticisms. This was perhaps the only home where her spiritual ideas met no resistance. This brief interlude is well described in a letter Mrs. Eddy received from Fred Ellis in 1901:

Letter from Fred Ellis

> How many times I have thought of writing a line to try whether you still remember your old friends, Mrs. Ellis and her son, with any such interest as has ever gathered about my recollection of you and of our acquaintance, to me so delightful, in those far away days at Swampscott....
>
> I have kept the even tenor of my way, teaching school with a persistence that would be monotony but for the stimulus and cheer that come through association with children. I have my own four and my thousand and more in school, to keep me feeling young....
>
> And you, you, what can I say! Words fail when I think of the marvellous work thou hast wrought!
>
> It may be presumption in me to address you. I do so, not in the light of the magnificence of your achievement, but out of my cherished remembrance of those precious evenings in the little sitting-room at Swampscott, when the words of Jesus, of Truth, were so illumined by your inspired interpretation.
>
> All that may have passed from your memory, but not from mine.
>
> Accept my heartfelt wishes for your further success, and for your peace of mind under the irritating assaults of malicious enemies.

Mrs. Eddy did not forget, and in her reply to Mr. Ellis she wrote: "Do you forget your Christmas present to me—that basket of kindlings all split by your hand and left at my door? I do not."

Though Daniel had been a very poor provider, Mary had managed to get by with income from her writing. But all of her time was now given to God's work and there was no remuneration. In her words, "Before entering upon my great life-work, my income from literary sources was ample, until declining dictation as to what I should write, I became poor for Christ's sake."

One day when Mary was with the Phillipses, Daniel came to the door expecting to be forgiven once more. The mild Mr. Phillips was infuriated at the audacity of such a faithless husband and raised his cane to strike him; whereupon Mary interceded. But she did not receive her husband again. She had made her last attempt to salvage their marriage, so Daniel Patterson wandered out of her life. He went first to the Tiltons to confess his sins and his sorrow. He agreed not to leave Mary destitute, and promised to provide her with two hundred dollars a year, which he did for a short time in small irregular amounts.

Abigail wrote Mary making a very generous offer to build her a new home of her own and to settle an income upon her, but in return she required that Mary give up her theory of divine healing. She may as well have requested that she stop breathing.

*   *   *

Mary was embarking upon a new life, although it would be two more years before she resumed the name Glover and seven more before she obtained a divorce from Dr. Patterson. In the fall she returned to the *Reminiscence of George Clark* pleasant boarding house of Mrs. Clark on Summer Street which was but a short distance from her dear Quaker friends. The reminiscences of Mrs. Clark's son George afford a picture of Mrs. Patterson in the fall of 1866.

> She was a beautiful woman with the complexion of a young girl, her skin being fair, the color often glowing in her cheeks as she talked; her eyes were deep blue, becoming brilliant and large under emotional interest, and her hair falling in a shower of brown curls about her face.
>
> She usually wore black but occasionally violet or pale rose

...And I remember well a dove-colored gown trimmed with black velvet that she wore in the summer. I remember the colors because she suggested a flower-like appearance; she had a refreshing simplicity about her which made one think of lilies. . . . Usually she was reserved, though her expression was never forbidding. But when she talked, and she talked very well and convincingly, she would often make a sweeping outward gesture with her right hand, as though giving her thought from her very heart.

My mother was much interested in Spiritualism and used to entertain the Spiritualists. . . . My mother and Mrs. Patterson would occasionally get into a lively argument, and both expressed themselves most positively on opposite sides of the question. They never fell out about it, for they were both too well used to such divergence of view among their friends. They respected each other, I may say they had too much affection to quarrel. But their arguments were highly entertaining to me, and I often wondered how persons holding such opposite views could shake hands so amiably over their differences.

Mrs. Patterson sat at the head of Mrs. Clark's table of fourteen and was always listened to with interest when she cared to talk. According to George she was admired and liked by all though her statements sometimes caused protracted arguments.

On her left sat a young man from Stoughton named Hiram S. Crafts. He was an expert heel-finisher and had come to Lynn to work in a shoe factory. He was also a spiritualist, but unlike Mrs. Clark, he was persuaded by Mrs. Patterson's arguments against spiritualism and became very interested in her theory of scientific healing.

In Mrs. Clark's parlor in the evenings some played whist, but there was always a group gathered round Mrs. Patterson, questioning and listening. She was gaining the scientific certainty that all causation is infinite Mind and had proved in numerous cases of healing the truth of her conclusions. Every evening her most interested questioner and listener was Hiram Crafts. With Mrs. Patterson's encouragement he soon felt that he, too, could heal according to her theory. So late in the fall he and his wife returned to their home in Stoughton where he planned to practise metaphysical healing.

Shortly after their departure Mrs. Patterson received an urgent letter from Mrs. Crafts requesting her to come to them and help her husband to commence practice.   First What a problem—how to teach frail mortals   student from her spiritual height! In her words:

> I discovered, in 1866, the momentous facts relating to Mind and its superiority over matter, ... Yet there remained the difficulty of adjusting in the scale of Science, a metaphysical *practice*, and settling the question. What shall be the outward sign of such a practice: if a divine Principle alone heals, what is the human modus for demonstrating this, — in short, how can sinful mortals prove that a divine Principle heals the sick, as well as governs the universe, time, space, immortality, man?
>
> When contemplating the majesty and magnitude of this query, it looked as if centuries of spiritual growth were requisite to enable me to elucidate or to demonstrate what I had discovered: but an unlooked-for, imperative call for help impelled me to begin this stupendous work at once, and teach the first student in Christian Science.

"Start where you stand" is the beginning of the road to accomplishment, and circumstances caused Mary to make that beginning. The trials she was to encounter in teaching divine Science to mortal consciousness were beyond comprehension. Bitter, bitter experiences lay in the path of the chosen of God who would give her life for others. As 1866 drew to a close the greatest teacher in the history of the world embarked upon her teaching mission,—a mission which caused her to write: "If the Master had not taken a student and taught the unseen verities of God, he would not have been crucified."

*   *   *

THE MOVE TO STOUGHTON

The first of the new year found Mrs. Patterson in East Stoughton, sixteen miles due south of Boston, living with

Hiram and Mary Crafts. She gave him his tuition, and as Mr. Crafts wrote later, "She furnished our parlor, and gave us the use of her furniture free of cost while she remained with us."

Hiram's success in healing was phenomenal, due largely to the unremitting help from his teacher. In 1901 he wrote: "She never taught me in my mental practice to hurt others, but only to heal the sick and reform the sinner. She taught me from the Scriptures, and from manuscripts that she wrote as she taught me." She also healed the more difficult cases and those who sought help from the teacher rather than from the young doctor. James Ingham and Alanson C. Wentworth were two residents of East Stoughton who later wrote testimonials of their healings by Mrs. Glover.

The larger town of Taunton, Massachusetts, sixteen miles distant and thirty-two miles south of Boston, offered greater promise for the young man; so in April of 1867 the Crafts and their mentor moved there to new and larger quarters. Mrs. Patterson wrote to her sister Martha, "The Doct. here is just beginning at great expense in a new place . . . but all that come to him sick he cures."

Move to Taunton April, 1867

Having adopted the proper title according to the gracious simplicity of those days, Mr. Crafts inserted the following advertisement in a Taunton newspaper:

To the Sick

Dr. H. S. Crafts

Would say unhesitatingly, *I can cure you,* and I have never failed to cure Consumption, Catarrh, Scrofula, Dyspepsia, and Rheumatism with many other forms of disease and weakness, in which I am especially successful. If you give me a fair trial and are not helped, I will refund your money.

A few weeks later on May 13, his advertisement included a testimony from Mrs. Abigail Raymond of Taunton which read as follows:

Testimony of Mrs. Raymond May, 1867

In giving to the public a statement of my peculiar case, I am actuated by a motive to point out the way to others of relief from their sufferings. About 12 years since I had an internal abscess, that not only threatened to destroy my life at that time, but which has ever since continued to affect me in some form or another internally, making life well nigh a burden to bear. I have consulted many physicians, all of whom have failed to relieve me of this suffering, and in this condition, while growing worse year by year, about three weeks ago I applied to Dr. H. S. Crafts, who, to my own, and the utter astonishment of my friends, has, in this incredibly short time, without medicines or painful applications, cured me of this chronic malady. In conclusion, I can only quote the words of a patient who was healed by his method of cure: "I am convinced he is a skillful Physician, whose cures are not the result of accident." I reside in Taunton, at Weir street Railroad Crossing.

> Abigail Raymond

The cures of the "skillful physician" most certainly were not the result of accident. With the constant help of his teacher he was healing all manner of disease and most particularly cases that the regular schools had failed to cure. Hiram Crafts was an apt pupil, but his spirituality and his faith in God did not begin to approximate that of Mrs. Patterson, so he did not always practise wholly according to her method and her instructions. On February 23, 1902 he wrote to Calvin Frye:

> Mrs. Eddy never instructed me to rub the head, or body, or manipulate in any form. But when I was a Spiritualist, I used to use water and rub the head, limbs and body. So, sometimes when I was studying with her I would try it, but I did not say anything to her about it.

He did not need to say anything to her about it. If it was in his thought, he could not keep it from her. But Dr. Quimby had used the material application of rubbing and water, and at this point Mrs. Patterson saw no harm in it. So, she allowed her first pupil this material crutch upon which to lean,—even including it for some of her next students, before she learned that it was a vehicle that could be used for evil.

Late in July Mary received word from her sister Martha that Ellen, Martha's daughter, was lying at the point of death. She was suffering from what her physicians   Visit to called enteritis of the severest form, after Sanbornton Bridge typhoid fever, and had been given up by three   July , 1867

89

physicians. Mary went at once to her old home in Sanbornton Bridge where Ellen lay. The house her father had built belonged now to George Sullivan who had inherited all of his father's property at the death of Mark Baker in 1865.

George's wife said that when Mary arrived "Such a change came over the household. We all felt...'the angel of the Lord appeared and glory shone round.'" Mary's step-mother, Mrs. Elizabeth P. Baker, wrote of Mary's visit to Ellen:

Healing of Ellen Pilsbury August, 1867

> In a few moments after [Mrs. Glover] entered the room and stood by her bedside, she recognized her aunt, and said, "I am glad to see you, aunty." In about ten minutes more, Mrs. Glover told her to "rise from her bed and walk." She rose and walked seven times across her room, then sat down in a chair. For two weeks before this, we had not entered her room without stepping lightly. Her bowels were so tender, she felt the jar, and it increased her sufferings. She could only be moved on a sheet from bed to bed. When she walked across the room at Mrs. Glover's bidding, she told her to stamp her foot strongly upon the floor, and she did so without suffering from it. The next day she was dressed, and went down to the table; and the fourth day went a journey of about a hundred miles in the cars.

There was some rejoicing at Ellen's recovery, but it was muted; for Mary's family was not unlike Jesus'—"neither did his brethren believe in him." Her brother George was a bitter old man. His marriage had not been a happy one; he was now blind, and he would not allow Mary to help him. Abigail, who had done so much to help Mary in the past, resented her independence and rejected her now. And they were all embarassed by her unorthodox ideas.

So, four days after healing Ellen, Mary returned to Taunton. She had persuaded her niece to accompany her and to continue treatment with Dr. Crafts. Perhaps she felt that Ellen's interest would convert her family. But, Alas!

Ellen Pilsbury was from the town's first family and was accustomed to refinement and gracious behaviour. Mary Crafts' background was common and vulgar. Her contact with greatness for the past several months which could have elevated her life to new heights, instead had caused a smouldering resentment. As soon as Mrs. Patterson had left for Sanbornton Bridge, Mrs. Crafts' smouldering emotions had burst into flames, and she had made life miserable for her husband. When aunt and niece arrived, they came into a very hostile household. Ellen reacted with hostility toward her aunt. She packed her bags and returned home, convinced that her family was right about her aunt's behaviour and companions, making the break between Mary and her family permanent.

Not only was the rift with her family wider and deeper, but her wonderful beginning with her first student was in ruins. Hiram's career was at an end; his wife was returning to East Stoughton.

Only a few months before, Mrs. Patterson's marriage had ended in disaster, and the wound was not yet healed. The members of her family, once so close and loving, were now all distant and hostile. Almost a year's work of teaching spiritual healing lay in ashes. In the summer of 1867 she was alone as her poem records:

ALONE

No answering tone, no gentle smile,
Life's joys to share or griefs beguile—
Their sunshine o'er its shadows fling,
Those hours have fled with life's glad spring,
And left this heart a sea-shell's moan
Repeating ever all alone!
   O weary heart, O tired sigh,
   Alone to live! Alone to die!

Love's golden chain and fervent vow
Are broken, and forever now!
O, can he bask in fortune's ray—
Who took from out my skies their day—
Or love to learn, and willing own—
He's made a heart forever lone?
   O weary heart, O tired sigh,
   Alone to live! Alone to die!

When cruel men kept all my gain,
Oft stored in tears, through toil and pain,—
I've sought the home my childhood gave—
A moment's shelter from the wave—
Then those when sick, whose pain I bore,
A *Sister!* drove me from the door.
  O weary heart, O tired sigh,
    So wronged to live—alone I'd die!

Yet not alone, for oft I see
Bright forms that look in love on me,
To thee, thou lost ones, and my own—
I call, O leave me not alone!
When answering tones this music pour—
Thy God is with thee ever more;
  O better bliss, that knows no sigh,
    O love divine, so full, so nigh.

And o'er the harpstrings of the soul
Sweet sounds this trembling echo roll,
Thy love can live in Truth, and be
A joy, and immortality;
To bless mankind with word and deed—
Thy life a great and noble creed.
  O glorious hope, my faith renew,
    O mortal joys, adieu! adieu!
              Aug. 13th. 1867

THE MONTHS IN AMESBURY

Mary Patterson had looked back upon her unhappy marriage
for the last time. She may have hoped that her refusal to accept Daniel's behaviour would have caused a true reform on his
part, but no such reformation had occurred. In bidding adieu
to mortal joys she dropped the name Patterson and resumed
her former name of Glover.

For a temporary refuge Mary returned to her friends the
Winslows in Lynn. She longed for peace and quiet in which to
write and to pursue the work God had given her to do. The

Winslows suggested the quiet little town of Amesbury about forty miles to the north where they had a friend Mary could contact.

Thus, in the fall of 1867 Mary Glover knocked at the door of Mrs. Mary Esther Carter in Amesbury, Massachusetts. Mrs. Carter, the Winslow's friend, could not accom- Move to modate Mrs. Glover, but she kindly recom- Amesbury mended the nearby home of Capt. and Mrs. Autumn, 1867 Nathaniel Webster. Captain Webster was a retired sea captain who was presently superintendent of a cotton mill in Manchester, only visiting his home in Amesbury every other Sunday. But Mrs. Webster was seldom alone in their fifteen room house. Mother Webster, as everyone called her, was devoted to spiritualism and was known as a "drawing medium" and a "healing medium" in the terminology of that day. She was also sympathetic, charitable, and hospitable and constantly had a house full of boarders including invalids, unfortunates, and charity patients. When Mrs. Glover introduced herself and explained her situation, Mother Webster said, "Glory to God! Come right in!"

Mrs. Glover did not believe in spiritualism, but she had found that those who did were often easier to interest in her science than were those of orthodox faith. Mother Webster was much impressed with Mrs. Glover's spirituality and with the healings she performed. She gave her a lovely room and accorded her special household privileges. For many months Mary was able to devote herself to writing. Her spiritual interpretation of the Bible begun at the Ellises' in Swampscott grew to great proportions. These copious writings were footsteps for Science and Health which was still in embryo, but her babe that would come forth after nine years had its beginning in this early manuscript on Genesis wherein she wrote, "The time for thinkers has come." Occultism and the supernatural had no part in Mrs. Glover's Science. Of these early compositions the author says:

Before writing this work, SCIENCE AND HEALTH, she made copious notes of Scriptural exposition, which have never been published. This was during the years 1867 and 1868. These efforts show her comparative ignorance of the

stupendous Life-problem up to that time, and the degrees
by which she came at length to its solution; but she values
them as a parent may treasure the memorials of a child's
growth, and she would not have them changed.

It would appear that Mrs. Glover went to Swampscott to
spend the Christmas holidays with her friends the Ellises, for
the following appeared in the *Lynn Reporter* early in January.

INVOCATION FOR 1868

Father of every age!
Of every rolling sphere!
Help us to write a deathless page
Of truth, this dawning year...
Mary Baker Glover
Swampscott, Mass., Jan 1st.

Back in Amesbury Mrs. Glover was writing a deathless page
of truth, and these are the copious notes that show the steps of
Original version her progress up to the solution of the great
Christ My Refuge Life-problem, and which she would not have
February, 1868 changed. But one of her writings of that period
she *has* changed. On the fifteenth of February her original
version of *Christ My Refuge* appeared in the *Lynn Reporter*
in eight stanzas.

Over the voice-harp of my soul
There sweeps a hand—
Beyond this mortal, weak control—
From some soft band

Of ministries; a white-winged throng
Of thoughts illumined
By God, and breathed in raptured song
With love perfumed.

And in this unveiled presence grew
A ladder bright
Rising to bear me upward to
A world of light.

Not from this earthly home afar,
    But nearer Thee,
Father, to shine a loving star
    O'er crystal sea.

Over the waves of doubt and fear—
    Time's Galilee—
Aid me to walk, Christ ever near
    To strengthen me.

And fix my sight on God, the Rock
    Upon my shore
'Gainst which the winds and waves may shock
    O, nevermore.

I am no reed to shake at scorn
    Or hate of man;
I am no medium but Truth's, to warn
    The creedish clan.

'Gainst their oppression and their wrong;
    To crucify
The Christ whose deeds they must prolong,
    To hold Him nigh.

Mrs. Glover and Mrs. Webster became close friends, although the latter comprehended little of the truth Mary was imparting to her. But she did witness many Healing of healings as did the others in her house, until Mary M. Gale Mrs. Glover was the talk of the small town. May, 1868 One such healing was that of Mrs. Mary M. Gale of Manchester who was a friend of the Websters. Mrs. Gale was critically ill with pneumonia on May 30 when she sent Mrs. Glover a telegram asking her to come to her. Mary went immediately to Manchester and healed Mrs. Gale. While there she saw a copy of *A Dictionary of the Bible* by William Smith which had recently been published and which interested her very much.

Mary was not satisfied with healing all who sought her aid. She longed to impart to others the principle of this healing.

She had proven that this could be done and that others could
practise mental healing successfully in the few
months she had instructed and assisted Hiram
Crafts. She needed another student to work with,
so as spring turned to summer she wrote an advertisement:

Advertisement
July 4,
1868

ANY PERSON desiring to learn how to heal the sick can receive of the undersigned instruction that will enable them to
commence healing on a **principle of science** with a success
far beyond any of the present modes. No medicine, electricity, physiology, or hygiene required for unparalleled success in the most difficult cases. No pay is required unless this
skill is obtained. Address MRS. MARY B. GLOVER, Amesbury, Mass. Box 61　　　　　　　　　　　　tf--June 20

Because she had found some receptivity among spiritualists,
she placed her advertisement in their publication, *Banner of
Light*. But the time for Mary to move on had arrived with or
without a place to go or a student to teach. Mrs. Webster's son
had brought his three children from New York to spend each
summer school vacation with their grandparents in Amesbury
ever since his wife had died three or four years earlier. He
thought the influence of Mother Webster's friends and patients
undesirable for his children, so he preceded their visit each
year and evicted all her tenants. He arrived toward the end of
June in 1868, and Mrs. Glover, with all the rest, was put out
into the street.

Three of them, Mrs. Glover, a Mrs. Richardson, and an
eighteen year old lad named Richard Kennedy, stood together
discussing where to go. Mrs. Richardson knew a kindly woman
who lived nearby and who, she was sure, would give them a
night's lodging. Therefore the trio went to the home of Miss
Sarah Bagley on Main Street.

Miss Bagley was a well-educated, cultured New England
spinster, and the refinement of her home was refreshing to Mrs.
Glover. The others moved on, but Mary remained with Miss
Bagley for several weeks. While there she received grateful
letters from Mrs. Gale in Manchester together with a gift of
Smith's *Dictionary of the Bible*. In the latest edition of Science
and Health there is a reference from this volume.

Miss Bagley was interested in Mrs. Glover's science, but the young man she had met at the Webster's, Richard Kennedy, was even more interested. He would come by in the evenings after his day's work that he might learn from Mrs. Glover and enter into the metaphysical discussions. Mrs. Glover did not yet know that he was destined to become her second student, and neither he nor she had any inkling of the temptations that would beset his path and the part he would play in the drama of Mrs. Eddy's earth experience.

Second student

Sarah Bagley was related to the poet, John Greenleaf Whittier, and they were friends. He had been critically ill the previous winter and was suffering again from incipient pulmonary consumption when Miss Bagley took Mrs. Glover to visit him. They found him huddled over the fire, feverish and coughing, though it was a warm summer day. Mrs. Glover remarked that the atmosphere seemed better outside than in, and he replied that if Jesus Christ lived in Amesbury, he would have to have brass-lined lungs to survive. But he responded to Mrs. Glover's ideas as they conversed, for her spirituality touched upon a chord in the poet's thought. Before long, "the sunshine of his former character beamed through the cloud," and when they rose to go he took both of Mary's hands in his own and said, "I thank thee, Mary, for thy call. It has done me much good. Come again." And indeed it had! He was completely healed. He was out and around the next day, which the neighbors noted, for the change was so sudden and remarkable.

Healing of Whittier Summer, 1868

When the estate of Squire Bagley, Sarah's father, had been settled it was learned that his fortunes had faded and there was little more than the house for his daughter's inheritance. In order to meet expenses Sarah had taught school for a time, had opened a shop in her home, and was presently doing sewing; but her meager funds would not permit a guest in the house. Mrs. Glover's financial situation was even more difficult than Sarah's. For two years she had been doing Christ's work, healing all manner of disease, and yet she scarcely had a cent with which to pay for the necessities.

She had been endeavoring to instruct Mrs. Gale in Manchester, who was most appreciative. On the eighth of August the latter had written, "I feel dear Mrs. Glover that I owe you all I am able to do for you and then my debt would never be discharged." She offered lavish financial assistance; but when Mrs. Glover accepted and moved to Manchester, Mrs. Gale was shocked. Mrs. Glover was learning that you cannot trust mortal mind, because it cannot trust itself; but she was in a very difficult, unpleasant situation. She thought of going to her son, George Glover, in the West, but by the tenth of September she was in East Stoughton. She wrote Sarah Bagley from there saying, "O, I am tired! tired! When will my rest come?"

*   *   *

THE STOUGHTON YEARS

> ...for now shalt thou go forth out of the city, and thou shalt dwell in the field.
>
> Micah

Mrs. Glover had met the Wentworth family shortly after moving to the Craft's home in East Stoughton. The younger daughter, Lucy, wrote, "When Hiram Crafts brought her to our fireside, we just felt as if an angel had come into our home." When she returned to Lynn, they had invited her to come to live with them, but it was in September of 1868 before she accepted the invitation.

Mrs. Glover had many friends and acquaintances in Lynn and spent part of 1868 there, probably both before and after
Healing of moving to Stoughton. During one of these visits
escaped maniac an escaped lunatic burst into the house where
c.1868 she was staying, badly frightening the woman of the house and her daughter. When Mrs. Glover responded to the woman's call, the man raised a chair to strike her, but she faced him fearlessly and compassionately. She spoke to him, and he dropped the chair pointing upward as he approached saying, "Are you from there?" He fell on his knees at her feet, sobbing, with his head in his hands. When he looked up, he said, "That terrible weight has gone off the top of my head," and he departed in his right mind.

Sixteen years later, in 1884, Mrs. Eddy was living on Columbus Avenue in Boston when this same man called on her. He had returned to the asylum, had been discharged as cured, and gone to live in the West. His healing had been instantaneous and permanent; he had married and had children. And now he had traced his healing to Mrs. Eddy and her Science and had come to express his gratitude.

Another of Mrs. Glover's early healings in Lynn was that of Mrs. Abigail Winslow. She had paid her dear friends a brief visit,—perhaps before deciding to move to Stoughton, and wrote of this visit:

Healing of Mrs. Winslow Lynn, 1868

> When I went there Mrs. Winslow was very lame and sick, had not walked upstairs naturally for years and given up trying to go out at all. I stopped two days and when I came away she walked to the Depot with me almost a mile. They were one and all urgent for me to stay, but I am not of their opinion. I don't want society.

Mrs. Glover had instead chosen the humble home of Sally and Alanson Wentworth. Supporting a large family on a very small farm had not been easy for the Wentworths, and Mr. Wentworth's ill-health had made it even more difficult; for he was unable to work. Their income had been supplemented by his wife who had become a "rubbing doctor," devoting much of her time to caring for the sick. Husband and wife were both deeply grateful to Mrs. Glover for Mr. Wentworth's healing. Several years later he wrote of it as follows:

> I cheerfully give my testimony to the wonderful efficacy of the Science Mrs. Glover teaches, in its application to my case. I was the melancholy victim of sciatica in the hip for many long years; at times I could neither lie, sit, nor stand without great suffering. When I first saw Mrs. Glover she told me she could cure me; but I must say it seemed impossible, after suffering so long and trying so many things, that I could be healed without medicine or application of any sort. Yet such was the case. I improved until my hip disease left me, and I am completely rid of it.
>
> Alanson C. Wentworth

Stoughton, Mass. 1873.

I was also cured of an inveterate habit of smoking and chewing tobacco.

A.C. Wentworth

Mr. Wentworth was an opinionated Bible scholar who loved Mrs. Glover's explanations. Mrs. Wentworth was eager to learn her method of healing in order to improve her own work. Nineteen-year-old Celia leaned on Mrs. Glover because of delicate health. Seventeen-year-old Charles and his friends sought Mrs. Glover's company for companionship. And the youngest Wentworth, thirteen-year-old Lucy, idolized Mrs. Glover. She told Sibyl Wilbur:

> I loved her because she made me love her. She was beautiful and had a good influence over me. I used to be with her every minute that she was not writing or otherwise engaged. And I was very jealous of her book. We talked and read together and took long walks in the country. I idolized her and really suffered when she locked her door to work and would not let me come to her. After she had worked for hours she always relaxed and threw off her seriousness. Then she would admit us, my brother Charles and me, and sometimes a school friend of Charles. The boys would romp in her room sometimes rather boisterously, but she never seemed to mind it. Our times alone were quieter. When she finally left our house it seemed to me my heart would break.
>
> ...she made a great deal of me. Yet her influence over me was always for good. We read good books and talked of spiritual things. She loved nature; she was cultivated and well-bred. Her manners seemed to me so beautiful that I imitated her in everything. I never missed anyone as I missed her.

Mrs. Glover subscribed to two magazines, particularly for Charles' benefit, and she bought a backgammon board and taught them to play; but in this busy, active household she had to lock her door to work, which she did regularly, devoting most of her time to her writing. She was instructing Sally Wentworth and often helping her with difficult cases, but she longed for a student that would seek the principle of her teaching. She had also learned that younger people were often more tractable than their elders, or as she has so beautifully worded it, "While age is halting between two opinions youth makes rapid and easy strides forward."

The previous March Sally Wentworth had written her in Amesbury. The newsy letter had included the sentences: "Hiram Crafts and wife made us a call last Sunday. He says he has not given up doctoring." So now the teacher wrote to her first student asking whether he would be willing to take up the work again. His reply of November 27 read in part: Letter from Hiram Crafts November, 1868

> I should be willing to do all you ask if I was in different circumstances. You know how things stand with me, after all the trouble that we have had I feel the same interest in the developing of Truth and its principles. I know that I am not perfect and am willing to acknowledge that fact. But it would be impossible for me to come over there to help you at present. I should have no peace at home if I did. I have been through one hell and don't want to go through another. . . . Your letter was opened and read before I got it, if you send another have it delivered to me.
>
> As to Doctoring again I do not think now that I shall ever do any more of it. If I was alone, perhaps it would be different. But as it is I must live out this miserable life in darkness and error.

If Hiram Crafts was not willing to take up the work for Truth, another young man was. Richard Kennedy, whom she had first met at the Webster's in Amesbury, visited her in Stoughton and wrote her frequently. Mary's letters to him for the next year or more, which he never shared with anyone, amounted to a mailorder course of instruction. But her main work during all the long months in Stoughton was her writing.

In her teaching she allowed both Sally Wentworth and Richard Kennedy to rub the head as Quimby had done. She also allowed Mrs. Wentworth to copy the fifteen questions she had put to Dr. Quimby several years earlier; but these questions and answers were becoming increasingly inadequate, so she wrote a preface to give them a more spiritual meaning. Mary had endowed Dr. Quimby with her own ideal and then made him think it was his own. But she herself did not yet see this clearly.

She did, however, find it necessary to formulate her own questions and anwers in teaching her students, and the thirty-five Questions and Answers in Moral Science given by Mrs. Glover and preserved by Sally Wentworth are very different from the Quimby paper. The earliest version in Mrs. Wentworth's handwriting is entitled, "Rudiments. The Science of Man. by Mary M. Glover. For the learners."

One day William Scott came hurriedly to the Wentworth house and implored Mrs. Glover to come quickly. His father, John

Healing of   Scott, was in critical condition. After   several
John L. Scott remedies had failed, they had sent for Mrs. Went-
c.1869   worth. When Sally Wentworth had arrived, she was so alarmed by his condition that she said she dared not take the case and urged William to go for Mrs. Glover. Mary came immediately and found Mr. Scott vomiting, rolling on the floor, cursing violently, and at times shrieking in agony. Two medical doctors had just left his room saying there was no hope. Mrs. Glover told him she could heal him if he would cease and be calm. He did as requested. In less than an hour the pain was entirely gone, the vomiting had ceased, and the bowels which had not moved in two weeks acted normally. By the time Mrs. Glover left he said he felt perfectly well, and he was at work the next day.

But Mr. Scott's real healing was of his character. A few days later his wife told Mrs. Glover that he had never caressed his children as other fathers did, but on the night of his recovery he had taken them in his arms and told them he loved them. With tears streaming down his cheeks he told his wife he was going to be a better man. The grateful wife said, "Oh, how I thank you for restoring my husband to health, but more than all, I am grateful for what you have done for him morally and spiritually."

Mrs. Glover's work was never like that of her students. In 1909, after reading of a student's experience in healing, she said:

> No such experiences ever come to me. I reach the results without intermediate steps. If anyone was said to be ill in the next room, I wouldn't have to treat, I would just *know* the Truth about them and they would seem to be no more sick or dead than you are. I cannot tell you how I do it, but I have none of the experiences recorded by others, though I enjoy

reading them.

By June of 1869 Mary had completed the volume she was working on. She wrote to a friend in Rumney:

> I have just sent a work to the press for publication entitled—Science of Soul—I mean you shall read it sometime. I have written this and notes on the entire book of Genesis within the last year and this, besides laboring for clothes and other expenses with teaching. I am worn almost out, have lost my love of life completely and want to go where the weary have a rest and the heavy laden lay down their burdens.

The petty annoyances of personal life harassed the revelator to this age, and poverty plagued her every footstep, but the rewards of spiritual discovery were a recompense. She could look back and say, "The search was sweet, calm, and buoyant with hope, not selfish nor depressing," She wrote to Sarah Bagley a few days later with a more triumphant note:

> My volume is finished, Sarah, and ready for the press and the outcry that will follow it: first the ridicule, then the argument, and lastly the adoption by the public, but it may be long ere the public get it. . . . I only wish I were able to launch into the fullness of Christ, embrace the whole world in my love.

Historians seem to know nothing about this volume, *Science of Soul,* but it is certain that it was not published. Mrs. Glover paid Lucy Wentworth's cousin Kate Porter seven dollars to copy it for her, but copying was all she did for Mrs. Glover. Behind her back she ridiculed and mocked her. And she was not alone in this; she was joined in her mockery by the oldest Wentworth son, Horace, who was married and lived nearby. Though their unkind remarks were not made to Mrs. Glover nor in her presence, she was not deceived. Her teachings were being derided and resisted while the healings she performed in East Stoughton, Amesbury, and Lynn were as miraculous as those by the Sea of Galilee and the Hills of Judea. She was truly "Seeking and Finding" as she recorded in her beautiful poem *Christ and Christmas:*

> What the Beloved knew and taught,
>   Science repeats,
> Through understanding, dearly sought,
>   With fierce heart-beats;

During these early years of Mrs. Glover's work she healed all manner of sickness and disease—most of the cases at Healing of crippled man Lynn—c. 1869 death's door and considered hopeless. If all these healings were written down, they would fill many books; for the streets of Lynn resounded with her cures. She told of one such case in these early days of her poverty:

> I was walking along the street in Lynn—I walked because I hadn't a cent to ride—and I saw this cripple with one knee drawn up to his chin; his chin resting on his knee. The other limb was drawn the other way, up his back. I came up to him and read on a piece of paper pinned on his shoulder: help this poor cripple. I had no money to give him so I whispered in his ear, "God loves you." And he got up perfectly straight and well. He ran into the house of Mrs. Lucy Allen, who saw the healing from her window, and asked, "Who is that woman?" pointing to Mrs. Glover. Mrs. Allen replied "It is Mrs. Glover." "No, it isn't, it's an angel," he said. Then he told what had been done for him.

When Mrs. Glover was called to a case, her ability to perceive mortal thought revealed the cause of the sickness immediately, and her spiritually uplifted thought usually healed it just as immediately in one treatment—never more than three. She was never wrong, and she never failed.

But she did have one experience which looked like failure temporarily, but which was really a beautiful incident for her own enlightenment and progress, and for ours. She told this experience to the last class she taught in November, 1898, and there was not a dry eye when she finished:

> In her early experience when she healed the sick, the most desperate cases, before getting to them,...none would acknowledge that she did it. She was troubled at this, for she feared God would not get the glory, and Christian Science be

slow in becoming established. One day she was sent for to go to a dying man and before starting to his house she knelt by her bed and asked God that the patient might not be healed till she got there, so that God's power be acknowledged and Him glorified. She said, "When I got there, I couldn't do a thing. I went home, and put my face upon the carpet, and there I stayed, until I found Jacob's ladder, from the bottom to the top. Then I saw that God, in His own time and way, would take unto Himself the glory, and it was not for me to say."

The case was healed and the man recovered.

She also asked this last class how they would heal instantaneously. After all had answered she said, "Now let me tell you how *I'd* heal instantaneously. It is not so much to realize the presence of Love—but *LOVE! Love* enough, and you'll raise the dead! *I've done it!*"

While Mrs. Glover was healing the most desperate cases till the streets of Lynn rang with her works and the folks of Amesbury expected her to walk on the water, she was faced with the problem that Henry David Thoreau had voiced a few years earlier, i.e., "Can a man feed and clothe himself gloriously, who keeps only the truth steadily before him? who calls in no evil to his aid?" On July 1, 1893 Mrs. Eddy said to her artist at the easel:

Oh, Mr. Gilman! I sometimes used to wonder, Why does not God provide for my needs? I who was raising the incurably sick (to medical sense) to health and strength so speedily as to cause amazement, even from death's door; and, in the families of the wealthy, while I was often hungry for the want of simple things that I craved, ordinarily considered necessities of life, because I lacked the material means for obtaining them. But God in His graciousness was testing me, that was all. You see, at that time I thought it would be wrong to take anything for doing such Christly work. I thought it was a gift from God to be able to heal as Christ healed and that I ought not to take money for it. . . . I worked and healed four years in this way without money and without price; and then God having tested me, He showed me a better way."

105

This better way shown by God to the woman of the apocalypse has cast down the power of Babylon, that great city, so that there is much weeping and wailing in the world, but rejoicing among the saints. Every student of Christian Science, after he has demonstrated health, is faced with the problem of supply, and this is a greater problem for the worldly wealthy than for those who suffer lack, "because thou sayest, I am rich ...and have need of nothing; and knowest not that thou art wretched, and miserable, and poor, and blind, and naked." If thou wouldst be rich, learn and follow the better way that the woman has set forth, for through her teachings and example we find the gold tried in the fire.

*   *   *

THE PARTNERSHIP

While Horace Wentworth was ridiculing and scoffing in East Stoughton, young Richard Kennedy was applying himself assiduously in Amesbury. His eagerness was a joy to the teacher, and she poured out to him freely all that she was teaching to Sally Wentworth, and perhaps more; for he was an apt pupil with an exceptionally keen intellect. Though she had formulated much more for her second and third students than she had for Hiram Crafts in his brief experience with her, she was nonetheless feeling her way as she went along. She wrote:

> ...in the beginning, to know how the students could mentally practise on the sick puzzled me. I had not by any *material* means or method demonstrated on the sick the power of divine Science and did not believe that my students at the start could reach my purely mental attitude of healing. I thought they must approach it from their standpoints and gain the results of Truth on themselves before they could practise through prayer and heal the sick.

Still believing that Quimby's healing was somewhat akin to hers, she included his material method of rubbing the patient's head as an intermediate step for her students, instructing them in application:

...first to leave your own belief or body, then you will be in principle and there be able to speak to another in this principle, in which immortality controls the body. If this wisdom be not yet fully attained, the next method is by rubbing the head, while at the same time take yourself utterly away from all thought of his complaints or their locality in matter...

Mary had very severe experiences ahead before learning that *any* physical contact is an avenue for mesmerism. But that lesson lay in the future. The present lesson was a proper and adequate sense of supply,—or how to feed and clothe oneself gloriously without forsaking Truth.

Experience had taught her that even the barest necessities were unobtainable without money. The attitude of society toward money was that it was wordly and had no place in Christ's Church,—often considering that all lucre was "filthy lucre." Mrs. Glover was learning, as she later wrote in the scientific statement of being, that *"All* is infinite Mind and its infinite manifestation." Then every so-called worldly or filthy thing must be redeemed, not denied. In time she gave her followers this beautiful, spiritual definition of money:

The Coin of Christian Science
GOLD—The silent thoughts of Truth and Love which heal the sick.
SILVER—The spoken word of Truth and Love which casts out evil and heals the sick.
CURRENCY—The written word of Truth and Love published and distributed throughout the world healing sickness and sin. But this currency must be backed up by a gold reserve in human character.

In 1870 Mrs. Glover had to make practical application of what God had been revealing to her about substance and supply. God was teaching her what He had spoken to Isaiah centuries earlier: "Thus saith the Lord, thy Redeemer, the Holy One of Israel; I am the Lord thy God which teacheth thee to profit, which leadeth thee by the way that thou shouldest go."

Mary had had an agreement with Hiram Crafts for a small percentage on his practice, but she had realized nothing from

this agreement. She had a similar agreement with Sally Wentworth, and by early 1870 Mrs. Wentworth was earning fifty
dollars a week from her practice; but once again Mary was not
paid. She wrote in retrospect:

> I taught Mrs. Wentworth Christian Science more from
> sympathy than for money, for she had told me that owing to
> her husband's long illness and inability to work they were
> poor. My terms for tuition were a small percentage on her
> practice. But I made no demands for this, and took no *legal
> action* to obtain it.

The time had come when Mary was called upon to make
God's business more businesslike. On the twentieth of February she entered into an agreement with Richard
Kennedy *in writing*. The young man had been
studying Mrs. Glover's Science for two years,
and he was eager to enter the full-time practice of mental healing. He was also eager to sign his name to the statement: "In
consideration of two years instruction in healing the sick I hereby agree to pay Mary M. B. Glover one thousand dollars in
quarterly installments of fifty dollars commencing from this
date." He valued his instruction very highly, and Mrs. Glover
had great hope for his future.

Contract with Kennedy February, 1870

The time had also arrived for Mary to move on from East
Stoughton. Her home town of Sanbornton Bridge had been renamed Tilton the previous year in honor of its
first family and their industry, but Sanbornton
Bridge or Tilton was no longer Mary's home.
Over the past several years Lynn had become home to her, and
now she thought of returning there. But that was a little farther
in the future,—the present was calling her back to Amesbury.

Return to Amesbury Spring, 1870

Sarah Bagley was very desirous of instruction by Mrs. Glover
in healing the sick. Mary had suggested that "Dickie" instruct
her while she had been instructing him, but either he had not
tried or he was unsuccessful. So Mrs. Glover made arrangements toward the end of February to return to Amesbury.
After she had bidden all the family a fond farewell, Mr. Wentworth took her to the depot and thanked her cordially for what
she had done for him and his family. Her goodbye to Lucy had
been particularly touching and with great affection. She had

held her in her arms and looked long into her eyes. Then she said sadly, "You, too, will turn against me some day, Lucy." Her words were as prophetic as Jesus' when he said to Peter, "before the cock crow, thou shalt deny me thrice."

After arriving in Amesbury, the next six weeks were spent in teaching Sarah Bagley and Richard Kennedy. At the end of that time, on the twenty-third of April, Miss Contract with Bagley signed an agreement to pay Mrs. Glover Sarah Bagley twenty-five per cent of all the money she earn- April, 1870 ed by healing in return for the instruction. And that instruction enabled her to make a very comfortable living for the rest of her life. Mrs. Glover later reduced the percentage to ten, and then even lower. But when Mrs. Glover had to renounce her teaching of physical manipulation as a method and forbid its further use by her students, Miss Bagley was not able to follow the teacher's instruction. In 1876 their contract was cancelled by mutual agreement, and Sarah was left behind with the cast-off beliefs that the discoverer was forced to discard. She never renounced her teacher and over the next twenty years purchased numerous copies of Science and Health for friends and patients. When she took a copy to John Greenleaf Whittier he examined it slowly and carefully and then said to Sarah, "Well, you will never be able to understand one-tenth part of it during your lifetime."

During the weeks in Amesbury Mrs. Glover and Richard Kennedy had been making plans for the future. The previous September he had written her, "In my future ex- Partnership perience with the world, Mary, I do not expect to with Kennedy obtain applause and popularity. This could not June, 1870 be, for truth will have its opposite, and in this will be contention and strife." For one so young Richard was surprisingly dedicated to the work at hand,—that of establishing the scientific mental healing of moral science; and he also had the buoyancy and enthusiasm of youth. What a joy and a help to the teacher! Mary had written Sarah Bagley from Stoughton after receiving a particularly appreciative letter from Richard, "Was there ever a more glorious nature, a more noble soul than Richard Kennedy possesses." Once again she was endowing another with her own qualities and ideals, but for the time being this endowment was lifting the young man to new heights. In the spring Mary made plans to return to Lynn where she was well known and to bring her young student with her to demonstrate her teaching. Their agreement was that she would supervise his practice and teach her method of healing to others. They drew up a legal partnership agreement regarding the healing practice. But this partnership did not include Mary's teaching and writing. That was solely between Mary and God.

In May Mary and the fledgling doctor left Amesbury. In Lynn they stayed temporarily with her friends Mr. and Mrs. Oliver until they should find suitable quarters. This was accomplished quickly, and by June they were located at No. 2 Shepard Street occupying the second floor of a large house opposite Lynn Common on the corner of South Common and Shepard Streets. The success of this venture was almost immediate. Mary wrote Sarah Bagley on the fifteenth of July:

Letter to Sarah Bagley July, 1870

> I have all calling on me for instruction.....Richard is literally overrun with patients....We enjoy our *moments* of leisure more than can be named. On the evening of the fourth our rooms were filled with company to hear the concert given on the common by the brass band.

At this time Mrs. Glover's business cards read simply:

MRS. MARY M. GLOVER
TEACHER OF
Moral Science

and the first business she attended to was rewriting the questions and answers she had developed for her pupils into textbook form. This was copyrighted in 1870 as "The Science of Man By Which The Sick are Healed, or Questions and Answers in Moral Science." Here again God's business was being run in a businesslike way, for her class-book was protected by copyright even though it was not printed at this time.

Copyright Science of Man 1870

The first section of this class-book was handed to each pupil in manuscript form at the beginning of class. This manuscript consisted of twenty-five questions and answers which are very similar to the twenty-four questions in Recapitulation in the latest edition of Science and Health, although the terminology is sometimes different and often broadening and helpful. For example:

> 7th Ques. What is matter?
> Ans. ....matter held as shadow is the idea of God, but matter held as substance is a belief and error.
> 13th Ques. What is sense?
> Ans. It belongs to the Soul and not to the body, and this sense gives the idea of truth and never errs.

There were yet two remnants of Quimbyism not yet eradicated from Mrs. Glover's thought. One was the belief that the healer takes on the ills of his patients. This did Letter to not seem to affect young Dr. Kennedy whose Mrs. Ellis office was filled with sick and suffering in- July, 1870 dividuals, but the spiritually sensitive teacher and director of his work who was responsible for all the healing was affected. She wrote to her friend in Swampscott, Mrs. Mary Ellis, on the twenty-third of July:

> Never did the life that seems appear so small to me as this year, and never the life that is so vast, so glorious. ....My own health is greatly affected by the many sick ones that surround me but if I can aid them out of the dark places my feet have trod I am happier even though I suffer physically.

By mid-July Richard was overrun with patients, and by mid-August Mrs. Glover was preparing to teach her first class. She placed the following advertisement in the Advertisement *Lynn Semi-Weekly Reporter* on August 13: August 1870

> MRS. GLOVER, the well-known Scientist, will receive applications for one week from ladies and gentlemen who wish to learn how to HEAL THE SICK without medicine, and with a success unequaled by any known method of the present day, at DR. KENNEDY'S OFFICE, No. 71 South Common Street, Lynn, Mass.

Mrs. Glover required each student to sign a contract before entering the class. The first two students to enroll by signing
Contracts
August
1870 such an agreement on the fifteenth of August were George H. Tuttle and Charles S. Stanley, the brother and husband of a woman who had had treatment from Dr. Kennedy and been healed of tuberculosis in an advanced stage. Daniel and Addie Spofford signed a contract two days later on the seventeenth of August; however, only Mrs. Spofford attended class in 1870. Mrs. Glover's original agreement for class instruction was as follows:

> We, the undersigned, do hereby agree in consideration of instruction and manuscripts received from Mrs. Mary Baker Glover, to pay annually on the income that we receive from practising or teaching the science. We also agree to pay her one thousand dollars in case we do not practise or teach the above-mentioned science that she has taught us.
>
>   G.H. Tuttle, Charles S. Stanley

These two young men were far from exemplary students, but they do depict the problems the teacher encountered. George Tuttle was a young seaman just returned from Calcutta who joined the class because his sister wanted him to, with little if any thought about the subject matter. When, after a few lessons, he cured a girl of dropsy, he was so alarmed that he dropped the study completely. Stanley, on the other hand, was an argumentative, dogmatic Baptist determined to disrupt every lesson with constant disagreement. Mrs. Glover had to dismiss him before the three week course ended. Neither young man had paid his tuition in full, but Stanley set himself up as a doctor and practised mental healing for several years.

Jesus taught his message to the simple fishermen, and Mrs. Glover taught hers to the shoe workers from the factories and shops of Lynn.

Early in the fall Mr. and Mrs. Spofford called upon Samuel Putnam Bancroft who was foreman in the shoefactory of Ban-
Second class
November
1870 croft and Purington where Daniel Spofford was employed. Mrs. Spofford had been treated by Dr. Kennedy and been greatly benefitted. She was entering the fall class of the wonderful woman who taught

Dr. Kennedy, and the Spoffords were eager for Mr. Bancroft to do the same.

After an interview with Mrs. Glover, Samuel Bancroft enrolled in the class as did a number of others. The contract had been eliminated and the tuition changed. Mrs. Eddy later wrote:

> I could think of no financial equivalent for an impartation of a knowledge of that divine power which heals; but I was led to name three hundred dollars as the price for each pupil in one course of lessons...a startling sum for tuition lasting barely three weeks. This amount greatly troubled me. I shrank from asking it, but was finally led, by a strange providence, to accept this fee.

This amount continued to be her tuition charge throughout the nineteen years of her class teaching; however, she had a great many charity scholars,—as many as seventeen in one class. In this November, 1870 class Mrs. Miranda Rice was admitted free, because she could not obtain the money from her well-to-do husband, but her sister, Miss Dorcas Rawson, who was a shoe worker, paid the full amount. George Allen paid in full. Seventeen-year-old George Barry paid only one-half but was receipted in full.

Samuel Bancroft has left an interesting description of this early class:

> The class meetings were held at Mrs. Glover's house, on the corner of South Common and Shepard Streets, and the course consisted of twelve lessons. Before studying we were treated by Dr. Kennedy, in order to render us receptive and to acquaint us with the physical methods used, after which Mrs. Glover was to teach us the spiritual methods.
>
> Dr. Kennedy's treatment consisted of a manipulation of the head and solar plexus. The theory, as we understood it, was that these were considered the most sensitive portions of the body. Mrs. Glover taught us, however, that there was no sensation in matter. To some of us this seemed a paradox.
>
> After being treated by Dr. Kennedy, pupils were given a manuscript of questions and answers, a portion of which we were required to study and, as far as possible to memorize each day.

We were also given private instruction between lessons when such seemed needed. Mrs. Glover was a faithful teacher, and even gave her pupils a treatment, if requested. This did not consist of manipulation, however, but of silent or audible argument.

While [the] course of instruction consisted of twelve lessons, we were never really graduated. Every meeting with her was a lesson; every letter received from her. This continued for years. I have never known of any of her loyal students to complain of not receiving full value for money paid, or asking to have it refunded. For my own part, I will say that from my limited practice in healing I received many times the amount I paid her, besides enjoying over fifty years of almost perfect health.

At the end of the class the students were given another manuscript entitled "The Soul's Enquiries of Man" which is the second part of *The Science of Man,* an essay of instructions for advancement in Moral Science.

Bancroft, the shoe manufacturer, voiced the general public opinion when he learned that his nephew had studied with Mrs. Glover: "My boy, you will be ruined for life; it is the work of the devil." But the students were inspired and exalted by their instruction and quite dedicated to future work.

The Spoffords moved immediately to the South where Mrs. Spofford began to practise metaphysical healing. Samuel Bancroft suggested that the class meet for discussions, and the home of Susan and Clark Oliver became their meeting-place as indicated in this letter:

Lynn, Dec. 4th

Mr. Bancroft:

Dear Sir,—I was sorry you did not get my word sent you to meet with the class Sat. Eve at Mr. Oliver's. You first proposed it and I acted upon your suggestion, naming it to Mr. O. He was delighted and said, "have them meet here," and accordingly they did. Mr. Allen went to your place of business the day before to inform you, but found you not.

The class meets every Sat. eve. at 7 o.c. at Mr. O's. I have a little Bible that I purchased for you about a week since and will be happy to send it to you by Dr. Kennedy at your next meeting at Mr. Oliver's.

Very truly,

M.M.B. Glover

P.S. You see I do not forget you and you must not forget yourself.

Mrs. Glover enjoyed a visit from her nephew, George Baker, in December of 1870. He had just graduated from the New Hampshire Conference Seminary. During his visit his aunt wrote in his autograph album:

> If an avalanche roll from its Alp, ye tremble at the will
> of Providence;
> Is not that will concerned when the sere leaves fall from
> the poplar?
> A thing is great or little only to a mortal's
> thinking.

Early in the new year Mrs. Glover received a letter from a very promising young man. Twenty-five year old Wallace W. Wright, a bank accountant and son of a Univer- Final salist minister, was considering entering her next identification class and asked her to respond to the nine ques- with Quimby tions he included in his letter. His sixth question and Mrs. Glover's answer are of special import, because it is the last time she was to relate her discovery to Quimby's theory:

> Question 6—Has this theory ever been advertised or practised before you introduced it, or by any other individual?
> Answer—Never *advertised* and practised only by one individual who healed me, Dr. Quimby of Portland, Me., an old gentleman who had made it a research for twenty five years, starting from the stand-point of magnetism thence going forward and leaving that behind. *I* discovered the art in a *moment's time,* and he acknowledged it to me; he died shortly after and since then, eight years, I have been founding and demonstrating the science.

Mary knew that Dr. Quimby started from the standpoint of magnetism. But, alas! She knew too little about animal magnetism and had yet to learn that that had been the basis of his entire practice. Quimby did not understand the basis of his

115

own practice, and because of his benevolent nature neither he nor his one ardent disciple had any comprehension of its potential use for evil instead of good. But experience would soon teach her this difficult lesson.

In the meanwhile Mr. Wright enrolled in her next class, which convened in April, and proved to be a student of con-
Third class
April
1871 siderable talent. At the close of the course he said that the last lesson alone was worth the entire tuition. He went to Knoxville, Tennessee to assist Mrs. Spofford who was doing very well in that city.

Shortly afterward Richard Kennedy asked Mrs. Glover whether she had heard the reports of Wallace Wright's success in the South. When she said that she had and that she had expected it from him, the color came to Richard's face and a momentary look of indescribable envy. He made a derogatory remark about Wright, ending with, "I hope he will do well, but I am afraid you will be sorry you ever took Wright for a student of metaphysics." But because Richard was affable and Irish, youthful and buoyant, Mrs. Glover disregarded the incident and his words as merely a passing remark. She did not see the wanton petulance he was beginning to cherish in thought, for he intentionally cloaked it with an air of innocence. It would be another year before their partnership would be legally terminated, but the dissolution had begun in Kennedy's thought.

*   *   *

MALICIOUS MALPRACTICE

And there appeared another wonder in heaven; and behold a great red dragon.
                 Revelation

From the beginning Mrs. Glover's partnership with Kennedy was a financial success. At the end of their first year, after first deducting all expenses such as rent, etc., her share of the receipts was $1,744. But her main interest was in the work, not the money. Kennedy was a popular young doctor, busy constantly. Many other students were beginning to practise in a small way with good success. Two students, Mrs. Spofford and

Wallace Wright, were practising full-time in Knoxville, Tennessee with very good success.

The summer season had arrived, and New Englanders were thinking of vacation trips. In a letter to a student Mrs. Glover remarked casually, "Yesterday morning Richard took a fit to go to Portland." His purpose for such a trip did not dawn on her at this time. She made a trip to Tilton for a visit, but wrote from there on July 11, "They were glad to see me on my arrival, but really all is so changed since I were here that I feel as if I never wanted to come again." Mary's heart was in her work and with her students.

What Richard Kennedy learned about Quimby and mesmerism while in Portland is conjectural, but the results of his clandestine malpractice began to appear startlingly in Mrs. Glover's experience. It was some time before she traced this wickedness to its source, and even when she did, she could scarcely credit it.

With her spiritual insight and unusual abilities why did she not see it sooner? In exposing Kennedy in the third edition of Science and Health she gives two reasons for the fact that he was able to deceive her as long as he did:

> Carefully veiling his character, through unsurpassed secretiveness, he wore the mask of innocence and youth. . . .
> We have never departed from one cardinal point of metaphysics, namely, never to encroach on the rights of mind . . . never to enter another's thoughts more unceremoniously than his dwelling. . . . to read mind only when it appeals to you for help.

Until now all her students had appealed to her for help, and she read their thoughts as easily as she heard their words. They were anxious to be healed, and she never failed to heal them. Or they sought her help with difficult cases, and again she never failed to heal. But strange things began to occur.

One morning Mrs. Glover fell downstairs, and Kennedy carried her up bleeding and unconscious. The young girl who lived on the third floor of the same house was sent to get Samuel Bancroft, who came immediately and treated as he had learned to do from his teacher. In a short time she was up and around and came to the supper table (occupants of all three floors had made arrangements for meals together) as usual.

It had become proverbial that friends and patients were benefited and often cured just by Mrs. Glover's presence or by talking with her. Then one day one of her best friends said, "I hope you will excuse me, but I cannot see you, I suffer so in your presence." This friend had always proclaimed that she felt better in Mrs. Glover's presence. In Mary's words:

> We were pained at the change and her altered manner, and insisted on her telling us what was our offense. She replied, "In the many years I have known you I was never cognizant of your doing wrong, but you make me suffer now, and I do not love you as I did." We parted in mystery, and our lives have ever since floated apart down the river of years. We could not beg the friendship we hoped to deserve, and never knew until long afterwards the silent influence by which that student, whom we were benefiting daily, severed our friendship.

But no experience leaves us where it found us, and because of such sore trials Mrs. Eddy could instruct the children of earth:

> Would existence without personal friends be to you a blank? Then the time will come when you will be solitary, left without sympathy....Friends will betray and enemies will slander, until the lesson is sufficient to exalt you;...The author has experienced the foregoing prophecy and its blessings.

Mrs. Glover had expected to hear from Wallace W. Wright soon after he left for the South, and though she had heard reports of his immediate success, nearly three months elapsed with no letter from him. When one finally arrived in midsummer, she opened it eagerly and was shocked at its contents. It was an abusive epistle which said in part:

Letter from W. W. Wright August, 1871

> Restored to myself again I shall be more willing to overlook in you the pains I have already suffered in bearing the load you have put upon me. I ask you to refund to me this amount (five hundred dollars), and I will retire from the

cause, but still consider that I am not restored to my former position.

Wright insinuated in the same letter of August 24 that the relationship between Mrs. Spofford and Dr. Kennedy was improper. Mrs. Glover answered immediately say- Letter from
ing she did not want to hear such gossip, giving   Wright
him helpful counsel including the statement,   August, 1871
"You are now in a chemical." But her counsel, her love, and her guidance were not effective as they had always been before. A second letter from Wright described graphically what Kennedy's malpractice had accomplished though neither he nor his teacher had any inkling of the cause at this time:

> The chemical you say I am in has been with me most of the time since I took this up, as I am "floored" in arguments with myself, and cannot sustain the positions your MSS. take. And my conversations with Mrs. S. are far from satisfactory, as the weight of my argument crushes any she is able to bring forward on the side of Science.

It may have been the weight of Wright's arguments that caused Mrs. Addie Spofford to make a trip to   Letter from
Lynn to see her teacher in the fall. When she   Mrs. Spofford
returned to Knoxville she wrote on October 2:   October, 1871

> When I reached home, I found my practice was much run down. I shall have hard work to bring it up again, but I don't regret my journey, for I gained so much, spiritually while with you....
> Be with us, dear Mrs. Glover and help us; for I am strangely drawn to this field of labor.

Later in the fall Wright returned to Lynn and called on Mrs. Glover, threatening to ruin the cause of metaphysical healing unless she paid him the five hundred dollars he demanded. Kennedy denounced Wright's conduct, but he was not able to hide completely from the thought of his teacher the fact that it pleased him.

Her experience with Wallace Wright might well have influenced the poem she wrote on receiving some beautiful grapes, for he had shown beautiful promise in the classroom. And now

how bitter! The poem appeared in the November 4 issue of the
Poem   *Lynn Transcript:*
November, 1871

LINES ON RECEIVING SOME GRAPES
By Mary Baker Glover

Beautiful grapes would I were thee,
   Clustering round a parent stem,
The blessing of my God to be,
   In woodland bower or glen;

Where friend or foe had never sought
   The angels "born of apes,"
And breathed the disappointed thought,
   Behold! They're sour grapes.

And such, methinks, e'en Nature shows
   The fate of Beauty's power—
Admired in parlour, grotto, groves,
   But faded, O how sour!

Worth,—unlike beauty—fadeless, pure,
   A blessing and most blest,
Beyond the shadows will endure,
   And give the lone heart rest.

The youthful George Barry had first gone to Dr. Kennedy
with bleeding lungs, hoping to be cured of consumption. He
had regained perfect health after instruction from Mrs. Glover
and was most enthusiastic about Moral Science. Barry was
naive, and Richard Kennedy remarked to his teacher, "Barry
is a fool, and you will find how you will come out with him."
But Richard maintained a genial attitude on the surface which
cloaked the intent of his words, so Mrs. Glover simply replied,
"If he is what you say, he is harmless, and with our experience,
that is a great consideration."

By the end of the year Kennedy and Wright were conspiring
together, and Mrs. Glover's metaphysical work was beginning
to reveal the crimes being committed against her and to expose

the criminals. She wrote:

> One day we heard them [Kennedy and Wright] plotting
> to injure us, and opening the door suddenly on them, said,
> "We have overheard the conversation of these conspirators."
> They arose, and blandly looking us in the face, one after the
> other declared we were mistaken, and they entertained the
> highest respect for us.

Their lies were followed by Wright's letter to the *Lynn Transcript* of January 13 entitled "Moral Science alias Mesmerism" which was a lengthy attack on Mrs. Glover and her Science. Mrs. Glover replied in the same newspaper the following week, and Wright con- tinued the attack with further letters claiming that Mrs. Glover taught mesmerism. After several letters over as many weeks, Wright ended by saying that "Mrs. Glover and her science were virtually dead and buried."

Wright's attack 1872

*   *   *

BEGINNING THE BOOK

...and thou shalt go even to Babylon; there shalt thou be delivered; there the Lord shall redeem thee from the hand of thine enemies.

Micah

In the heat of the controversy there was great progress. Mrs. Glover turned to her Bible for guidance one morning and opened to Isaiah 30:8. From that moment her one main purpose was her book, for God had said to her through Isaiah, "Now go, write it be- fore them in a table, and note it in a book, that it may be for the time to come for ever and ever."

Began Science and Health February, 1872

She was in the sixth year of practising and teaching since her discovery, and the child in her womb was no longer embry- onic. Her practice and experiments had proved the truth of her theory, and her fidelity to God was beginning to unravel the mysterious occurrences of recent months. She has recorded that she could not have written Science and Health sooner than she did. Her eyes had to be opened to malicious malpractice. Her education through experience was increasing her understanding every day. It would be three more years before the birth of her babe that would "be for the time to come for ever and ever;" but the nine pregnant years were necessary for the full and proper development of the infant idea. How well she understood this process when she told her students in 1904: "We understand best that which begins in ourselves and by education brightens into birth."

Mary wrote in her notebook, "Commenced writing the *Science of Life* in February, 1872." This was *the* great forward step, but there were other benefits ensuing from this battle early in this new year. Mary had endeavored to meet the evil she had glimpsed in Kennedy's character in the same way she had treated sickness, but it had been totally ineffective. She had learned that the sick can be comforted, but the sinner must be challenged. So she confronted Richard with his sins. Of this she said:

> A stolid moral sense, great want of spiritual sentiment, restless ambition, and envy, embedded in the soil of this student's nature, metaphysics brought to the surface, and he refused to give them up, choosing darkness rather than light. . . . Carefully veiling his character, through unsurpassed secretiveness, he wore the mask of innocence and youth. But he was young only in years; a marvellous plotter, dark and designing, he was constantly surprising us, and we half shut our eyes to avoid the pain of discovery, while we struggled with the gigantic evil of his character, but failed to destroy it. . . . The second year of his practice, when we discovered he was malpractising, and told him so, he avowed his intention to do whatever he chose with his mental power, spurning a Christian life, and exulting in the absence of moral restraint.

Kennedy's malpractice had brought the searchlight of Soul upon mesmerism, and she now saw it clearly. She understood for the first time that Quimby's practice had been benevolent mesmerism and that any manipulation was an avenue for malicious mind. She lost not one minute in instructing all her students to delete the one short passage from their manuscripts that permitted manipulation. But she lost many of her students over this issue, and first and foremost among the dissenters was Richard Kennedy.

In the midst of Wright's attacks in the newspaper Mrs. Glover received a letter from Daniel Spofford in Knoxville written on the twentieth of January: Letter from D. Spofford January, 1872

> I have for a long time had a desire to write to you on matters relating to science; it seems as though I too should be in the good work; although I am in business at present such may not always be the case. . . . I would prefer to feel that I was doing some good and striving to advance the Truth. . . . What I wish is that I might be sufficiently taught to at least attend to all of the outside patients wherever we may be situated. . . . Mrs. Spofford is having wonderful success and has recently completed cures that had been given up by the MDs. . . . I think she meets with success in nineteen cases out of twenty. . . when W W Wright says We meet with but little success he lied for he should have said I and told the reasons, which were primarily that he was practicing mesmerism. . .

There was one disturbing note in Mr. Spofford's letter, and that was the request that his wife should not be informed regarding his application for class instruction. Mrs. Glover sent her response to Mrs. Spofford.

Mrs. Glover never broke with her students who were malpractising but endeavored always to exhort, instruct, advise, guide. As she wrote to Sarah Bagley, "nearly all my time I have done little else than try to change this vile nature in them and to sustain them and Letter to Samuel Bancroft Spring, 1872 the cause." But Richard Kennedy would not be guided nor sustained. Early in March he refused to pay another cent and tore up his contract. Mrs. Glover went to Peabody to stay temporarily with a new student, Peter Sims and his wife; and it appears that she visited several other places including Swampscott before returning to Lynn. Richard spent his time alienating all of her students. During this time she wrote to Samuel Bancroft:

Tuesday M.

Dr. Bancroft:

Dear Student,—By which sacred name I call you. "Thou art near" and yet some considerable distance away—which meaneth "and yet so far." I shall write even though I have not much to say, and do you ask why is this? I answer, because I am a fish out of water; when I am dragged away from wisdom and love into the grosser abyss of folly and hate, then I am not a fish at home. Truth is, I am so tried by the malice of my students, that up to this time, or a little prior to it, I have done nothing but love and praise, that I am losing my happiness and consequently my health in the dark labyrinth into which I gaze and stand upon the brink, thinking momently, will my students plunge therein? Yes, Mr. Bancroft, they have taken even this step of late. If you call I will tell you about it. Please call tomorrow, Wed. eve., and I will be here. Soul and body are one in Science only we are the soul. This I have just learned, but how can I make you see a demonstration that you can't give.

Oh, how I have worked, pondered and constantly imparted my discoveries to this wicked boy that I shall not name and all for what? God grant me patience. Mrs. Susie Oliver told me once Richard said he thought I had suffered so much from bad students if he did not well it would kill me, but it won't. I most fear it will ruin my sweet disposition.

I may as well jest over the absurd striplings that turn to rend me, to threaten me with disgrace and imprisonment for giving to them a discovery that money cannot pay for, but a little good breeding might have helped at least to reward the toil, and scorn, and obscurity, by which it was won for them.

Adieu
Mary

Give my teacherly love to Mr. S.P. Bancroft as one of the good ones so far.

In spite of her trials Mary had managed to complete the first sixty pages of her new manuscript by the time she re-turned to Lynn a few weeks later. Very shortly thereafter, on the eleventh of May, the *Dissolution of Co-partnership* between Mrs. Glover and

Partnership terminated May, 1872

her student, Richard Kennedy, was published. Richard sought other quarters while Mary stayed for the time being at the Shepard Street address.

She continued working on her book while Kennedy opened a new office and with his deceptive geniality and boyishness worked constantly to separate her students from her and win them all as his patients and staunch supporters. Mrs. Glover had not always attend- ed the class meetings, but now in an effort to keep her students loyal to Truth she had meetings in her rooms as is evident from this letter to Samuel "Putney" Bancroft:

Letter to
Bancroft
Spring, 1872

> Friday Morn
>
> Dear Student,—I drop you a line fearing Mr. Allen may for-get, and yet it seems to me he has told you of my class meet-ing, and something has been said to you that is false and you are not feeling your very best. Come, dear Putney, and tell me if you have aught against me. I have thought from what you once said that you regarded me as an adopted sort of a mother. I am this the same as ever. If you knew the false-hoods I have heard that I said and I never thought of saying them, you would put little confidence in the folks *over there* or in anyone.
>
> Come yourself and wife on Sabbath next at four P.M. to No. 2 Shepard St. I shall have some that do not belong to our class.
>
> I wish you would bring over a letter from the Swampscott P.O. and let me pay you for the cartage.
>
> Enclosed please hand to Mrs. Currier or Frothingham for my last board there.
>
> In haste,
> M.M.B.G.
>
> P.S. I expected to leave when I came to Lynn, but three suc-cessive circumstances hindered me. I have since seen the wis-dom of it. Will tell you all about it. We have an instrument in the parlor again. The Berry family will be here and we shall have music from you all.

Very shortly she did leave Lynn, visiting first in Tilton and then with her stepmother in Derry, New Hampshire. When she returned her loyal students presented her with a beautiful family-size Bible and a copy of *Cruden's Complete Concord-ance* to the Scriptures.

Her book was now Mrs. Glover's one concern. She had stopped teaching when she began it, so with no classes and no practising student with her she had no need for such large quarters. But she did need peace and quiet for her writing. And write she did for the next three years. In retrospect she wrote of this period:

> Such a flood tide of truth was lifted upon me at times it was overwhelming and I have drawn quick breath as my pen flew on, feeling as it were submerged in the transfiguration of spiritual ideas.

But the peace and quiet for such writing was not easily found. In August of 1872 she moved to Mrs. Chadwell's on Shepard Street, and later in the year she boarded with her student Miss Dorcas Rawson and her mother which was temporarily more satisfactory.

But she was pursued and harassed and at times overwhelmed by the wicked malpractice of Richard Kennedy. Student after student succumbed to his mesmerism, never knowing they were mesmerized. Following is a typical case that Mrs. Eddy recorded:

> A young lady whom we had restored from hopeless disease to health, he drew to his office, told her she was not restored, and prevailed on her to visit him and he would remove her remaining difficulties. She was in perfect health, and her mother had said so to us. He treated her three times and pronounced her cured. The change was immediately apparent, she grew rapidly ill. Then, by his mesmeric mental treatment, he made her believe that we had caused her relapse, and when her mother sent for us to visit her daughter she was unwilling to be treated by us. Knowing nothing of what this malpractitioner had done, we were astounded at the result, but thought no more of it until we heard of her death. This mesmerist held her with his mind as the serpent holds his victim, until she was dying, and then he stood in a remote part of the room while her friends surrounded her bed, and with her expiring breath she said to them, "Dr.

[Kennedy] did all for me that anyone could."

Mrs. Glover had taught her students the power of mind over matter and how to apply it to heal the sick and relieve the suffering, never dreaming that anyone would pervert the principle for evil instead of good. She did not see at once that all the disaffection was traceable to Kennedy, but when she did she wrote:

> ...the history of one of our young students...diverged into a dark channel of its own, whereby the unwise young man reversed our metaphysical method of healing, and subverted his mental power apparently for the purposes of tyranny peculiar to the individual....His motives moved in one groove, the desire to subjugate; a despotic will choked his humanity....The habit of his misapplication of mental power grew on him until it became a secret passion of his to produce a state of mind destructive to health, happiness or morals. His power to heal failed because of his sins, and if he succeeded with the power of will to remove one disease, it was succeeded by a more malignant one. His mental malpractice has made him a moral leper that would be shunned as the most prolific cause of sickness and sin did the sick understand the cause of their relapses and protracted treatment, the husband the loss of his wife, and the mother the death of her child, etc.
>
> ...We had not an enemy in the city where we introduced this young student and built him up a practice. He commenced his malpractice or demonology, and then, among the many patients that we procured and healed for him, not one, to our knowledge, remained our friend after they were subject to his silent influence.

While the floodtides of Truth were pouring in to Mrs. Glover's consciousness on the one hand, the awfulness of evil was constantly at its heels. "In speaking of this experience she told us that she walked the floor for three days and nights with the perspiration pouring from her," wrote a student of her Divinity Course of later years. But she was also able to tell later students that when these experiences cease to bless, they will cease to occur.

From the first Mrs. Glover was guided in her work by visions. A few that she told to students have been recorded, though not always in detail or specifically.

> The first visions were always of water and in proportion as I would walk over the wave or struggle through it with an old rickety bark and the waters subside would be the success of our Cause. Then came in an interval of serpents. Then it went back to water again. Then came all manner of beasts.

Mrs. Glover's early students looked upon her teachings as a method of healing for the purpose of regaining their health or **Vision of 1872** of entering upon a business venture, though her religious and moral views were always foremost. She followed her class instruction with precept upon precept that they might learn that continued success depended upon the purity of their own lives. After Richard Kennedy's divergence into mesmerism with no moral demands, one after another dropped away or turned against her. She had a vision at this time in 1872 that strengthened her in her work:

> I was pitched out of a boat into the sea and went down. While going down a clear consciousness came to me that I could have no human aid and must go to the bottom. When I reached the bottom (out of the depths He called me) the view was terrific. Green slime covered it and the most horrible reptiles hissed around me, but immediately a ray of light came down through the water and there burst in upon me the most gorgeous sunlight, "and there was no more sea."

1873 found Mrs. Glover moving from boarding house to boarding house, living with one student and another. The one student who was most helpful was young George Barry. He spent many hours househunting, helped her with her moving, ran errands, and most important of all, devoted himself to copying her manuscript. George was not aware of it, but Mrs. Glover made out a will leaving all her estate to that young man.

In mid '73 Mary was back in Mrs. Clark's boarding house on Summer Street where she had lived the first time with Daniel Patterson in the summer of 1866. After several more weeks of industrious writing she had her manuscript ready to present to a publisher. George Clark, too, wanted a publisher, for he had written a sea story for boys; so one day in the fall he accompanied Mrs. Glover to Adams and Company on Bromfield Street in Boston. George was jubilant on the way home, for his story had been accepted for publication, and Mrs. Glover rejoiced with him speaking encouragingly about his future. But her *Science of Life* had been rejected, for the publisher could see no possibility for profit in it.

George Clark accompanied Mrs. Glover on another fall day in 1873. This time it was to a courtroom in Salem on the fourth of November. It had been seven years since   Divorce from
Daniel Patterson had deserted his wife when   Dr. Patterson
they had been residing at Mrs. Clark's boarding   November, 1873
house; and she now made the separation legal and permanent with a bill of divorcement.

Mrs. Glover renewed her efforts on her manuscript, rewriting and revising; "and the dragon stood before the woman which was ready to be delivered, for to devour her child as soon as it was born." Richard Kennedy followed her every footstep avidly. The previous year, on September 8, 1872, he had written to Sarah Bagley:

> Last Friday night Mrs. G. had a gathering of her students, she has something new on foot this time, or at least she is going to make a new movement, and this is the movement. She intends throwing out great inducements to all those who gather about her in this hour of her peril. She is the centre around which all the orbits must revolve and when one sees fit to step out from her circle they lose their equipoise and are known no more among men. How fearful to think of don't you almost shake with fear and awe at her terrible sublimity. But after all I ought not to speak of her she is not worth notice.

Perhaps Kennedy did not speak of her often, but he noticed her every move and hounded her every footstep. During the writing of Science and Health Mrs. Glover   Letter to
moved time and time again, because the wicked   Bancroft
thought of the malpractitioner followed her   Thanksgiving Day
from household to household stirring the thought of her companions, disturbing the harmony and the peace and quiet, in

addition to breaking up her body of students. It was probably November of 1873 that she wrote this letter to Putney Bancroft:

Thanksgiving Day

Friend Bancroft,—They tell me this day is set apart for festivities and rejoicing; but I have no evidence of this except the proclamation and gathering together of those who love one another. I am alone today, and shall probably not see a single student. Family ties are broken never to be reunited in this world with me. But what of those who have learned with me the Truth of Moral Science; where do they find their joys; where do they seek friendship and happiness? Shall I see one of them today? Will they love to gather themselves around me to talk of loftier joys and be getting ready to receive them; to talk of a home in heaven where love fills the thoughts and good will reaches the finest sense of all the spirit calls around them. Is one hungry and they feed them? thirsty, and they give them drink? naked, and they clothe them? sick, and they visit them? a stranger, and they take them in, or in prison, and they come unto them? Years have passed since I have been keeping this law of Love inasmuch as was possible in this wicked world, but now, I in turn look in vain for others to do to me as I have done unto them. My spirit calls today, but who of all my students hear it? Who of you are thinking of the hungry and the stranger today? Would you give me meat at your boards of turkey? Oh! no! for you would then offend the world by entertaining a guest of God. No! you cannot supply this literally and this is not my want—but you cannot supply this spiritually, say you, and this is my want. The literal and spiritual go together, if you did the one to triumph over this world you would do the other and inasmuch as ye do it to the least of these little ones ye do it to Truth also.

Now, dear student, do you understand me? Do you think I want an invitation to dine out today? Oh no, you cannot so misconstrue the meaning; but I wish you all were awake in this hour of crucifixion, awake to the sense of the hour before you and the oil you need in your lamps at that coming of the Bridegroom.

I regret to inform you our regular class meetings are broken

up. If you call on me I will tell you all I know as the cause
of this. May God bless you, my dear student, and hold you
lovingly in the paths of His testimony.

M.M.B. Glover

In the spring of 1874 Mary was ready to present her manuscript to a publisher once more, and again it was rejected. But
she was not deterred. She started revising and rewriting once
more.

Mrs. Glover said that she had never made a specialty of
healing, laboring instead in whatever direction God led her.
But she was ever ready to respond to calls for   Testimony of
help. One of her students, Mrs. Miranda Rice,   Mrs. Rice
called for Mrs. Glover at the birth of her young-   1874
est child. Her testimony, which was later published, said in
part:

> ...Slight labor-pains had commenced before she arrived.
> She stopped them at once, and requested me to call an
> accoucheur, but to keep him below stairs until after the
> birth. When the doctor arrived, and while he remained in a
> lower room Mrs. Eddy came to my bedside. I asked her how
> I should lie. She answered, "it makes no difference how you
> lie," and added, "Now let the child be born." Immediately
> the birth took place, and without pain. The doctor was then
> called into the room to receive the child, and he saw that I
> had no pain whatever. My sister, Dorcas B. Rawson, of Lynn
> was present when my babe was born, and will testify to the
> facts as I have stated them. I confess my own astonishment. I
> did not expect so much, even from Mrs. Eddy, especially as I
> had suffered before very seriously in childbirth....For sev-
> eral years I had been troubled with *prolapsus uteri,* which
> disappeared entirely after Mrs. Eddy's wonderful demonstra-
> tion of Christian Science at the birth of my babe.
>
> Miranda R. Rice

Lynn, Mass., 1874

A few testimonials were published at one time or another,
but scores of Mrs. Glover's healings were never published and
scores more never even recorded.

Another mother in Lynn brought her young son, Stanley,

to Mrs. Glover saying that she feared it was too late. The
Healing of brain fever, etc. little child had brain fever and she was afraid he was already gone. Mrs. Glover took the child in her lap and asked the distraught mother to leave and return in an hour. Mrs. Glover turned her thoughts to the Truth of being and after a time became aware that the child was sitting up in her lap looking into her face. He said, "Me is tick," and Mrs. Glover answered, "No, you are *not* sick, you are well." He repeated, "Me *is* tick," angrily and struggled in her arms trying to strike her, until she stood him on the floor while she talked to him of Truth and Love. When he began to sob, she took him in her arms and talked to him tenderly. He was healed of brain fever and perverseness, and even more. Mrs. Glover sent him to answer his mother's knock on the door, and thought for a moment she would have another patient as his mother appeared near collapse in her astonishment. Stanley had been paralyzed from birth and had never walked before.

But while these marvellous healings were occurring in Mrs. Glover's presence, the strange occurrences of the past two years did not cease. For the record Mary penned the following:

A young lady from Boston, who was suffering from ill-health and a peculiar grief, became our student and recovered her health and happiness. Our friendship flowed smoothly; nothing ever occurred to interrupt it, but the argus eye of the mesmerist was on her. He enquired her out thoroughly, and learned that we were strongly attached to her; that was enough. One evening she called on us to present us with a beautiful pair of vases. On leaving she startled us with the remark, "I shall probably never come to see you again, but shall always love you the same as now." We replied, "That will be a poor proof of it, when we reside so near you." She had no reason for her remark, and claimed none, and we concluded it was merely mirthfulness. We parted with the usual affection, but have never seen her since, and certain unmistakable proofs have convinced us that the aforesaid mesmerist influenced her feelings and action.

By summer Mary had completed her manuscript to her own satisfaction and had it copyrighted on the seventh of July. Shortly thereafter she was able to make arrange- *Science of Life* ments with a printer to print the book at her   copyrighted expense. In her notebook she wrote: "Septem-   July 7, 1874 ber 6, 1874. Sent my mss. to the printer to commence work. The work is entitled *The Science of Life*."

It was another year before Science and Health was published, but at this juncture she thought her labors were behind her and that she could turn her attention in another direction.

*   *   *

THE CAMBRIDGE PLAN

And the dragon stood before the woman which was ready to be delivered, for to devour her child as soon as it was born.
                                        Revelation of John

One day during the writing of Science and Health Mrs. Glover had received a letter from Wallace W. Wright. He was still confused by malicious mesmerism as is evident from its contents:

> It is evident to me that you desire Dr. Kennedy to leave the city, and I think, also, it would be for your interest to accomplish this end. The relations between he and I are probably of a different nature from what you suppose, as I owe him a debt on the past which, if driving him from Lynn will accomplish, it can and shall be done. He thinks that I am your greatest enemy, and favors, if either, his side. Let him continue to think so; it will do me no harm. For my part, I rather a person would come out boldly and fearlessly, as you and I did, facing each other, than to sneak like a snake in the grass, spitting his poison venom into them he would slay. I have said I owe Dr. Kennedy on an old score, and the interview I had with him last evening has increased that debt, so that I am now determined, if it be your object also, as two heads are better than one, to drive him from Lynn.
>
> Why should we be enemies, especially if we have one great

object in common? Perhaps we can be united on this, and the result may be that this city will finally be rid of one of the greatest humbugs that ever disgraced her fair face. All this can be accomplished; but, as I said before, it is necessary to be very cautious, and not let the fact of our communicating together be known, as a friend in the enemy's camp is an advantage not to be overlooked.

In reply Mrs. Glover said:

. . . We will help you always to do right; but with regard to your proposition to send Dr. Kennedy out of Lynn, we recommend that you leave this to God; his sins will find him out. . . Even though so falsely accused, we shall never swerve from the right. If defrauded, and set at naught, God will one day justify his children. You said Dr. Kennedy denied his indebtedness to us. We can show you, under his own signature, his agreement with us that he has broken, and a note he has never paid of seven hundred and fifty dollars.

Richard Kennedy had not forgotten that he had paid only two hundred fifty dollars on his one thousand dollar note, and the dark plot he built around this obligation is well nigh inconceivable. But Mrs. Glover's thought since the dissolution of their partnership had been constantly on her book. The suggestion of driving Richard Kennedy or anyone else from the city, she did not entertain for one second; however, she did at times long to escape from the constant harassment of her dissolute students.

Now that her manuscript was in the hands of the printer, she could entertain thoughts of a new beginning in another city. After much deliberation she settled upon Cambridge, Massachusetts as a promising location for the planting of her standard.

She needed a demonstrator, a loyal student, to accompany her. Her time must be given to "planting the standard" and Beginning in Cambridge December, 1874 she must have one practising student to whom she could refer patients and new students for help and consultation. George Barry was very busy on the book business, and few were qualified. The mantle fell upon Samuel Putnam Bancroft and was a very serious step in that young man's life. He wrote in his diary on the seventh of December:

> Today, I take another step and one which I take with fear and trembling, but in which I feel that I am obeying the call of wisdom which call I dare not disobey. I have today come before the world as a demonstrator of the Science of healing the sick by the power of Soul over matter, as taught by Mary M.B. Glover, and which I believe to be the true Science of Man.

Bancroft opened his office in Cambridge in December. The plan was that George Barry would move there with Mrs. Glover as soon as a suitable tenement could be located, and once the venture was established Bancroft would bring his wife to Cambridge. Mrs. Glover selected the wording for Putney's business card which read:

S. P. BANCROFT
SCIENTIFIC PHYSICIAN
Gives no Medicine

Bancroft, George Barry, and Mr. Hitchings, a real estate agent, were all engaged in finding the right place for Mary Glover's next move, but George was also much in Boston on the book business, which took precedence. It was not the business of Mrs. Glover and her students, however, that foiled all their efforts in Cambridge, including her plans to visit and lecture there prior to moving. An entry in Samuel Bancroft's diary on the eleventh of January in 1875 described the unexpected events of one day that occupied the time of everyone concerned:

> I received a letter today from George Barry giving me an account of a strange experience which my teacher passed through on Friday last, and which he was present to witness. It seems he called on her with Mr. Hitchings, and, on rapping, heard a voice, hardly above a whisper, say "Come in." On

entering, she arose to meet them, but fell back, lost consciousness, and to their belief, was gathering herself on the other side. George went after Mrs. Rice, who came, and immediately a change took place. George had called on her mentally to come back, but Mrs. Rice called loudly, as for someone afar off, and the answer came, faintly at first, but stronger and stronger, till she was able to sit up and have the Bible and manuscripts read to her, and, finally recovered.

Mary still did not know that all of the malicious attacks against her were traceable to Kennedy's work, but circumstances and events plus her own spiritual vision gradually revealed to her the character and method of evil. Later in the month she wrote the following letter to Samuel Putnam Bancroft:

Letter to Bancroft January, 1875

Lynn, Jan. 22nd.

Dear Student,—I am sad, sad at your want of practice, but think the one principal reason I have discovered. I know it is not in you, that your moral claims are sufficient for success, but I have seen in spiritual vision the enemy at work, and today I learn from Mr. Prescott the whole case. Kennedy is hounding your footsteps. He has been going to Cambridgeport for weeks past constantly, on the pretence that he has patients there, but I know he never visits patients in that way. Where your circulars have gone he has got hold of the minds and turned them away from their purpose to give you a call.

Now, I have tried to have Prescott help you, and he is interested for you, but Dick's magnetism of mind reaches him, and just as he concludes to study he will hear something that turns him away; the fact is, he is the most impressible person to mental influence I about ever saw, and because I have no power to do wrong as Dick has we are not equally matched, and so it is with my good students. He injured Ingalls so that Ingalls injured himself to meet him.

I am almost tired to death of so much effort made against me and nothing on the right side to weigh in the scale of Truth for me and the cause.

Now, go about your own way, dear Student, but do not stand still; make a stir; go to the sick and heal them if they

do not send for you. Be meek, but dignified in your acts, and
work, that is all my resort, and I know no other for you.
> Lovingly,
> Your Teacher,
> M.B.G.

In 1875 Mrs. Glover knew not the depths of the evil to which
Kennedy had lent his thought, nor the subtle maliciousness to
which Prescott was exposed; for Kennedy was living in Prescott's house. Nor did she know at this point how to combat
the intentional wickedness of evil minds. She did know that
you cannot fight evil with evil, so her only resort was to keep
working for good. But infinite Mind had uncovered the evil and
shown her its workings, and Mind would in time reveal to her
how to meet it. Almost every day she could see Dick's influence, even on her loyal students, confusing and nullifying
them. Before the end of the month she was to see his malicious
endeavor discourage and nullify her prize student, Samuel
Bancroft. Bancroft never did see the issue of malicious animal
magnetism clearly, but he was much affected by it nonetheless. By the end of January he had given up the Cambridge
venture in despair and written Mrs. Glover a letter expressing
regret at being one more student to disappoint her. A portion
of her response read:

Dear "One More,"—
   You refer to the injury your failure will be to me, and the
cause; I am more sensible of that than you are; my students
have done me irreparable injury while I have been doing all
in my power, under the circumstances, for them. When I
suffer for Truth, they desert me, and when I send out their
names, endorsed by myself, they disgrace my recommenda-
tion by a failure or turning into mesmerism and working
against me.
   Why is all this? . . .
   They love more the ties of the flesh than those of the Spirit,
and always hold on to the former, if they conflict with the
latter. I am not censuring anyone. I am only explaining for
your good what hinders your success, as you do to the sick
what stands in the way of their recovery, you know better

than they; I know better than you, and yet your spiritual perception of the way is far beyond some others. . . . Not curing and keeping until cured your first patients was where you lost. ...Do not let it be thought you left because you were driven out. Call it your family, as it was in reality. Had you not laid up first your treasures in earthly things you would have been free to work on under difficulties, but you chose not to take the footsteps of Science, and because you are better than Kennedy you have no prosperity in wrong. I could not help you when I desired to more than I ever did or I should have done more than I have.

In love,
M.B.G.

*   *   *

CHRISTIAN SCIENCE EMERGES

Mrs. Glover was living in Lynn,—in the boarding-house of Amos Scribners on Broad Street,—when the Cambridge plan collapsed. She had hoped to plant her standard in a more favorable location, but in reality her standard had already been planted. The establishment of moral science, the teaching and successful practice in healing the sick, and then the perversion of her teaching for wicked purposes were all part of its history.

The divine reality of science in its purity had unfolded in Mary's consciousness, and experience was teaching her what mortal man would do with this priceless gift. She had learned that only the Christian thought could be trusted with the omnipotence of divine Science. Thus it was in 1875 that Christian Science emerged from her founding footsteps as the saviour of the world.

For many months Mrs. Glover had been considering the establishment of a home for students as well as for herself which Purchase of would become a center of scientific activity. As house in Lynn she looked out her window one day she saw that March, 1875 a sign had recently been placed on a house across the street which read "For Sale." It seemed providential. Arrangements were made for the purchase, and very soon thereafter Mary moved,—not to Cambridge,—but across the street.

Mrs. Spofford, who had recently returned to Lynn, had seemed strangely estranged from her teacher, and it was rumored that the Spoffords were estranged from one another and had separated. Daniel Spofford was also in Lynn endeavoring to practise metaphysical healing from what he had gleaned from his wife's manuscripts. In February Mrs. Glover had kindly sent him an invitation to attend her next class free of charge.

The purchase of the house had depleted Mary's funds and there were still mortgage payments to meet, so it was necessary to rent out her rooms to meet expenses. She kept only a small attic room for herself and the second floor front parlor for a classroom. There a class of four, including Daniel Spofford, met in April.

In the classroom Daniel Harrison Spofford justified Mrs. Glover's hopes. He was a sincere, dedicated, intelligent young man desirous of pursuing the path of righteous-   Letter from
ness, as this letter he wrote to his teacher on the   Spofford
twenty-sixth of April during the course of in-   April, 1875
struction indicates:

> Many, many times each day I ask myself, do we students realize what is held out for our possession. . . .Do we realize that we are moving to a position which while here, if we are faithful, brings us from the world probably nothing but trials and rebuffs? but that in ages to come these meetings in the upper chamber will have passed into history and that we will be blessed or cursed according to our fidelity in the preserving of Truth, until time shall be at an end. . . .O that I might be worthy; that I might have lived the life of righteousness to enable me to give to you, be it ever so little, of that living water which you must so desire to drink.

Mrs. Glover's teaching was in consonance with her forthcoming book. The terminology "Science of Man" and "Moral Science" had largely given place to "Christian Science",—the term she employed to express the spiritual Science of Mind-healing.

Mary had learned that another book titled *Science of Life*
was already in print, so a new title for her volume was essential;
Science and Health but it was not immediately forthcoming. When
copyrighted   it did come she was certain of its rightness and
June 2, 1875   copyrighted the new title on the second of June.
Of this new name she wrote:

> Six weeks I waited on God to suggest a name for the book
> I had been writing. Its title Science and Health, came to me
> in the silence of night, when the steadfast stars watched over
> the world,—when slumber had fled,—and I rose and recorded
> the hallowed suggestion. The following day I showed it to my
> literary friends who advised me to drop both the book and
> the title. To this, however, I gave no heed, feeling sure that
> God had led me to write that book, and had whispered that
> name to my waiting hope and prayer. It was to me the "still,
> small voice" that came to Elijah after the earthquake and
> the fire.

Mrs. Glover was constantly sharing her inspiration openly
and freely with those around her, while the serpent was just as
Vision regarding constantly working in secret to thwart her every
Science and Health move. Mary had a vision regarding her book at
c.1875   this time which she did not fully understand
until later, but she told a class in 1888 that that vision was
just as visible to sense as they were.

> She saw a beautiful maiden clad in pure white standing
> at the altar being wedded to a terrible sensuous man. She
> cast herself down weeping and implored that it should not be,
> but she was forced back.

She recognized this man when he entered her experience
some three years later, but she did not know until long afterward that he was an accomplice of the mesmerist.

Daniel Spofford opened an office in Lynn as soon as his
course of instruction was completed and was outstandingly suc-
Healing of   cessful from the outset. At last Mrs. Glover had
Mrs. Ethel B. West a capable, practising student devoting all his
c. 1875   time to the cause, although he was not unlike
all the other students in turning to his teacher for help with

difficult cases. For example, the woman with whom Spofford boarded also had her small granddaughter Ethel living with her. One day Ethel fell down a deep stairwell at school and was gravely injured. When the child was brought home in an unconscious condition, Spofford offered to heal her, and to the relief of the alarmed grandmother he did so in a very short time. Ethel then thought it would be "smart" to return to school, but the alarm at her appearance was so great that it affected the child as seriously as had the fall so that she was taken home unconscious a second time. This time Daniel Spofford's work seemed to be ineffective, and he went immediately to Mrs. Glover for help. At the moment his teacher was apprised of the situation, the child was instantaneously healed, and her healing was complete and permanent.

Thirty years later Ethel West became a student of Christian Science, but at the time, despite her healing, the family was strongly prejudiced against Mrs. Glover be- Resolutions cause of the lies and malicious rumors gossiped of students and spread about Lynn. Mary kept on with her June, 1875 work, letting future ages speak for her accomplishments, but her loyal students were endeavoring to counteract the misconceptions and extend her teachings. On the first of June eight students drew up and signed the following resolutions:

Whereas, in times not long past, the Science of Healing, new to the age, and far in advance of all other modes, was introduced into the city of Lynn by its discoverer, a certain lady, Mary Baker Glover,

And, whereas, many friends spread the good tidings throughout the place, and bore aloft the standard of life and truth which had declared freedom to many manacled with the bonds of disease or error,

And, whereas, by the wilful and wicked disobedience of an individual who has no name in Love, Wisdom, or Truth, the light was obscured by clouds of misinterpretation and mists of mystery, so that God's work was hidden from the world and derided in the streets,

Now, therefore, we students and advocates of this moral science called the Science of Life, have arranged with the said Mary Baker Glover to preach to us or direct our meetings on the Sabbath of each week, and hereby covenant with one another, and by these presents do publish and proclaim that we have agreed and do each and all agree to pay weekly, for one year, beginning with the sixth day of June, A.D. 1875, to a treasurer chosen by at least seven students the amount set opposite our names, provided, nevertheless, the moneys paid by us shall be expended for no other purpose or purposes than the maintenance of said Mary Baker Glover as teacher or instructor, than the renting of a suitable hall and other necessary incidental expenses, and our signatures shall be a full and sufficient guarantee of our faithful performance of this contract.

(Signed)

Elizabeth M. Newhall	$1.50
Dan'l H. Spofford	2.00
George H. Allen	2.00
Dorcas B. Rawson	1.00
Asa T. N. MacDonald	.50
George W. Barry	2.00
S.P. Bancroft	.50
Miranda R. Rice	.50

Before the end of the month these students had adopted Mrs. Glover's advancing terminology and agreed to call themselves Christian Scientists.

The printer had had the manuscript for months and months. Seven hundred dollars had been paid in advance, and still the book was not out. Finally, Mrs. Glover yielded to the growing conviction that she must include in the last chapter some of what she had learned about malpractice, even though she was still working daily for Richard Kennedy, hoping that his eyes might be opened so that he would forsake mesmerism and turn again to the Truth.

After fulfilling her painful task of composing a partial history of mental malpractice, she loaned the manuscript to Prescott, possibly hoping that if Dick saw the exposé it might cause reform. She had gone clear to the bottom of the sea of iniquity in her vision of 1872, but she was far from the bottom in dealing with it in her human experience.

The manuscript was stolen from Prescott's house! Kennedy

was probably responsible, and most likely Prescott challenged him. In the following account Mrs. Eddy did not name Prescott, but it is most probable that this is the history of Kennedy's revenge on that student:

> He ruined a promising student, who was somewhat addicted to intemperance before he learned metaphysics, but when he left our class was thoroughly reformed, and labored in turn to help others abandon their cups. He had totally abstained from strong drinks, and lost his appetite for them, when [Kennedy] went to board with him. Shortly afterward they had a slight altercation about their teacher, in which the mesmerist was shown up in no favorable light. Subsequently the reformed student called on us, appeared dejected, and not as courageous regarding himself as usual. We questioned him, and he replied, "I have at times an impetuous desire to drink liquor. I cannot account for this, for I detest it, and have no relish for it; still this strange feeling that I must get intoxicated comes over me at stated periods with an overwhelming force." Being ignorant at that time of the cause of all this, we suggested it might be the chemicalization by which chronic errors sometimes pass off. He replied, "I have treated it for that metaphysically, but without success." A sudden interruption closed our conversation, and we saw him no more; but in three months from that time we learned that he was a demoralized man and a confirmed sot. He never was that before...

Had Mary known what she later learned about this student's experience, she might have used stronger language in the manuscript she prepared for the printer. Nevertheless, her exposure of animal magnetism completed the volume, and the book now went forward.

The Sunday meetings held in pursuance of the students' resolutions were very well attended, but because the dissidents were endeavoring to take advantage of public meetings, Mrs. Glover saw fit to discontinue them after five weeks. Nonetheless, the summer of 1875 was a period of rich fulfillment. In Samuel Bancroft's words:

> I consider the summer of 1875 the most harmonious period

of the twelve years from 1870 to 1882, during which Mrs. Eddy had continued to reside in Lynn. I never knew her so continuously happy in her work. Although she was writing, teaching, and preaching, and occasionally treating some severe case beyond a student's ability to reach, her physical and mental vigor seemed to be augmented rather than depleted. I can picture her now as she stood, erect and stately, on the raised platform of the little hall on Market Street, unwearied and undismayed, while curious questioners strove to confound her...On such occasions we were very proud of our teacher.

The Revelator had seen in prophetic vision the woman of the Apocalypse, "And she being with child cried, travailing in birth, and pained to be delivered." The nine long pregnant years of the woman's travail were coming to an end, and the pain of the labor was behind her. The earth had prepared a place for the woman in the founding of the United States of America,—and now the woman had prepared a place for her child. She had developed a family of loyal Christian Scientists who would welcome, love, and cherish her offspring that God had named Science and Health, and she had provided a home for her child and family. The home now had a sign over the door with an open Bible, a cross and crown, and the words "Mary B. Glover's Christian Scientists' Home."

HIRAM CRAFTS   144   SALLY WENTWORTH
Mrs. Eddy's first student.

CHAPTER XII

THE BIRTH OF THE CHILD

*And she brought forth a man child, who was to rule all
nations with a rod of iron: and her child was caught up unto
God, and to his throne.*

Revelation of John

1875

GEORGE Barry had asked permission to call Mrs.
Glover "Mother," and she treated him as a son. One
evening in July he and Miss Florence Cheney Letter from
visited Mrs. Glover. The next day, July 27, Miss Miss Cheney
Cheney wrote: July, 1875

> I enjoyed one of the pleasantest evenings that I must ever
> remember as among the happiest, and most profitable I have
> known. For truly, dear Mrs. Glover, you call out all the good
> in my nature; not alone, I think, by your teachings, but your
> very presence inspires one with a respect and love for the
> pure, the beautiful and true; making one more fully realize
> the blessed privilege of living a noble, unselfish life.

Before long George wished to marry Florence Cheney and
Mary was pleased at the prospect. For George's sake she taught
Miss Cheney gratuitously in a small class she held in August,
that she might help to give a spiritual impetus to their marriage.

They were both devoted students and George continued to
fulfill the role of son that he had adopted, performing numerous
small services in addition to being a good worker for the cause.

George Barry was doing what George Glover had never done,
but the ties of the flesh were a fleeting part of Mary's experience. Her babe was of the Spirit, the new-born of Truth, Science and Health. For as Isaiah had foreseen, "a virgin shall

145

conceive and bear a son, and shall call his name Immanuel."
Christendom had thought that the virgin Mary had fulfilled
this prophecy, as indeed she had in part. But Jesus was the
messenger and not the message. The name Jesus is not synonymous with Immanuel. Jesus is synonymous with Joshua, being
the Greek translation, and means *saviour*. Immanuel means
God with us.

The pure, virgin consciousness of another Mary was now
bringing forth her son and his name, Immanuel, is clearly
stated on page 210 in this first edition in the words "'I' is God,
and not man." And in another passage, "if Christ, Truth, has
come to us in demonstration...it is 'God with us.'"

Mary Glover presented her child to the world on the thirtieth
day of October in this joyous year of 1875. Mankind should
First edition have been singing with the angels, "unto us a
Science and Health child is born, unto us a son is given: and the
October, 1875 government shall be upon his shoulder: and his
name shall be called Wonderful, Counsellor, The mighty God,
The everlasting Father, The Prince of Peace." Angels knew
that this child was destined to rule absolutely, imperatively,
finally; and so did his mother, Mary Glover.

Mary rejoiced at the birth of her babe. She said of the nine
long years of labor:

> From 1866 to 1875, I myself was learning Christian Science
> step by step—gradually developing the wonderful germ I had
> discovered as an honest investigator....I was reaching by
> experience and demonstration the scientific proof, and scien-
> tific statement, of what I had already discovered. My later
> teachings and writings show the steady growth of my spiritual
> ideal during those pregnant years.

And of the first appearance of her book she wrote:

> The first edition of my most important work, Science and
> Health, containing the complete statement of Christian Sci-
> ence,—was published in 1875.

The complete statement of Christian Science had been given
to the world, but the human garments in which the young child
was clad were far from perfect. Mrs. Glover recorded in her
notebook "490 typographical errors in words besides para-

graphs and pages wrong, and punctuation." To a student she wrote, "There are grammatical errors in Errata and some in the book doubtless that I have not touched...Our next printer should have a proof reader who is *responsible* for this."

As soon as the book appeared Mary began planning for a second edition in which all the errors would be corrected. But they had the book, and now its promotion and distribution were of primary importance.

But the dragon was wroth with the woman and persecuted her. The summer and fall of 1875 seemed to be a lull in the storm while her child was caught up unto the Second vision throne of God. But Mary had a second vision regarding of the terrible sensuous man and knew it Science and Health pertained to her spiritual conception:

> She stood with a beautiful babe in her arms clad in beautiful garments of spotless white, and this same man came and tore the *lower* part of the garment away and dragging it in the mire took it and put it about the neck of a *negro*.

HOUSE ON BROAD STREET IN LYNN, MASSACHUSETTS

Purchased by Mrs. Glover in March, 1875.

CHAPTER XIII

ASA GILBERT EDDY

*Asa Gilbert Eddy—the impersonation of integrity in the
Science of Man.*

Mary Baker Eddy

1876

ASA and Betsy Smith Eddy reared their seven children on their farmstead in Londonderry, Vermont
where Asa farmed in the summers and worked as a cooper
during the winters. But the Eddys were far from a typical
New England farm family. Eddy, as a common noun, is strictly an English word. Noah Webster, that jewel among philo-
logists, recorded, "I find this word in no other language." His
definition is: *a current of water running back, or in a direction
contrary to the main stream,—in a circular direction;* and the
verb eddy means *to move circularly.* Metaphysically a circle
represents infinity without beginning or end; water symbolizes
mental activity,—a current of water, a channel of thought.
Thus Eddy stands for mental activity contrary to the main
stream, tending to move toward infinity: and Betsy Smith
Eddy fulfilled the name her husband had given her.

Their next to youngest son, Asa Gilbert, was the closest to
his parents and responded most to the progressive ideas of
his unusually capable mother. Betsy's children learned to do
all things methodically and well with no lines drawn between
men's work and women's work. Gilbert farmed with his father,
taught writing in the winters, and became interested in a marvellous new invention which was lessening labor and drudgery,
—the sewing machine, taking the agency and traveling
throughout Massachusetts. Gilbert was a fluent writer whose
diction and penmanship both were beautiful. He also had a

148

natural artistic ability with a pencil which delighted the children of his acquaintance.

He was the favorite friend of seven-year-old Mary Godfrey,
and also the best friend of her parents, Mr. and Mrs. George
Llewellyn Godfrey, of Chelsea. For the past several years Gilbert Eddy had been a frequent visitor in their home, and in
recent years his health had become a deep concern to Mrs.
Godfrey; for severe heart trouble was threatening to make him
a hopeless invalid.

                    *   *   *

At this time in Lynn there was great rejoicing at Number 8
Broad Street, for Mrs. Glover had brought forth her child and
presented him to the world.

There was additional rejoicing in that house, albeit less spiritual, for another child had arrived at that address in October
of 1875. A daughter had been born to the young couple who
rented the second floor, Mr. and Mrs. William Nash. Although
the Nashes were not remotely interested in Christian Science,
they were exceedingly fond of their landlady and named their
newborn infant Flora Glover.

Early in the new year Mary Glover received a most gratifying
response to one of the many complimentary copies of Science
and Health that had been sent out. Amos Bron-   Letter from
son Alcott has been little acknowledged by the   Alcott
world, though his literary peers in New England   January, 1876
recognized his spiritual genius. Henry David Thoreau said that
Alcott was the sanest man he ever knew, and Ralph Waldo
Emerson once wrote of him, "Wonderful is his vision. The
steadiness and scope of his eye at once rebuke all before it,
and we little men creep about ashamed." In time to come the
name of A. Bronson Alcott will be remembered beyond his
contemporaries because of his response to and appreciation of
Science and Health and its author. On the seventeenth of
January he wrote Mrs. Glover:

> Accept my thanks for your remarkable volume entitled
> "Science and Health," which I have read with profound in-

terest and let me add, the perusal has awakened an earnest
desire to know more of yourself personally.

The sacred truths which you announce, sustained by facts
of the Immortal Life, give to your work the seal of inspiration—reaffirm in modern phrase the Christian revelations. In
times like ours, so sunk in sensualism, I hail with joy any
voice speaking an assured word for God and Immortality.
And my joy is heightened the more when I find the blessed
words are of woman's divinings.

...May I then enquire if you would deem a visit from me
an impertinence? If not, and agreeable to you, will you name
the day when I may expect the pleasure of fuller interchange
of view on these absorbing themes.

Three days later, following the proposed visit, Alcott wrote
in his journal:

> [Mrs. Glover] receives me cordially at her house, and I
> have an interesting visit. I find her one of the fair saints,
> whose attractions have drawn about her a little circle of
> followers which meets for fellowship at her house fort-
> nightly...
>
> I find her a devoted student of the New Testament, a
> Christian in the truest sense, an idealist in apprehending
> the supremacy of mind over matter, and a faith in Spirit
> transcending any contemporary whom I have been fortunate
> to meet. I shall cultivate further acquaintance with a person
> of such attractions mentally and spiritually.

Their meeting gave Mrs. Glover hope. An exceptionally well-
educated man was spiritual enough to understand and endorse
Science and Health and eager to present it to the acknowledged
literary leaders of New England. But when Alcott introduced
her volume and her science to his literary circle, the response
was less than enthusiastic.

At a later date Mary healed the elderly gentleman of a severe
form of rheumatism which had confined him to his chair.
Alcott once said, "If I were younger, I would help that woman."
But a revolutionary science that required action and demonstration also required youth, ardor, and stamina. It was too
demanding for the aged philosopher; so, though his kindliness

never waned, his interest did. Mary's disappointed hope was forced to turn once again to God and not man. But the help for which she yearned came from another and unexpected direction.

*   *   *

When the new year was still young and baby Flora Glover was about four months old, a crisis occurred for the new father. His wife and baby were both ill. Young Mr. Nash sent a distressed call for help to his favorite aunt who lived in Chelsea. Thus Mrs. Godfrey entered into the experience of Mary Baker Glover.

At the dinner table, (Mrs. Glover boarded with her tenants) Mary asked Mrs. Godfrey about her heavily bandaged swollen finger, and was told that she had run a needle deep into it and that it was very badly infected. Mrs. Godfrey also said that she had been to several doctors all of whom wanted to amputate the finger, which she would not allow, even though they warned that it would cost her the loss of her entire arm.

The following morning Mrs. Godfrey ran excitedly into the next room in her nightgown exclaiming, "William, look at my hand!" William was not surprised that her finger was nearly normal and remarked that it was probably Mrs. Glover's work. But his aunt was overjoyed and from that moment turned unreservedly to Mrs. Glover as her physician.

Mary offered to teach Mrs. Godfrey, but the latter declined, being perfectly satisfied to rely wholly upon Mrs. Glover for healing. She was, however, most eager to have her dear friend come to study and be healed. So it was that in March of 1876 Asa Gilbert Eddy came to Lynn for healing and was greatly improved at the first visit. He came again to Lynn to be taught. The class of two students was distinguished in *Science of Man* that it was the first class held wherein the stu-   published dents were able to study from *printed* books.   February, 1876 Mrs. Glover's class-book, *The Science of Man*, in revised form from the original, had been published on the fourteenth of February. She soon began considering the inclusion of her class-book within the pages of the second edition of Science and Health, but little did she know what intricate snares were

151

being set in her path in that regard by the deep designs and dark plots of her former student and junior partner.

Mrs. Addie Spofford had fallen completely under Kennedy's control. When Mrs. Glover had urged Daniel Spofford, or Harry as she called him, to seek a reconciliation, she learned from him that Mrs. Spofford's only terms were a complete vindication of Richard Kennedy. But despite his marital difficulties Daniel Spofford was very sincere and successful in his work. By the time Mr. Eddy came to study, Dr. Spofford was maintaining offices in Lynn, Haverhill, Newburyport, and Boston, and was the most successful student in selling Science and Health.

To Gilbert Eddy, Christian Science was a revelation from God and its author an angel on earth. He had found the Christ and was ready to follow whithersoever it might lead without so much as a backward glance. He left Boston for Lynn and listed himself in the city directory as A. G. Eddy, Christian Scientist, —the first individual in the world to so proclaim publicly. From that moment he devoted all his time and energy to the practice of Christian Science and never wavered in his fidelity. Dr. Eddy, as he soon became known, was small of stature and, as had been his dauntless mother, always handsomely dressed. His strength of character and unimpeachable integrity were not readily recognized, but they lay behind his gentle manner and pleasant smile and ere long would offer strength and support to his teacher.

CHAPTER XIV

CHRISTIAN SCIENTIST ASSOCIATION

O sing unto the Lord a new song; sing unto the Lord, all the earth.

Psalm of David

1876

THE entrance of Asa Gilbert Eddy into the ranks of the Christian Scientists scarcely made a ripple. Dr. Eddy's mild manner was so self-effacing that it went practically unnoticed at the time that he was the first to call himself a Christian Science practitioner. Daniel Harrison Spofford was unquestionably the foremost among Mrs. Glover's practising students, and there was no challenge nor thought of such from the newcomer.

Thus far Daniel Spofford had proved to be the most capable of Mrs. Glover's students, and he had met with the greatest success. It is not at all surprising that she made arrangements with him on the eleventh of April to enlarge his activities by taking over the Christian Science Publishing Company. He would assume full responsibility for the sale of Science and Health and handle all the money in connection therewith. He made an agreement to pay Barry and Newhall $1700 *from any sums accruing beyond $1200.* In addition he would be the publisher for the next edition or anything else she might write. Six days later, on April 17, a contract was signed in which Spofford also agreed to pay Mrs. Glover a ten per cent royalty on the net list price for the balance of the first edition.

Contract with Spofford April, 1876

The net list price was $2.50. The first edition was supposed to have cost $1000, but because of the numerous changes and corrections had amounted to $2285.35. Two students, George

Barry and Elizabeth Newhall, had invested close to $1700 toward its publication. Obviously the publication of Science and Health was in its infancy, but Harry was as convinced as was Mary that it was God's gift to mankind and had a great future. Never before had a man the opportunity that was placed in Harry Spofford's hands.

Some time after this George Barry began to behave very peculiarly. In Mary's own words:

> A noticeable change commenced in the young man very unlike the fruits of metaphysics. Our students saw it as well as ourself; they also noticed his neglect of the business that belonged to him, and the losses it caused us. We noticed the change in his disposition, and certain mental symptoms foreign to his constitution, and wholly unlike himself.

Before long George Barry left Mrs. Glover's home and her circle of students. Forgotten were the sentiments and debt he had felt and once expressed poetically in a letter to his teacher and adopted mother:

> O mother mine, God grant I ne'er forget,
> Whatever be my grief or what my joy,
> The unmeasured unextinguishable debt
> I owe to thee, but find my sweet employ
> Ever through thy remaining days to be
> To thee as faithful as thou wast to me.

Mary was mystified. From the time of her discovery of Christian Science nearly ten years earlier she had had no difficulty in seeing in a person's thought the cause of their disease or difficulty. She could do this with those present or absent, and she even had unfailing success in reading the thoughts of patients of students whom she had never met nor seen. In the latter case, however, the remedy was dependent upon the student's progress as she wrote in her first edition of Science and Health:

> Whenever we have taken charge of a practice to establish a student, it was not necessary for us to see the patients to heal them; if the student was not advanced spiritually, we failed to benefit the sick so much in connection with him.

Mrs. Glover was constantly being called upon for help and was busy every minute. She had neither the time nor the inclination to dwell upon George's disaffection, but she was perplexed by it. Reading the human mind had been as easy for her as following a man's track along a dusty path. In George's thought she saw no tracks to follow. Though she knew it not, the man responsible was assiduously covering and obliterating his tracks in order to deceive her, but that man was not George Barry. It was Richard Kennedy.

Kennedy was working not only to separate Barry from his teacher, but to get his accomplice into Barry's position, that is, in Mrs. Glover's home as her very closest helper. Sad to say, he accomplished his purpose. It was five years later after many trials before she wrote the following about Kennedy's mesmerism of George Barry:

> During a period of about five years the mesmerist evidently nourished his hatred and purpose to destroy that young man, and from no cause apparent but our interest in his welfare. He finally accomplished his purpose, and broke up his business relations with us through the aid of his accomplice, who was interested to obtain his position. Their united mesmerism severed a friendship that might have been profitable to us both. We doctored him gratuitously, and his friends when he requested it, gave him business chances that others coveted, etc. He having seen but about seventeen summers when we first knew him, his business mistakes cost us months of labor. He copied for us, and we offered to pay him, but he always refused, saying he was not doing us the good that we were doing him; and that was true, although he was then a good worker for the cause, and rendering us many small services. For his sake we taught the lady whom he wished to marry gratuitously, and endeavored to realize the obligations of the word mother that he had asked permission to call us. . . . Had we understood then, as now, the demonology carried on by the aforesaid mesmerist, that young man would have been saved what will be to him the saddest recollection in his whole history.

Mrs. Glover had seen much of the result of Kennedy's work, but she had thought that it was accomplished by manipulation, with the mesmeric influence he exerted over his patients when rubbing their heads. Part of what she had added to the final chapter of Science and Health read:

> The science of healing is incapable of evil, but this opposite practice is as clearly proved capable of great mischief, and even crime; able, while it lays high claims to right, secretly to work out a hidden wrong...."more subtle than all other beasts of the field," it coils itself about the sleeper, fastens its fang in innocence, and kills in the dark. We thank Wisdom, that revealed this great error to us before these pages went to press, that the years we have labored to bless our fellow-beings be not wholly lost through this trespass upon the blessing of mental healing.
>
> We knew of no harm that could result from rubbing the head, until we learned it of this mal-practice, and never since have permitted a student, with our consent, to manipulate.

Mary had also added to the first edition of Science and Health, "Never trust human nature in the dark, if this nature is so dark it covers its footprints." But she had yet to uncover many of these hidden footprints through the lessons of bitter experience.

At this point in Mary's experience it seems as if the mal-practitioner was always way ahead of her. But his work was in the dark, and his footprints such that even he was afraid to have them seen. Such iniquity and workers of iniquity are destined for oblivion.

Mary's work was in the open for all the world to see and for the benefit of all humanity. Her footprints are fadeless. In the words of a poet:

> Footprints, that perhaps another,
>   Sailing o'er life's solemn main,
> A forlorn and shipwrecked brother,
>   Seeing, shall take heart again.

Pursued and harassed by all the machinations of malicious minds, the revelator to this age took the forward steps that are imperishable. One hundred years earlier our founding fathers had pledged their lives, their fortunes, and their sacred honor to found a *new order* which would provide "liberty and justice for all." Many who so pledged were persecuted and destroyed, but the idea came forth and grew from that simple "Declaration of Independence" into a great nation.

In the small town of Lynn, Massachusetts, unnoticed by the world, on Independence Day, July 4, 1876, Mrs. Glover and six of her students made a solemn pledge which is also destined to grow into greatness. This small beginning embraces the only means for preserving and maintaining the freedom and the great nation our fathers envisioned. Of this momentous step Mrs. Eddy wrote simply,"The first Christian Scientist Associationwas organized by myself and six of my students in 1876, on the Centennial Day of our nation's freedom."

C.S.A.
founded
July 4, 1876

The Constitution and strict By-Laws were written by Mrs. Glover. Jesus' mission had renamed Israel, *Christianity*. Mary's mission had renamed Christianity, *Christian Science*. The preamble to the Constitution states:

> This association was organized in the summer of 1876, on the centennial day of our Nation's Independence. Christian Science and purely mental healing were founded in 1866 by Mrs. Mary Baker Glover, author of "Science and Health," published in 1875. Said author gave to Christianity its new name after her discovery, to wit: that a Divine principle and given rule applicable to every condition of man, and constituting the Divine plan of his salvation from sin, sickness, and death exist in the order of eternal Life, Truth, and Love, and that Jesus demonstrated for man's example and his redemption, this holy principle of Divine Science, healing the sick, casting out devils, error, and raising the dead; clearly showing by this divine understanding and proof, the indivisibility of Science and Christianity.

The signers of this new declaration of freedom were as relentlessly pursued and persecuted mentally as had been their predecessors physically a century earlier. Nearly all were overcome by the enemy, but the idea came forth and grew from that humble beginning.

CHAPTER XV

CONTINUED PERSECUTION

And his tail drew the third part of the stars of heaven, and did cast them to the earth.

Revelation of John

1876

A FRIEND of Mrs. Glover who had witnessed the work of the malpractitioner asked her why, since she had discovered Christian Science and uncovered its abuse, she did not control the minds of individuals or community to disbelieve the falsehoods. Her answer was:

> We have neither divine authority, nor the power to control minds for any other than their own benefit, and we are giving the results of our moral, spiritual and metaphysical researches to the world as fast as possible, but the footsteps of falsehood and error are swift, those of honesty and Truth slow, and strong. The community must understand the science of being to appreciate it, and they must detect the wicked mal-practice to appreciate that; therefore the true verdict is not yet given, and Truth can wait, for it is used to waiting.

But the malpractitioner had no such inhibitions in his hidden work. His primary target was Mrs. Glover, and he pursued her constantly with his wicked thought after each forward step on her part.

It was only a few days after the founding of the Christian Scientist Association that Mary experienced a "violent seizure." But no attack of malicious mind leaves us where it found us. Turning to God in physical suffering is always a spiritually exalting as well as a healing experience. At this time Mary found even more. She *discovered* Gilbert Eddy. He had been called when she had fallen unconscious. He came immediately and brought her

Letter to Hattie Baker July, 1876

158

out of it, greatly impressing her as being "calm, clear and strong, and so kind." She wrote of the experience to her cousin Hattie in Boston on the fourteenth of July, adding:

> Never before had I seen his real character, so tender and yet so controlling. Hattie, you would change your views of him if you were to read him spiritually.

Mrs. Glover was very pleased to have another capable practitioner in the ranks, but Dr. Eddy was far from replacing Daniel Spofford as is evident from her October 1 letter to the latter: Letter to Spofford October, 1876

> My joy at having one living student, after these dozen years of struggle, toil and defeat, you at present cannot understand, but will know at a future time when the whole labor is left with you. . . .

Mary had taught a class of five students in June. Now she taught another of seven students in October. She was working on the revision of Science and Health. On the surface it looked as if everything was progressing; but the dragon was at work. Though Mrs. Glover as yet knew not his means and method, she did sense it. On the twenty-second of October she wrote to Daniel "Harry" Spofford, "my student, in my lonely chamber I read the coming storm. I feel it gathering." In the same letter to her "one living student" she said: Letter to Spofford October, 1876

> Press on: You know not the smallest portion comparatively, of your ability in science. Measure your stature in Christ; do not count on your powers as man, and do not rob God by denying them. . . .
>
> I feel like a tired and wounded soldier of the cross, taken to the rear; but my wounds are enlivening my soldiers, I do believe; if so, God give me more—and teach me all I need—and make me more of a blessing; poor, weak and unworthy, on one hand, august and glorious on the other! Pray for me dear student.

Mary had true humility, and she also had the one thing that most infuriates the world and the worldly,—conscious worth,—

that which man cannot give nor take away. But she was tired and wounded and more than willing to step down and let her "one" student take the lead.

Behind his mask of youth and innocence Richard Kennedy was gloating. He had brought George Barry under his will, and now he was working on Daniel Spofford. Saint John had seen the great red dragon cast to the earth the third part of the stars of heaven, and Mrs. Glover was experiencing what John had foreseen.

Kennedy she had left with his manipulation, and though she worked for that "wicked boy" that he might see the light, she did not connect him with Spofford's odd behaviour nor with the physical attacks she suffered.

Out of suffering and struggle always comes progress. Mary's spiritual footsteps at this time brought forth one of her most "Hymn of Science" beautiful poems, "Hymn of Science," which
December was published in the *Lynn Transcript* of Decem-
1876 ber 2.

HYMN OF SCIENCE

Saw ye my Saviour? Heard ye the glad sound?
　　Felt ye the power of the Word?
　　　　'Twas the Truth that made us free,
　　　　And was found by you and me
　　In the Life and the Love that are God.

Mourner, it calls thee—come to this Saviour:
　　Love wipes your tears all away,
　　　　And will lift the shade of gloom
　　　　And for thee make blessed room
　　Where the darkness hath yielded to day.

Sinner, it calls thee; all who are thirsty
　　Drink of its life-giving stream:
　　　　'Tis the Spirit that makes pure,
　　　　That exalts thee, and will cure
　　Every sorrow and sickness and sin.

Strongest deliverer, friend of the friendless,
God of all being divine:
Thou the Christ, and not the creed:
Thou the Truth, in thought and deed:
Thou the water, the bread, and the wine.

In later years this was set to music and is known and sung to-day all round the world. It has healed many a weary sufferer as it did Mrs. Glover at its inception.

This beautiful woman, fairer than the world had ever known, was not without suitors. Several men had asked for her hand in marriage since she had divorced Daniel Patterson, but to one and all the answer was the same. There was no place for marriage in Christian Science and her mission for the world. As 1876 drew to a close one more man proposed marriage to her, but her answer to Gilbert Eddy was "No," as it had been to all the others.

Though Mrs. Glover rallied from each attack, the mesmerist did not let up. Mary was always his primary target, but his secondary target now was Daniel Spofford. Spofford did not succumb to the demonology as readily as had many others, but he felt it. Mrs. Glover thought he was jesting when he would say, "I feel as if I were mesmerized."

When Daniel Spofford began to worship Mary personally instead of turning to Principle, she was very distressed. And when she suffered a physical relapse she felt that Letter to it came from Spofford, as indeed it did, al- Spofford though it did not originate with him. Not until December, 1876 later was the "hidden foe" and the mortal who was trying to influence Spofford to leave her, revealed. On the thirtieth of December she wrote to her student:

Dr. Spofford won't you exercise reason and let me live or will you kill me? Your mind is just what has brought on my relapse and I shall never recover if you do not govern yourself and TURN YOUR THOUGHTS wholly away from me. . . .It is a hidden foe that is at work read Science and Health page 193 1st par.

No student nor mortal has tried to have you leave me that I know of Dr. Eddy has tried to have you stay you are in a

mistake...There is no cloud between us but the way you set
me up for a Dagon is wrong and now I implore you to turn
forever from this error of personality and go alone to God as I
have taught you.

Mary had taught all her students how to work metaphysically and asked them often to support her and her cause. She
turned particularly to Spofford for support, but what she had
written earlier was still very true:

> Pioneering what is new, or of great value to the world, is
> like a traveller on the desert of Arabia in company with one
> who becoming alarmed, his heat and sufferings increase and
> his courage fails; but the explorer, despite the hardships,
> and convinced he will come out right, accepts the situation
> more calmly, and encourages his friend, assuring him the only
> danger is his fear, then points anew the path; at length they
> reach an oasis, where, resting and slaking their thirst, they
> are ready with new vigor to push on. But here the more help-
> less traveller turns to his guide, saying, "Are you not some-
> times alarmed on this desert route?" "Yes," is the ready re-
> sponse; "but," replied the other, "you told me my danger
> consisted in my fear, therefore you have no more practical
> Wisdom than myself;" forgetting his guide carried the bag-
> gage, met the intricacies of the way, and was attacked by
> brigands, plundered, and hindered in his course, his fellow-
> travellers following not, until the danger was over. Bearing
> others' burdens, if you undertake more than you can well
> carry, and are tried or over-wrought, they name it a hopeless
> task, and desert you; few arms are extended to your support,
> until you can help yourself and others, and have no need of
> aid.

The question George McLaren of Boston wrote to Mrs. Glover was probably often in her heart:

> Dear Sister Mary of Lynn, Author of a Wonderful Book...
> you have thrown down the gauntlet to Prof. Tyndall. And you
> have called the world to battle on this issue. Who is to be
> your Armour bearer in this battle of Life?

Who indeed!

CHAPTER XVI

THE SPIRITUAL MARRIAGE

And they sung as it were a new song...and no man could learn that song but the hundred and forty and four thousand, which were redeemed from the earth.

Revelation of John

1877

ON the thirtieth day of December in the year of 1876 Mary felt almost overcome by the weight of the burdens that her students cast upon her. The bright promise of Science was always before her, but so few were working for it and so many hindering the work she was doing that she knew not where to turn. That night she had a dream:

Dream of December 30 1876

> She seemed to be standing on one side of a beautiful field of wheat. As she was rejoicing in its promise, dark swinish forms seemed to move underneath it; their uprooting instincts were destroying thought. She could not cross the field as she intended. Terror and abhorrence chained her to the spot. Then on the other side of the field she saw Gilbert Eddy's manly form. "Come on, Mary," he said, "I will help you."

To Mary this dream was a message from God. The next day she sent the following note to Dr. Spofford:

Marriage to Dr. Eddy January, 1877

Dear Student,

> For reasons best known to myself I have changed my views in regard to marrying and ask you to hand this note to the Unitarian Clergyman and please wait for his answer.

Your Teacher
M.B.G.

On New Year's Day, January 1, 1877 Mary Baker Glover and Asa Gilbert Eddy were united in marriage.

Mrs. Eddy's students were stunned. Her only explanation to them was that this was a spiritual marriage entered into to promote her work.

Jesus said, "I have yet many things to say unto you, but ye cannot bear them now." No doubt a true concept of marriage was one of these things, but that age was incapable of separating marriage from sex or of comprehending spiritual unity; so he merely implied that it was better not to marry for those who could understand. Proclaiming celibacy without understanding produces an arbitrary state which is neither respected nor profitable.

Mary's understanding of sex and spiritual unity dated from her discovery in 1866, but she did not thrust advanced views upon an unprepared public. Her "precious volume" offered good advice for happier marriages under Jesus' precept, "Suffer it to be so now, for thus it becometh us to fulfill all righteousness."

She had added therein, "yield obedience to common forms, until you reach the understanding of their spiritual significance." Having reached the understanding of the spiritual significance of marriage, she had chosen not to marry in the world's way. But here was something else. A man had understood the spiritual significance of marriage and had proposed a spiritual union wherein they would work side by side for the cause of Christian Science to bring forth the divine idea, man. Mr. and Mrs. Eddy set an example before the world of a new and spiritual concept of marriage. In the next edition of Science and Health she wrote:

> The pleasing prospect of the final realization that all is spiritual presents a no less striking contrast to the unblushing farce of 'materialization' than will the past history of 'free love,' when it shall be compared with the future history of the chastity that must follow the spiritualization of all things.

After her marriage Mrs. Eddy wrote to Daniel Spofford:

I have done what I deem the best thing that could be

done under the circumstances, and feel sure I can teach my husband up to a higher usefulness, to purity, and the higher development of all his *latent noble* qualities of head and heart.

To Mary, Gilbert Eddy was as helpful as her own right hand. He had a capacity for accomplishment and a remarkable sense of order, thanks to his capable mother. His strength, which was unseen because of his quiet gentle manner, was felt by his patients and now became a rock for Mary. For the first time she had one student upon whom she could lean and who could support her without collapsing.

It was decided that Dr. Eddy would turn his practice over to Dr. Spofford and devote all his time to helping Mary with her work. With the exception of the additional practice, Daniel Spofford would continue as before, as healer, and agent and publisher for "the book."

Mary found Gilbert a tremendous help, and she was soon relying heavily upon his good judgment. The unity and strength of their marriage was a blessing indeed, for the storm that Mary had felt the previous fall was about to break upon her with all its fury.

CHAPTER XVII

BEGINNING OF THE FLOOD

And the serpent cast out of his mouth water as a flood after the woman, that he might cause her to be carried away of the water.

Revelation of John

1877

MARY'S dream of the previous December had given her guidance, and she had been quick to follow. Obedience to God made her footsteps sure and strong. She stressed the great importance of obedience when she said to her students, "God is the fountain of light, and He illumines one's way when one is obedient. . . . Be sure that God *directs* your way; then, hasten to follow under every circumstance."

Was there not another lesson in Mary's dream? From childhood she had had the ability to see thoughts, motives, and purpose in those around her. Now she was *feeling* something deeper which appeared in her dream as dark swinish forms. The conscious thought of her loyal students had been good, and the appearance was promising, but something underneath was destroying this promise. Something swinish was uprooting the field she had sown and so carefully tended.

This swinish element in human nature would exact a heavy toll before she learned what it was, how it operated, and how to meet it. But when God bade her to rebuke students, she understood that it was to stir the latent tendencies in the heart in order to bring them to the surface for destruction. And do you not think that she recalled this dream when she wrote for a later edition of Science and Health, "In the soil of an 'honest and good heart' the seed must be sown; else it beareth not much fruit, for the swinish element in human nature uproots it."

In the first edition of Science and Health Mrs. Eddy had written:

> To make a specialty of healing is really impossible for us, when our time, means, and health are required for the fuller investigation of this subject; to teach, write, establish practices for students, or halt, perhaps, at measures to be adopted, because of persecution.

The demands on Mary's time were so great that she had the hope that Dr. Eddy might take over the teaching. To this end she called upon her old friend from Albion, Sarah Crosby, who was now a successful court reporter, to take complete stenographic notes of the course she taught to a small class in February.

Some time earlier Mrs. Crosby had written for her friend's aid because of an injury to her eye, and Sarah's testimony of the healing, which had been immediate, appeared in Science and Health. Mary charged Sarah nothing for the healing, but her friend did not reciprocate with her services. She had written before coming that she feared Mary would feel she had grown worldly and sordid, and Mary *was* astounded at the love of money and lack of interest in the metaphysical teaching which she encountered. It proved to be a most unsatisfactory arrangement for both of them. Sarah was unhappy with her pay, and Mary found the twelve hundred transcribed pages worse than useless. Of this she wrote:

> A shorthand writer made more than twelve hundred pages out of our instructions of twelve lessons, but rendered those pages wholly unfit for use by a misapplication of our terms, and omitting our full explanations, whereby a material or physical statement is given a metaphysical explanation when describing disease and the method of its cure.

This problem with Sarah was minor compared with the uprooting of her work that the swinish element was doing. Richard Kennedy knew that his teacher's spirituality made her so sensitive that she had *felt* the ills of her students and his patients when they were working together. Her students were an avenue through which the malicious malpractitioner could attack her health and remain hidden. And lo, of a sudden, she experienced such severe pain through the thoughts of her new students that she could scarcely carry on her work.

But that was not all of the water (mental activity) out of the serpent's mouth. He was not through with George Barry. In Sued by George Barry March, 1877 March that young man sued Mrs. Eddy for twenty-seven hundred dollars and attached her house. His bill of particulars demanded pay for everything he had done for her for the past five years, even listing accompanying her on a walk.

Attorneys were hired, a trial date set for September, and Mrs. Eddy fled from the persecution in Lynn. She left no forwarding address, but she wrote Daniel Spofford Letter to Spofford c. March, 1877 just before leaving with her husband:

Dear Student—This hour of my departure I pick up from the carpet a piece of paper write you a line to say I am at length driven into the wilderness. *Everything* needs me in science, my doors are thronged, the book lies waiting, but those who *call on me mentally* in suffering are in belief killing me! *Stopping my work* that none but me can do in their supreme selfishness; how unlike the example I have left them! Tell this to Miss Brown, Mr. McLauthlen, Mrs. Atkinson, and Miss Norman but do not let them know they *can call* on me thus if they are doing this ignorantly and if they do it consciously tell *McLauthlen* and *them all* it would be no greater crime for them to come directly and thrust a dagger into my heart. They are just as surely in belief killing me and committing murder.

The sin lies at their door and for them to meet its penalty *sometime. You can teach* them better, see you do this.

O! Harry, the book must stop. I can do no more now if ever. They lay on me suffering inconceivable.

Mary

If the students will continue to think of me and call on me, I shall at *last* defend myself and this will be to cut them off from me utterly in a spiritual sense by a bridge they cannot pass over and the effect of this on them they will then learn.

I will let you hear from me as soon as I can bear this on

account of my health; and will return to prosecute my work
on the Book as soon as I can safely. I am going far away and
shall remain until you will do your part and give me some
better prospects.

Ever truly,
Mary

It was imperative that Daniel Spofford give her better prospects. Their contract of the previous April had required that he
pay her a royalty of ten per cent of the net   Letter from
list price of the book, said royalty payable semi-   Spofford
annually, and that he render her a monthly   March, 1877
statement of sales. Nearly a year had elapsed and these terms
had not been fulfilled, although he had spent five hundred
dollars of the receipts for advertising purposes. Spofford had
acknowledged that he had been remiss and had written:

> I know you would do nothing which you did not conscien-
> tiously think right and pertaining to the greatest good of the
> greatest number, even if necessary to the sacrifice of your
> own self-interest. I have not done right by you in not report-
> ing, according to agreement, the sales of your book. Truth
> may again be buried beneath the accumulating dust of cen-
> turies by the stopping of your labors. I want the books sold,
> and would gladly have any one you might sanction take the
> same off my hands if you think best, as it undoubtedly is.

He wanted to make amends and continue in his position, so
Mrs. Eddy made no change. But his sincerity and fidelity were
soon to be tested. The trials his teacher was enduring, however,
were far greater.

The attacks on her health continued and almost overwhelmed her. A few years later she learned the cause and
recorded of Kennedy's work, "This malprac-   Letter to
titioner tried his best to break down our health   Spofford
before we learned the cause of our sufferings."   April, 1877
But in the spring of 1877 she had not learned this, and she
appealed to Harry Spofford for help on the seventh of April:

> I sometimes think I cannot hold on till the next edition is
> out. Will you not help me so far as is in your power, in this
> way? Take Miss Norman, she is an interesting girl and help

her *through*. She will work for the cause but she will swamp me if you do not take hold. I am at present such a tired swimmer, unless you do this I have more than I can carry at present. Direct your thoughts and everybody's else that you can away from me, don't talk of me.

Twelve days later Mrs. Eddy was able to write a very lengthy business letter to Spofford who had promised, among other things, to mark all the errors in two copies of the first edition of Science and Health.

April 19, 1877

My Dear Student,...I will consider the arrangement for embellishing the book. I had fixed on the picture of Jesus and a sick man—the hand of the former outstretched to him as in rebuke of the disease; or *waves* and an ark. The last will cost less I conclude and do as well. No rainbow can be made to look right except in colours and that cannot be conveniently arranged in gilt. Now for the printing—would 480 pages include the Key to Scriptures and the entire work as it now is? The Book entitled Science and Health is to embrace the chapter on Physiology all the same as if that chapter was not compiled in a separate volume; perhaps you so understand it. If the cost is what you stated, I advise you to accept the terms for I am confident in the sale of two editions more. There can be a net income over and above it all. If I get my health again I can make a large demand for the book for I shall lecture and this will sell one edition of a thousand copies (if I can stand it). I am better, some. One circumstance I will name. The night before I left, and before I wrote you those fragments, Miss Brown went into convulsions from a chemical, was not expected to live, but came out of it saying she felt perfectly well and as well as before the injury supposed to have been received. I thought at that time if she was not "born again" the Mother would die in her labours. O, how little my students can know what it all costs me. Now, I thank you for relieving me a little in the other case, please see her twice a week; in healing you are *benefitting yourself*, in teaching you are benefitting others. I would not advise you to change business at present the rolling stone gathers no moss; persevere in *one line* and you can do much more than to continually scatter your fire. Try to get students into the field as practitioners and thus healing will sell the book and introduce the science more than aught but *my* lecturing can do. Send the name of any you can get to study for the purpose of practising and in six months or thereabouts we will have them in the field helping you. If you have ears to hear you will understand. Send all letters to Boston. T.O. Gilbert will forward them to me at present.

Now for the writings you named. I will make an agreement with you to publish the book the three years from the time you took it and have twenty-five per cent royalty paid me; at the end of this period we will make other arrangements or agreements or continue those we have made just as the Spirit shall direct me. I feel this is the best thing for the present to decide upon. During these years we shall have a treasurer such as we shall agree upon and the funds deposited in his or her hands and drawn for specified purposes, at the end of these three years if we dissolve partnership the surplus amount shall be equally divided between us; and this is the best I can do. All the years I have expended on that book, the labours I am still performing, and all I have done for students and the cause gratuitously, entitle me to *some income* now that I am unable to work. But as it is I have none and instead am sued for $2,700 for what? for just this, I have allowed my students to think I have no rights, and they can not wrong me.

May God open their eyes at length.

If you conclude not to carry the work forward on the terms named, it will have to go out of edition as I can do no more for it, and I believe this hour is to try my students who think they have the cause at heart and see if it be so. My husband is giving all his time and means to help me up from the depths in which these students plunge me and this is all he can do at present. Please write soon.

As ever,
Mary

Send me the two books that are corrected and just as soon as you can, and I with Gilbert will read them.

Please tell me if you are going to have the chapter on Physiology in a book by itself that I may get the preface ready as soon as I am able.

I do nothing else when I have a day I can work. Will send you the final corrections *soon.*

Think of me when you feel *strong* and well only, and think only of me as well.

Ever yrs. in
Truth
Mary

This hour surely was to try her student who thought he had the cause at heart. But his trial was not simply being willing to pay the author a high royalty. He could have done that easily, for most of his sales were at the retail price, saving him the usual thirty to forty per cent discount to booksellers. His trial came from the same source that was constantly attacking Mrs. Eddy's health. And these attacks on her health had not lessened. Before the end of April she wrote Spofford again:

April, 1877, Sunday

Dear Student: I am in Boston to-day feeling very very little better for the five weeks that are gone. I cannot finish the Key yet. I will be getting myself and all of a sudden I am seized as sensibly by some other's belief as the hand could lay hold of me. My sufferings have made me utterly weaned from this plane and if my husband was only willing to give me up I would gladly yield up the ghost of this terrible earth plane and join those nearer my Life. . . . Cure Miss Brown or I shall never finish my book.

Truly yrs.   M.

Kennedy's attacks against those close to Mrs. Eddy were unlike his attacks upon her. Instead of endeavoring to implant in their thought suggestions of pain and suffering, he reached out to their thought with suggestions of doubt of their teacher, of her motives, of her spirituality, and of her revelation. Though Richard Kennedy is no longer the perpetrator, the malicious attack on the Revelator to this age separates many a promising student from Science by separating in his thought the Revelator from her revelation, either by doubt, neglect, or lack of true appreciation. The attack on Daniel Spofford was not as subtle as the present day attacks of malicous mind, and his letter of May 30 indi-

Letter from Spofford May, 1877

cates that he succumbed completely to the erroneous suggestions:

May 30, 1877

Mrs. Eddy: . . . It is not healing a few sick or teaching a dozen students a year but the preparing of the "ark" for the saving of God's people. Nineteen months since the book was first issued and not corrected yet . . . and the "writing on the wall" is . . . "you have proven yourself unworthy to be the standard bearer of Christian Science," and God will remove from you the means for carrying on this work. . . . I consider that I have a perfect right to appoint meetings, or place in practice those you have taught. . . . I suggest that you give that book and the copyright unconditionally to some one, any one; and see if God will not prosper it. . . . You have said "if you only had two to stand by you you would carry this cause." I propose to carry it alone expecting no one but God to stand by me.

Daniel

Lamentations IV, 6, 7, 8

Mrs. Eddy had thought that she at last had two students to stand by her, and now it was obvious that she had only one,— Asa Gilbert Eddy. It was also obvious that Spofford was no longer working with her or for her. It was not so much that their partnership must be terminated as that it had terminated already. Whether his statement that "God will remove from you the means for carrying on this work" was a suggestion from Kennedy or a product of his own confused thoughts, he did not leave it to God, but endeavored to implement it himself. When Mrs. Eddy requested that he return to her the books on hand, he refused to do so and closed them out at a fraction of their value. When she demanded the money that he received for them, he again refused and paid the entire proceeds of six hundred dollars to Barry and Newhall.

On the second of July Spofford wrote Mrs. Eddy his parting letter:

Final Statement

Boston, July 2, 1877

The number of copies of Science and Health on hand May 1, 1876 were   765
Disposed of as per reports   679
                                                        ———
                                                         86

Left with you to sell Jan. 3, 1877   26
Left with you to sell Feb. 12, 1877   12
Left with you to sell Feb. 24, 1877   <u>48</u>
                                                           86

...I do not consider that I have had a well made book to handle. 3 months ago the interest was such that large quantities of new ones would have found a ready sale provided the essential corrections had been made, but on your writing me that I could have the new books only by paying you a royalty beyond all reason and justice or "you would let the book go out of edition" I saw that the motive actuating you in this 'cause' was such that in justice to myself and the Principle of Christian Science no successful business relations could be maintained for any length of time between us.

Under the influence of mesmerism Spofford expected to supercede Mrs. Eddy as the leader of the Christian Science movement. He foolishly expected her to give him the copyright to Science and Health now that he had removed from her the means for republishing. He even signed an agreement with Barry later in July to pay him four hundred dollars more if at any time he should "receive control of the said book 'Science and Health'."

The time was not distant when Mrs. Eddy would see that Richard Kennedy was fascinated with evil and with motiveless malignity was experimenting with the projection of thought to control other people's minds. But in the fall of 1877 Kennedy, in the utmost secrecy that he maintained all his lifetime, was smiling at his success as she reacted to the behaviour of Daniel Spofford and George Barry. He gloated at George Barry's trial when Spofford testified as a witness for Barry and both testified against their teacher; and he "remarked in the court-room with a malignant sneer, to a Christian scientist, Now what do you think of your Mr. Barry?"

Kennedy's work was the exact opposite of his teacher's and so was his life. All that he did was hidden and covered up while all she did was in the open for everyone to see. All her years were a sacrifice to the world for the benefit and progress of mankind. But temporarily her work came to a stop, for once more it was necessary, as she had written, to "halt...at measures to be adopted, because of persecution."

She taught no more classes in 1877 and stopped temporarily on her revision of Science and Health; but she was ever encouraging newcomers to enter the ranks, to study, and to practise.

One such newcomer was Clara Choate, a young wife and mother who had been healed by Dorcas Rawson. Mrs. Choate has left a word picture of the Leader at that time:

> One of my most precious memories of Mrs. Eddy is an interview I had with her in 1877. . . . I had been wonderfully healed. . . She emphasized this work of Christian healing as laying the foundation for *Science and Health,* as we then termed the Cause, more often than its present name of Christian Science. . . . she said. . . "To be a good healer or a true follower of Christ you must demonstrate the law of God, for His law does overcome disease. In overcoming this you overcome sin." I replied, why this will be glorious; and she remarked in her sweet, winsome and persuasive manner, "Your enthusiasm is just what I need to carry forward this work of healing to the hearts of the people, for healing is what *they* desire and what you and I and dear Gilbert and others of my students must give them. I must turn my attention from now on, to other departments of the work. . . which I am trying to systematize. We must have system."
>
> . . . The healing was the need of the hour, she strongly urged, just the faithful, patient healing work, by a life devoted and willing.
>
> . . . As she sat so unconsciously stately in her modest rocking chair. . . with eloquent upturned face, beaming with the glorious hopes of a soul inspired, I felt she was pleading for the sick world, the *whole sick world*. . . I resolved to join the class as she proposed and remember the joy of my decision and the "God bless you my dear girl" which she so tenderly and impressively uttered as she accompanied me to the door . . . All the way home I marvelled at her *faith* in God, at her divine leading and still feel to this day Mrs. Eddy really walked and talked with God.

CHAPTER XVIII

ENTER THE ACCOMPLICE

*And . . . the dragon . . . persecuted the woman which brought
forth the man child.*

Revelation of John

1878

EDWARD Arens (pronounced Ahrens) was in the class
that Dr. Eddy taught in Clara Choate's home in January
or February of 1878. By mid-February Mrs. Eddy was defending Arens to other students, but that was not so when she first
met him. She shrank back from accepting him, for she recognized him immediately as the sensuous man of her visions two
or three years earlier. She was overpersuaded, however, by Dr.
Eddy who had been favorably impressed by Arens' eagerness
in class and by Arens himself who was as intentionally in-
gratiating as his ambitious powerful personality would allow.

In 1907 Richard Kennedy told an interviewer "that after
their partnership was dissolved she felt the pinch, and did the
best she could." Thirty years earlier a definite part of Kennedy's malicious thought projection to Mrs. Eddy was that of a
relapse to the poverty she had experienced. As she struggled to
meet the unusual demands on her resources and to overcome
the lack of funds, his thought projection to her students was,
that she was greedy for money. The effect of this was already
evident in Barry's and Spofford's accusations against her.

Since the time of Jesus no one had cared as little for money
and wordly things as had Mary Baker Eddy, but her students
failed to appreciate her sacrifices for them and the cause. As
she had written to Daniel Spofford, "I have allowed my students to think I have no rights, and they cannot wrong me! May
God open their eyes at length."

176

Before long Edward Arens proposed to do that very thing. Whether it was his persuasive aggressiveness or the combined secretive thought of this accomplice and of Kennedy, the originator of the dark drama of 1878, matters little. Kennedy was seeing the manifestation of his mental malpractice in Mrs. Eddy's acceptance of Arens into her home as a trusted associate in the position George Barry had held. She had written to a student in February:

> ...the effect I saw on Mr. Arens when you were here was owing to the influence of Mesmerism...I wish you could see what a nervous desire he has to do us good and you would like him.

She was right about the mesmerism but did not then know how much it was affecting her.

Mary had leaned very heavily on her husband who was always beside her helping in his quiet way. In contrast to Gilbert's mildness, Arens proposed to forge ahead aggressively and clear the way for the teacher by taking matters into his own hands, acting as her counsel, and relieving her of some responsibilities. The assistance was not unwelcome to someone as harassed as Mrs. Eddy had been.

Arens knew about her contract with Kennedy and the others, that she had never collected, and he convinced her that she was allowing her students to do wrong. In the third edition of Science and Health she wrote:

> In the interests of truth we ought to say that never a lawsuit has entered into our history voluntarily. We have suffered great losses and the direst injustice rather than go to law, for we always considered a lawsuit, of two evils, the greatest. About two years ago the persuasions of a student awakened our convictions that we might be doing wrong in permitting students to break their obligations with us, refuse the payment of their notes, and to deny their considerations when they were filling their pockets by their claims to be practising that for which they refused to pay us. The student who argued this point to us so convincingly offered to take the notes and collect them, without any participation of ours; we trusted him with the whole affair, doing only what he told

us, for we were utterly ignorant of legal proceedings.

As always Mrs. Eddy's main interest was the cause of Christian Science. She turned over her 1870 contracts from Kennedy, Stanley, and Tuttle to Arens and resumed work on the revision of Science and Health. She devoted her time also to new students, to loyal students, and to the Christian Scientist Association which convened about once a week, occasionally at a student's home, but more often at Number 8 Broad Street.

Both Mr. and Mrs. Choate had become interested and active in Christian Science. One meeting of the Association which stood out in Mrs. Choate's memory was held in the Eddy's parlor in the spring of 1878. The members present in addition to Mr. and Mrs. Eddy and Mr. and Mrs. Choate included Miss Dorcas Rawson, her sister Mrs. Miranda Rice, Samuel P. Bancroft, his brother Henry Bancroft, Mrs. E. N. Taylor, and perhaps two or three others. When they came to the question and discussion period, Samuel Bancroft raised the question that has continued to be a vital issue to the present day. He said, "Should we say, or can we truthfully say, we as individuals are perfect, pure, holy, or infallible now?" Clara Choate recalled the following:

> Mrs. Eddy arose quietly and with dignified composure of manner, in a firm, convincing though seriously pleasant voice, asserted, "I am infallible, I am infallible now, *we* are infallible now."
>
> ...we students were all...surprised and to some degree shocked...Mr. Bancroft began an earnest expostulation *against* such a statement...Other students present sided with him...Even dear Dr. Eddy in his quiet, patient manner and tender voice... [tried] to enter a conciliatory compromise...But Mrs. Eddy heroically stood her ground, and with a gracious decision still declared, "I am infallible *now*."
>
> The power of this truth thus uttered by her was not lost upon the students and was more or less felt by all present. One said she had come with a headache, another with fear of spine, another with throat and a cough, and so each one thinking of their troubles, suddenly found the *air* changed, and their conditions also changed to their immediate consciousness of relief from evil. One or two *felt* worse which Mrs.

Eddy said was as good as if they felt better. This great thought had started an upheaval then and there. The solid ground of old beliefs was broken. The stir of love, of hate, smiles and tears in even that small company seemed like a battlefield between Truth and error. Mr. Bancroft almost in temper, with apparent disgust coldly left the meeting, Mrs. Eddy kindly saying, "I have told the Truth."

This battle between Truth and error within the ranks was minor compared with the onslaught against Mrs. Eddy from without. The case with George Barry was still unsettled. From the time of his defection Daniel Spofford began working against his teacher, endeavoring to draw her students away from her. Early in 1878 she had written to a student, "I have been so besieged for a whole year that my *native* sense at times seems almost yielding and I almost fear the end my besiegers desire will come, unless I have an armistice."

The student, Mr. Atkinson, endeavored to arrange an armistice with Spofford who rejected the idea, saying that he hoped the subject of reconciliation would never again be mentioned. In his attempt to alienate the students from Mrs. Eddy, Spofford was calling on them mentally (and often in person) to desert their teacher and follow him as the new leader of the Christian Science movement. This malpractice had some effect on their health as well as their work, causing Mrs. Eddy to bring it out in the open and discuss it, as she was wont to do with everything. To one student she wrote, "Take up Spofford thus: He cannot affect his Teacher or her students to make them sick or turn them away from Truth and their Teacher." To another who was in frequent contact with Spofford she wrote, "Guard well your own and your dear family's symptoms, and when you feel doubts of me, or physical ailments, take [Spofford] up with the contradictions of his arguments and the symptoms will disappear."

Miss Lucretia Brown was a middle-aged spinster from Ipswich who had been a semi-invalid since a severe injury received in girlhood. She had been marvellously healed by Mrs. Eddy when she began studying Christian Science in 1877. She had also been helped by Daniel Spofford, but turned to Dorcas Rawson for assistance when Spofford defected. When she suffered an unaccountable relapse in the spring of 1878 both Miss Rawson and Miss Brown feared that it was caused by the mesmerism Daniel Spofford was practising.

Though Spofford was but another tool in Kennedy's hands, the mesmerism he practised unravelled one more step in the uncovering of evil. In the second edition of Science and Health Mrs. Eddy wrote:

> Mesmerism is practised through manipulation—and without it. And we have learned, by new observation, the fool who saith "There is no God" attempts more evil without a sign than with it. Since "Science and Health" first went to press, we have observed the crimes of another mesmeric outlaw, in a variety of ways, who does not as a common thing manipulate, in cases where he sullenly attempted to avenge himself of certain individuals, etc. But we had not before witnessed the malpractitioner's fable without manipulation, and supposed it was not done without it; but have learned it is the addenda to that we have described in a previous edition, but without manipulating the head.

Arens lost no time, from the moment he gained Mrs. Eddy's confidence, in filing suit against Richard Kennedy. He acted in her name and, supposedly, on her behalf. The case came up in Judge William Parmenter's court on the fourteenth of March. The judgement awarded Mrs. Eddy the seven hundred fifty dollars still owing plus interest and costs. Kennedy immediately filed an appeal.

Almost immediately Arens filed several other suits involving Mrs. Eddy and Christian Science. The method of evil at this juncture seemed to have been the old game of "divide and conquer." Daniel Spofford was basically sensitive and sincere and had been the most devoted and successful practitioner of Christian Science. The best, perverted, becomes the worst, and Spofford was now the most potent tool the enemy had found and the endeavor was to keep him that way.

Some of what Arens did in Mrs. Eddy's name was without her knowledge and consent. The case he now filed against Spofford for unpaid tuition may have been one of those actions. A second case filed against Spofford most definitely was begun without her knowledge. Arens called on Miss Lucretia Brown affirming to her that Spofford's malpractice was the cause of her problems and that Mrs. Eddy desired that she sue the malpractitioner at a court of law. Mrs. Eddy disapproved when she learned of the case, but *Brown vs. Spofford* was already filed and Mr. Arens was acting as Miss Lucretia's counsel, so the Teacher supported her student's action.

Mrs. Eddy was not averse to bringing the practice of malicious mesmerism to public notice. Whether it accomplished anything in that day other than notoriety for Mrs. Eddy and Christian Science is doubtful. The notoriety together with the conflict with Spofford was what Kennedy desired, but despite the malicious intent all things do work together for good. The "Salem Witchcraft Trial" of 1878 was the first public exposure of malicious mental malpractice in the present era. Public understanding of the issue is necessary to its elimination whether the evil practice be called mesmerism, hypnotism, ancient or modern necromancy, or witchcraft. And the case did provide court records and newspaper accounts for future generations to study.

Litigation was not the only area of Aren's influence in Mrs. Eddy's affairs. He was most insistent and persuasive in his argument that her class-book for teaching and practising Christian Science should not be included in Science and Health. He convinced some students and may have affected her decision temporarily. His attacks on her babe, Science and Health, which began as friendly persuasion became wicked malpractice and blatant theft a few years later. After rescuing her child from these attacks, her comment was most charitable:

> When I revised "Science and Health with Key to the Scriptures" in 1878, some irresponsible people insisted that my manual of the practice of Christian Science Mind-healing should not be made public; but I obeyed a diviner rule.

Her class-book, already published as the *Science of Man,* was not included in Science and Health as the chapter entitled Recapitulation until the third edition three years later. The second edition was a near disaster. When the proofs came from the printer, the Eddys were confronted with a confused mass,

181

full of countless errors.

After struggling with the wretched material for some time, Dr. Eddy called upon John Wilson whom he knew to be a printer of some repute. Mr. Wilson responded by going over the confused mass of proofs with Mrs. Eddy. Though the damage was beyond repair, he showed her how she might salvage about one hundred seventy of the pages so that the money expended would not be totally lost.

W. F. Brown and Company had not done a good job on the first edition, so they had gone to Rand, Avery and Company for the second, hoping of course for improved workmanship, only to meet with a far worse situation. The careless printing errors were a grave disappointment and a severe financial setback, but the cause of the problem lay with her recalcitrant students and their malicious mental malpractice.

EDWARD J. ARENS

CHAPTER XIX

BLESSING FOR CURSING

But I say unto you, Love your enemies, bless them that curse you, do good to them that hate you, and pray for them which despitefully use you, and persecute you.

Jesus

1878

THE slim volume that Mrs. Eddy was able to salvage was entitled "Science and Health Volume II," although the printer had entitled the contents on nearly Second edition every left hand page "Metaphysics *versus* Physi- Science and Health ology." This second edition of Mrs. Eddy's book October, 1878 had an ark and waves in gilt on the cover and became known as the "ark edition."

About a week before the ark edition came off the press in October of 1878, Mrs. Eddy sought to implement her words in *Miscellaneous Writings:* "If, consciously or unconsciously, one is at work in a wrong direction, who will step forward and open his eyes to see this error? He who *is* a Christian Scientist, who has cast the beam out of his own eye, speaks plainly to the offender and tries to show his errors to him before letting another know it."

Mrs. Eddy had not ceased endeavoring to cast the beam out of her own eye from the time she had written Quimby many years earlier, "Dr., I have a strange feeling of Letter to late that I ought to be *perfect* after the com- Kennedy mand of science, in order to know and do the October, 1878 right." On the eighth of October she wrote to Richard Kennedy:

183

Dr. Kennedy

I do not like to blight the future of a young man. I do not like to see year by year your opportunities to do better passing away never to return...and will spare every blow in my power if only you will cease to commit in secret the sins you are committing. Your promise to pay me for tuition is not of as much importance to me, or to you, as your debt to God, to Truth. You have said this Truth has saved your life (or that which is called life) and yet you are making it no returns for all this, by acknowledging in your life that you love Truth and adhere to it sufficiently to do as you would be done by....

Now I come to you again with that spirit of forgiveness which you cannot understand, to ask you, if the world knows more of the error of your past, you will cease to commit the sin against the Holy Ghost by doing in secret what you would not have revealed, by trying to injure the helpless who know not what you are trying, and so stop the terrible malpractice you have fallen into. If you will, you shall not be publicly exposed, and I for one will take back the straying lamb, and help you to prosper, and go on in the path of Truth....

Now do not place the false unction to your heart that any sinister motive, or motive to benefit myself prompts this letter, for it does not. I can take care of myself and the dear ones God has given me and the malpractice is powerless to harm me....I hope God will govern your resolves this time and bless you from that hour.

M. B. Glover Eddy

Kennedy's debt to Mrs. Eddy was important as the bait in the trap he was about to spring. But he covered his footprints carefully in all his wickedness and maintained an outward attitude of injured innocence. He did not respond to Mrs. Eddy's letter. On the day that it was written he wrote to Sarah Bagley whom Mrs. Eddy had instructed along with Richard in Amesbury almost ten years earlier and who was completely beguiled by him. In reference to Mrs. Eddy, Kennedy wrote, "the Devil will never get his own until he has her. She is really malicious in her intentions. She does her wickedness knowingly and hence I have no charity for her."

Daniel Spofford was also the recipient of a letter written by

Mrs. Eddy on October 8, 1878. She wrote to him as follows:

Dear Student,

Won't you make up your mind before it is ever too late
to stop sinning with your eyes wide open? I pray for you, that
God will influence your thoughts to better issues, and make
you a good and a great man, and spare you the penalty that
must come if you do not forsake sin. I am ready at any time to
welcome you back, and kill for you the fatted calf, that is,
destroy in my own breast the great material error of rendering
evil for evil or resenting the wrongs done us. I do not cherish
this purpose toward any one. I am too selfish to do myself
this great injury. I want you to be good and *happy in being
good* for you never can be happy without it. I rebuke error
only to destroy it not to harm *you,* but to do you *good.* Whenever a straying student returns to duty, stops his evil practice
or sin against the Holy Ghost, I am ready to say, "neither do I
condemn thee, go and sin no more." I write you at this time
only from a sense of the high and holy privilege of charity,
the greatest of all graces. Do not mistake my motive, I am not
worldly selfish in doing this, but am only desirous to do you
good. Your silent arguments to do me harm have done me the
greatest possible good; the wrath of man has praised Thee. In
order to meet the emergency, Truth has lifted me above my
former self, enabled me to know who is using this argument
and when and what is being spoken, and knowing this, what
is said in secret is proclaimed on the house top and affects
me no more than for you to say it to me audibly, and tell me
I have so and so; and to hate my husband; that I feel others;
that arguments cannot do good; that Mrs. Rice cannot; that
my husband cannot, etc., etc. I have now no need of human
aid. God has shut the mouth of the lions. The scare disappears when you know another is saying it and that the error is
not your own.

May God save you from the effects of the very sins you
are committing and which you have been and will be the victim of when the measure you are meting shall be measured
to you. *Pause,* think, solemnly and selfishly of the cost to you.
Love instead of hate your friends, and *enemies* even. This
alone can make you happy and draw down blessings infinite.

Have I been your friend? Have I taught you faithfully the way of happiness? and rebuked sternly that which could turn you out of that way? If I have, then I was your friend and risked much to do you good. May God govern your resolves to do right from this hour and strengthen you to keep them.

Adieu,

M. B. Glover Eddy.

There was no response from Daniel Spofford.

DANIEL HARRISON SPOFFORD

CHAPTER XX

KENNEDY'S UNBELIEVABLE PLOT

He deviseth mischief upon his bed; he setteth himself in a way that is not good; he abhorreth not evil.

Psalm of David

1878

K ENNEDY'S unpaid tuition meant very little to Mrs. Eddy. Her concern was for his welfare and progress. She would have been happy to drop the lawsuit against him with the slightest sign of sincerity or repentance on his part. But she received no such sign.

Kennedy's trial by jury was scheduled for early November. With his unpaid promissory note and his accomplice he had set an intricate snare to entrap and discredit, if not destroy, the Revelator to this age.

Arens had once been arrested on a swindling charge. The charge was not pressed, but this record leaves a suspicion that he may have provided Kennedy a contact with the criminal world. However it was managed, Kennedy, with calculated discretion, stayed in the background, and Arens stayed close to the Eddys in his trusted position in their household. They, of course, knew nothing of the questionable aspect of his background while he played his role as a zealous disciple with a nervous desire to do good for Mrs. Eddy.

The Eddys were the victims of Kennedy's plot, though at the time Daniel Spofford appeared to be. Spofford was merely a dupe in the incredible scheme. Early in October he was visited by a burly, evil-looking man named James Sargent who informed him that he had been hired to murder Dr. Daniel Spofford. He also said that he did not intend to do it (although he had received some of the pay), but had reported the situation to a state police detective named Pinkham. Both Sargent, who had a criminal record, and Pinkham urged Spofford to secrete himself in a house in Cambridgeport owned by Sargent's brother,—which Spofford did on the fifteenth of October.

Very shortly thereafter an article appeared in the newspapers entitled "Mysterious Absence" which began, "Dr. D. H. Spofford, the Christian Scientist, has been missing since Tuesday, October 15, and much alarm for his safety is manifested." A few days later another article appeared stating that Spofford's body had been identified in the morgue.

On the twenty-ninth of October Sargent appeared at the door of Number 8 Broad Street and, because of his impertinent remarks, was turned away by Dr. Eddy who had never before seen the man. What a shock to have this convict admitted to their home a few minutes later by the state detective who arrested Gilbert Eddy and E. J. Arens and took them to jail. The thunderbolt aimed at Mrs. Eddy followed. Newspapers blared forth with the statement that Eddy and Arens had been arrested for having conspired to murder Spofford, who had by now reappeared. A portion of the letter that Gilbert wrote to Mary from the jail said:

> You have doubtless seen the charge and I need not say so to assure you that it is wholly untrue. I saw D. H. Spofford when the trial was called and he could not look me in the face. ...Do not fear for me or Mr. Arens. God doeth all things well...and I have enjoyed myself during this experience so far, having as I have the assurance of being accounted worthy to suffer persecution for the Master's sake. Now Mary Dear be of good cheer for though this is not the experience we should have chosen yet the Master who knoweth better than we hath said it worketh out a more exceeding and eternal weight of glory.
>
> Yours in Love,
> Gilbert

Inflammatory articles continued in the Boston newspapers with such statements as: "All three [men] emanate from the notorious Scientists' home, on Broad Street, in Lynn." And, "Finding that they could not dispose of their rival by any process of law, the Eddy combination...visited Boston and bargained with a Portland street "bummer," to put Dr. Spofford out of the way, in other words to MURDER HIM IN COLD BLOOD."

Daniel Spofford was the plaintiff against Eddy and Arens at the preliminary hearing in the Boston Municipal Court on the seventh of November. The chief witness was James Sargent who wove a fantastic tale of false-hoods. The elaborate detail of his story was cor-roborated by a procession of witnesses, mainly prostitutes from his sister's house of ill-fame in that city, and convicts.

Hearing of November 7, 1878

Not knowing what the accusations were, Dr. Eddy offered no defense to the fantastic story of malicious intrigue told by the motley group of criminals and prostitutes,—a story of false accusations against Dr. Eddy,—lies from beginning to end. This hearing is reminiscent of the false accusations against Jesus of Nazareth to which he answered not a word, and of Jesus' hearing in the high priest's palace where they sought false witness against him.

But the plot of 1878 was obviously planned and master-minded, for the preliminary newspaper articles were well-timed and organized. Now the newspapers carried this lurid story of lies which spread rapidly beyond Boston, and writers and readers alike judged, condemned, and sentenced the Eddys, never having heard them.

In the third edition of Science and Health Mrs. Eddy noted the articles about Spofford's disappearance and continued:

> Then similar articles flashed out from the press, couched in the same covert malice, and showing no special sympathy for Mrs. Eddy and Christian scientists in general when dropping down to state that Dr. Eddy and E. J. Arens had been arrest-ed for conspiring to murder D. Spofford. But the murdered man was alive and well, hidden away... The leading dailies in the city, the "Boston Journal," etc., belched forth those damaging articles all over the United States and into Europe before the rebutting testimony could be furnished. Those scurrilous communications were evidently all given to the press at the same time that they might be used simultaneous-ly, knowing that any decent moderation would have pre-vented respectable papers publishing such slander. The plot

was laid so adroitly that my husband's counsel advised him to keep silent and give no clew until he had unearthed the diabolical plot. . . .

The purpose of the plotters was evidently to injure the reputation of metaphysical practice, and to embarass us for money at a time when they hoped to cripple us in the circulation of our book.

Mrs. Eddy was embarassed for money. All of their funds had gone into salvaging the second edition of Science and Health which had been out only two or three weeks, when she suddenly had to hire an attorney and, on his advice, detectives. It is not surprising that the Eddys believed Daniel Spofford to be the instigator of the plot, for that, too, was part of the master plan.

Neither is it surprising that the import of the next episode of this drama did not impress Mary at the time, for her thoughts were turning to God in this trial and her efforts were to help her husband and to raise money for his release. But it was far from coincidental that Richard Kennedy's trial for non-payment of his note to Mrs. Eddy came up on the eighth of November, the day following the preliminary hearing,—on the very day that the newspapers were filled with the lurid details of this incredible falsehood.

Kennedy's jury trial November, 1878

The papers left not the slightest doubt of the defendants' guilt and vividly portrayed the Eddys as criminals and charlatans. Little wonder that the jury reversed the judge's decision and released Kennedy from his obligation.

Col. Russell Conwell, the Eddys' attorney, was endeavoring to get to the bottom of the plot before the case came up before the grand jury of the Superior Court on the third of December. All the evidence pointed to Spofford as the plotter, and his previous behaviour surely did not exonerate him. But from the perspective of years Mrs. Eddy wrote, "I am glad to say that I now believe Mr. Spofford was wronged, and unwittingly drawn by his enemies into that conspiracy."

In the next edition of Science and Health the chapter exposing Kennedy's malpractice was enlarged from 15 pages entitled "Mesmerism" to 46 pages titled "Demonology." In that chapter Mrs. Eddy wrote, "Never but one of our students was a voluntary malpractitioner; he has made many others."

RICHARD KENNEDY
From a photograph taken in Lynn, Massachusetts in 1871.

CHAPTER XXI

BEGINNING PREACHING

The spirit of the Lord God is upon me; because the Lord hath anointed me to preach good tidings unto the meek; he hath sent me to bind up the broken-hearted, to proclaim liberty to the captives, and the opening of the prison to them that are bound.

Isaiah

1878

O N the twenty-fourth of November, with the conspiracy-to-murder trial still pending, Mrs. Eddy, by invitation of the pastor, began preaching at the Baptist Tabernacle on Shawmut Avenue in Boston. Mrs. Eddy wrote of this period in *Retrospection and Introspection:*

Preaching in Baptist Tabernacle

The congregation so increased in number the pews were not sufficient to seat the audience and benches were used in the aisles. At the close of my engagement we parted in Christian fellowship if not in full unity of doctrine.

Our last vestry meeting was made memorable by eloquent addresses from persons who feelingly testified to having been healed through my preaching. Among other diseases cured they specified cancers. The cases described had been treated and given over by physicians of the popular schools of medicine, but I had not heard of these cases till the persons who divulged their secret joy were healed. A prominent churchman agreeably informed the congregation that many others present had been healed under my preaching, but were too timid to testify in public.

One memorable Sunday afternoon, a soprano,—clear,

strong, sympathetic,—floating up from the pews, caught my ear. When the meeting was over, two ladies pushing their way through the crowd reached the platform. With tears of joy flooding her eyes—for she was a mother—one of them said, "Did you hear my daughter sing? Why, she has not sung before since she left the choir and was in consumption. When she entered this church one hour ago she could not speak a loud word, and now, oh, thank God, she is healed!"

Richard Kennedy was pleased but never satisfied with his successes at injuring the Revelator and her cause. She wrote of his wicked work:

> From the time we dissolved partnership with the aforesaid mesmerist, because of his depravity, he avowed his intention to injure us, and we have the testimony of those who have heard him say that he would follow us to the grave for that purpose.

Being constantly surprised by Kennedy's diabolical plotting did not deter Mrs. Eddy from her purpose, but the fiendish harassment did force her higher in her demonstrations of spiritual power and protection. In the winter of 1878 the conspiracy-to-murder trial weighed heavily on the Eddys, but Kennedy, undetected, had accomplished his aim. His malicious intent was now bent upon pursuing Mrs. Eddy into the Baptist Tabernacle.

The malpractitioner influenced young men of his acquaintance to attend the meetings and take front seats. As soon as the services had well begun they would get up and leave one at a time just to disturb the meeting. Finally the minister, Dr. Williams, seeing their intentions, placed himself near the door. When they began their exit, he arose and locked the door, ordered them back to their seats, and threatened them with arrest for disturbing the services.

After those disturbances had ceased, as Mrs. Eddy was preaching one day, a stone came crashing through the glass and landed at her side. A venerable gentleman arose and implored that she not attempt to go on with the service, to which she replied that she feared no harm and called upon them to stand still and see the salvation of God. Then suddenly, though there were no clouds to be seen in the sky, a heavy thunderbolt burst which shook the house. Members of the audience saw the lightning playing all around Mrs. Eddy while her voice was heard above it all proclaiming, "He uttered His voice, the earth melted." They were troubled no more with attempts to disturb the meetings.

The youthful Mrs. Clara Choate accompanied Mrs. Eddy to one of the early meetings,—probably the first. Her recollections provide a word picture of that occasion:

Reminiscences of Mrs. Clara Choate

> I consider this. . . meeting one of the *great* events in the history of Mrs. Eddy's work. She told me going home she had been led to do this thing by Spirit, and her obedience to God had led her aright, some feeling she would shipwreck her Cause by holding the meetings in this very orthodox church. . . . She told me she was up all night holding to God lest error darken and discourage us in this undertaking, and we cried for joy when the meeting proved a success. I was proud of Mrs. Eddy. She looked the queen, so graceful. . . her face aglow, a new inspiration in her tone and manner, an indescribable power I have never seen with another. Even the hard face of the Reverend softened as he looked at her, and it seemed hard for him to utter any disagreement from her conclusion of God and man. "Why," he said, "if what you say is true, you will have *man live forever.*" Other questions. . . came up. . . Each subject was met and overcome so that Mrs. Eddy remarked she had *purified the temple.*
>
> On our way home I asked if she was hungry. And then she revealed to me her strength in Truth outside of matter and replied, "I have a meat to eat ye know not of." . . . Again I asked, "Are you tired?" She turned upon me a radiant face, glowing with health and in charming freshness of voice and manner said, "Do I look so?" I again was convinced that neither loss of sleep nor absence of food mattered to this wonderful woman, whose close and real association with God met every need.

CHAPTER XXII

BEGINNING THE CHURCH

For many successive years I have endeavored to find new ways and means for the promotion and expansion of scientific Mind-healing.

Mary Baker Eddy

1878

O N the third of December the Grand Jury of the Superior Court accepted the incredible story of James Sargent and his colleague, George Collier. To their indictment Dr. Eddy and E. J. Arens said they were not guilty.

Dr. Eddy's attorney was preparing the defence in great detail in order to refute totally Sargent's fabrication with facts. And, at the Eddy's expense, detectives were en- Letter from deavoring to get to the bottom of the malicious George Collier plot. But no doubt it was Mrs. Eddy's walking and talking with God for spiritual guidance which produced the next bit of evidence in the case. In mid-December Dr. Eddy received the following letter:

Taunton, Dec. 16, 1878

To Dr. Asa G. Eddy and E. J. Arens,—Feeling that you have been greatly ingured by faulse charges and knowing thair is no truth in my statements that you attempted to hire Sargent to kill Daniel Spofford, and wishing to retract as far as possible all things I have sed to your ingury, I now say that thair is no truth whatever in the statement that I saw you meet Sargent at East Cambridge or any other place and pay or offer to pay him any money; that I never hurd a conversation between you and Sargent as testified to by me. Whether Daniel Spofford has anything to do with Sargent I do not know. All I know is that the story I told on the stand is holy faulse and was got up by Sargent.

George A. Collier

In the first month of 1879 the charges against Dr. Eddy and Arens were dropped. The Superior Court record regarding this reads:

> This indictment was thence continued to the present January term, and now the District Attorney, Oliver Stevens, Esquire, says he will prosecute this indictment no further, on payments of costs, which are thereupon paid. And the said Arens and Eddy are thereupon discharged, January 31, 1879.

Lawyer Conwell planned to arrest and prosecute Daniel Spofford, but that was not the course that Mrs. Eddy's experience was to take. Her preaching in the Baptist Tabernacle was stimulating interest in Christian Science in Boston, and her footsteps turned in that direction. Dire as their personal situation had been, it had caused the Leader to rise higher. In her words:

> Abiding by the rules of metaphysics prevents any results from the attacks of the mesmerist, not beneficial even to the individual, that do not lift him higher, enlarging his power, and unfolding his latent capacity to meet and master error. Metaphysics sustains and increases by use the power of Truth. This fulfils the Scripture, "They shall take up serpents."

Were it not for Mrs. Eddy's pen, the charges of conspiracy to murder would have remained a blot on the name of Eddy and a total enigma to future generations. The next edition of Science and Health published the facts of the case in the chapter "Demonology," which detailed Mrs. Eddy's experience with Kennedy's malpractice. She wrote of the case as:

> ...one of the most diabolical conspiracies that ever disgraced the annals of history, and which we have evidence was carried on by the hidden influences employed in the foregoing plots. ...
>
> The State removed the aforesaid detective, the other two principal witnesses were taken to jail on previous charges;

but those individuals evidently most guilty, and who, it is believed by competent judges, instigated the plot, had sheltered
themselves behind so many circumstances, and so wrought
back of others in all they did, they have not yet been tried
by human law, and await their sentence from a higher
tribunal.

*   *   *

In the first edition of Science and Health Mrs. Eddy had
written:

> The mistake the disciples of Jesus made to found religious
> organizations and church rites, if indeed they did this, was
> one the Master did not make; ...
> No time was lost by our Master in organizations, rites, and
> ceremonies, or in proselyting for certain forms of belief:...
> We have no record that forms of church worship were insti-
> tuted by our great spiritual teacher, Jesus of Nazareth, and
> we learn the improbability of this, in the science of God, that
> he taught and demonstrated.

Mary had learned through bitter experience in endeavoring
to give her wonderful discovery to the world that only the
Christian consciousness was prepared to use rather than abuse
or misuse the wonderful science of being. For over twelve years
she had worked diligently to present her marvellous message,
with little assistance and much hindrance from pulpit and
press. In the second edition of Science and Health she had
written:

> We have not a newspaper at our command through which
> to right the wrongs and answer the untruths, we have not a
> pulpit from which to explain how Christianity heals the sick,
> but if we had either of these, the slanderer and the physician
> would have less to do, and we should have more.

Christ's Church does not require organization, but the students did; so they had formed the Christian Scientist Association. This was a help to their growth, but it was restricted to

Mrs. Eddy's students, and she needed a broader platform from which to proclaim her message to humanity. The series of meetings in the Baptist Church in Boston had been most gratifying. On the twenty-fourth of January, shortly before they terminated, Mrs. Eddy wrote to Clara Choate, "I have lectured in parlors 14 years. God calls me now to go before the people in a wider sense." Though she had been lecturing for many years, the era of her preaching began in the Baptist Tabernacle in the fall of 1878.

In February the Scientists arranged for a room in the Parker Memorial Building on Berkeley Street in Boston, and Mrs. Eddy continued to preach each Sunday. On the twelfth of April the Christian Scientist Association recorded, "On motion of Mrs. M. B. Glover Eddy it was seconded and unanimously voted, that we organize a church to be called 'Church of Christ'." But in the spring of 1879 Mr. and Mrs. Eddy *were* the church, commuting every Sunday to Boston to hold services. A young man who was attracted to these meetings described them as follows:

Church beginning April, 1879

> While Mrs. Eddy, the eloquent, earnest pleader for her infant Cause was the chief object of interest, it was the gentle, yet evidently strong nature of Asa Gilbert Eddy which formed a necessary "background," and seemed to make the meetings altogether complete.

This young man, Arthur True Buswell, and a friend, James Ackland, roomed with the Eddys in Lynn while they studied in Mrs. Eddy's class that summer. Neither was able to pay even a third of his tuition, and the class of two was little smaller than average size during these years of intense persecution. Size meant nothing to Mrs. Eddy. As she later wrote, "A small group of wise thinkers is better than a wilderness of dullards and stronger than the might of empires." She had two intelligent, earnest pupils who were learning under her tutelage to be wise thinkers.

Both students were deeply impressed with the spiritual unity expressed by the Eddys' marriage. Their companionship and cheerful cooperation were doubly evident in this summer of 1879, for all of the domestic chores as well as the work for the cause fell upon their shoulders.

By the time the charter for the church was obtained in August these two new students were deeply imbued with Mrs. Eddy's spiritual teaching and eager to practise their new-found truths. The first directors of the Church of Christ, Scientist, which was to be established in Boston, were Mrs. Eddy, Edward A. Orne, James Ackland, and Arthur T. Buswell. !.

Mrs. Eddy's church, however, was not a material organization to be established in Boston or any other city. Her church was "the structure of Truth and Love" to be builded in individual consciousness. Every student whose thoughts were resting upon and proceeding from divine Principle was a missionary for her church. Every practitioner of Christian Science was a pillar in the temple of our God. And her church was to embrace every city on earth until all the globe manifested New Jerusalem.

SAMUEL PUTNAM BANCROFT

199

CHAPTER XXIII

FIERY DARTS OF THE WICKED

*The mild forms of animal magnetism are disappearing, and
its aggressive features are coming to the front.*

Mary Baker Eddy

1879

MRS. Eddy's successor has clearly described evil as
that "imp of darkness" which trots right alongside the
unfolding truth of being as the negation of the true idea. Jesus
said that the son of man is come to destroy the works of darkness, and in the 1870's and 80's Mrs. Eddy was learning from
necessity *how* this is to be done.

In the 1970's a young man has given demonstrations in which
he bends metal, moves objects, causes objects to disappear,
and other such phenomena through mental power alone. He
has caused a stir among physical scientists, but Christian Scientists are able to understand his performances for the explanation is in their textbook. A century earlier Richard Kennedy was applying himself to such mental feats, and Mrs. Eddy
was, with God's guidance, solving the mystery and giving that
solution to her students and to posterity.

Unlike the twentieth century accounts of innocent, public
demonstrations, Kennedy's works were clandestine and all
maliciously directed against the Revelator to this age. Clara
Choate, who was very close to Mrs. Eddy at that time, has
written about these experiences of our leader:

> ...myriads of unlooked for events occurred to perplex her.
> One very annoying thing constantly beset her, viz., her
> books, valued trinkets, and belongings constantly disap-

peared. She could scarcely lay down her purse, or money, or jewelry, over which she executed great protection, before they would disappear.

More than physical, human care and protection is requisite to protect our belongings. *That* Mrs. Eddy exercised to the utmost, and it was not sufficient. The strange disappearances had first to be understood scientifically, and this, added to the attacks on her health, her money (their bank had failed), her income, her home, her students,—did not make her task an easy one. Little wonder she wrote that Kennedy was constantly surprising her. But step by step she was learning to solve the problem of iniquity, and her footsteps and solutions are recorded in the progressive revisions of Science and Health. Her evaluation of this record is evident in her statement that he who had all the editions of the textbook would have a "treasure-trove."

Mrs. Eddy was finding the Way and showing it to her followers, but the students of that day did not seem able to follow the mental footsteps of the Wayshower nor to comprehend what she discovered and uncovered. She shared all she learned, and many witnessed her experiences resulting from malicious malpractice. They knew of Kennedy's denial of his teacher and reversal of her teachings, yet relative to the disappearance of her belongings Mrs. Choate wrote in later years, "I do not think the thief was ever detected."

In the fall of 1879 her two newest pupils had learned more than had others about malicious mental malpractice, for the teacher had experienced and learned more. They were apprised of the work of the mesmerists, but did not fear it as so many students did; so the teacher had great hope for these two missionaries. It was arranged that James Ackland would go to Philadelphia, Pennsylvania and Arthur Buswell to Cincinnati, Ohio.

Among the older students there was very little appreciation of the unceasing efforts of Mr. and Mrs. Eddy. They would take all Mrs. Eddy gave and constantly ask for Cincinnati more with no thought of remuneration. This lack plan of appreciation, added to the attacks from the 1879 mesmerists, caused the Eddys to plan to leave the battlefield in Massachusetts after settlement of the lawsuits, which were still dragging on. Their intent was to join Arthur Buswell in Cincinnati, and to that end their household goods were crated and made ready for shipment. Buswell wrote that it was a relief to be in this fresher atmosphere away from the "mental furnace" of Lynn and Boston. About this time Mrs. Eddy heard again from her son George Glover who wanted to see the mother he had known only from a picture and letters since childhood. She wrote him to meet them in Cincinnati where they would soon be moving.

Early in October George Barry was awarded $350 instead of the $2700 he sought, which was a great relief to the Eddys. To the Kennedy jury-verdict of the previous November Mrs. Eddy's attorney had filed exceptions which were allowed. But now that case was dropped, for, lo, Kennedy's note for $1000 which was still largely unpaid and was the subject of the litigation had mysteriously disappeared from the attorney's office.

The Cincinnati plan was all arranged, but Mrs. Eddy was God's weathervane, and the winds of God began to blow in another direction. Critics say that she was changeable, but her true followers know that it was always God's leading that caused her to change direction, and they share their Leader's appreciation of the poem:

CONSECRATION

Laid on Thy altar, my Lord divine,
    Accept my gift this day for Jesus' sake;
I have no jewels to adorn Thy shrine,
    Nor any world-famed sacrifice to make.

But here I bring within my trembling hand
    This will of mine—a thing that seemeth small,
And only Thou, dear Lord, canst understand
    How, when I yield Thee this, I yield mine all.

Hidden therein Thy searching eyes can see
    Struggles of passions, visions of delight,
All that I love or am, or fain would be—
    Deep loves, fond hopes, and longing infinite.

It hath been wet with tears and dimmed with sighs,
   Clinched in my grasp 'til beauty it hath none.
Now, from Thy footstool, where it vanquished lies,
   The prayer ascendeth, O may Thy will be done.

Take it, Oh Father, ere my courage fail;
   And merge it so in Thine own will that e'en
If in some desperate hour my cries prevail
   And Thou give back my gift, it may have been

So changed, so purified, so fair have grown,
   So one with Thee, so filled with peace divine,
I may not know, or feel it as my own,
   But gaining back my will, may find it Thine.

*   *   *

Mary sought always to do God's will, and there was no criticism from James Ackland or Arthur Buswell when she wrote them toward the end of October that things had changed and she felt she should stay in Boston. Buswell wrote in reply from Cincinnati that he was not surprised and that he had felt from the first that she should remain. He had an inkling of the difficulties in her path, for he wrote, "You seem to be aware of 'some trials' awaiting your labors there. I hope our little band—the apostles—will rally around and sustain you."

About the first of November the Eddys rented their house in Lynn for the winter and moved to two furnished rooms on Newton Street in Boston. The previous winter Preaching at Mrs. Eddy had spoken to her congregation every Hawthorne Hall Sunday without a cent of remuneration. For all November, 1879 they had received the students had not even arranged to pay her fare from Lynn to Boston each week. She had built up the church and helped them to organize, but she had also declined to accept the pastorate. Perhaps her decision to move away had aroused a sense of appreciation, for they were most grateful when she began preaching in Hawthorne Hall on the thirtieth of November. The church arranged to pay her five dollars per week, and on December 1 she accepted the second call to become its pastor.

Before the first meeting at the Hawthorne rooms George Glover arrived in Cincinnati. Not finding his mother there, he proceeded to Boston. She had written him about some of her trials because of the mesmerists, and the story as he told it in 1907 was as follows:

Within a week of my arrival in Boston I learned strange things. The strangest of these was that rebellious students were employing black arts to harass and destroy my mother.

The longer I remained with mother the clearer this became. Pursued by evil influences of the students, we moved from house to house, never at rest and always apprehensive. It was a maddening puzzle to me. We would move to a new house and fellow lodgers would be all smiles and friendliness. Then, in an hour an inevitable change would come; the friendliness would vanish under the spell of black magic, and we would be ordered to go. But mother made it all very clear to me.

It was Kennedy that mother talked of most. He was a master hand at the black arts, as mother pictured him to me, until at last I made up my mind to cut him short in his evil work. But I kept my plan to myself. One morning I slipped my revolver into my overcoat pocket and left our boarding house.

I had never seen this man, but I knew where he had offices, and I walked straight there. He was doing business as a healer, and his name lettered on a brass plate, was on the door of his office. Every detail of that visit is as clear in my mind today as if it took place only a week ago.

The girl who admitted me asked me if I was a patient, and I answered, "Yes." She then led me straight to Kennedy's office, on the second floor of the house, opened the door, bowed me into the room, and hurried away. Kennedy was before me seated at his desk.

He looked up smilingly and asked, "Are you in need of treatment?"

Pulling out my revolver I walked up to him, pressed the cold muzzle against his head, and said, "I have made up my mind that you are in need of treatment."

There, while he looked like a jelly-fish in terror, I gave him his one chance to live. I told him that my mother knew of his

black art tricks to ruin her, and that I had made up my mind
to stop him or kill him.

"You needn't tell me that you *aren't* working your games of
hypnotism to rob her friends and drive mother into mad-
ness," said I. "My word to you is this: if we have to move to
another boarding house I will search you out and shoot you
like a dog."

I shall never forget how that man pleaded for his life at
the end of my weapon, and swore that the black art accusa-
tion was false, and my mother had deceived me.

But it did the business all right. We were not ordered out
of another boarding house that winter.

Kennedy was not the only malpractitioner aiming his fiery
darts at the Discoverer and her discovery during the winter of
1879-80. Edward Arens had left the Eddys, had not partici-
pated in beginning the church, and had drifted away from his
best friends, teachers, and mentors. He had moved to Boston
and begun teaching and practising confused metaphysics. Mrs.
Eddy recorded:

> On Christmas Morning of 1879 Mr. Arens called on us.
> After a mutual exchange of kind congratulations tears filled
> his eyes, and he said: "I have been hating you dreadfully,
> Mrs. Eddy, and am here to confess it, for I now know the
> cause. When I was feeling so hard towards you it occurred
> to me it was the aforesaid mesmerist [Kennedy] producing
> this effect, and when I met it as that metaphysically, it des-
> troyed it, my feelings changed at once, and I feel the same
> friendship for you as before." We assured him that we should
> have the same interest in his welfare as ever, so long as he
> did right, and hoped he would always escape the snare of the
> spoiler.

But Arens did not make any effort to do right. Shortly after
this visit he began enacting the visions Mrs. Eddy had had of
him several years earlier. He began tearing away from her babe
the *lower* part of the beautiful garment of spotless white.

Every metaphysician learns that "the healer in Christian
Science carries two lines of thought, first, the approximation
to the truth, and second, the final truth." The final Truth, of

course, is absolute Christian Science which is the present perfection of being. The approximation is the argument applied to the human circumstance that needs healing, and is definitely the *lower* part. If one practises only the mental argument to obtain results, without basing those arguments upon the unchanging Principle of divine Science, that practice will devolve into mesmerism. It may be benevolent mesmerism, but in Arens' case it was not.

He was using Mrs. Eddy's teaching "manual of the practice of Christian Science Mind-healing" which he had insisted she not include in Science and Health, in a way of his own. A student named Joseph Morton was rooming in Boston with Arens. The latter would read aloud a statement from Mrs. Eddy's class-book, *The Science of Man,* and ask Morton to restate it without changing the meaning. Sentence by sentence Arens was pirating Mrs. Eddy's writings for publication as his own.

Mrs. Eddy could not help but think of Kennedy and Arens when she wrote in her sermon *Christian Healing:*

> The preparation for a metaphysical practitioner is the most arduous task I ever performed. You must first mentally educate and develop the spiritual sense or perceptive faculty by which one learns the metaphysical treatment of disease; you must teach them how to learn, together with what they learn.

However, it was the dullness of her loyal students as much as the wickedness of the disloyal which caused her to add, "I have never yet had a student who has reached this ability to teach; it includes more than they understand."

CHAPTER XXIV

TEACHING AND HEALING IN THE 1880'S

Since the author's discovery of the might of Truth in the treatment of disease as well as of sin, her system has been fully tested and has not been found wanting.

Mary Baker Eddy

When the people heard the good news, they came unto her; and she received them, and spoke unto them, and healed them that had need of healing.

1880

WHILE Arens was busy plagiarizing Mrs. Eddy's class-book, she was at the same time incorporating it into the next edition of Science and Health as the chapter titled "Recapitulation." The new edition of the textbook which she was preparing for publication was by far the most important of her activities, but it was not easy to find the time, peace, and quiet necessary for this work.

George Glover was a disappointment to his mother. She had hoped that he would be a help to her in her great mission, but he was a rough, boisterous mining prospector with little interest in the mental realm or even in literacy. However, during his visit his mother made a deep and lasting impression upon her son. In talking about his family, George told about his mother's namesake, his three-year-old daughter, Mary Baker Glover. When he said that the child was cross-eyed, his mother exclaimed, "You must be mistaken, George; her eyes are all right." In February, after George had returned home to Deadwood, South Dakota,

Healing of Mary Baker Glover

207

he related this conversation to his wife while little Mary was asleep. They wakened the child and found that her eyes were straightened. In later years Mary B. Glover Billings wrote:

> Mother has a picture of me taken before this incident, showing my eyes crossed. This healing was often told me by my father and mother, and is at this time verified by my mother, who is with me.

After George returned to the mid-west, the Eddys moved to a house on Shawmut Avenue in Boston together with Mr. and Mrs. Choate. The Choates, their son, and Mrs. Choate's sister occupied the first and third floors, and Mr. and Mrs. Eddy had the second floor. George Choate was away much of the time endeavoring to practise Christian Science healing in Portland, Maine. On one of his visits home he asked Mrs. Eddy's advice on a case he was treating but not curing, even as the disciples had sought Jesus' aid in their failures.

Mrs. Eddy examined the case mentally (miles are no deterrent to Mind), and told him the belief latent,—that the difficulties were produced by a fall several years earlier. The effects of her mental examination and spiritual potency were immediate as described in this letter George wrote on his return to Portland:

> April 2, 1880
>
> Last Saturday, when I was at home, and you examined my patient, she had the most wonderful chemical, or something of the kind, that I ever heard of. She was sitting talking with some ladies, and felt a little faint, her head ached, and she said she would go to bed, when she felt a crash, just as when she was thrown from a carriage, and knew nothing for four hours. Great black and blue spots, just where she was bruised years ago when she fell, appeared, and she acted and talked like a person under the influence of morphine. After the discoloration was gone, the cuticle came off in scales, and she is better than ever now, and walks without a cane. Has been out to ride to-day. What can it be? What does it mean?
>
> G. D. Choate

Though George and Clara Choate were both endeavoring to practise Christian Science, the world held many attractions for them. Their depth of interest in Science and sincerity in spiritual endeavor were somewhat less than that for which the Teacher yearned, so her hopes turned once again to a new student who offered greater promise.

James Howard had entered into the study of Science with the earnestness that Daniel Spofford had shown. He was one of the class of two that Mrs. Eddy had taught in February and was the outstanding member of the new Church of Christ, Scientist, which met every Sunday afternoon at Hawthorne Hall. With the rest of the congregation, he witnessed many healings as a result of Mrs. Eddy's sermons.

Healings that had resounded through the streets of Lynn at the beginning of her ministry to suffering humanity were now pealing through the streets of Boston, giving   Healing of Henry
hope to the weary and attracting many hopeless   A. Littlefield
sufferers to Hawthorne Hall. Some that came in   c. 1880
on crutches, left carrying them over their shoulder. A young man named Henry Littlefield who had been a printer in Boston before his severe illness was carried in on a stretcher. He was one who was carried in and walked out; after which he was able to resume his trade. And he was also the one out of ten who came back to acknowledge his healing and testify to the Truth. In his words:

> I was born in 1846. I was attacked by inflammatory rheumatism in my early thirties in such form that even the bed clothing was burdensome and painful. I had heard about Mrs. Eddy's meetings in Hawthorne Hall, and at the very worst stage of the belief I was taken there on a stretcher. After the service, Mrs. Eddy came down from the platform and greeted personally the small group of about a dozen people who were there. When she came to me and shook my hand and spoke to me, I felt the healing and responded by telling her that I was healed. I walked out of the hall rejoicing, and that belief never made itself real to me again.

In the spring of 1880 a woman came to Mrs. Eddy with a

problem very different from that of Mr. Littlefield. She had
Healing of   been seeking help of physicians for nineteen
Hanover P.   years for her son who had been born deaf and
Smith   dumb. The boy, Hanover P. Smith, had been in
an institution for deaf mutes when his mother took him to Mrs.
Eddy who healed him quickly. Perhaps nineteen-year-old Hanover was the youngest member of Mrs. Eddy's class of five students that May; and he was also the most eager to enter into
the public practice of Christian Science.

Despite the demonology Mrs. Eddy was constantly encountering and which she was exposing fully in her revision of Science and Health, the good word, the gospel of Christian Science, was finding its way to receptive individuals. The church
was growing and had put out a circular which read in part:

> This church is designed to perpetuate the teachings of
> Jesus, to reinstate primitive Christianity, and to restore its
> lost element of healing.

These words fell like manna upon the ears of one young
woman who had longed for healing and understanding. Julia
Bartlett was the first of Mrs. Eddy's students to remain loyal
to our Leader and an active practitioner of Christian Science
all the years of Mrs. Eddy's sojourn with us. Her introduction
to Christian Science is worth the telling.

JULIA BARTLETT'S STORY
(in her own words)

> There are pleasant memories of my childhood days, of the
> dear parents' wise and loving care, and the joy and happiness
> they brought into my life. . . .
> Suddenly the change came. After one week's illness my
> dear father passed on. . . My mother survived him but three
> years. . . .
> We were left six fatherless and motherless children. I, the
> eldest, was sixteen years of age, while the youngest was but a
> babe of three years, a delicate little girl who needed much a
> mother's care and love, as did all. . . . We were able to make
> remuneration for all that was done for us, but that seemingly
> made no difference. The sad, little faces told the story of the

hardships that were endured, and while my heart ached for the little ones more than for myself I was powerless to save them from it.

As time went on and I was beyond the schooldays, my thought continued to open to the Truth sufficiently, to drop some of my old theological views, . . . I felt there was a truth beyond what I knew or had been able to find, and more and more there was a longing and reaching out for it, trying to find it. . . .

At this stage of experience I was taken very ill and at different times my life was despaired of by physicians. . . . Completely shut out from the world for five years, helpless on my bed, weakened by suffering, I could still be patient and cheerful and not a complaining invalid. . . . Twice I was removed on my bed to different cities to be treated by other physicians. All were most interested and kind, and I appreciated their efforts, but material remedies could not heal me.

After seven years there was improvement, but no hopes were given of a final recovery. . . one day a letter came from a friend telling the first I had ever heard of Christian Science. This was in April, 1880, when the Science was little known. She also sent a little circular giving account of the first Christian Science Church. . . which said "This church is designed to perpetuate the teachings of Jesus, to reinstate primitive Christianity, and to restore its lost element of healing."

I asked my friend to recommend a practitioner to take my case, and at the same time I sent for the book Science and Health. She went to Mrs. Eddy for advice, and she put me under the care of her husband, Dr. Asa G. Eddy. I began to improve immediately and was getting my freedom. I felt like one let out of prison. The fetters of material beliefs and laws were giving way to the higher law of Spirit and the sufferings were correspondingly disappearing. I never could describe the sense of freedom that came with a glimpse of this glorious Truth. The world was another world to me. All things were seen from a different viewpoint and there was a halo of beauty over all.

In the eyes of the students the little church was progressing and all was well. From Mrs. Eddy's standpoint the progress was far from satisfactory. Physical healing is but the first step: purification of thought, motive, and character must follow. But most of the students were completely satisfied with only the physical healing, and more often than not called upon their teacher for help with that. Bickering and jealousies from within and malice from without were driving Mrs. Eddy once again into the wilderness, so on the twenty-third of May she preached a farewell sermon. The students were stunned and temporarily united in requesting her to remain with them. To their resolution she responded by agreeing to stay and preach through the month of June. But her work on the revision of Science and Health demanded her undivided attention. It was imperative that she leave the students to their own devices and give her time unreservedly to God's work.

SARAH BAGLEY   DORCAS RAWSON

Two of the students Mrs. Eddy taught in 1870. She lived in each of their homes for short periods.

CHAPTER XXV

MALPRACTICE FULLY FATHOMED

The author's own observations of the workings of animal magnetism convince her that it is not a remedial agent, and that its effects upon those who practise it, and upon their subjects who do not resist it, lead to moral and to physical death.

Mary Baker Eddy

1880

JOSEPH Morton left Arens to study with Mrs. Eddy. He told of Arens' antagonism to Christian Science, his discrediting of Mrs. Eddy, and his plans for Expulsion plagiarizing her writings. At a meeting of the of Arens Christian Scientist Association on the second June, 1880 of June he convinced the membership that Arens should be expelled, although Mrs. Eddy took no part in the expulsion.

Before her departure from Boston at the end of June she had taken a new step. On the twenty-sixth of June she had given official notice through her student James Beginning Howard of a meeting to form a corporation to be of College called the Massachusetts Metaphysical College. June, 1880

The Eddys spent the months of July and August in Concord, New Hampshire, near the scenes of Mary's childhood. She could not totally abandon her flock and kept in touch through her one trusted student James Howard. He was the only one who knew their whereabouts.

The summer of 1880 was truly another wilderness experience for the Woman of the Apocalypse. Of the demonology she was encountering she wrote:

Because this error was so remote from the border lands of

213

metaphysical science we never fully fathomed its working until the summer of 1880, and to our Father we owe it that we
have found the facts of immortal Mind more than equal to
meet the fables of mortal mind...

Finding the way to meet these fables was no easy task. On
the twenty-third of July she wrote to James Howard, "I have
passed into and out of HELL since I saw you last."

For the first time Mrs. Eddy saw clearly that Richard Kennedy was the one perpetrator back of all the wickedness that
had been heaped upon her and her students. She almost lost
hope for his reform, but she did not stop working to that end.
She did gain hope for the reform of those who she now understood had been perverted by Richard's malicious mental
manipulation. In her "Demonology" chapter she wrote:

> We have not exposed one half the wickedness that has been
> committed unseen, and the purposes achieved by it and the
> falsehood uttered of us in order to accomplish those purposes.
> We wait, before doing this, with the hope that the perpetra-
> tors thereof will repent and forsake their sins forever. Some of
> the individuals before referred to offer indications of this re-
> form, and favor the hope that God is wresting them from the
> iron control of the hopeless sinner who has instigated and car-
> ried out this programme of crimes so far as it has succeeded.
> May Heaven aid those whom he has lured from positions of
> usefulness and rectitude of conduct into the gloom of his own
> night of sin...

As the Discoverer uncovered the hidden way of malice she
recorded this knowledge that others might benefit from her experience. This of course was further exposure of Kennedy's
means and methods:

> ...by reversing the arguments of Truth, he attempts to
> make sickness through a silent mental process, even as the
> metaphysician restores health by the opposite mental
> process. In his mental argument to frighten an individual and
> build up a belief of disease, he includes another one, namely
> to make that individual believe that someone else is doing
> this, and he cannot be healed unless he is treated for the

effects that individual is supposed to be producing on him. This last infirmity of sin is possible only to mesmerism... Mesmerism can make mortals believe a lie, but metaphysics cannot; it can only make them unbelieve it....Sensuality, envy, malice, hatred, and revenge must cooperate in the individual mind that can carry out demonology as aforesaid.

By August Mrs. Eddy was gaining the mastery over the evil she had uncovered. She wrote to Clara Choate on the fifth of the month:

I...now have mastered one part of this earth-problem. In *all* the different malpractices I *now* see first the individual that comes to me or my husband before they go further. So one step follows another of light in this glorious path if we walk in the light.

She wrote again to James Howard. That young man had a wife and family to support and had not yet entered upon the full-time practice of Christian Science. In an effort to help him to cast his net on the right side the Teacher wrote offering five of the rooms in their house in Lynn rent free when their summer tenants vacated. She was looking forward to the fall even though her work made every day a busy one.

Anyone who has had a vision knows that he can not be mistaken as to the meaning. The import of the message is vividly clear at the moment. Mrs. Eddy's vision early in August doubtless meant far more to her than we will ever know. Gilbert Eddy recorded simply: "A vision of passing over the wave without sinking into a particle."

Vision of
August 7
1880

Most probably she was meeting or had met the attacks of the enemy, understood his wickedness, and was overcoming it. In the forthcoming revision of Science and Health she stated:

...a silent mental process of impregnating into the mind, and thence into the body, suffering, disease, fear, hatred, sensuality, etc., is "Satan let loose," the sin that "standeth in holy places," more subtle than all other beasts of the field, a crime at which every one should shudder either to become the victim or the perpetrator. We hope the years that we have labored to help the human race through the curative agent of mind have also furnished the means to stop this trespass on mental healing.

Having traversed faithfully the realm of metaphysics, and found in this field of inquiry the mental cause and its physical effect, we ought to understand, and do, what we are saying. You would not deny the mathematician the right to say what has wrought an example incorrectly, or deny the musician who gives the true tone the ability to detect the discord.

Even as Judas Iscariot was the one disciple who betrayed the Master, Richard Kennedy was the one individual who reversed the teachings of the Revelator to this age. But he was the tool of sin and not the sin itself. He fulfilled the position Jesus described when he said:

> ...whoso shall offend one of these little ones which believe in me, it were better for him that a millstone was hanged about his neck, and that he were drowned in the depth of the sea. Woe unto the world because of offences! for it must needs be that offences come; but woe to that man by whom the offence cometh!

A decade or more later Mrs. Eddy wrote that "sin created the sinner." The impersonalization that was to come in her work and her writings was suggested in this passage on the penultimate page of "Demonology":

> The re-establishment of the Christian era, or the medieval period of metaphysics, will be one of moderation and peace; but the reinauguration of this period will be met with demonology, or the unlicensed cruelty of mortal mind, that will compel mankind to learn metaphysics for a refuge and defence.

CHAPTER XXVI

BACK IN LYNN

In the first century of the Christian era Jesus went about doing good. The evangelists of those days wandered about....

The ideal of God is no longer impersonated as a waif or wanderer; and Truth is not fragmentary, disconnected, unsystematic, but concentrated and immovably fixed in Principle.

Mary Baker Eddy

1880

SEPTEMBER found the Eddys back in Lynn, but the Howards had not yet elected to move there. They were still undecided about leaving Boston, however Howard was unanimously elected president of the Christian Scientist Association at its first fall meeting.

Julia Bartlett was often in Lynn during the fall of 1880 and has painted a word picture of this time:

> I never had seen a Christian Scientist, but my one desire above all others was to see and know the one through whom all this great good had come to the world and to be taught the truth by her...In about four months from the time I first heard of Christian Science I applied to Mrs. Eddy for class instruction...She made an appointment with me at her home in Lynn, and when I went there...Dr. Eddy waited on me...She came in almost immediately...and said she would not keep me waiting. I felt her love which always made her thoughtful for others, and was perfectly at ease in her presence. She was beautiful, but rather more slender...than at a later period. I think what most impressed me at this first meeting was her spirituality and the place she occupied in the

world, and yet she met me just where I was, so simply and sweetly, mindful even of the little things for my comfort. . . .

My first instructions from Mrs. Eddy began September 30, 1880. This class consisted of only three members. . . but she spoke of how much she enjoyed teaching this little class. Her teachings were a wonderful unfolding of Truth to her students. I can seem to see her now as she sat before us with that heavenly spiritual expression which lighted her whole countenance as she expounded the truth. . . In teaching one member of the class she told me she always saw a halo over his head, then she said, "Dear, I see white roses in your thought." When the class was through, my friend [Mrs. Ellen Clark] who first told me of Christian Science and who was also in the class, and I lingered a little and were sitting beside our dear teacher while she was talking to us of mortal mind's hatred of Truth and the evil to be overcome. She mentioned an incident of a person coming to her door armed against her, but he was not able to perform his evil work. [Could this have been Edward Arens the previous Christmas?] We were seeing a little what it meant for her to stand where she did—a representative of Truth before a world of error—the cost of it and the glory of it, but we said in a playful, childlike way that amused and comforted her, "They shall not touch you; *we* will help you." My greatest joy today is that I may have been the means of lightening her burdens somewhat in the years that followed. . . .

The first Christian Science Sunday service I ever attended was at this time and was held in the little parlor at 8 Broad Street, Lynn. There were about twenty people present. Mrs. Eddy preached the sermon which healed a young woman sitting near me of an old chronic trouble which physicians were unable to heal. Her husband, who was present with her, went to Mrs. Eddy the next day to thank her for what had been done for his wife. . . .

I was much interested in conversation with other students to learn somewhat of their experience before Science and Health was published or there was anything in print on this Science. They said that whenever they were to see Mrs. Eddy they would take pencil and paper with them and at the first opportunity would write down what she said to them, and they pondered over those words and treasured them. They had wonderful cases of healing and their work was easily done until all at once they were not successful...Then our great Leader discovered that evil minds were at work to hinder the progress of Truth in its healing power and that the students must be taught how to meet and overcome this evil. As this was done, their patients began to improve and their work went on as before.

After class Mrs. Eddy advised me to go to my home in Connecticut and have a little experience in healing, which I did. During this time I often went to Lynn to attend the meetings of the Association and to aid our dear teacher as I could in the work of the Cause.

Probably some of the early students Miss Bartlett talked with after that first service were Dorcas Rawson and Miranda Rice. They had been in Mrs. Eddy's second class in the fall of 1870 and had been practising now for ten years. They had experienced the prophecy in Revelation wherein Satan was bound for a season and then loosed again. Mrs. Eddy's discovery of the scientific statement of being had bound the dragon and nothing was impossible. No case was too difficult to cure. The healings of that day were miraculous and immediate, and that day was as a thousand years. "But when the thousand years are expired, Satan shall be loosed out of his prison."

Richard Kennedy's reversal of all that his teacher had taught him, his misuse of mind power, had loosed Satan from his prison. For nine years Mrs. Eddy had been struggling with the effects of his malicious malpractice, and now she saw clearly what it was and how it operated. She also saw that every student must meet and solve this problem. Those who close their eyes to it become tools of the enemy, and they invariably stop following their Leader.

Mrs. Eddy taught another small class in November. Of the new students Julia Bartlett was the most dedicated as this letter from her teacher indicates:

8 Broad Street, Lynn
December 17th, 1880

My own dear Child:
You will pardon me I know for not writing sooner. I have

Sunday services, two meetings sometimes in the week, and writing, have calls all the time and so do neglect what I love to do—answer you at once. I am more than glad when I hear anything favorable from a student these times "that try men's souls." I have not seen Mrs. C. yet nor heard from Mr. S. You dear can do much in every direction and when you are getting a bit disheartened come to Mother. I will try to help you. Please remember in a *scientific way* the members of your class. If you love me, feed my sheep, our dear Master said. Write often and unless your letter needs an immediate answer you need not be surprised if it does not get it. I am so busy now until after my book is published.

Love from my husband
Ever your affectionate Mother,
M. B. G. E.

The publication of her book was far from the only thing that kept Mrs. Eddy so very busy. Two days after this letter was written she wrote in her notebook:

December 18, 1880. Commenced services at the Hawthorne rooms. The salary proposed was ten dollars by Mrs. Choate, but they said they would wait to see how much was collected of arrears before settling on the amount. I said I should not state my salary but leave it to them to say how much it should be, but that I should not take more than five dollars per week, and could not agree for one year as duty might call me away.

While Mrs. Eddy was working on all fronts, the evil that Kennedy had loosed was spreading. Before the end of the year Arens caused a pamphlet to be published which was largely verbatim extracts from *The Science of Man* and Science and Health interspersed with his confused metaphysics. The *lower* part of the garment that he had torn from its proper setting was taking him deeper and deeper into mesmerism. The attempts to destroy Mrs. Eddy's babe, Science and Health, were soon to grow very wicked in the endeavor to prevent the woman's child from being caught up unto God and to his throne.

CHAPTER XXVII

ASA GILBERT AROUSED

You are not aroused to this action by the allurements of wealth, pride, or power; the impetus comes from above—it is moral, spiritual, divine.

Mary Baker Eddy

1881

ON the thirty-first day of the first month of 1881 the Massachusetts Metaphysical College received its charter from the state of Massachusetts "to teach Pathology, Ontology, Therapeutics, Moral Science, Metaphysics and their adaptation to the treatment of disease." The seven charter members were Mrs. Eddy, James Howard, Samuel P. Bancroft, William F. Walker, James Wiley, Edgar F. Woodbury, and Charles J. Eastman, M.D.

College chartered January, 1881

On the same day the charter was issued business of greater importance was being transacted in Cambridge. Mrs. Eddy had called upon Mr. John Wilson at the University Press and told him the story of the publication of Science and Health, displaying copies of the first and second editions. Dr. Eddy had contacted Mr. Wilson the previous April, but the bid he had received at that time was now obsolete, for their former printer had destroyed all the usable plates.

After covering everything else Mrs. Eddy explained their financial situation, said she could give him a few hundred dollars but not half the cost in advance; that she knew she could sell the book as he would produce it, to meet the cost, but could not pay in full on delivery. To his own utter astonishment from that day forward, Mr. Wilson accepted the order without a moment's hesitation. Thus began a long and fruitful relationship between these two upstanding New Englanders, both of Scottish ancestry.

Though busy with her book, college, teaching, and students, Mrs. Eddy did find a few moments for a young friend, Miss

Letter to
Alice Sibley
1881 Alice Sibley, whom she had met two years earlier. This letter written to the sixteen-year-old Miss Sibley sometime in February of 1881 shows her continuing interest in young people and also her devotion to duty as Mother to the whole human family:

> That word embraces to my mind all the graces. I wish O! I wish, but vainly, I had my fancy free to write you a little offering, but will some time. I have no broken wing only a folded one. Now dear Go forth into the fields, drink in the breeze, be happy and free. O the bliss of freedom! I would I were a child again, but you, dear one, are now both child and woman; you are, in other words when I descend to pet names, my naughty wild girl, wayward in goodness, impulsive as the March wind and sunny as the flowers. . . . I hope you will remain at your best all the time next Sabbath and not get impatient with me because I have passed the hay day of Life and have now no time for the sweet joys of friendship but must show my love for you all working at the treadmill of metaphysics.

By spring the Howard family had moved to Lynn and were residing with the Eddys at 8 Broad Street. And in the spring Mrs. Eddy was teaching a class which included several students who had left Arens in search of true metaphysics. One of these, Mrs. Elizabeth Stuart, told of Arens' bitter attacks against Mrs. Eddy and of how he ordered his students to work against her mentally.

Gilbert Eddy was incensed. That anyone could do such a thing was almost inconceivable; but that this man whom he had taught, befriended, and defended would maliciously attack his spiritual benefactor was an outrage.

When Arens published a second pamphlet a short time later claiming authorship under the title *The Understanding of Christianity, or God* to material almost completely lifted from Mrs. Eddy's writings, Dr. Eddy rose in righteous indignation.

He wrote a foreword to the Science and Health now in press, which began:

TO THE PUBLIC

While this third edition of "Science and Health" was in press a certain man set afloat a pamphlet, the contents of which he took from Mrs. Eddy's works published in 1870 and 1878, all of which can be found in this edition, in chapters "Recapitulation" and "Platform of Christian Scientists." This pamphlet is prefaced with the following pretext: "In preparing this work we have made use of some thoughts contained in a work by Eddy," and then went on to repeat her words *verbatim,* in over thirty pages, as the following extracts will show.

After several pages of examples including some unhealthy original statements by Arens, he continues:

Mrs. Eddy's works are the outgrowths of her life. I never knew so unselfish an individual, or one so tireless in what she considers her duty. It would require ages and God's mercy to make the ignorant hypocrite who published that pamphlet originate its contents. His pratings are colored by his character, they cannot impart the hue of ethics, but leave his own impress on what he takes. He knows less of metaphysics than any decently honest man.

The proof of these last statements was not merely by induction. Elizabeth Stuart and her friend Jane Straw had left Arens to study with Mrs. Eddy. After completing Mrs. Eddy's class they had written and signed the following statement on the fifteenth of April:

We studied Mrs. Eddy's system of metaphysical healing of Edward J. Arens but he did not understand it as we have since learned. And we did not learn of him how to heal the sick according to metaphysics.

On the eighth of July Mrs. Stuart wrote Mrs. Eddy advising her not to take the legal action against Arens that she was contemplating. Her letter also said:

Keep quiet, don't give things to the *Public*, work *silently* and we will work with you; vanquish him that way, for he is daring, at the same time, with the smoothest face and most angelic expression, praising you when he knows it will tell in his favor. . . . I would not even append to my Book what your husband has written, true as it is, but reserve all that for some other time and place; don't place it within the same covers with that which is so sacred.

Mrs. Stuart was merely repeating the same human opinion that had caused Mrs. Eddy to resist the exposure of evil in the first edition of Science and Health,—the same evil that said to Jesus, "Let us alone. What have we to do with thee?" But Mrs. Eddy had followed a diviner leading in 1875, and she did so now. Her mission was not to keep quiet, but to give to the public. Until now her voice had been the only one raised against evil. Now her husband joined her in the exposure and denunciation of malpractice.

JAMES ACKLAND

CHAPTER XXVIII

THE THIRD EDITION

God has bidden me to uncover this wickedness, and I follow His voice.

Mary Baker Eddy

1881

EARLY in the year James Ackland in Philadelphia had printed and Mrs. Eddy had copyrighted her manuscript for "Private Direction for Treating Disease Met- Private aphysically." This, however, was as a defence Direction against the plagiarism of Arens. The real help printed 1881 to the student was the new edition of the textbook which would soon be forthcoming.

While it was still in press she received a most welcome letter from Arthur Buswell in Cincinnati. Miranda Rice had paid him a visit, and he was inspired by her account of the progress of the Scientists in Boston. In this letter of July 14 he went on to say that Mrs. Rice had shown him how much they needed the leader there and what a mistake it would have been had she moved to Cincinnati.

On August 17 the book was ready for delivery. Mrs. Eddy presented the first copy to her tenant and student James Howard. He was also placed in charge of sales Third edition and promotion, although Gilbert Eddy was the published publisher. The second copy may have been pre- August, 1881 sented to the youthful Hanover Smith, for he spent much of the summer in the Eddy's home in Lynn.

The first and second editions were not unattractive as far as the binding and outward appearance were concerned, but now for the first time Science and Health was every whit whole. The typography and printing were equal to the binding.

225

The new edition was in two volumes. The frontispiece in
Volume I was a picture of Jesus raising Jairus' daughter. This
had first appeared in the second edition in 1878 and continued
to appear in many subsequent issues including the revised
sixth and sixteenth editions.

The page following the title page has three quotations as
follows:

"God is Love."

I John iv:8

"There is nothing either good or bad but thinking makes
it so."

SHAKESPEARE

I, I, I, I itself, I,
The inside and outside, the what and the why,
The when and the where, the low and the high,
All I, I, I, I itself, I."

The poem, too, had appeared in the second edition, and with
the addition of the word "Anonymous" in the sixteenth printing, continued to appear through hundreds of editions until
it was replaced in 1908.

Following Gilbert Eddy's foreword was a statement repudi-
ating the mental malpractitioners and their work which was
signed by thirty students in addition to Asa Gilbert Eddy.
Among these was Mrs. Margaret Dunshee whose home in
Charleston had been the scene for the organization of the
church in 1879 when she was made treasurer. Some names such
as Dorcas Rawson and Miranda Rice went back to 1870, and
many were new students in the past year or two including
James Howard and Julia Bartlett.

For the first time Mrs. Eddy's teaching manual, *The Science
of Man*, was included within the pages of the textbook under
the title "Recapitulation." The first sentence reads: "This
chapter is from our class-book, first edition, 1870." The twen-
ty-two questions are similar, many identical, to the twenty-
four in the last edition of the textbook. The two that have

been added are the tenets of Christian Science and question number ten, "What is Mind?" Expanded answers have enlarged the chapter to thirty-three pages from the original nineteen in this edition, but one answer has been shortened.

The answer to: "Does metaphysical science include medication, hygiene, mesmerism, or mediumship?" covered two pages and read in part:

> We regret to say it was the malpractice and terrible crimes of a young student that called our attention to this question [manipulation] for the first time and placed it in a new moral and physical aspect. By thorough examination, we learned that manipulation hinders instead of helps mental healing; it also establishes a mesmeric connection between patient and practitioner, that gives the latter opportunity and power to govern the thought and actions of his patients in any direction he chooses, ...The crimes of that student have since reached beyond his patients and, without manipulating, gone forth on their errands of envy and revenge, to draw others into the vortex of ruin...Before we discovered, in 1872, the malpractice aforesaid...we had given no thought to the subject of a counteracting mental malpractice, and had it to meet unprepared. ...We now understand that never another of our students would have gone astray from the strait and narrow path but for the continued mesmeric influences of that one, employed months, and even years, upon certain individuals whom he wished to turn away from Christian science, until at last they yielded to the hidden agent, and thought and did as he directed, and he boasted of his power over them. Future history will reveal him, and his inauguration of a power which, if it be not discovered, is fatal to the health, life, or prosperity of the individual. The solution of Salem witchcraft has come, and its remedy is metaphysics instead of a gibbet.

This is future history, and the story must be told and understood.

CHAPTER XXIX

ENTER CALVIN FRYE

Hast thou been driven by suffering to the foot of the mount?

Mary Baker Eddy

1881

FROM outward appearances no one would have selected Calvin A. Frye as an outstanding prospective student for Christian Science, but there had been an inner preparation of the heart which the world cannot see. It was, in his experience, as Mrs. Eddy had written in the new edition of Science and Health: "the ripening of mortal man through suffering will drop his false sense of life and intelligence."

Calvin Frye was a year younger than Mrs. Eddy's son, George Glover, and he had been ripened through suffering. When he was still a child his mother had been afflicted with insanity and was at times institutionalized. His father was lame and partially incapacitated from a severe illness early in manhood. Calvin had married at the age of twenty-six, but had returned to the family home one short year later after the premature death of his wife. He had the companionship of a widowed sister, Lydia Roaf, but the picture of life in this sad household was drab indeed,—an unending round of toil and care with little to lighten the load or dispel the gloom.

A brother, Oscar Frye of Boston, attended some of the meetings at Hawthorne Hall with his wife. They contacted Clara Choate on behalf of the senior Mrs. Frye. Very shortly after Mrs. Choate agreed to take the case the mother was completely restored to health and sanity.

There was great rejoicing in that home in Lawrence, Massachusetts. The sunlight of Christian Science healing had gladdened the hearts of all, but it penetrated deepest into the receptive thought of Calvin. As soon as he could arrange it he went to Lynn to study with Mrs. Eddy.

Both Mr. and Mrs. Eddy were favorably impressed with Mr. Frye's sincerity and felt that he could be depended upon. A few months later Dr. Eddy made a trip to Lawrence, unbeknown to Calvin, for the express purpose of inquiring into his record. This quiet young man did measure up to and fulfill their expectations. In later years Mrs. Eddy told him that he had done more than any other, except herself, for the cause of Christian Science.

CALVIN A. FRYE
From a photograph taken about 1882.

CHAPTER XXX

ENVY AND REVENGE

And the dragon was wroth with the woman, and went to make war with the remnant of her seed.

Revelation of John

1881

WHEN a criminal is exposed or a vicious beast cornered, it will fight furiously. The third edition with its exposure of malicious animal magnetism and the one who inaugurated its supposed power, also said, "the wounded or cornered beast turns on its assailant." The fury of Richard Kennedy was loosed on his assailant. Behind his mask of innocence and amused indifference revenge burned hot, adding fury to the malice aimed as always at the Revelator. But now others felt his wrath for they had openly denounced him. The first paragraph of their statement of repudiation of his work read as follows:

> The undersigned, in justice to ourselves, hereby publicly state that we believe the abuses denominated mesmerism and malpractice are carried on by some claiming to be metaphysicians; but while our knowledge of metaphysics enables us to defend ourselves and others from their attacks, we are by no means committing their crimes, for our power lies not in mesmerism, but Truth; it is not animal magnetism, but moral and spiritual strength.

Thirty-one names were appended to this statement. Their knowledge of malpractice was extensive, because they had witnessed their dear teacher's trials and heard her explanations. But their understanding of animal magnetism was very small.

Few withstood the malicious attack loosed upon them, for they did not recognize the enemy's deadliest weapon, but accepted as their own, the unhealthy thoughts of his creating.

Nor did they understand another tool of the enemy—that of whispering behind a man's back. If they had, they would have comprehended Jesus' instruction, "if thy brother shall trespass against thee, go and *tell him* his fault." True Christian Scientists understand Mrs. Eddy's strict compliance with the Master's method and see her rebukes as nothing more than calling the individual's shortcomings to his attention and thus bringing them out into the open for destruction. Are we guilty of saying behind a man's back what we would not say to his face? Our Leader was not.

By the first of October James Howard had moved from Number 8 Broad Street, but neither he nor his seven fellow-conspirators gave any outward sign of discon- Rebellion
tent. All eight were, however, absent from a reg- October
ular meeting of the Christian Scientist Associa- 1881
tion at the Eddy's home on the evening of October 26. In the absence of the president, James Howard, Putney Bancroft read a letter the eight had prepared and signed five days earlier:

> We, the undersigned, while we acknowledge and appreciate the understanding of Truth imparted to us by our Teacher, Mrs. Mary B. G. Eddy, led by Divine Intelligence to perceive with sorrow that departure from the straight and narrow road (which alone leads to growth of Christ-like virtues) made manifest by frequent ebullitions of temper, love of money, and the appearance of hypocrisy, cannot longer submit to such Leadership; therefore, without aught of hatred, revenge or petty spite in our hearts, from a sense of duty alone, to her, the Cause, and ourselves, do we most respectfully withdraw our names from the Christian Science Association and Church of Christ (Scientist).
>
> S. Louise Durant,
> Margaret J. Dunshee,
> Dorcas B. Rawson,
> Elizabeth G. Stuart,
> Jane L. Straw,

Anna B. Newman,
James C. Howard,
Miranda R. Rice.

October 21, 1881

Two of the signers had been loyal, faithful practitioners since that early class in the fall of 1870. Affidavits from two of the signers in defence of Dr. Eddy in the "conspiracy to murder" trial had just been published in the third edition as had Mrs. Rice's testimony of healing. Two had recently come from Arens' misteaching to the fountainhead and had signed a statement to that effect. Seven of the eight signers had affixed their names to the repudiation of malpractice which said, "our knowledge of metaphysics enables us to defend ourselves and others from their attacks." It was not their knowledge, but their fidelity which was tried and found wanting. The paragraphs in Science and Health had stated further in defence of their teacher:

> And we are fully convinced that no one can reach the height in metaphysics that our teacher, the author of "Science and Health," has reached, and progress as she is progressing, and be a moral or mental malpractitioner.

Little more than two months had passed since that statement had appeared in print. Talking about malpractice and meeting its attacks are two different things. In the Divinity Course in later years Mrs. Eddy told her students, "All there is of man is what is left after animal magnetism has gotten through with him; now measure your height." In 1881 there was very little height left to measure in many of the students that Richard Kennedy had set about to destroy.

CHAPTER XXXI

THE MOUNT OF TRANSFIGURATION

And thou, O tower of the flock, the strong hold of the
daughter of Zion, unto thee shall it come, even the first
dominion; the kingdom shall come to the daughter of Jeru-
salem.

Micah

October, 1881

THE letter of withdrawal fell like a bomb on the
stunned membership. Mrs. Eddy made no reply but sat
in silence. The twenty members who were present drew up the
following resolution and voted to send it to each dissenter:

> That your unchristian communication of October 21st 81
> renders you liable to Church discipline as you have broken
> our covenant in that you went not to the individual whom
> you abused. To tell her that you had aught against her. That
> you had assumed the appearance of full fellowship with her.
> ...You are liable to expulsion. You are hereby notified to
> appear before the Church of Christ (Scientist)...on Mon-
> day, Oct. 31 at 5 P.M. to answer for your unjust proceedings.

Mrs. Eddy withdrew from the meeting and the others quietly
dispersed,—all but two. There were two new students who remained with their teacher and her husband. They were Mrs.
Abbie K. Whiting and Mr. Calvin A. Frye. Their names, together with that of Asa Gilbert Eddy, will be remembered as
long as time lasts.

When Jesus went up onto the mount of transfiguration, he
had three faithful disciples with him. Now, more than eighteen
hundred years later, three loyal disciples were watching with
our Leader all that long night, burdened and sorrowful. Mrs.

Eddy was ascending the mount in their presence and, like Jesus, she was transfigured before them.

As morning dawned she suddenly arose from her chair and stepped out into the room. Her eyes beheld what her students could not see, and she began to speak, but not to them. Her face shone, and her words were so stirring that her students wept; but they picked up pencils and endeavored to record some of her words:

> Is this humiliation, the humility the oppressor would heap upon me! O, the exaltation of Spirit!
>
> I have made thee ruler over many things.
>
> Height upon Height! Holiness! Unquenchable light! Divine Being! The Womanhood of God!
>
> Well done, good and faithful, enter thou into the joy of thy Lord.
>
> One woe is passed, and behold, another cometh quickly; and no sign shall be given thee. Sufficient unto the day is the evil thereof.
>
> Woe, woe unto my people! The furnace is heated, the dross will be destroyed.
>
> And the false prophet that is among you shall deceive if possible the very elect, and he shall lead them into forbidden paths. And their feet shall bleed upon the jagged rocks. And the briars shall tear the rags from them. For they are not clothed with a garment of righteousness.
>
> And I will give to thee, daughter of Zion, a new heritage and a new people.
>
> Her ways shall be ways of pleasantness and ways of peace.
>
> Oh, blessed daughter of Zion, I am with thee. And none shall take my words out of thy lips. Thou art my chosen, to bear my Truth to the nations, and I will not suffer another messenger to go before thee.
>
> And this Absalom shall perish and this backsliding Israel shall eat the bread of bitterness.
>
> And I will lift thee up Oh daughter of Zion. And I will make of thee a new nation for thy praise.
>
> Get thee up! Depart, depart. This people are a stiff necked people.

When our Leader stopped speaking, she put down her hand and said, "Why, I haven't any body."

It was at this point that Julia Bartlett, who had been absent the night before, arrived at 8 Broad Street. She wrote:

> I was in Salem at the time and could not attend the meeting, but the next morning on hearing what had transpired I took the first train for Lynn, desiring to be with my dear teacher and to be of some service in her hour of trial. Dr. Eddy admitted me to the house. I found Mrs. Eddy seated by the table and the two students who had spent the night with her sitting near. I quietly took a seat near them as did Dr. Eddy also, and listened to Mrs. Eddy who was talking with a power such as I had never heard before. They were wonderful words she was speaking while we young students were receiving of the great spiritual illumination which had come through her glorious triumph over evil.
>
> ...When she was through, she said, "I want you three to stay with me three days." She said she did not know what might be but felt there would be a great deal for us.
>
> Those three days were wonderful. It was as if God was talking to her and she would come to us and tell us the wonderful revelations that came. We were on the Mount. We felt that we must take the shoes from off our feet, that we were standing on holy ground. What came to me at that time will never leave me.

The students who were with Mrs. Eddy during her trial and transfiguration had much to ponder. Was not her experience like that of Saint John, who on this plane of existence beheld spiritual reality—a new heaven and a new earth? And was not her countenance radiant as had been those of Moses and Jesus in spiritual exaltation?

What is the meaning of her words, "Why, I haven't any body"? To the students with her she had a body that they could see. It may be that they could not have felt her body had they tried. In a translation from the Greek of *The Acts of John* accredited to his student, Leucius, we find: "Sometimes when I would lay hold of him (Jesus), I met with a material and solid body, and at other times, again, when I felt him, the substance was immaterial, and as if it existed not at all."

The solution to life's problem, including the belief of a mortal body, is what Mrs. Eddy was working out for herself as well as for all mankind. In the first edition of Science and Health she had written:

> Belief produces the results of belief, and the penalty it affixes will be as positive as the belief that causes it; therefore, our remedy lies in reaching the bottom of the thing, in finding out the error or mind that produces the discord we see on the body, and not to honor it with the title of law, and then yield obedience to it.

The remedial part of this sentence she changed in the second edition to read:

> ...therefore, our remedy lies in reaching to the bottom of the thing, in finding out the error in mortal mind that produces the discord of mortal body.

In the third edition she had changed it further to read:

> ...our remedy lies in reaching to the bottom of the thing, in finding out the error of belief that produces a mortal body.

The moment of Mrs. Eddy's exaltation was not time for experimentation or inquiry by her students. But let us now state that situation in the form of a syllogism:

MAJOR PREMISE: "To be on communicable terms with Spirit, persons must be free from organic bodies." (S.&H. 74:3).

MINOR PREMISE: On October 27, 1881, the person known as Mary Baker Eddy was on communicable terms with Spirit.

CONCLUSION: Therefore, on October 27, 1881, Mary Baker Eddy was free from an organic body.

Consequently her statement, "Why, I haven't any body."

The names of the three students who were with their teacher when she was free from an organic body,—the names Asa Gilbert Eddy, Abbie K. Whiting, and Calvin A. Frye are destined to become as familiar to posterity as are those of Peter, James, and John who witnessed their teacher's spiritual exaltation;

albeit the nineteenth century record is no more detailed than the Biblical account. Nevertheless, all Christendom will be grateful for the record they did leave of their teacher's transfiguration on the mount. And wherever this story is told, the name of Julia S. Bartlett, who shared in the afterglow, will not be left out.

HOMES OF THE MASSACHUSETTS
METAPHYSICAL COLLEGE
Right to left 569 and 571 Columbus Avenue, Boston. The former was leased by the Eddy's in April, 1882. Mrs. Eddy moved to 571, which is slightly larger, about two years later.

CHAPTER XXXII

DEPART, DEPART

Nevertheless I tell you the Truth; It is expedient for you that I go away.

Jesus

1881

MRS. Eddy went personally almost as a penitent to the eight defectors, but not one of them would so much as open the door. She wrote to her young friend Alice Sibley, who had recently turned seventeen:

Letter to Alice Sibley October, 1881

My little friend is never forgotten by me, however many friends or *enemies* come between us....never forget me, will you? I am hanging yet, even as a monkey hangs from a branch, in all respects except the hinder appendage.

Take care of the company you keep, be not deceived in anyone. Attempt no more than is thy duty, teach people to be unselfish and bear their own burdens, at least, while you are willing to do more than they. Do not make my mistake, to take upon yourself all the baggage of this journey onward, but correct people's taste if not their conscience in that they think to make others their handy slaves. All this is a "new tongue," is it not, dear little one? but I mean it and you need it. . . .

None of the eight dissenters appeared at the church meeting of October 31. For Dorcas Rawson and Miranda Rice Mrs. Eddy had long borne the baggage and the burdens of the journey onward. And to James Howard she had given much aid, economic as well as spiritual. By the end of October she had had three

Visions of October 1881

238

visions involving James Howard and Richard Kennedy:

NUMBER ONE: I saw a great huge elephant, a watch dog and K—. The elephant followed me into a house, and pursued me from room to room until I got into my last room, and the dog was watching outside for me. Then the vision disappeared.

NUMBER TWO: I saw K— and H—. And K— looked to me, shaking his finger, and said pointing to H—, "This is the elephant that shall crush you into fragments beginning on your limbs." Then I looked at H— and over his head was written "Absalom" in blue luminous letters, and at his left side were dark clouds rolling up over their heads passing toward K—.

NUMBER THREE: Saw H— sitting, bowing his head with his hands to his face, holding his head and I knew what he was saying, and it was telling the students who had signed that letter, "Don't give Mrs. Eddy a chance to talk to you; turn away from her and I will lead you," and by his side stood K— governing his thoughts. After the visions she heard a voice crying, "Save my people!" repeated three times. Later the voice said three times, "Mine hour hath come!"

The hour had come and it was marked by more desertions from the ranks, but the loyal followers were more certain than ever of Mrs. Eddy's spirituality and leadership. *Ordained November 1881* The next week, on the ninth of November, they ordained their leader pastor of the Church of Christ (Scientist). It was a simple ceremony with Mrs. Whiting officiating.

A week later, on November 16, the Christian Scientist Association met at the Choate's home in Boston. Mrs. Choate, Abbie Whiting, and Samuel P. Bancroft had drawn up the following resolutions which were adopted: *Resolutions November 1881*

Resolved, That we the members of the Christian Scientist association, do herein express to our beloved teacher, and acknowledged leader, Mary B. Glover Eddy, our sincere and heartfelt thanks and gratitude for her earnest labours in behalf of this association, by her watchfulness of its interest and persistent efforts to maintain the highest rule of Christian love among its members.

Resolved, That while she has had little or no help, except from God, in the introduction to this age of materiality of her book, *Science and Health,* and the carrying forward of the Christian principles it teaches and explains, she has been unremitting in her faithfulness to her God-appointed work, and we do understand her to be the chosen messenger of God to bear his truth to the nations, and unless we hear "Her Voice," we do not hear "His Voice."

Resolved, That the charges made to her in a letter, signed by J. C. Howard, M. R. Rice, D. B. Rawson, and five others, of hypocrisy, ebullitions of temper, and love of money, are utterly false, and the cowardice of the signers in refusing to meet her and sustain or explain said charges, be treated with the righteous indignation it justly deserves. That while we deplore such wickedness and abuse of her who has befriended them in their need, and when wrong, met them with honest, open rebuke, we look with admiration and reverence upon her Christ-like example of meekness and charity, and will, in future, more faithfully follow and obey her divine instructions, knowing that in so doing we offer the highest testimonial of our appreciation of her Christian leadership.

Resolved, That a copy of these resolutions be presented to our teacher and leader, Mary B. Glover Eddy, and a copy be placed on the records of this Christian Scientist Association.

There were other protestations of loyalty. Arthur Buswell wrote her on the twenty-second of December that he had "explicit faith in our leader and consider her love and labor as divine." But her leadership now was to leave them. She had had instructions from on high, "Get thee up ! Depart, depart;" and she set about working to that end.

A special church meeting was called for the twenty-fifth of December at which time two new members, one of whom was Julia Bartlett, were admitted to the purged ranks of her infant church.

One of Mrs. Eddy's remarkable healings should be mentioned here. Although it probably occurred a little earlier, it took place at Number 8 Broad Street which she was soon to leave for the last time:

Teamster healed

At Lynn, when Mrs. Eddy lived there, a teamster passing
her house was thrown to the ground so that a heavily loaded
wagon ran over him. One wheel crossed his body, crushing it.
Men who carried him into her house regarded him as dead...
The commotion caused by the accident attracted Mrs.
Eddy's attention; and she went downstairs to where the body
was and...treated silently. In a short time...the injured
man became conscious, sat up, stood up, declared he was
not hurt and walked back to his team.

Another occurrence of interest should be mentioned before
the final departure from Lynn. That is the Eddys' visit to
Ralph Waldo Emerson. We have this record that   Visit with
our Leader wrote at a later date to Miss Lane,   Emerson
one of her students: c. 1881

Now beware of what our Master warned his students
against, *viz*. *'The doctrines of men'*. Waldo Emerson was a
man fitting a niche in history well, and we all in Mass. love
him; but he was as far from accepting Christian Science as a
man can be who is a strict moralist. Bronson Alcott is far
in advance of him. I saw Emerson some months before his
demise; went for the purpose of *healing* him. Let no one but
my husband, Dr. Eddy, who went with me, know it. As soon
as I got into the deep recesses of his thoughts I saw his case
was hopeless. I can work only by God's graces and by His
rules. So when I said, in reply to his remark, "I am old and
my brains are wearing out from hard labor"—and then chat-
tered like a babe— "But you believe in the powers of God
above all causation, do you not?" he answered, "Yes," and
this followed in substance: but it would be profane for me to
believe a man does not wear out. I don't believe God can or
wants to prevent this result of old age. Now Miss L., what
would this be for an item of history—that Normal Class
Students from the only College or School in our land teaching
the supremacy of Mind over all error should relapse into
studying the ethics of one who died in that belief? Can you
find in any work higher ethics than in *Science and Health?*

*   *   *

241

It was mid-January before the Eddys finally left their home in Lynn, but the farewell meeting with her few faithful followers was on Christmas night in 1881. The students were deeply moved by her parting words and her reading of John 17:

> I have manifested thy name unto the men which thou gavest me out of the world: thine they were, and thou gavest them me; and they have kept thy word.
>
> For I have given unto them the words which thou gavest me; and they have received them, and have known surely that I came out from thee, and they have believed that thou didst send me.
>
> I pray not that thou shouldest take them out of the world, but that thou shouldest keep them from the evil.
>
> As thou hast sent me into the world, even so have I also sent them into the world.
>
> O righteous Father, the world hath not known thee: but I have known thee, and these have known that thou hast sent me.

The men which infinite Mind had given to the Leader had failed her one after another. The "Womanhood of God" was beyond their comprehension, and the demands of this higher understanding were left unfulfilled. Following James Howard's leadership to apostasy, the "men" in the ranks were mostly women. But woman's day was dawning.

In the Key to the Scriptures which Mrs. Eddy had been working on for several years she had identified the second river of Eden as "The rights of woman acknowledged morally, civilly, and socially." This "channel of thought" met with much resistance from the Adam, but the Eve was more receptive to the advancing idea.

Upon four of the women in the church Mrs. Eddy placed the responsibility for leading her flock in the Mother's absence. To one of the four, Miss Julia Bartlett, she mailed a poem which she had written on the eve of her departure, with the request that it be read to the Church:

TO THE CHURCH OF CHRIST, SCIENTIST

With Love's battle flags unfurled,
With hope's cause before the world,
We are going on.
Though the storm clouds thunder o'er us,
Though the path seems dark before us,
Though the foeman strive to kill us
We are going on.
For our Master led the way,
Fought the fight and won the day;
Follow, follow all who may,
Going on, going on.

Stand ye only back, who dare
Not the cross of Christ to bear;
We are going on.
Triumph's star above us gleaming
Victory on our foreheads beaming,
For fresh duties hourly reaching,
We are going on.
To fulfill each hope and aim,
Conquer sickness, sin and blame,
And each erring heart reclaim,
Going on, going on.

From the darkness of the night;
Into morning's golden light;
Sisters labor on;
With the aid of God's own Science,
With no heed of hate's defiance,
Truth and right my sole reliance,
I shall labor on.
                    Your loving Teacher
                    Mary Baker Glover Eddy

CHAPTER XXXIII

ENTRY INTO JERUSALEM

And when he was come into Jerusalem, all the city was moved, saying, Who is this?

Matthew

1882

L YNN was the cradle of Christian Science and for that will be as remembered as Bethlehem, but as 1882 dawned the infant had outgrown his cradle. Mid-January found the Eddys in Washington, D.C. where Dr. Eddy spent much of his time researching the copyright laws as a protection for Science and Health. On the twentieth of January Mrs. Eddy wrote to Julia Bartlett:

Letter to
J. Bartlett
January, 1882

January 20, 1882

Julia S. Bartlett
My Dear Student:
Your precious letter I have just finished reading and *never* was I more thankful than to hear that *one* of my students whom I know is exercised by love to God and man is at work after the long night of struggle. Like Jacob you have wrestled and prevailed and now I will rest in hope once more. This sheet is all I have unpacked. Like the stone for Jacob's pillow was your entrance into our church and the dear associations with it. O! my darling girl, all I ask is that the ladder of light shall rest upon it and on this ladder you go up higher until the things that eye hath not seen appear and we meet in Spirit no more to part.

There should be a substitute for me to lead this people and now, dear student, I ask you will you take this place, not that you can unloose the [latchet] of my shoes, not that

244

you can fill my place, but only that I think you rather more fit for it than any one whom I leave. Now do not yield to temptation and say you cannot but, "if you love me keep my commandments."

The charge is simply this—see that the Christian work of this church is preserved and dear Mrs. Whiting will help you. She has qualities of inspiration that are glorious and this is needed. Now, dear, remember that Mrs. Choate is a sister in our church and doing much good for our cause in selling books and bearing testimony for Christ.

This I beg that you "love one another even as I have loved you," that no root of bitterness springs up among you. That no pride comes up or vain inquiry "who shall be greatest" but remember: I have made myself the servant that I might lead others to Christ.

Farewell, may our Father bring us together again to co-operate in His cause.

Lovingly—

M. B. G. Eddy

Mrs. Eddy was advising her students as Jesus had advised his:

And he [Jesus] came to Capernaum: and being in the house he asked them, What was it that ye disputed among yourselves by the way? But they held their peace: for by the way they had disputed among themselves, who should be the greatest. And he sat down, and called the twelve, and saith unto them, If any man desire to be first, the same shall be last of all, and servant of all.

Mrs. Eddy had made herself the servant of all, and her life was one of self-sacrifice. Her students could no more fill her shoes than the disciples could fill those of Jesus, but several had thought that they could, and most were more concerned with their own stature than with *following* their leader. Pride and contention over "who should be the greatest" made them poor soldiers in the war to overcome error with Truth. In a letter to Mrs. Choate, the Leader wrote:

This is the whole of the disaster in all cases,—that my students will not accept in time my advice, or take only a part of it. What would a general do in a fight with such soldiers or officers? It would defeat every battle, and so it is doing.

But Mrs. Eddy moved forward with or without the support of her students. Soon after their arrival in Washington she had
Teaching in a circular and the following card printed:
Washington
February, 1882

> You are respectfully invited to attend
> A Course of Lectures
> by Mrs. Eddy, Author of "Science and Health,"
> At 13 First Street, N.E.
> Commencing Feb. 10th   First Lecture Free

Col. and Mrs. Eldridge J. Smith who had been studying Science and Health and corresponding with its author since 1876 were in attendance. And they were far from alone in this freer atmosphere removed from the malpractice of Lynn, Boston and environs. The audience at these Washington lectures numbered about fifty.

By the end of the month her lecture course was completed. She wrote to Clara Choate on the twenty-fifth of February:

> I have worked harder here than ever, 14 consecutive evenings I have lectured three hours...besides what else I am about. Get to bed at 12, rise at 6, and *work*.

"Besides what else I am about" covered a great deal of territory, not the least being the healing that occurred wherever Mrs. Eddy went. One instance of healing during her sojourn in Washington, D.C. was as follows.

Mrs. Eddy aroused the interest of the clergyman whose church they attended in Washington. He requested the privi-
Healing of lege of calling upon her, which was granted, and
cancer he listened with interest to her explanations of
1882 the Bible and Christian Science. As the dinner hour approached, he requested the privilege of remaining for

the sociability, explaining that he could not partake of the re-
past because a stomach ailment of many years had developed,
according to the physicians, into cancer of the stomach causing
him to confine himself to a fluid diet exclusively.

Mrs. Eddy said that this was a good time to test the facts
they had just been discussing. His reply was that he could
hardly afford to do that for the sake of killing himself, to which
she voiced the Truth and asserted his ability to eat in comfort.
At the table he completely forgot his fears and partook heartily
of the meal, afterward exclaiming, "What have I done? Will I
ever survive?" Mrs. Eddy assured him that he could not suffer,
and he did not, nor ever again.

A few days after the Eddys' arrival in the capitol city, the
youthful Charles J. Guiteau was found guilty of assassinating
President Garfield. Mrs. Eddy analyzed the case, but she did
not leave it there. Orders had been issued that only relatives
would be allowed to visit the prisoner, but the *Washington
Post* stated on February 13:

> A number of people were granted the privilege yesterday
> of looking at Guiteau in his cell, but only a few were allowed
> to converse with him, and none on matters relating to his exe-
> cution or the trial.

One of the few was Mary Baker Eddy. Her account of this
situation is the starting point for the present-day metaphysician, for he must understand her strict classi-   Visit to
fication of the mental stages of crime in order   assassin
to solve the problem of the insane criminality   February, 1882
of these latter days.

> The mental stages of crime, which seem to belong to the
> latter days, are strictly classified in metaphysics as some of
> the many features and forms of what is properly denominat-
> ed, in extreme cases, moral idiocy. I visited in his cell the
> assassin of President Garfield, and found him in the mental
> state called moral idiocy. He had no sense of his crime; but
> regarded his act as one of simple justice, and himself as the
> victim. My few words touched him; he sank back in his chair,
> limp and pale; his flippancy had fled. The jailor thanked me,
> and said, "Other visitors have brought to him bouquets, but

you have brought what will do him good."

* * *

James Ackland was expecting the Eddys to come to Philadelphia in March and had made preparations for their stay.

Teaching in Philadelphia March, 1882

Very early in the month Mrs. Eddy was teaching a group of students in that city. She wrote of this activity to Col. and Mrs. Smith in Washington. She also encouraged them to continue their meetings, stating:

> Do not as you love me and love Truth omit your Sunday meetings. A real revival in Metaphysics is going on in Boston because my dear students there are carrying out my advice to keep up these meetings in my absence. . . . *Heal the sick.*

About the same time, she wrote to Julia Bartlett who was now living and working with Mrs. Whiting in the Boston area.

Letter to J. Bartlett March, 1882

The two women were meeting with success after a period of difficulties and sore trials. Mrs. Eddy's letter of March 14 said:

> *My very dear Student:*
> You don't know how much joy your letters give me. I knew it was best for me to do as the husbandman, go away and then see if you all did not add many more talents to those you already had. Yes, dearest one, you and Mrs. W. are deserving all praise.
>
> > Lovingly my dear child
> > Mother Mary

Shortly after Mrs. Eddy had left them, the students had published in the *Lynn Union* the Resolutions adopted the pre-

Letter to Clara Choate March, 1882

vious November. Great success in their work followed this public acknowledgement of and affirmation of loyalty to their leader. The women were carrying the work forward. Woman's hour had come. On the fifteenth of March Mrs. Eddy wrote from Philadelphia to Clara Choate who was also living and working in Boston:

> It is glorious to see what the women *alone* are doing here for temperance. More than ever man has done. This is the

period of *women,* they are to move and carry all the great moral and Christian reforms. I know it. Now darling, let us work as the industrious Suffragists are at work who are getting a hearing all over the land. Let us work as they do in love "preferring one another." Let us work shoulder to shoulder each bearing their own part of the burdens and helping one another and then the puny kicks of mesmerism will give up the ghost before such *union.*

To Mrs. Choate the "kicks of mesmerism" loomed rather large. Though she resisted successfully, her husband did not and his metaphysical practice grew poorer and poorer. His situation had not improved since Mrs. Eddy had written of it to James Ackland in February:

His wife told me when I was there she should have to give up getting him patients he so neglected them and every time injured the cause. I pity him from the depths of my heart but can do no more than I have done for him. It is demonology and his old appetite for liquor that they bring back. He would do well but for *them.*

As George Choate succumbed to the work of the mesmerists, Clara turned more zealously to her work. She was successful at healing, and her youth and enthusiasm were magnetic. She wrote to Mrs. Eddy of lecturing and of teaching small classes. Soon she was writing of being overwhelmed with practice and of overflow meetings with the seats all filled and many standing.

On the twenty-sixth of March the *Boston Globe* ran an unbiased full-page article on Christian Science. Everyone was discussing the topic. An air of excitement pervaded the city when the Eddys returned midst much acclaim the following week.

Favorable publicity was accorded the formal reception that Mrs. Choate gave for Mrs. Eddy on the evening of April 5. The warm welcome from the faithful and the fashionable, plus the atmosphere of excitement throughout the city caused Mrs. Eddy to write to James Ackland, "This was my entry into Jerusalem. Will it be followed with the cross?"

CHAPTER XXXIV

BEGINNING IN BOSTON

The star of Bethlehem is the star of Boston.

Mary Baker Eddy

1882

MASSACHUSETTS Metaphysical College had appeared over the door of Number 8 Broad Street in Lynn early in 1881, but in the students' eyes it had its beginning in the new location in Boston. April of 1882 was devoted to finding this new location.

During the search for suitable quarters the Eddys stayed at the Parker House in Boston. One spring day Mrs. Eddy Morphine received a most gratifying letter from a physi- habit cian who worked for Associated Charities of Cin- healed cinnati,—one Otto Anderson. M. D. He had written on April 22 telling of his introduction to Science and Health and relating his experience with Christian Science:

Having been together daily in the same office with your disciple, Mr. A. T. Buswell, for the past four months, I have learned to respect him professionally and love him individually. . . .

I am an "old school" practitioner, have served as surgeon in two European navies and have practised medicine for about ten years in New York and Brooklyn until my health compelled me to relinquish my profession. I became a victim of the Morphine habit and had to take as high as thirty grains, of the most diabolical drug that ever was manufactured, daily. My physicians who treated me declared me consumptive and banished all hope of recovery. In the month of December last year, I made the acquaintance of Mr. Buswell and commenced assisting him in the discharge of his noble duties. He being a metaphysician and I Allopathic we naturally often discussed the matter and as drugs did me no good, I stopped taking any whatever, save Morphine without which I thought it impossible to get along. I, to my great astonishment, commenced to gain in flesh and am by this time 20 lb. heavier in weight than I was on January 1st. Recuperating, my ambition and energy returned in proportion, I felt in my mind that I could stop my loathsome habit and I performed the wonderful feat in a week without any discomfiture worth mentioning (the case standing alone in our medical records). I have administered one quarter of a grain of Morphine (hypodermically) to Mr. Buswell without the slightest physiological effect, clearly proving the existence of metaphysical laws.

Toward the end of April Julia Bartlett had an interesting experience:

One day as I was returning from a call on a patient I could not dismiss the thought that there was a need for me to see Mrs. Eddy. I told Mrs. Whiting, and she said, "If I felt that way, I would go to her by all means." This I did, and when she opened the door to let me in, she said, "You are just the one I want to see."

This day marked the beginning of a new epoch for Julia Bartlett. Mrs. Eddy had just recorded: "Took the lease of the house at 569 Columbus Ave. April 25th, 1882. Rent $83.33." This ample four-story house was to be the location of the college. Julia Bartlett and Abbie Whiting were two of the four students invited to reside at the college with the Eddys. Miss Bartlett wrote:

It was in April, 1882, that we entered the College...

Mrs. Eddy's time was filled with the great work which lay before her—in teaching, conducting Sunday services, Friday night meetings, writing, receiving callers, and many other duties connected with the Cause, and Dr. Eddy was constantly of assistance to her. Aside from him there were four students with her at the opening of the College—Mr. Hanover

P. Smith, Mrs. Whiting, myself, and one other. . . .

There were so many pressing needs and so few to meet them that the moments were precious. There was work to be done at all hours.

Letters of appreciation and reports of healing and progress were coming from all quarters. One morning's mail brought an interesting letter from an old friend, Mrs. Mary Godfrey of Chelsea. On the ninth of May she had written:

Letter from
Mrs. Godfrey
May, 1882

I feel as if I owe you a debt which will never be paid when I look at my thimble finger of my right hand.

She went on to say that perhaps she had made partial payment by sending her Asa Gilbert Eddy, "for I don't believe you could have found a better one anywhere." Neither she nor Mrs. Eddy even dreamed of what another month would bring.

Mid-May had not arrived before Mrs. Eddy was teaching a class. Julia Bartlett's narrative continues:

Mrs. Eddy soon taught a Primary class and invited Dr. Eddy and me to sit through this, the first Primary class taught in College. . . .she said there were questions in our thought which had to be answered. . .It was all a rich feast for us, for which we were most grateful.

This first Primary class in the new college location began on the twelfth of May, little over a fortnight after leasing the building. But this first class was the last that would see the participation of Asa Gilbert Eddy.

CHAPTER XXXV

MENTAL MURDER

*One woe is passed, and behold, another cometh quickly;
and no sign shall be given thee.*

Revelation of Mary Baker Eddy

1882

MRS. Eddy's vision of a beautiful young maiden being
wedded to E. J. Arens over her objections had been
fulfilled. Because of this marriage Mrs. Eddy had lost three
fine students, Mr. and Mrs. Benjamin F. Atkinson and their
daughter Adelma. Mr. Atkinson, a member of the Massachusetts legislature, had publicly praised Mrs. Eddy in the spring
of 1879 after the barrage of adverse publicity against her and
Christian Science. But the following year all three Atkinsons
tendered their resignation from the Christian Scientist Association, and the daughter became Arens' bride. It is less surprising that his character was undetected by the Atkinson
family than that he was able to deceive Mrs. Eddy as long as
he did. He may have been only a tool in Kennedy's hands, but
he was a willing and wicked one.

In the summer of 1881 Mrs. Eddy had suffered gastric pains
with all the symptoms of arsenical poisoning. When she had
defended herself from the "poison" of Arens' hatred, the
physical effects had disappeared.

From the time that Arens had published pages of Mrs.
Eddy's writings as his own, the Eddys had felt that he must
be restrained, and to that end Gilbert had first exposed his
actions in the foreword to Science and Health. Arens was undeterred. He forged ahead with his malpractice, "treating" to
help one person and to hinder another. The garment of Truth

is every whit whole.

During the winter while Dr. Eddy was making a thorough study of the copyright laws and Mrs. Eddy was teaching and lecturing, they both were obliged to guard constantly against the same symptoms of arsenical poisoning. In the spring, whether it was that Arens' malice was bent more upon Gilbert Eddy or that the blows aimed at the Revelator fell short of their mark due to her spirituality, wounding those nearest her, Gilbert's suffering increased alarmingly.

He missed some of the sessions of the course she was teaching, but declared repeatedly that he was coping with the situation and could handle his own case. His words were more to keep from burdening his wife than a statement of fact. In every spare moment Mary went to him and her silent treatment gave him relief. She also asked students to work for him.

One student in the May class who had just related a story, was sent by the teacher to Dr. Eddy to repeat her experience with the hope that it would break the mesmerism affecting him. Mrs. Delia S. Manly told that as a child she had seen a bird hypnotized by a snake. The bird circled closer and closer calling out louder and louder. When it was nearly within the snake's striking distance, her brother had thrown a stone between them breaking the spell and releasing the bird.

Mrs. Eddy had no doubt of the cause of Gilbert's suffering, but her students had not her spiritual intuition and did not fully appreciate hers. Instead of following her lead and working diligently in the direction she indicated, they let doubts grow and began casting about surmising other causes for Dr. Eddy's illness, overlooking her words in Science and Health: "because disease is a belief, a latent thing of mind, before it appears as matter, we are never mistaken in our metaphysical diagnosis of disease."

In the third edition of Science and Health Mrs. Eddy had quoted from R. K. Noyes, M.D. of Lynn in his *History of Medicine for the Last 4000 Years:*

A drug or substance can never be called a healer of disease; there is no reason, justice, or necessity in the use of drugs in disease. I believe that this profession, this art, this misnamed knowledge of medicine, is none other than a practice of fundamentally fallacious principles, impotent of good, morally wrong, and bodily hurtful.

The Eddys were well acquainted with Dr. Noyes and his associate, Dr. Eastman. Both Mr. and Mrs. Eddy had taken a course in obstetrics from Dr. Noyes and been certificated before leaving Lynn. Although the course of her college was not to follow her recently printed prospectus, it would appear that she endeavored briefly to align Christian Science with general medical practice. The 1882 prospectus for the Massachusetts Metaphysical College read:

Mary B. G. Eddy
Professor of Obstetrics, Metaphysics, and Christian Science

Rufus King Noyes, M.D.
(formerly resident surgeon of the Boston City Hospital)
Professor of Surgery and Accouchement

Charles J. Eastman, M.D.
Professor of Medical Jurisprudence

Mrs. Eddy taught the metaphysical, never the physical, aspect of obstetrics. Science and Health then said, "The obstetrics of metaphysics is its highest branch and one with which teacher and student should be familiar." Mind so changed the direction of her experience that the two gentlemen listed never taught at all in her college. But in May of 1882 she called them to examine Dr. Eddy and substantiate her diagnosis. The substantiation was only partial, and of very little, if any, help in convincing her students of the correctness of her analysis.

On the second of June Dr. Eddy felt much improved, and he and Julia Bartlett went out for a street car ride which he enjoyed as a pleasant change. Hanover Smith and another student were with him that night as he rested in his chair, finding it more comfortable

Death of
A. G. Eddy
June, 1882

than his bed. After he had been quiet for some time they went to him and found that he was gone. At a later date Mrs. Eddy was able to write:

In 1882 he passed away, with a smile of peace and love resting on his serene countenance. "Mark the perfect *man,* and behold the upright: for the end of *that* man is peace."

But in 1882, in the wee small hours of June 3, Mrs. Eddy was grief-stricken. The students, including Dr. Eddy, had not comprehended her instructions sufficiently to resist vigorously malicious mesmerism. Her words to Clara Choate had never been more graphic: "This is the whole of the disaster in all cases—that my students will not accept in time my advice."

Even in her grief she saw the situation clearly and knew that she must leave a record for future generations to study that they might understand what her present students could not fathom.

The first thing she did on the morning of June 3 was to send Hanover Smith to deliver a message to Edward Arens who lived nearby. She wrote of this:

After the death of [my] husband, Dr. Eddy, I sent for one of the mental malpractitioners to come and look on his calm, dear face. The messenger, who stood at the door and delivered my request, said that on hearing it, he grew deadly pale and clutched at the door to stand. He never came.

Next she wrote to Benjamin F. Atkinson, Arens' father-in-law:

With the cold form of [my] beloved husband lying on his bier in my desolated home I appeal to you once more, and if you are not darkened to the sense of the awful crimes I know you will stop them by every influence in your power.

I have power to discern the cause of his death...and what I say the future will declare, namely: that Edward J. Arens has caused the death of my husband in connection with his co-operators so far as I can clearly discern in my diagnosis of the case.

Her work of June 3 was not finished. She next sent for a reporter from the *Boston Globe* whose account of her story appeared the next day with the caption:

Mesmerism or Arsenic
A Strange Claim by Mrs. Eddy Regarding
Her Husband's Death

Mrs. Mary B. Glover Eddy, the founder of Christian Science, sent for a reporter to come to the Metaphysical College, 569 Columbus Avenue, yesterday. She wished to make a statement. Mr. Eddy, her husband, had died that morning, and she appeared much overcome at the event, and could scarcely control herself enough to make the following statement: Her husband, she said, had died with every symptom of arsenical poisoning. Both he and she knew it to be the result of a malicious mesmeric influence exerted over his mind by certain parties here in Boston, who had sworn to injure them. She had formerly had the same symptoms of arsenical poison herself, and it was some time before she discovered it to be the mesmeric work of an enemy. Soon after her marriage her husband began to manifest the same symptoms and had since shown them from time to time; but was, with her help, always able to overcome them. A few weeks ago she observed that he did not look well, and when questioned he said that he was unable to get the idea of this arsenical poison out of his mind. He had been steadily growing worse ever since, but still had hoped to overcome the trouble until the last. After the death the body had turned black.

The next day was no easier for Mrs. Eddy. The students expected her to bear up serenely and unflinchingly whatever the calamity. Meeting Delia Manly alone in the hallway, Mrs. Eddy put her head on this student's shoulder and wept, saying, "I feel that there is something in your heart that will understand what is in mine."

Drs. Noyes and Eastman performed an autopsy and found no trace of poison in the body. This showed that mesmeric poison could produce the same result as material poison without the telltale evidence, but for the neophytes in metaphysics it further confused the issue. The Teacher had to substantiate further the facts for the Scientists of the future who could follow her mental lead, so once more she called in reporters,—this time from the *Boston Post,* the *Herald,* and the *Journal.* The most detailed account appeared in the *Post:*

My husband's death was caused by malicious mesmerism. Dr. C. J. Eastman, who attended the case after it had taken an alarming turn, declares the symptoms to be the same as

those of arsenical poisoning. On the other hand, Dr. Rufus
K. Noyes, late of the City Hospital, who held an autopsy over
the body to-day, affirms that the corpse is free from all material poison, although Dr. Eastman still holds to his original
belief. I know it was poison that killed him, not material
poison, but mesmeric poison. My husband was in uniform
health, and but seldom complained of any kind of ailment.
During this brief illness, just preceding his death, his continual cry was, "Only relieve me of this continual suggestion,
through the mind, of poison, and I will recover." It is well
known that by constantly dwelling upon any subject in
thought finally comes the poison of belief through the whole
system. . . . I never saw a more self-possessed man than dear
Dr. Eddy was. He said to Dr. Eastman, when he was finally
called to attend him: "My case is nothing that I cannot
attend to myself, although to me it acts the same as poison
and seems to pervade my whole system just as that would."

This is not the first case known of where death has occurred from what appeared to be poison, and was so declared
by the attending physician, but in which the body, on being
thoroughly examined by an autopsy, was shown to possess no
signs of material poison. There was such a case in New York.
Every one at first declared poison to have been the cause of
death, as the symptoms were all there; but an autopsy con-
tradicted the belief, and it was shown that the victim had
had no opportunity for procuring poison. I afterwards learned
that she had been very active in advocating the merits of our
college. Oh, isn't it terrible, that this fiend of malpractice is
in the land! The only remedy that is effectual in meeting this
terrible power possessed by the evil-minded is to counteract
it by the same method that I use in counteracting poison.
They require the same remedy. Circumstances debarred me
from taking hold of my husband's case. He declared himself
perfectly capable of carrying himself through, and I was so
entirely absorbed in business that I permitted him to try,
and when I awakened to the danger it was too late. I have
cured worse cases before, but took hold of them in time. I
don't think that Dr. Carpenter had anything to do with my
husband's death, but I do believe it was the rejected students—students who were turned away from our college be-

cause of their unworthiness and immorality. To-day I sent for
one of the students whom my husband had helped liberally,
and given money, not knowing how unworthy he was. I
wished him to come, that I might prove to him how, by
metaphysics, I could show the cause of my husband's death.
He was as pale as a ghost when he came to the door, and refused to enter, or to believe that I knew what caused his
death. Within half an hour after he left, I felt the same attack
that my husband felt—the same that caused his death. I
instantly gave myself the same treatment that I would use in
a case of arsenical poisoning, and so I recovered, just the same
as I could have caused my husband to recover had I taken
the case in time. After a certain amount of mesmeric poison
has been administered it cannot be averted. No power of
mind can resist it. It must be met with resistive action of the
mind at the start, which will counteract it. We all know that
disease of any kind cannot reach the body except through
the mind, and that if the mind is cured the disease is soon
relieved. Only a few days ago I disposed of a tumour in twenty-four hours that the doctors had said must be removed by
the knife. I changed the course of the mind to counteract the
effect of the disease. This proves the myth of matter. Mesmerism will make an apple burn the hand so that the child
will cry. My husband never spoke of death as something we
were to meet, but only as a phase of mortal belief. . . .I do
believe in God's supremacy over error, and this gives me
peace. I do believe, and have been told, that there is a price
set upon my head. One of my students, a malpractitioner,
has been heard to say that he would follow us to the grave.
He has already reached my husband. While my husband and
I were in Washington and Philadelphia last winter, we were
obliged to guard against poison, the same symptoms apparent at my husband's death constantly attending us. And
yet the one who was planning the evil against us was in Boston the whole time. To-day a lady, active in forwarding the
good of our college, told me that she had been troubled almost constantly with arsenical poison symptoms, and is now
treating them constantly as I directed her. Three days ago
one of my patients died, and the doctor said he died from
arsenic, and yet there were no material symptoms of poison.

The reporter may not have been accurate in all his details, but the message for the metaphysician of today is unmistakable. In that day, however, the only students interested in learning from the details were the malpractitioners.

Arens seemed to have a fascination with arsenic which even penetrated to his writings. Midst the muddle of correct and incorrect metaphysical questions and answers in his next pamphlet, these two questions appeared:

Question 12. Is it arsenic that kills?
Question 13. In what way is mind the cause of death which is said to be produced by poison?

A year later he was still pursuing the subject and wrote, "It is said that arsenic kills; but it would be very difficult for anyone to prove how it kills, since persons have had all the symptoms of arsenic poisoning without having taken any arsenic."

"Whatsoever a man soweth, that shall he also reap." In her reminiscences Mrs. Manly wrote that "Mr. Eddy was a dear, courteous, gentle character, and it seemed as though he couldn't conceive of anyone doing him an injury." With a peaceful smile on his face he passed away quietly in his sleep. Arens, on the other hand, had his own wicked thoughts to reap. If he had been the student of metaphysics that he professed to be, he would have heeded Mrs. Eddy's words about malpractitioners in the third edition of Science and Health:

They should have feared for their own lives in their attempts to kill us. God is supreme and the penalties of their sins they cannot escape.

On the same page of the third edition Mrs. Eddy also said:

Since God has shown us our way in Christian healing, our mind often heals involuntarily. The malpractitioners know this, and many a time have asked us about their patients to direct our thoughts to them, knowing the benefit therefrom.

Even with all the malpractice and its dire effects, this was the first case Mrs. Eddy had lost since her discovery of Science sixteen years earlier. This loss caused her to make one important change. She ceased working metaphysically for her second student, Richard Kennedy. Several years later she told a class not to labor indefinitely with a chronic sinner as she had done. According to notes of students in that class:

She [Mrs. Eddy] had labored with a chronic sin in a student for ten years. It would have been better for him had she ceased her endeavors at the end of three years. One should never interfere with God's methods. . . . The sin is the sinner and brings its own suffering. If the sinner will not give up the sin, do not interfere with the penalty. . . .

The orthodox hell would be none too hot, or too long, for one who attempts wilfully to defile the Truth, or to lead others astray. "God will make the wrath of man to praise Him."

By the fifth of June the hardest tasks of this heart-rending ordeal were behind her. At the funeral service conducted by a Unitarian minister for Dr. Eddy, Mrs. Eddy joined in singing "Nearer My God to Thee." Her voice was clear and sweet, and to the students she seemed uplifted above the sense of death.

Alone in her chamber her thoughts went back to previous partings and griefs. The poignancy of the present situation was not unlike that of her experiences in 1849, and her thoughts dwelt upon her loved mother as well as dear, dear Gilbert. In her Journal she wrote:

MEETING OF MY DEPARTED
MOTHER AND HUSBAND

"Joy for thee, happy friend, thy bark hath past
The dangerous sea, and safely moored at last—
    Beyond rough foam.
Soft gales celestial, in sweet music bore—
Mortal emancipate for this far shore—
    Thee to thy home.

"You've traveled long, and far from mortal joys,
To Soul's diviner sense, that spurns such toys,
    Brave wanderer lone,
Now see thy ever-self; Life never fled.
Man is not mortal, never of the dead:
    The dark unknown.

"When hope soared high, and joy was eagle-plumed,
Her pinions drooped; the flesh was weak, and doomed
    To pass away.
But radiant hopes around thy death-couch spread,
Majestic forms and rainbow glories shed
    O'er Life's long day.

"Intensely grand and glorious this sphere;
Beyond the shadow, infinite appear
    Life, Love divine.
Here mortal yearnings come, but all are stilled,
And home where peace is won and hearts are filled,
    Thine, ever thine.

"Bearest thou no tidings from our loved on earth,
The toiler tireless for Truth's new birth,
    Earth's unbeguiled.
Our joy is gathered from a parting sigh,
This hour looks on that heart with pitying eye:
    What of my child?"

"We parted in death's dream, I woke to life.
She deemed I died, and could not know the strife
    It was to fill
That waking with a love that steady turns
To God; a hope that ever upward yearns,
    Bowed to His will.

"Years had passed o'er thy broken household band,
When angels beckoned me to this bright land,
    With thee to meet.
She that is left bent o'er my chilling brow;
Rears the sad marble to my memory now,
    In lone retreat,

"By the remembrance of her earthly life,
And parting prayer, I only know my wife,
    Thy child, shall come—
Where farewells cloud not o'er our ransomed rest-
Hither to reap, with all the crowned and blest,
    Of bliss, the sum.

"When Soul's rapt sense the heart-strings gently sweep
With hope divinely fair, the high and deep,
　　　To call her home.
She shall mount upward unto purer skies;
We shall be waiting in what glad surprise,
　　　Our spirits' own."

ASA GILBERT EDDY

CHAPTER XXXVI

EVENT OF IMPORT

Oh, blessed daughter of Zion . . . Thou art my
chosen, to bear my Truth to the nations.

Revelation of Mary Baker Eddy

1882

THE death of Gilbert Eddy marked the nadir of Mrs. Eddy's earth experience. At this low point she turned first to her son asking him to come to stay with her. George Glover did not come, answering briefly that his wife was not willing. Arthur True Buswell, to whom she turned next, responded immediately and came to her aid.

Christian Scientists are indebted to Arthur Buswell for the record of the fact that Mrs. Eddy had brought her husband back twice from the dream of death before his final departure. The night of his death Dr. Eddy had apparently been gone for several hours before the students were aware of it and finally notified their teacher.

The work of the Movement was such that all at the college worked at all hours, and none so tirelessly as the Leader. With the weight of loss and grief added to the burden of work, she was near exhaustion; but even now she saw that "whom the Lord loveth he chasteneth." She confided one day to Delia Manly:

> You who have suffered recent affliction know how to sympathize with me. I would not dare to give way to grief before the other students. Dear Gilbert, I could be happy with him in a hut, but God means that I shall rely on Him alone.

Arthur Buswell suggested that Mrs. Eddy make use of his

home in Barton, Vermont for a much needed rest, to which she agreed. So he made the necessary arrangements while she took care of the pressing business which included the completion of the class which had been in progress. She was soon on her way to northern Vermont with a young woman companion she dearly loved and Mr. Buswell, leaving the college in the care of Julia Bartlett and Abbie Whiting.

There is a pamphlet titled *The Latter Days;with Evidence from The Great Pyramid* which was published in London, England in 1895. This pamphlet states the end of the present era to be December 3, 1910. It also states that July 10, 1882 marks an important event in English history. This event was as unnoticed by the world as had been the beginning of "The Great Step" in January of 1844, but both events mark the inception of great changes in human progress. If that household in Barton had only known it, they were witnessing the travail of the Woman and the birth of this new epoch. Mary Beecher Longyear has recorded some of Arthur Buswell's reminiscences of Mrs. Eddy at this period: *[margin: Event of historical import]*

> Mr. Buswell relates that her great struggle was known to his household, but that she carried it through alone, though they often watched outside her door. After a night of agony she would emerge from her struggle with a radiant face and luminous eyes, and they would hesitate to speak to her for fear of disturbing the peace which enveloped her.

July 10, 1882 probably marked the very greatest depth of despair into which Mrs. Eddy was plunged as she struggled with doubts and agonized over how she could or should fulfil her mission. Only an inkling of this struggle crept into her letter of July 16 to Clara Choate: *[margin: Letter to C. Choate July, 1882]*

Barton, Vt., July 16th.

My darling Student:
I have not forgotten you. Oh no, not until this heart ceases to beat can that be. The services you are rendering to God and man are engraven upon my memory as with the point of a diamond.

265

I am up among the towering heights of this verdant state, green with the leaves of earth and fresh with the fragrance of good will and human kindness. I never found a kindlier people. I am situated as pleasantly as I can be in the absence of the *one true heart* that has been so much to me. O, darling, I never shall master this point of missing him, all the time, but I can try, and am trying as I must—to sever all the chords that bind me to person or things material.

How are you getting on? *Well, of course.* I did not name it to any one whom I should take with me, but dear little Alice Sibley went with me and has hovered round me like a flower of light. She sends much love to you and will inclose a word herself.

The beauties of our trip are familiar to me but Alice was almost wild over them. We will be ready for work when we return after having such a nice vacation. Write me all about the dear cause. This is my birthday, a day of such moment to the race and of *such* a *history* to one. I love to return and the time will soon pass. I dread to return but the days glide by.

Ever lovingly,
M. B. G. E.

"Such a *history* to *one."* Do these few words mean that her history, or the story of her great and noble life was known to no one but herself? That was probably the case at that time, and even at this late date mortals are still endeavoring to usurp Her position as Leader of her cause while diverting the fruits of her great labors to their own selfish ends.

Mrs. Eddy knew that her birthday, July 16, 1821, was a day of moment to the race. But did she know that that year of such import was recorded in stone? Scholars of the "Bible in Stone" measure the "time line" which begins at 4000 B.C. in lunar years and solar years. According to these pyramidologists, Epoch I is 6000 *lunar* years ending in 1821 A.D. Is it surprising that the Woman of the Apocalypse with the moon (matter) under her feet should first appear in that year? From then on the time must be measured in *solar* years.

A few days after writing to Clara Choate Mrs. Eddy answered a letter from Julia Bartlett which had told her of affairs at the college:

Barton, Vermont, July 19th

My darling Student:

Your letter was very welcome and I thank you very much for the good care you take of *your* College. I can't yet feel much interest in anything of earth. I shall try and eventually succeed in rising from the gloom of my irreparable loss but it must take *time*. *Long after* I shall smile and appear happy shall I have to struggle *alone* with my great grief that none shall know, if I can hide it. I think of you at the fort and always as little, or rather great heroes and pray that my coming shall be a joy and not a sorrow to you. I know you will hail it but O! I hope I shall be more useful to you than a *mourner* is apt to be. I shall never forget dear, dear Gilbert. His memory is dearer every day but not so sad I think as when I left home. It is beautiful here. The hills, vales, and lakes are lovely, but this was his native state and *he is not here*. The lady companion is very comforting with her merry manners and kind heart. I long to see you and dear Mrs. W. Will inclose a line to her. Has H. gone? and do you hear from him and what? Are the meetings successful and won't you help dear Mrs. Choate in every way that you can and do yourself no harm? Write soon and often and

I am ever thine—

Lovingly,

M. B. G. E.

Dear Mrs. Whiting was helping Julia Bartlett to care for the college, but she was struggling against the enemy's attacks and passed away a short time later,—another loss on the field of battle.

In Barton, Vermont, the "toiler tireless, all unbeguiled," as Mrs. Eddy had called herself was gaining ground in her struggle with the demons of darkness. In her years of toil for "Truth's new birth" she had had few earth ties. Now she had none. It was as she had said to Mrs. Manly, "God means that I shall rely on Him alone." If her heart had been in her work till now, it was no longer. Her heart, her yearnings, and her life were in Spirit. And in this Life of Spirit she saw and clearly understood her own identity. For many years she had known her mission and devoted herself to it com-

Identity revealed

267

pletely. She had known *what* she was to do. Now for the first time she knew *who* she was. The Woman of the Apocalypse, the Revelator to this age, the woman Jesus had revealed to John on the Isle of Patmos was Mary Baker Eddy,—and *she knew it.*

Mary Baker Eddy had a mission to fulfill, but the total severing of earth ties affected her method considerably. For ten years she had been on the defensive against the attacks of the false prophet and all the lesser luminaries that he had lured into a life of malicious mental malpractice. Now she would take the offensive. For ten years she had worked for Richard Kennedy to heal him of his sins. Now the sinner must learn from his own suffering. From now on her work would be for the sole purpose of establishing Christian Science on the earth. Those who would rally to her standard would have to be a help meet for her Cause or fall by the wayside.

On the twenty-seventh of July she wrote again to Clara Choate:

Barton, Vt., July 27, 1882

My precious girl and faithful Student:
    I was glad to hear from you and hope you will move round the world like a haunting presence doing all the good that I know you are so capable of doing. Hold the Fort, for I am coming. Be wise as a serpent and harmless as the doves that are cooing over my window. I hope my forty days in the wilderness are almost over. But when I shall return depends on circumstances.
    My lecture made a big stir. A Rev. Methodist called on me the next day and talked pretty much all the A.M., and an M.D. talks of studying. I will teach you anew when I return and know I shall have an interesting old head lecturer and healer student again. Alice sends lots of love, Dr. Buswell the kindest regards, and please remember me in love to your husband; and darling Warren, give him a kiss,
Ever as ever,
Your loving Teacher,
Mary B. G. Eddy

Her revelation from God in July of 1882 gave her a courage and strength she had never before possessed, but it did not eliminate the anguish and quavering in her heart. On the twenty-eighth of the month she wrote to James Ackland:

> I thought...I would write you a few lines telling you in brief how I am changed. I see it in the mirror and my heart tells me it every hour. ...But I question my ability to walk over all, only as God gives me aid that I never have had before.

Her trials were far from over, but in meeting them God did give her that aid that she had never had before.

ARTHUR TRUE BUSWELL

CHAPTER XXXVII

A HELPER

*God able is to raise up seed—in thought
and deed—to faithful His.*

Mary Baker Eddy

1882

GILBERT Eddy was irreplaceable. For more than five years he had been by his wife's side in every undertaking from publishing, teaching, and meeting malicious animal magnetism, to domestic chores. No one could fill his shoes. And yet Mrs. Eddy needed a helper who would be always at her side. If the battles thus far had been difficult, what would be encountered in the all-out war which loomed in the pathway ahead?

Her thoughts turned to her three students who had been with her on the mount the previous October,—Gilbert Eddy who was gone; Abbie Whiting who was at the college in Boston; and Calvin A. Frye in Lawrence, Massachusetts. July had scarcely passed when Mr. Frye received a telegram from his teacher requesting him to meet her at Plymouth on her return to Boston. Calvin was there, and he was by her side every day from that time onward.

There is no record of the conversation between Mrs. Eddy and Calvin Frye while on the train that sixth day of August in 1882. Did she reveal to this student the fact of such moment to the race that Mind had so recently revealed to her, i.e., her own identity as the Woman of the Apocalypse? However that may be, outside of God's two witnesses, Jesus of Nazareth and Mary Baker Eddy, the world has not seen such fidelity to duty as was manifested in the devotion of Calvin Frye for the ensuing twenty-eight years.

Christians say the Bible is the word of God. Mrs. Eddy said that God spoke to her through the pages of that book. Her several worn copies read like a diary of her life, for she has penned dates and pertinent passages in the margins. On the day of her return to Boston God spoke to her through the Scriptures in verification of her recent revelation. She penned in her Bible: "August 6th 1882 returned Boston opened to Isaiah 54." These words must have lifted her heart:

Return to Boston August, 1882

> Sing, O barren,...
> Enlarge the place of thy tent,...
> For thou shalt break forth on the right hand
> and on the left,...
> Fear not;...
> For thy Maker is thine husband;...
> For the Lord hath called thee as a woman forsaken
> and grieved in spirit,...
> No weapon that is formed against thee shall
> prosper; and every tongue that shall rise against
> thee in judgment thou shalt condemn. This is the
> heritage of the servants of the Lord, and their
> righteousness is of me, saith the Lord.

Hanover P. Smith
Born deaf and dumb; healed by
Mrs. Eddy in 1880

CHAPTER XXXVIII

BACK IN BOSTON

Enlarge the place of thy tent, and let them stretch forth
the curtains of thine habitations; spare not, lengthen thy
cords, and strengthen thy stakes.

Isaiah

1882

BACK in Boston Mrs. Eddy was quick to implement the words she had written to Clara Choate. Both Choates, Clara and George, together with Alice Sibley, Mrs. Sarah H. Crosse, and Rev. Charles Barbour, were in a class that began on the sixteenth of August.

From the moment of Mrs. Eddy's return the college became a beehive of activity. There were soon Sunday services and weekday parlor talks open to the public, plus meetings for the students. In addition to the Leader's unceasing activities which included another class in October, the several students who resided at the college were also practising and receiving patients there.

Mrs. Eddy's offensive approach to the malicious mesmerism that had hounded her every footstep since 1871 is evident in the minutes of a meeting of the Christian Scientist Association on the eleventh of October:

> The subject of nothingness, commonly called mesmerism, was approached but was thought to be unworthy of consideration. The president, Mrs. Eddy, thought there was a great excess of talk about the error, she said "all there is to mesmerism is what we make of it."

As her good work increased and spread, the attacks from malicious minds increased and were devastating. But the re-

272

ducing of malicious animal magnetism to its native nothingness
continued and increased with each new onslaught.

Mrs. Eddy made herself readily available to students and
newcomers alike. One of the newcomers was Janet Colman who
was a member of the class of fourteen that Mrs. Reminiscences
Eddy held in January of 1883. Mrs. Colman's   of Janet
recollections of the Leader at that time state: Colman

> I never shall forget my first experience when my mother
> and myself called upon her. After talking with her for a while,
> I said I would like to study with you, and then the wondrous
> purity of the one before me came to my thought, and I added,
> if I am good enough. Such a look as came into her face, and
> she answered that for my answer, she would teach me. I never
> had been in such an atmosphere of thought in my life before.
> I felt my own shortcomings. It was unfolded to me a glimmer
> of the divine inspiration which encircled her, and this is what
> gave me the blessed privilege of becoming her student,
> which I never have regretted. I can truthfully say, that the
> light that shone into my thought has never left me, and I
> never doubted our Leader's inspiration or her wisdom in
> guiding our Cause. Such wisdom is not of this world.

The purity which Janet Colman felt in Mrs. Eddy's presence
was the most essential quality for successful healing and the
most difficult for students to attain. And why?   Statement
Because it required watching every single thought   signed
and rejecting from consciousness every suggestion   January, 1883
that was less than perfection. To this end of watching, the three
students at the college who were accomplishing most for the
movement, Julia Bartlett, Arthur Buswell, and Calvin Frye,
signed their names on the twenty-third of January to the
following statement:

> We the undersigned hereby promise to keep a close guard
> on our thought and action and never by word or deed know-
> ingly influence a resident of this College, or anyone, to a
> wrong result.

In 1883 Mrs. Eddy was in her sixty-second year which was
considered elderly in the nineteenth century, but those who

knew her then said she had the youthful appearance of a woman in her thirties or early forties. Julia Bartlett wrote:

> I can see her now as she looked at this time,—her face radiant with that spiritual beauty that never could be put on canvas. Her light brown hair which was naturally curly was arranged becomingly. Her eyes had a wonderful spiritual expression, and she had the fair, delicate complexion of youth with often a pink color in her cheeks...

Mrs. Eddy had been consciously and scientifically purifying her consciousness for nearly twenty years. The pure in heart shall see God, and every day she was seeing more and more of the light of reality,—of scientific being. She also was endeavoring to impart this light to her students as Miss Bartlett recorded:

> Sometimes she would show us how it would be with us and others when farther advanced in our understanding of Truth. ...
>
> One time when two or three of us were with her she began to talk to us in an unusual way, and I listened to her every word lest I should lose any. It was a wonderful, beautiful glimpse of the real that she was unfolding to us until one of the students present questioned her: then she stopped and said, "O, you can't understand me." I said "Do, please, go on. We will try." She replied, "But you can't."

"If I have told you earthly things, and ye believe not, how shall ye believe, if I tell you of heavenly things?" Jesus' words were equally applicable to Mrs. Eddy's experience. For years she had been proving by demonstration that mind alone affects the body, but students could not let go of general belief sufficiently to see that this was true in every aspect of experience. Nor could they believe when she would tell them of earthly things to prove her point. This is illustrated by one of Mrs. Eddy's earlier experiments.

Cleanliness had always been of utmost importance to Mrs. Eddy. In an era when all clean people bathed regularly once a week, she had bathed daily. After discovering Science and learning that cleanliness was mental not physical, she used this

as one area of experimentation to prove the truth of her discovery. In later years she told the following to Calvin Frye who
recorded it January 25, 1890:

> From daily baths she entirely stopped bathing and never
> bathed for seven years. One of her students who roomed with
> her, one night said upon retiring, "Oh, Mrs. Glover, how
> sweet you smell," to which she replied, "Why, I use no
> cologne." "No, I don't mean that," was the reply, "but how
> sweet and clean your person is." Mrs. Glover said, "Well, now
> I will tell you. I have not bathed for seven years." "Oh, don't
> tell any one that," was the reply, "for if you do, people will
> think you the dirtiest person that ever lived."

Her own students could not apply the Science they were
studying; so she left the paragraph in Science and Health regarding "the daily ablutions of an infant" almost unchanged
from the first edition to the last. In 1883 she wrote in a sermon,
"The cool bath may refresh the body...and so satisfy man's
belief; but it cannot purify his mind, or meet the demands of
Love. It is the baptismal of Spirit that 'washes our robes and
makes them white in the blood of the Lamb;' that bathes us in
the life of Truth and the truth of Life."

If they could not comprehend the earthly things, how could
they understand the heavenly? Julia Bartlett's record is not
surprising:

> In later years, when I talked with Mrs. Eddy, she said no
> one knew how much was revealed to her every day, but there
> was no one to whom she could talk it; they could not under-
> stand, not even her most advanced students...She was so
> far above the world she was utterly alone in it, and some-
> times felt that loneliness and would express the desire for the
> time to come when she could voice the Truth she saw.

She gave the students just as much as they could take, but
she knew that it would be future generations that would
comprehend her teachings and her life. She   Vision of
must now so educate her students spiritually   January
that they were able to preserve and pass on to   1883
future generations that which they themselves did not under-

275

stand as well as to practise and perpetuate that which they did. The growth from their own practice would increase their understanding more than aught else could. The task of educating mortal mind (which is unconscious of itself) out of itself is full of perils. Did her vision of January, 1883 depict the task before her?

> VISION OF JANUARY, 1883: A bridge over unconscious mind with weak rail which protected from running off the bridge—fear of it—steeds were unmanageable—team struck against the rail—it bent and she leaped out of the team and the others followed and got on the bridge.
> Next saw a poor bridge full of holes which she avoids in passing over and showed them how to pass over safely.
> Afterward was out in the stream of mortal mind alone and went to the very verge of a cataract and was going over but climbed up again safely by catching hold of the water.

Mrs. Eddy could avoid the holes in the bridge over unconscious mind and show her students how to pass over safely, but few followed her example and instructions. When there was greatest danger, she *alone* was resisting the current of mortal mind. Alone, but not alone, for God was ever with her guiding her footsteps,—even to catching hold of the very water (mental activity) that was endeavoring to destroy her, thus enabling her to climb up safely. The serpent becomes a staff when it is handled.

CHAPTER XXXIX

A GHOST FROM THE PAST

O, blessed daughter of Zion, I am with thee. And none shall take my words out of thy lips. ...I will not suffer another messenger to go before thee.

Revelation of Mary Baker Eddy

1883

IT seemed that the malpractitioners were never inactive. While they were plotting new attacks early in 1883 Mrs. Eddy was warned in a vision of the coming storm.

Nearly two decades earlier Mrs. Eddy, then Patterson, had met Miss Emma Ware in Portland, Maine. Emma and her sister had both been devoted to Dr. Quimby and had acted as amanuenses assisting with syntax and orthography. Following his death his writings had been left in their care. Now at three o'clock on the morning of February 7, Miss Ware appeared to Mrs. Eddy in a vision, followed therein by Arens in the form of a gorilla:

Vision of February 7 1883

WEDNESDAY MORN, 3 O'CLOCK: Emma Ware. Saw a woman in a crowd whispering and when she came near me seemed to be friendly but was two-faced. Seemed to be influencing the people against me. Afterward saw a gorilla (Arens) who came to me as I was lying down and when I tried to get up he would push me down again and my limbs seemed bound that I could not stir; when I tried to speak he would put his huge paw over my mouth and stop me.

Since Kennedy's first reversal of metaphysical science, he had endeavored to discredit his teacher by attributing her discovery to Quimby. Eventually Mrs. Eddy learned this, even

277

though Kennedy was always clandestine, remaining in the background as he had in the conspiracy-to-murder plot. She suspected that he might have contacted the Ware sisters (one of whom had since married and moved to Scotland) in the summer of 1871 when he "took a fit to go to Portland." When George Choate was in that city practising Christian Science in March of 1880, his teacher wrote him regarding Emma Ware:

> get her that was E.W. (Now in Scotland) word to look out for K's mesmeric control that he will try on her to make her yield to his wishes; and another measure that he will take, and that is to get it through a third party into his hands.

Probably "it" was the Quimby manuscript,—the collection of Quimby's writings many of which were in Mrs. Patterson's handwriting and some of which were of Mrs. Patterson's composition either partially or totally. The danger she had foreseen in 1880 did transpire at a later date, causing Mrs. Eddy to write:

> Quotations have been published, purporting to be Dr. Quimby's own words, which were written while I was his patient in Portland and holding conversations with him on my views of mental therapeutics. Some words in those quotations certainly read like the words I said to him, and which I, at his request, had added to his copy when I corrected it.

Several students had been influenced by Kennedy to stir up Quimby's ashes, but little had come of it prior to 1882. Sometime in that year Julius Dresser entered the scene and fanned the flames of Arens' hatred. In the fall of 1882 Arens had written to Emma Ware. Her response of October 2 read in part:

> I remember Mrs. Patterson as a patient of Dr. Quimby and as a bright clever lady who took an interest in his theory. . . . I devoted myself to his instruction as long as he lived, but I never learned the art of healing.

Dresser and his wife came to Boston from the West because of the success of Christian Science, but instead of seeking out their former friend they went to her enemy, the mental murderer, Edward J. Arens. They studied with Arens, moved into his house, and opened offices there as practitioners of his version of Christian Science. On the eighth of February a lengthy letter by Dresser appeared in the *Boston Post* signed A.O. [Arens and Others?] which gave great praise to Quimby and criticism of "some parties healing through a mental method, which they claim to have discovered."

The third edition of Science and Health stated, "The mist that went up from the ground *alias* the darkness of supposition, would take the explanation of God and man out   Vision of of the hands of science and give it to a material   February 12 sense." This was the danger facing the Reve-   1883 lator,—the attempt to take the revelation away from God and credit it to a mortal man. Probably Mrs. Eddy's vision of a few days later was a reminder that Richard Kennedy was still the instigator of all the plots against her:

> VISION OF FEBRUARY 12: Saw Kennedy in prosperity surrounded by his friends and myself a mere skeleton wasted with consumption, and said he, "You have done this;" and he and his friends laughed at me.

Two days later Mrs. Eddy introduced the subject of this latest attack on her discovery to the Christian Scientist Associ- ation endeavoring to warn them of the coming   Minutes storm. Their minutes of February 14 read: February 14   1883

> There is a tidal wave coming. It is to be an attempt to wrest from me the fact of the origin of Christian Science and place it upon a mesmeric basis, giving to a former mesmerist the honor, thus endeavoring to get onto a Christian platform. But this tidal wave need not harm us, although it is an awful re- sponsibility to me. I give a great deal of time in the long hours of the night to study my duty, and how to carry it out.

A few days later Mrs. Eddy answered Dresser's letter in the columns of the *Boston Post*. This was followed by a second letter on each side. Midst the controversy her students glided on serenely, oblivious of the storm clouds, as is seen in Janet Colman's recollection of this period:

> We were very fortunate those who lived here in Boston,

when I first studied. Our beloved Leader met with us once a
week in a students' meeting, we would bring up our cases
and she would show us how to treat them; she lectured and
preached to us. She mothered us so kindly. ... It was such a
wonder to us at the lectures she gave, to see the learned men
of all denominations, Catholic and all, ply her with questions
and I heard two priests say after talking with her for a long
time, that they had never met her equal; they could not get
the best of her. When she was asked a question from the
Bible, no matter where it was, she would lift up her eyes for
a moment, and the answer would come as clear and true,
and those who had the slightest understanding of Truth,
would understand it.

Her days were given to her students and numerous activities
of the Cause, but the Leader's thoughts in the long hours of the
night dwelt upon her responsibility for protecting the spiritual
origin of the Science of Man.

She knew now what she had not known in the early days of
her practice; that is, that the metaphysical system which she
had attributed to Quimby was in reality a combination of his
ideas with her own. The line of demarcation came in February,
1866, when the Christ-consciousness raised her from her death-
bed. The magnitude of that event, which had not been seen at
the time, grew clearer with every upward step.

Mary's work truly began, not in Warren in 1864, but where
Jesus' left off. "His three days' work in the sepulchure set the
seal of eternity on time. He proved Life to be deathless and
Love to be the master of hate." He said to Mary, the first to
see him, "Touch me not, for I am not yet ascended to my
Father."

His most important instructions came after his resurrection,
but his disciples were able to follow him but a short distance
(to comprehend but little), and he was soon out of their sight.
In 1866 Mary Patterson had been ready to follow the Christ
higher and to lead the thought of the world above its former
self-imposed limitations, for she, too, had experienced resurrection. In her words:

> The accident occurred in the evening, on our way to a
> temperance meeting, and we were taken to our home on a bed

the next morning, and rose from it on the third day...

A dear old lady asked me, "How is it that you were restored to us? Has Christ come again on earth?"

"Christ never left," I replied; "Christ is Truth, and Truth is always here,—the impersonal Saviour."

Then another person, more material, met me, and I said, in the words of my Master, "Touch me not." I shuddered at her material approach; then my heart went out to God, and I found the open door from this sepulchure of matter.

In the seventeen years since her great awakening much had transpired. The sins of Richard Kennedy had caused her to see that Quimby's methods were really mesmerism practised from a humanitarian standpoint. Mesmerism does not emanate from the science of being, and it cannot be practised scientifically. Everything scientific is based upon one absolute Principle and is demonstrable, as in mathematics. Mesmerism, like witchcraft, is a denial of one absolute Principle with the supposition that everything can be reversed. Richard Kennedy's conscious, wicked reversal of the Discoverer's teachings had forced her to eliminate every vestige of Quimby's theory and methods from her Science. Now the very element that she had had to purge from her teachings was coming back to calm Christian Science as its own.

Mesmerism or hypnotism seems to heal the sick, but such healing is subject to relapse because the basis of these isms is duality. Quimby had not learned this and was endeavoring to do that which many hypnotists are attempting today;—i.e., to separate the good practice from the evil practice (the constructive from the destructive), and to apply the good only.

Those who are honestly endeavoring to practise white magic and to repudiate black magic will learn that the two are one and cannot be separated, because the basis of ancient and modern witchcraft or necromancy, alias mesmerism and hypnotism, is duality. Duality is the belief in two powers, opposite and equal and forever warring.

In her association with Quimby Mrs. Eddy had learned somewhat of the power of the human mind to accomplish good. From her experience with Richard Kennedy she had learned of the human mind's power to accomplish evil. She had suffered greatly from Kennedy's attacks and reversal of her teachings. Each severe experience had turned her to the reality of one power only and planted her feet more firmly upon the one Principle of existence. Every sharp attack had caused her to cast herself unreservedly upon the Omnipotence of Good with an ensuing elevation into a diviner atmosphere where human will cannot enter and could not harm her.

In her ignorance Mary Patterson had told Dr. Quimby that the science of mind was back of his treatment. In her Reminiscences she wrote:

> In his conversations with me and in his scribblings, the word science was not used at all, till one day I declared to him that back of his magnetic treatment and manipulation of patients, there was a science, and it was the science of mind...

She had believed this at the time, but she had since learned better. The human mind, good or bad, has no more bearing on the Science of Mind than the Ptolemaic theory that the earth was the center of the universe had on the science of astronomy. Copernicus, the Father of Modern Astronomy, was able to refute the latter belief. The refutation of the former rested on the shoulders of the Mother of Christian Science.

The world which had resisted Copernicus' discovery of astronomical law and order was now resisting her discovery of ontological law and order. Even her own students were healing more by faith than understanding. If they could review her experiences as she was now doing, they could not be misled by all the attacks against her and the attempts to obscure the Science of Man. She should have kept a record of her experiences and discoveries for a posterity which would have greater comprehension after her work had leavened the thought. She should have kept a journal of the history of Christian Science; but that history was still in the making. She would begin the record now.

CHAPTER XL

JOURNAL OF CHRISTIAN SCIENCE

Christian Science and Christian Scientists will, MUST, have a history.

Mary Baker Eddy

1883

THE Journal Mrs. Eddy envisioned in 1883 was to be more than a diary record of her thoughts and experiences. She would edit a bi-monthly newspaper for the promotion and extension of Christian Science as well as for recording its history. On the first of March Arthur Buswell was appointed to handle the advertising; Sarah H. Crosse was to be Mrs. Eddy's assistant.

Before the first issue was published, however, business of another nature must be taken care of. A year had elapsed since she and Gilbert had sojourned in Washington, Suit against D.C., largely for the purpose of studying the Arens copyright laws for the protection of Science and April, 1883 Health. That which they had planned to do together, she must now do alone; namely, restrain Arens in his plagiarism of her writings. Accordingly, on the sixth of April a bill of complaint was filed requesting an injunction against Arens to restrain him from publishing and circulating his pamphlet.

Eight days later all the students at the college were delighted to see the:

JOURNAL OF CHRISTIAN SCIENCE.

An Independent Family Paper, to Promote Health and Morals.

———•———

" For the weapons of our warfare are not carnal, but mighty through God, to the pulling down of strongholds."

VOL. I. { CHRISTIAN SCIENTISTS' PUBLISHING CO }   BOSTON, APRIL 14, 1883.   { TERMS $1.00 PER ANNUM. Postpaid, Single Copies, 17c. } No. 1.

The first article entitled "Prospectus" ended with the following paragraph:

> Dear reader, the purpose of our paper is the desire of our heart, namely, to bring to many a household hearth health, happiness and increased power to be good and to do good. To brighten so pure a hope will be to aid our prospect of fulfilling it, through your kindly patronage of the *Journal of Christian Science,* of which this is our first issue, and for which we are needing funds to establish its permanent publications.
>
> Mary B. Glover Eddy.

"A Case of Faith Cure" on page 2 was an item from *Medical News* telling of Sir Humphrey Davy's healing a paralytic patient by merely taking his temperature with a thermometer.

A very important column entitled "Answers to Questions" began in this first issue. Mrs. Eddy wrote not only the answers, but most of the copy for all eight pages. She drew frequently from her previous writings, both published and unpublished in these early issues, and her notebooks were a wonderful source. From there came the poem on page 3 which had been written August 1, 1882 when she was in Barton, Vermont after Gilbert's death. The circumstances enhance its meaning:

THE OAK ON THE SUMMIT

Ah! solemn mountain at whose feet I stand,
Clouds do adorn thy brow, skies clasp thy hand:
Nature and God in Harmony profound,
With peaceful presence have begirt thee round.

And thou majestic oak, from yon high place
Guard'st thou the earth, asleep in night's embrace?
Or from thy lofty summit, pouring down
Thy sheltering shade, her noonday glories crown?

Whate'er thy mission mountain sentinel,
O'er my lone heart thou hast a magic spell;
A lesson grave, of life, thou teachest me—
I love the Hebrew figure of a tree.

Faithful and patient be my years as thine;
As strong to wrestle with the storms of time;
As deeply rooted in a soil of love:
As grandly rising to the heavens above.

An article on page 5 titled "Timely Thoughts" bore the initials H.P.S.,—probably Hanover P. Smith. The last page and one-third were devoted to notices, advertisements, and "Christian Scientists' Professional Cards," the latter being those of Hanover P. Smith, Arthur T. Buswell, Julia Bartlett, Clara Choate, Janet T. Colman, Sarah H. Crosse, and seven others.

An inkling of Mrs. Eddy's busy days can be gleaned from a perusal of the advertisements. Her professional card reads: "Professor of Obstetrics, Metaphysics and Christian Science, Receives calls Mondays and Fridays from 3 to 5 P.M." An advertisement for the Massachusetts Metaphysical College said, "Students can enter at any time excepting the last week in June, the month of July, or the first week of August. Address for further particulars, Mrs. M. B. Glover Eddy, Pres't." A notice of Meetings and Lectures for The Church of Christ extended a cordial welcome to strangers to hear addresses by the pastor, Mary B. G. Eddy, every Sunday at 3 o'clock. Another notice announced free public lectures every Thursday at 7:30 P.M. "followed by discussion and practical explanation of Christian Science." A further notice stated that the Christian Scientist Association met on alternate Wednesdays at 3 P.M.

In addition to all of the labor for the college, plus the founding, editing, and publishing of the *Journal*, the Leader was revising Science and Health midst the work of the litigation with Arens. The lawsuit weighed heavily upon her. She had known from the first that Arens was a sinner, but so were all her other students to a greater or lesser degree. Like Jesus, she was not come to call the righteous, but sinners to repentance. Without repentance, however, sin increases and thought grows more material, sensual, and devious.

In the second issue of the *Journal* Mrs. Eddy wrote in a sermon, "The People's God," "Because God is spirit our thoughts must spiritualize to approach Him, and our methods grow more spiritual to accord with our thoughts." This sermon, which she also published in pamphlet form, began:

> Every step of progress is a step more spiritual. The great element of reform is not born of human wisdom:...The footsteps of thought, as they pass from the sensual side of existence to the reality and Soul of all things, are slow, portending a long night to the traveller; but the guardians of this night are the angels of His presence...

She was speaking of her own footsteps spiritward, and was confronted with the malicious claim that her great life work had been born of the human wisdom of Phineas P. Quimby. Arens had rushed a new edition of his pamphlet into print with an altered title and the following revision in the preface:

> In a former pamphlet similar in some respects to this one...I gave the credit of authorship of some thoughts which I took from another work to the wrong party. Having been informed since that time...that Dr. P. P. Quimby, of Portland, Me., was the author and originator of those thoughts, I transfer the credit to him.

In his defence filed in the Circuit Court in June, Arens alleged that Mrs. Eddy's works were not original but had been copied from Quimby's manuscripts. When the case came up in July, it was carried over to the fall term.

In the third edition of Science and Health Mrs. Eddy had written, "For the last ten years we have had no rest, and with unremitting toil have not had sufficient time to do the good we desired." The ensuing two years had presented even greater difficulties making twelve years of unremitting toil without rest. In August the tired Leader wrote to her friend Col. Smith in Washington:

> I flee to you, but my poor tired womanhood shuns the pity of it all. If only the warfare was open, and I had one strong nature like dear Gilbert's or your own to share my cares and burdens I could endure it better. As it is, I have all this superstructure of Christian Science resting on my shoulders and no moment yet of rest. I hope it all will not again go crashing down over my head and ears if I let go for a brief space, for if it does I shall not rebuild again at the awful cost

of the past two years.

About this time a Mr. George B. Charles journeyed to Boston. A brisk market for Science and Health had developed in the mid-west centering in Chicago, and he had come from that city for the purpose of studying Christian Science. But, Alas! Instead of going to the Massachusetts Metaphysical College, he went to A. J. Arens.

But the Leader's years of toil and travail were not to continue unabated. Perhaps twelve years were a fulfilment. However that may be, events were soon to take a turn in her favor.

MARY BAKER EDDY
Taken about 1883.

CHAPTER XLI

ARENS ARRESTED

Whoever uses his developed mental powers like an escaped felon to commit fresh atrocities as opportunity occurs, is never safe. God will arrest him.

Mary Baker Eddy

1883

S INCE the publication of the third edition in 1881, Science and Health had gone through two additional printings, the
Sixth edition fourth and fifth editions. The ensuing two years
Science and Health had extracted an "awful cost" in Mrs. Eddy's
September, 1883 experience, but they had also seen the sale of nearly three thousand copies of the textbook. A very ready market had developed for the new edition, the sixth edition, revised, which was published September 21.

Gilbert Eddy's foreword "To The Public" was dropped from the new revision. The chapter on "Demonology" was reduced
Key to from forty-six to thirteen pages, but of more im-
Scriptures portance was the addition. Mrs. Eddy had planned to add a "Key to the Scriptures" to her book nearly seven years earlier, but constant harassment by malicious mental malpractitioners had not allowed her "sufficient time to do the good [she] desired." The "Key" made its first appearance in the sixth edition as a dictionary of spiritual definitions. Following the words, "if you substitute the spiritual signification of a term for its material definition, or the bare word, it will elucidate the meaning of the inspired writer," was a twenty-three page glossary of Scriptural terms.

Many of the spiritual definitions are identical to those in her latest revisions, but not all. An entire page is given to the

definition of *Atonement;* three pages to the word *Devil;* a page
to *Matter;* and two pages to *Mind.*

On the twenty-fourth of September, just three days after the
sixth edition was off the press, the lawsuit with Arens was
decided in Mrs. Eddy's favor. With characteristic   Decision
aggressiveness Arens issued a statement to the   against Arens
Boston Globe declaring "that there had been no   September, 1883
decision whatever, and the suit was decided by an agreement
signed by the respective counsel."

This caused Mrs. Eddy to publish a detailed account of the
proceedings in the next issue of her *Journal* which was published October 6. The court's decree stated in effect that the
complainant's copyrights were valid, that the defendant had infringed them, that a perpetual injunction be issued against his
activities, and that he must pay the costs of the suit.

The injunction served upon Arens on the fourth of October
carried a penalty of ten thousand dollars for failure to comply.
The *Journal* went on to state:

> On Friday, October 5th. 1883—fitting day, one usually
> adopted for the execution of criminals,—the infringing books,
> to the number of (3800) thirty-eight hundred, or thereabouts,
> were put under the edge of the knife, and their unlawful
> existence destroyed.

Surely a sense of relief and rejoicing accompanied this legal
victory. At last the earth was helping the woman.   Vision
A vision a few days later held even greater   October 10
encouragement: 1883

> VISION OF OCTOBER 10, 1883—WEDNESDAY
> MORN: In a house in which there was a large number of my
> books stored and was a great smoke and cry of fire but I had
> no fear.

On the fifteenth of April in 1891 the house burned where
Science and Health lay on the table. The covers burned off,
but not one word was disfigured or destroyed when the book
was saved. Her response to the student concerned reveals how
deeply this moved the Leader:

> You may not learn through language my feelings when I

took that sacred Book rescued by the Divine hand from devouring flames, and through it saw the meaning of this rescue
in the type before me.

I have received presents from my beloved students that I
prize beyond all things that I ever before possessed. But dear
friend, your gift to me of my last revised *Science and Health*
saved from the fire that consumed all around it, but kindled
not on its sacred pages, is a gift dearer to me than aught else
this earth contains.

The vision of October 10 was encouraging, but another on
the following morning was a reminder that malicious mesmerism
Vision through Kennedy and Arens was still at work
October 11 against her. This vision included her faithful
1883 secretary and recorder of many of her visions,
Calvin Frye:

VISION OF OCTOBER 11—THURSDAY MORN:
Thought K—and A—were telling me how sick I was and growing old; told me to look in the glass and see how old and sick
I looked, and that I couldn't go out for the exposure would
give me a cold, and Frye was with me and he said, "How
fortunate that you can hear their talk, for you aren't afraid
of them now." They tried to prevent her from telling me of it
by loss of memory and made a law that if she told me she'd
suffer.

Arens had not ceased his wicked mental practice, but his
effectiveness against the Revelator was almost over. Without
the Truth he had pirated to lean upon, his spurious teaching of
Christian Science was greatly curtailed, and his threat to its
progress soon to be eliminated. If George Quimby had produced his father's manuscripts at Arens' trial, that issue, too,
would have been settled, but the warfare against the Revelator
was never out in the open. The calumniator worked in secrecy,
because his only power against her was in allegations and insinuations. In an effort to uncover whatever step he might be
plotting next Mrs. Eddy wrote for the December 1 *Journal,*
"Answer A Fool According to His Folly." A part of the three
column article reads:

Since we introduced our system of Metaphysical Healing

or Christian Science, some eighteen years ago, and taught ethics to students, we have been pursued by the envy, instead of gratitude, of those whom we have lifted above themselves. ...After years of this folly, certain ones are still at it, with fresh courage, over a new fabrication. This is it, that Mrs. Eddy is not the author of what she thinks, writes and does; but one Dr. Quimby is. ...

The second student we taught...was Richard Kennedy ...he went into court and swore to the effect that he had studied mental science with us, but had learned nothing.... He exhibited [Mrs. Eddy's] manuscripts in court to ridicule them...But since our system of healing has been fairly introduced and is in demand, he is reported as protesting with the same freedom that we are not the author of our works, but the said Quimby was. Now our manuscripts that he had held up for scorn are put on exhibition, and as somebody else's...We gave him when a student over three hundred pages of our manuscripts; and no matter how much he denies it, he knew when we wrote them. For years before we had our works published, we distributed our manuscripts to students and left written copies of our own works with the said Dr. Quimby. Where are they at this transmigration period?

Julius Dresser had stated in his letter to the newspaper that interested parties could examine Quimby's writings at his address in Boston for proof that Quimby was the originator of Christian Science. Were these some of the three hundred pages she had given to Richard Kennedy? Her article continues:

Another of our defamers, E. J. Arens, has recently been enjoined by the U.S. Circuit Court for printing our works... To our Bill of Complaint he replied, under oath, that he had not infringed our copyright; for the original manuscripts were the said Quimby's. The case was brought to court. Here the ringleaders had a chance to come out manfully and establish their claims, had they not been false; but because they were, not a single testimony could the defendant raise in defence of his barefaced falsehood, and Messrs. Kennedy and Dresser skulked, were modestly missing. ... these small animals are still gnawing in the dark at a woman's reputation, telling strangers who enter our city their falsehoods, and holding on

291

exhibition at one Mr. Julius Dresser's in Boston...certain writings that read like ours,—but he declares they are the said Dr. Quimby's. ...the son of that old gentleman says, over his own signature, that he has in Belfast, and that is not Boston, all of his father's writings. Query: Why were not those manuscripts brought forward in court? ...The truth was that they had no evidence that they dared bring legally.

To have produced either Quimby's writings or Mrs. Eddy's early writings, so liberally given to both Quimby and Kennedy and now being attributed to Quimby, for court examination would have greatly aided the Discoverer and been a death blow to Kennedy's lies. In earlier years both George Quimby and Emma Ware had been friendly with, and appreciative of, Mrs. Patterson. They would no more have denounced her activities than she would have repudiated Quimby's work had it not been for the wicked malpractice of Richard Kennedy. But under the influence of his malicious mesmerism they had grown hostile and now worked according to his silent bidding. Instead of bringing the disputed writings out into the open for scrutiny, they spent all their years in secreting and altering them, thus implementing the design of the false prophet to cast a doubt upon the background and the integrity of the Revelator to this Age. To this day some are influenced erroneously by Kennedy's dark plot, and even among serious students there are few with a clear understanding of the Quimby controversy.

CHAPTER XLII

WONDER OF
THE WESTERN HEMISPHERE

Chicago is the wonder of the western hemisphere.

Mary Baker Eddy

1883

IN 1882 Bradford Sherman was visiting in Boston where he witnessed a very impressive healing in Christian Science. He obtained a copy of Science and Health and began its study after returning home to Chicago. By the spring of 1883 he and his wife and their son Roger were all active practitioners of Christian Science healing in Chicago. They were wonderfully successful and overwhelmed with patients, so they appealed to a Science friend in Boston, Mrs. Caroline D. Noyes, to come to Chicago and join them in this work. Mrs. Noyes arrived in July of 1883 and was soon as busy as they. She had heard Mrs. Eddy lecture twice, but all these Chicago healers had learned to heal from the textbook alone. None had had class instruction.

Interest grew and spread rapidly as they healed and taught and sold copies of Science and Health. A large, eager, receptive audience developed in Chicago and environs which was ready to drink in any word from Boston. Mrs. Eddy chose Clara Choate to go to Chicago to teach a class because of her experience and speaking ability, but while that young woman was vacillating between her Leader's request and malicious suggestions, George Charles returned from studying "Christian Science" in Boston and permeated the area with Arens' mixture of metaphysics and mesmerism together with his wicked lies about the Discoverer.

The situation was improved somewhat by the arrival of
Caroline Noyes' friend, Miss Ellen Brown, who had recently
studied with Mrs. Eddy, but the "West" was still in need of
correct teaching. In her correspondence with Clara Choate Mrs.
Eddy wrote, "Now do not sell your tickets, . . .*wait* until I say
again go."

Mrs. Eddy was ever God's minuteman, ready to follow a
direction immediately, or to wait as the case might be. Her
timing was God's timing, and her students must
learn the same obedience. A vision early in
December seemed to be an omen for good.

Vision
December 9
1883

VISION OF DECEMBER 9—SUNDAY MORN: She saw
a river and in the river there seemed to be a black fish that
swam to where she was and came out of the water and came
and laid across her lap. There were a number of the students
around her and she turned to them and called their attention
to the fish and told them that it was a sign of good luck.

Capable, active students often caused the Leader more
problems than did the malpractitioners, because of their failure
to follow her lead and instructions. In fact, all of the students
seemed more concerned with the mental malpractice of other
students than with their own spiritual progress and regener-
ation. Clara Choate was young, eager, and successful in her
work, but rather than following her Leader's request she accepted the suggestion that the other students were working
against her and wanted her out of Boston. Early in December
Mrs. Eddy wrote to Clara:

> . . .no one here in this house has taken you up mentally or
> has any care one way or another about your going West. . . .I
> see what your fits and starts will end in. Christianity is fixed.
> Before you ever heard of Christian Science I had been com-
> missioned of God to lead his children out of the darkness of
> today. You never can do this until your life is changed as you
> well know.

But Mrs. Choate was unconvinced. In the middle of that
night she wrote Mrs. Eddy that she could feel the mental
pressure of the students trying to force her out of Boston and

that she definitely would not go to Chicago. Mrs. Eddy answered immediately:

> The battle of the demons, they think, has been fought and you are *conquered* because you rose up from their night's campaign resolved to do just what they told you. Now listen to me, the best friend you have on Earth, take back the resolve they made you form and go to *Chicago and Milwaukee*. Say as Luther said, "if there were as many devils between here and Worms as tiles on my house I would go."
>
> Will you do it? If you will not hear God's voice speaking through me they will conquer you and kill you just as they did Gilbert. *I know it.*

If Mrs. Choate had been as quick to obey God's voice as was her Leader, she might have been saved from her own indiscretions; but she did not go West and events soon took a turn for the worse in her affairs. In Milwaukee, however, there was a turn for the better.

In that metropolis Dr. Silas J. Sawyer had a flourishing dental practice, but a much greater interest in the Christian Science he had learned from the Shermans and from his own study of Science and Health. As the confusion of Arens' teaching spread throughout the community Dr. Sawyer and his wife contacted Mrs. Eddy in Boston who encouraged them to attend a course at the college which was to begin December 27.

An article in the *Journal* for February 2, 1884 (the first issue following the course) could very well have been written by Dr. Sawyer. It was signed, "A New Year's Student, Boston, Mass., Jan. 10, 1884," and read as follows:

> To the Readers of "Science and Health" and the "Journal of Christian Science"
>
> Dear Friends,—Time and again I have read the records of your success in applying the Truth you have gathered from these two sources, the book and the journal...
>
> But do you ever suspect what you miss of the *spirit* of that Word by not listening to it as it falls directly from the lips of its living and only interpreter, Mrs. Mary Eddy, the author of "Science and Health," and the editor of this journal?"
>
> The Science of God! ...

Only one of all the earth hath mastered it, and only one of all the earth can teach it.

Do you read over and over again a page of that deep work "Science and Health," following with eager wonder its clear close reasoning, and then acknowledge that you do not *understand* it?

But with her modulated, eloquent voice, her deep blue eyes, lighted by the inspiration of the subject, its interpreter would take you step by step from source to consummation, till with clasped hands and streaming eyes, as understanding dawned upon you, you would cry, "My Lord and my God!"

How do I know? I know by experience. ...some things I understand by reading the letter of their law: but the Science of God—the Science of Christianity,—is not one of them, and I have never yet met one who, by the most careful study of her books, had the *beginning* even of the wisdom that shineth in the faces and accompanieth the workings of her personally taught students. If you are seeking Truth go where it is taught —to the fountain head—to "the seed of the woman" which, in these latter days, is bruising the head of the wily serpent error, and bringing Love and Good home to the nations.

Before the end of February Mrs. Eddy was teaching a much larger class than she had had for many years. In the student body was a contingent from Chicago including the three Shermans and Mrs. Noyes. When the Teacher met Gideon Palmer Noyes, she told him she felt he would make a good healer and should enter the class with his wife. Mr. Noyes did not enter for he had just engaged in business in Chicago and did not feel free to drop it so suddenly. But he returned for instruction at a later date and became a very successful healer.

Chicago was saved from the enemy's slander, but it was unsatisfied. The clamor for teaching increased. As Mrs. Eddy considered all of her students, no one was qualified for the task. She finally made the decision to go herself.

CHAPTER XLIII

JULIA BARTLETT, MISSIONARY

That curative mission, which presents the Saviour in a clearer light than mere words can possibly do, cannot be left out of Christianity...

Mary Baker Eddy

1884

A LL the days at the college were so crowded with activity that much transpired before Mrs. Eddy's departure for Chicago. An unhappy event included Clara Choate.

Mrs. Choate had always roused the antagonism of other students, though some of it may have been envy because of her success and popularity. As 1883 drew to a close the situation had developed to almost solid opposition against her. Finally on the fifth of January Mrs. Eddy wrote to Mrs. Choate:

> This is my candid conclusion—that because the people are believing you the cause of pretty much all of their disasters, you had better withdraw from the Church and Association, and not attend our meetings of the students. I have fought in your defence seven years on this very question, and at the end of all this fidelity I hear of your accusing me publicly of working against you because I am envious of your popularity.

Mrs. Choate sent in her resignation immediately, but two days later wrote a repentant letter asking forgiveness. The membership, however, was unmoved. At their meeting of February 5 they refused her resignation and expelled her from their ranks. Mrs. Eddy took no part in the vote, but wept openly. Is it not possible that her tears were as much because of the stolidity and revenge of the other students as for Clara's shortcomings?

Perhaps the most difficult task imposed upon Mrs. Eddy by her exalted position was the necessity for rebuking the error in her students' thoughts. In any study and practice the most capable and advanced students get the most difficult problems and corrections. Ontology is no exception to this general rule, and the three students at the college who had signed the statement to watch their thoughts, Bartlett, Buswell, and Frye, probably received the severest rebukes of all. Calvin Frye was able to accept the corrections and grew spiritually because of them. This entry in his diary in 1884 was probably not his experience but rather Mrs. Eddy's words to him which he recorded:

> I was sad and sobbing at the thought of how imperfectly I was demonstrating this science in my own life and struggling to find my way when there came a voice saying "You don't need to struggle but simply to waken to see you are there." And immediately I could see those who had passed on in belief, and they were not dead but were right here about us, but I had not gained their point so as to be conscious to them, but as it were looked ahead to it. Neither did I seem to be in an abnormal state of mind at the time I saw this and yet it seemed as real and tangible as anything ever was.

Sad to say, Arthur Buswell reacted to the rebukes given for the perfecting of his character and criticized his Leader; but Julia Bartlett was able to take the severe corrections meekly, thus separating from the error rather than defending it. The Leader was not unaware of the severity of these lessons in purification and did what she could to make them easier. These two letters, of different date, to Miss Bartlett show her concern and her necessity:

> *My very dear Student:*
> My letter last written you was a message from a higher love than the human and was designed to do you more good than all praise can bestow. God grant me my desire.
> > With great Love,
> > M. B. G. Eddy

> *My precious Student:*
> Because I love you with unfailing affection I speak as I do and cannot apologize nor take back what I say lest it will

harm you.

So trust my love and God's holy, faithful means of blessing us—

Lovingly,
M. B. G. Eddy

Self-justification, which was using Arthur Buswell (and uses many others), was overcome by Miss Bartlett; but other forms of animal magnetism assailed her. She was harassed, not by lack of work, but of remuneration, until she thought she would have to leave the college for inability to pay her share of the expenses. Almost in despair she turned to her Bible for guidance and opened to the words, "Thou shalt remain in this house." Her resolve became firm and the problem not only evaporated but she was overwhelmed with successful practice. As she recalled this period:

About March, 1884, a young woman whom physicians were not able to heal was sent to me for treatment in Christian Science by a physician in New Hampshire who was attending her case. In nine days she returned to him a perfectly well woman and remained in his house two weeks. When this physician and those who knew the woman saw what Christian Science had done for her, a great interest was aroused... many...wished me to go to that place and take their cases. ...I sent them word that I...had all that I could do at the College. But they continued to urge...until finally I asked Mrs. Eddy what had better be done. She replied, "Write them you will go for one week," which I did and also that I would give them a talk...the first and second evenings...if they would engage a hall and do something for themselves in subscribing for the...Journal...

I found these people very ready to do what was asked... and the hall was well filled...When through, people crowded about making appointments for the next day until every minute...was spoken for. ...they were there promptly, beginning early in the morning and continuing through the day until late at night, with a room filled with people waiting perhaps two or three hours. ...

I was seeing and treating seventy patients a day, ...and although I could give each one but a few minutes of my time, most were healed quickly. [A] large number came from the surrounding towns begging that I take their cases, whom I had not the time to even see. I . . . sent a telegram to Boston for help, but could find no one to come.

Many people in New Hampshire were disappointed when Miss Bartlett left Littleton, but her work back in Boston was just as pressing and she could not stay any longer.

One man had travelled to Littleton from nearby Lyman, New Hampshire on behalf of his wife who had been ill for thirteen years, exhausting the skill of the physicians. Unhappily this gentleman, Ira O. Knapp by name, was among the large number Miss Bartlett was unable even to see. Mr. Knapp had been skeptical of this new manner of healing, but having decided to try it he was not to be deterred. He wrote directly to Mrs. Eddy asking her to take his wife's case and also his own as he had a minor ailment.

Their case was referred by Mrs. Eddy to Mrs. Mary E. Harris and is another episode; but essentially Julia Bartlett was responsible for introducing the Knapp family to Christian Science.

IRA OSCAR KNAPP   FLAVIA STICKNEY KNAPP

CHAPTER XLIV

I HAVE CHOSEN YOU

Ye have not chosen me, but I have chosen you.

Jesus

1884

ABOUT the time that Julia Bartlett was in New Hampshire the college was moving next door to a slightly larger house at 571 Columbus Avenue. But moving did not alter the busy schedule for everyone. In addition to all her other activities Mrs. Eddy spoke for private gatherings.

At the conclusion of one such lecture in a handsome private home, in the spring of 1884, Mrs. Eddy left the assembly and started upstairs. Almost unconsciously a young woman from the audience followed her through A new disciple the hall to the foot of the stairs, whereupon Mrs. Eddy turned and looked searchingly into her face. Her penetrating gaze, no doubt, read the woman's thought, for after a brief conversation she said, "I want you to come and see me. You are going to do a great work in Christian Science." This meeting, as the new disciple recalled it, was as follows:

> During the spring of 1884, I heard of several cases of Christian Science healing in Boston and was invited to attend a lecture which was to be given by Mrs. Eddy, in a handsome home on Monument Hill, Charlestown, Massachusetts. I went to the lecture weighted with care and nearly prostrated from the effects of watching for one year in the room of an invalid husband. During this lecture I lost all sense of grief, physical weakness, and prostration. It was long, however, before I understandingly realized that this was due to Mrs. Eddy's spiritual influence.

301

When Mrs. Eddy's lecture was concluded she arose and passed through the hall to go upstairs. Almost unconsciously I followed her to the foot of the stairway and as she reached about the fourth step she turned quickly and looked down into my eyes with a searching, penetrating gaze. She asked, "Will you come to see me?" and gave me her card. I replied "I do not know when I can come, Mrs. Eddy; I am so occupied." As I thought it was a matter of small consequence whether I saw her or not, I added, "Thank you, Mrs. Eddy, but I cannot tell whether or not I can come." Then she said, "I want you to come and see me. You are going to do a great work in Christian Science." After she had asked my name and address, which I gave her, I went away.

This young woman had no idea what her future was to be, but the Leader did. Mrs. Eddy, who read character, had seen in Augusta's eyes the earnestness, dedication, spirituality, and sincerity of her beloved student Julia Bartlett, combined with the ability, persuasiveness, assurance, and ardor of Clara Choate. A great work awaited the potential that Mrs. Eddy discerned in Augusta Stetson. It was several months, however, before Mrs. Stetson began this work, and it was many years before she realized that she had not chosen this course, but had been chosen for it.

CHAPTER XLV

STEADY PROGRESS

Progress is born of experience.

Mary Baker Eddy

1884

MAY of 1884 found Sarah Crosse and Calvin Frye in the West with their teacher; Julia Bartlett in charge of the college; and the *Journal* in the very capable hands of Mrs. Emma Hopkins who had studied with Mrs. Eddy the previous December. A card in the June issue read:

> The Editor of the *Journal of Christian Science* having been called to Chicago in the interest of the Science, the arrangement of the present number of the *Journal* was left in care of a student, to whose charge all imperfections and errors may be laid.—E.H.

The students who assembled in Chicago on the thirteenth of May came also from surrounding areas and included a Universalist clergyman and an M.D. If any had felt that the tuition of three hundred dollars was a high price to pay, they soon had a change of heart. In expressing her feelings, Mrs. Emma McDonald typified all of Mrs. Eddy's loyal students and even many who were disloyal. Mrs. McDonald wrote home to her attorney husband in Green Bay, Wisconsin, after the sixth lesson:

Teaching in Chicago May, 1884

> This grows more glorious every day. ... It seems to me now as though I was blind before, when I used to sit down and read the Bible. ... This Science makes God and the Bible a reality. ... The more I read the more I want to. ... In all the preaching I have ever listened to I have never gained as clear

a light as these six lessons have given me. ....If I went back home today I should feel as if I was repaid for all time and money. I would not give up the light I have for twice three hundred. ...I cannot write half I want to, perhaps I cannot say it all when I get home, I must live it.

The Sawyers expected Mrs. Eddy to come on to Milwaukee to teach another class. After learning that that would not be the case, they arrived in Chicago for the last five lessons together with Mr. and Mrs. A. J. Swarts and two or three others.

Following the course Mrs. Laura Sargent went home to Oconto, Wisconsin so inspired by the teaching that before long her town became the first in all the world to erect an edifice for Christian Science services. But all the teaching did not fall on fertile ground; "some fell among thorns, and the thorns grew up, and choked it, and it yielded no fruit." The first from this assemblage to choke out the Word of God was A. J. Swarts, and later, Ursula Gestefeld.

Mr. Swarts began immediately to organize classes of his own, and he wrote Mrs. Eddy at great length. In his epistles he said:

> Your visit here was prolific of good. Your teachings were the true bread. The soil was ready, and now the harvest is ripening, and the gathering is to be abundant. You have the Truth, and I rejoice to see you unmovable.
>
> All my classes are well unfolded spiritually ... They tell to anxious ones the fulness of the new, higher truths, and tell all that it is not to be confounded with spiritualism or mediumship. Good: and no class I teach shall hear me lower the standard — I do not allow mediumship or its cohorts dragged into the Metaphysics taught in my class.

Mrs. Eddy had told Dr. Sawyer and other of her students to begin teaching, but A. J. Swarts was not one of those students. Only five lessons, and those the last five, scarcely qualified him as one of her students and certainly not as a teacher. But even more, the seed had not been sown in an *honest* heart.

Perhaps Swarts' activity caused the Leader to designate *qualified* teachers, for she began the first Normal Course in the college on the eighth of August. The class consisted of ten of her older students including Julia Bartlett, Arthur Buswell, Calvin Frye, and Delia

First
Normal class
August, 1884

304

Manly. Mrs. Read of Roxbury, Massachusetts, was the first student to advertise her classes in the *Journal,* but Julia Bartlett was the first Normal teacher to hold a class. By the time Miss Bartlett's class convened, Mr. Swarts had issued a circular offering a course of instruction to be "chiefly as taught by the Massachusetts Metaphysical College," which course was to include "mediumship, clairvoyance and magnetism." He offered his twelve-lesson course for twelve dollars and compared this with the Boston price which he noted "seems much like extortion and speculation in truth." The five lessons he had attended had been given him gratuitously by the Teacher. What a mockery of appreciation and gratitude!

The Leader often tested the fitness of her students. Whether or not she had done so with Swarts, his unfitness was out in the open for all to see. Mrs. Hopkins' responsibility for the *Journal* may have been just such a test of her qualifications, and she had measured up to expectations. Mrs. Eddy made her the editor beginning with the September issue when she also made the *Journal* a monthly publication.

About the time of Mrs. Hopkins' first issue and Swarts' circular Mrs. Eddy was engaged in teaching a Primary class at the college. This was followed by another, two months later. Before the latter class convened on November 3, Mrs. Eddy contacted Augusta Stetson whose reminiscences state:

> About the first of November, 1884, I received a note from Mrs. Eddy, telling me that a class was to convene in the Massachusetts Metaphysical College and that she wished me to become a member of it. I went to see her, and told her that it would be impossible for me to enter a class; that I had spent much money and all my time during a year and a half in preparing myself to become a public reader and lecturer; and that my engagements were many and immediate. One engagement in particular would come during the class term and, as I was to appear with Professor George Blish of the Boston Blish School of Oratory, I felt that there was too much at issue for me to devote my time to the study of Christian Science, which, I confessed, had little interest for me.
>
> Mrs. Eddy then informed me that the class lessons would be from ten until one o'clock, and that the engagements I

had mentioned would come later than the class hours, so she saw no reason why I could not fill all my engagements and also take class instruction at the College.

The question of tuition, which was three hundred dollars, then arose. I told Mrs. Eddy that I did not feel that I could pay three hundred dollars to study a subject which I might not care to accept. She replied that I need not pay the tuition; that she had many students whom she taught gratuitously; and she felt sure that after I had gone through a class I would see that Christian Science was the Science and Truth of being.

Upon Mrs. Eddy's assurance that my engagement at Tremont Temple would not be interfered with, and that there was no tuition to be paid, I agreed to enter her class, and attended twelve lessons.

While Augusta's eyes were being opened to a new world, another disciple was coming to this new world through an entirely different approach. Ira Knapp had sought Christian Science healing for his wife the previous spring and had found it. But her miraculous recovery was only the bugle call to thought. Mr. Knapp wrote in retrospect to Mrs. Eddy:

Some years ago, before I knew Christian Science, I had a vision in a dream. Heaven, with all its splendor of light... seemed to open to me; but this was only for a moment; for I awoke in this dream, and wept and prayed, because I could not abide there forever.

Time passed on, until one day Christian Science dropped down at our door, to speak a word of peace; and in my glad moments I exclaimed: "It brings a message of Love." To my surprise a voice—nothing like a human voice—answered and said "Where shall I abide? Your house is occupied. Turn out your old tenants, and put on one measure of humility, and another measure, and yet another measure; and then I will abide with you, and Charity will abide with you."

I pondered this a few days and applied to you for instruction. Early one morning I was again surprised, with what seemed a mighty rushing wind, which no man could stay. It made the earth as a desert, and left me bare and naked; but before me was a great rock, square and upright;

and on its sides the word Truth appeared. On this rock I saw that I must build.

Not long after applying to Mrs. Eddy for instruction the Knapps received a telegram stating that their class would begin on the twenty-second of December. The message was sent from Boston December 16. The Teacher gave students sufficient notice for making arrangements and the necessary travel time but endeavored to allow no spare time for gossip and conjecture with friends and family.

After the third lesson Mrs. Eddy often assigned homework in healing to the class. Bliss Knapp recorded his parents' experience in this December class of 1884:

> One day during class, Mrs. Eddy asked every student to find a patient and report his healing the next day. Now, most of those pupils were strangers in the city, and the chief difficulty lay in finding their patients. Mr. Knapp voiced his perplexity to his landlady, when he returned to his lodging-house; and she remarked at once, "You can heal me: for I am totally deaf in one ear." In his joy at having found a patient, Mr. Knapp rushed up to his room, and in a burst of spiritual illumination, he exclaimed, "In all the realm of the real, there is no such thing as deafness." The woman immediately ran up the stairs after him, declaring, "I am healed." She said there was a report in that ear like a pistol shot, and her healing was instantaneous.
>
> When Mrs. Eddy made this request of the class for cases of healing, Mrs. Knapp remarked, "Oh, I am not good enough to do that." After Mrs. Knapp returned to the lodging house that day, she was passing along the hall and through an open door heard someone groaning. She entered the room, and found a woman who had been suffering severely for some time. The woman welcomed any help that Mrs. Knapp could give her; and in one treatment the patient was healed. Next day, when Mrs. Knapp was telling in class of this healing, Mrs. Eddy commented, "And you are the little woman who said you were not good enough to do that."
>
> Another member of the class sat up all night with a morphine patient and healed him in time to report the case next day. Every member of that class, but one, found his patient

and healed him in the required time. As the mantle of Elijah fell upon Elisha, so Mrs. Eddy poured out her spirit upon her pupils...

Two of the pupils had been members of the Chicago class the previous May and had come for additional instruction. They were Mrs. Emma McDonald and Mrs. Laura Sargent, and with them had come Laura's sister, Mrs. Victoria Sargent.

A newcomer to Christian Science who attended this December class was Captain Joseph Eastaman, whose introduction to the subject was very interesting. His last voyage after twenty-one years as a sea-captain was home from Peru to Boston to join his invalid wife. His colorful story is better told in the captain's own words:

Upon my arrival I found her much lower than I had supposed, and the consultations of physicians immediately secured only made it evident that she could not live long. ...One evening, as I was sitting hopeless at my wife's bedside, a friend called and asked, "Captain, why don't you get a Christian Scientist to treat your wife?" To my inquiry as to what that was, she replied that she did not know, but had heard that they healed many cases without medicine. "Anything that will heal my wife I will get if it takes all I own in the world," I replied. ...

So, like a drowning man grasping at a straw, with alternating hopes and fears besieging me on the way, I went to the college. In answer to my request for a personal interview, Mrs. Eddy kindly granted me an extended audience, though to my appeal for help she made the gentle announcement that she herself did not now take patients. At this my heart failed utterly, for I felt that none less than the founder was equal to the healing necessary in my case. As I was about to leave, she turned to me and said with much earnestness, "Captain, why don't you heal your wife yourself?" ...I stammered out, "How can I heal my wife? Have I not procured the best medical aid? What more can I do?" Gently she said, "Learn how to heal." Without hesitation I returned to the parlour for particulars. It seemed to me that it must require years of studying to learn Christian Science—and she whom I was trying to save would not long be here; but when I heard that the en-

tire term required but three weeks, I gathered courage, and
asked about tuition fees, which proved to be very reasonable.
In twenty minutes more, I had arranged to enter the class
about to open on the third day following.

My wife proved much averse to the plan; having in addition
to her fears with regard to Spiritualism, due caution on
account of the already heavy financial drain occasioned by
her prolonged illness. I was ready to spend every dollar to save
her, however, and continued firm in my resolve to go through
the class. ...

How much was due to my own changed thought, I cannot
tell; but after Christian Science was recognized in our
house—even before I entered the College—my wife began to
recover. Soon as I understood the rudiments, I began to treat
her; and, so quickly did she respond to the treatment, that
she was able to avail herself of the kind invitation of the
teacher to accompany me to the final session. That one lesson
dispelled her every doubt as to whether Christian Science
had any kinship with Mesmerism or Spiritualism—for which
she had strong antipathies...

At the time Captain Eastaman was treating and healing his
wife another new student was trying out her new-found knowledge,—the woman who had come so reluctantly, Mrs. Augusta
Stetson. Mrs. Stetson traveled to Maine to practise for four
weeks for reasons she related:

> At the close of the class term I thought I should like to test
> the power of Christian Science Mind-healing but feared to do
> so among my own people lest I should fail to demonstrate it.
> Though confident that the Science was demonstrable, I
> doubted that one so young as I in the work would be able to
> prove it. Just at this time a friend who was becoming inter-
> ested in Christian Science called to see me. She told me that
> her father and mother (seventy-five and seventy-six years of
> age) were both condemned by physicians to hopeless invalid-
> ism, her father requiring an attendant to prevent him from
> falling. The mother was declared by the best specialists to be
> a paranoiac, and much of the time was crying. These were my
> first patients. The daughter encouraged me to take them, say-
> ing, that they were aged and the physicians had given them

up as hopeless; that even if I had not the understanding to heal them, it would be different from taking the cases of younger and more useful persons. At the end of four weeks the old gentleman, with his wife beside him, drove his horses in a snow storm to the Sunday morning service at his church. He was a prominent man in the city of Skowhegan, Maine. The people of Skowhegan had known of the condition of this couple for a long time, and their sudden change from helplessness to health so startled the town that the lame, the halt, and the blind rushed to me for help, until I was overwhelmed with patients.

Two years earlier a young Skowhegan girl home from college had fallen and from that time been unable to rise or stand. For two years she had been in a helpless condition being lifted from bed to chair. The family sought Mrs. Stetson's help, but once again she felt inadequate:

The conditions were reported to me by her brother who came for me and asked me to go to her. The case seemed so serious that I feared to attempt it and refused to go. The next day the mother came and plead with me to come to her daughter. The mother's pleading so touched my heart that I granted her wish. I saw the daugher and gave her a treatment. The next day they came for me again, saying that the girl was greatly improved. This led to another treatment and in one week my patient was walking through the icy streets of Skowhegan.

From this time forward Mrs. Stetson found little time for anything other than Christian Science. She was not yet aware of it, but Mrs. Eddy's prophecy, "You are going to do a great work in Christian Science," had begun its manifestation in her experience.

An impressive member of the December class was Mrs. Josephine Curtis Woodbury. The Woodburys, who were socially prominent, had been interested in Christian Science for several years, Mr. Woodbury having been a member of Mrs. Eddy's first board of directors for the Massachusetts Metaphysical College in 1881. The talented and beautiful Mrs. Woodbury did not elect to study with Mrs. Eddy during the difficult, pioneering days, but by the end of 1884 when the movement was flourishing she decided to cast her lot with the Scientists. Her speaking ability and unusually attractive presence were decided assets. There were traits of character that needed healing, but that was true of everyone. Deterrents to the necessary healing and moral progress for Mrs. Woodbury were theories in conflict with Science which she had previously studied; i.e., mesmerism under Professor Carpenter and theosophy with Helen Blavatsky. But perhaps the greatest detriment to her spiritual growth was the fact that she concealed these former interests. Brought to the light of Science they could have been dispelled; kept in the dark they were nourished, foreboding ill for Josephine Woodbury and further trials for Mrs. Eddy and her Cause.

AUGUSTA E. STETSON

CHAPTER XLVI

MORE TRIALS

By the law of opposites, after the truth of man had been demonstrated, the postulate of error must appear.

Mary Baker Eddy

1885

THE good news was spreading far and wide and according to the law of opposites reaction was setting in. In reality there is no such law, but it seems to operate in human experience until we truly have but *one* God. Mrs. Eddy had first met up with it in Kennedy's malpractice against her, and now it seemed to be operating in all areas.

A notice in the Journal stating that schools claiming to be auxiliaries of the Massachusetts Metaphysical College were bogus was followed by another in the February issue implying that "Mind Cure" published in Chicago was plagiarism from Science and Health. Swarts' activities were not unlike those of Arens, but they were accompanied by an assault of another nature on another front,—a barrage from the Boston clergy. This was led off by the renowned Professor Townsend who challenged Mrs. Eddy's healing ability and offered her one thousand dollars to give sight to one born blind. She countered in the February *Journal:*

> ...to reward his liberality, I offer him three thousand dollars, if he will heal one simple case of opium-eating where the patient is very low and taking morphine powder in its most concentrated form, at the rate of one ounce in two weeks, and has taken it twenty years, and cure that habit in *three days,* leaving the patient *well.* I cured precisely such a case in 1869. Also Chas. M. Howe, of Boston, formerly

partner of Geo. T. Brown, Pharmacist, No. 5 Beacon Street, will tell you that he was my student in December, 1884, and before leaving the class took a patient thoroughly addicted to the use of opium—if she went without it twenty-four hours would have delirium—and cured her perfectly of this habit in forty-eight hours, with no bad results, and decided improvement in health.

Ironically, while some Bostonians were applauding Townsend's attacks, others were eye-witnesses to Mrs. Eddy's continued healing work on the occasional Sundays when she occupied the pulpit at Hawthorne Hall. Emma Hopkins wrote:

> There is no professional practitioner in the field of mental healing doing so many, so marvellous, and instantaneous cures as Mrs. M. B. G. Eddy. ...Not a Sabbath preaching of the Word of Life, but looses the bonds of some poor sick or crippled prisoners. One which came under our observation after the sermon of Jan. 18, was that of a man who went into Hawthorne Hall on crutches, but the power of the Truth as she gave it utterance, set him free from infirmities, and he went home without his crutches!

By the beginning of 1885 Emma Hopkins had her office and residence at the college; and Mrs. Janet Colman was out on the frontier, working for the cause in Chicago, moving on two or three months later to Wichita, Kansas. Mrs. Colman and four other students from Chicago were among the eight students in Mrs. Eddy's second Normal class on February 16. They, as well as all earnest workers, were stung by the next attack on their Teacher.

Boston was *the* center of culture; Tremont Temple was the most fashionable center in Boston; and Rev. Joseph Cook's Monday lectures one of Tremont Temple's most popular and influential occasions. On Monday, the twenty-third of February, Mr. Cook read a letter from his platform by Rev. A. J. Gordon which pertained to Mrs. Eddy and Christian Science. Among other unkind things, he read:

Attack by Gordon and Cook

I believe Christian Science to be of precisely the same

lineage as Spiritualism or Theosophy—from beneath, and
not from above. One has only to open the published volumes
of its lady apostle in this city to find such a creed of pan-
theism as has been rarely compounded.

Opening a volume is all that Joseph Cook could have done
prior to his bitter denunciation, having borrowed Science and
Health from a student the day before and having heeded not
the earnest request to meet with its author. While the hostility
of these critics was sharp and shallow, the wounds it inflicted
were deep and cutting. The Leader responded with a *Defence
of Christian Science* and a request to answer the charges from
the same platform. The day before this request was grudgingly
granted, she preached a stirring sermon to her church. The
Journal reported:

> March 15, the Rev. Mary B. G. Eddy preached a power-
> ful and awakening sermon from the text: "Thou art Peter,
> and upon this rock I will build my church; and the gates of
> hell shall not prevail against it." ... Many new converts were
> added to the faith, and the deep abiding interest of all was
> strengthened by the reassuring words of the faithful
> messenger of the Second Coming.

She was calling for a Peter, a rock, who would uphold her
understanding of man. For fourteen years she had had a Judas
to contend with, and now the Judas concept seemed ubiquitous.
Where were the Peters?

They did not come forth in her experience at Tremont
Temple the next day. She came unto her own and her own received her not. The world could not know how
she suffered from this encounter, but Julia Bartlett knew and has given us an inkling:

Tremont
Temple
March, 1885

> She was reluctantly granted ten minutes in which to meet
> all their false accusations with explanations of the truth of
> Christian Science. It was a hard ordeal for her, to encounter
> this hatred and antagonism to Truth, and when the time came
> I rode in the carriage with her to the Temple. When we
> reached there, we were met by Joseph Cook who was very
> abusive and insulting in his remarks to her, but she made no
> reply and took her place on the platform. The large house was

314

filled when she rose to speak, and the time was short, but her work was completed and she stopped at the end of the ten minutes allotted her, although she had not consulted her watch. As we were leaving I heard some say, "She is a wonderful woman." We rode quietly home. I saw she must be left to herself and her help came from a higher than human source. When we reached home she went to her room where she remained alone. I thought if I could only have shared some of the burdens how gladly I would have done it, and if the world only understood, these trials would not have been put upon her. No one but herself could know the burdens of that hour. At another time she expressed it in these words, "Never, never will a mortal again drink my cup."

Mrs. Eddy knew what Jesus had suffered, for she spent forty years on the cross. Those long years included triumphs as well as tragedy, but Monday, March 16, 1885 was a day of crucifixion. It was for her as she had written of Jesus:

> The burden of that hour was terrible beyond human conception. The distrust of mortal minds, disbelieving the purpose of his mission, was a million times sharper than the thorns which pierced his flesh.

The world did not understand, but Julia Bartlett did, and did what she could. The previous Christmas a few students had invited their Teacher into her reception room where their gifts to her were displayed. She turned almost immediately to Julia Bartlett and said, "I thought it was a picture." Julia, who was keeping a secret, replied, "I do not see why you should think it was a picture." "Well, I did," said Mrs. Eddy. Miss Bartlett then stated that there *was* a picture, but that it was not ready. "I thought so," Mrs. Eddy responded, and added that there had been a most beautiful, awe-inspiring picture of Jesus in her student's thought whenever she had seen her of late; and it seemed to have a history.

The fact was that Miss Bartlett had a cherished picture of Jesus (with a face beyond any she had seen in the most ideal renditions) which was said to be copied from the portrait carved on an emerald by order of Tiberius Caesar. This she was having copied for her Leader, but it was not completed.

In March the portrait was finished, but Miss Bartlett had not yet made the presentation. This sad day after the Tremont Temple experience seemed to be the proper time; however, Julia would not disturb her Leader and had to leave for a church meeting, so she asked another student to present it in her name when Mrs. Eddy returned from supper:

> Mrs. Eddy was so affected by it that she wished to see me at once and sent this student for me. When I met dear, dear Mrs. Eddy, she was deeply moved, and expressed her love and gratitude and joy. I could not say all that this picture brought to her thought of the real Christ Jesus as one who had suffered and triumphed over all claims of evil, but she at once rose above it, and I rejoiced with her...

The picture meant far more than Miss Bartlett ever knew. It was a symbol of her loyalty. "The real cross which Jesus [and Mary Baker Eddy] bore up the hill of grief was the world's hatred of Truth and Love." This gift of love from one loyal heart dispelled the gloom of the world's hatred that day.

The numerous gifts that the Leader received were all symbols to her, and she read in those symbols the thought of the donor. The cost in dollars was irrelevant, but the cost in giving was of utmost importance. Her card of thanks in the January *Journal* is interesting to consider:

> Daily obligations, a large correspondence, school in session, all pressing their demands on my time, may apologize for one public expression to you all my heartfelt thanks for your rare Christmas presents. From such a constellation of beautiful things, I can name only the central figures.

From this constellation of gifts she then named a few, but note that she did not say "a few," but rather "only the central figures." Among elaborate gifts why should she name "pocket-handkershiefs"? Was it not because she could distinguish the widow's mite? The thing of itself meant nothing; the thought behind it was all. This listing of Christmas gifts continued for several years and perhaps a few students learned from it. Those who had given of their earthly wealth and received no recognition may have been chastened or angered; but if they had given only of earthly wealth, their gift measured not at all in the scales of God. A gift from Mrs. Eddy on "giving" weighs mightily for all mankind for all time:

> Who doth but give me of his earthly wealth, gives to me that which cannot reach the heart and may but serve to stir my neighbor's envy: while he who gives me just a simple thought of Life, or Truth, or Love, gives to me that which I may give again, yet have and keep and use throughout eternity.

Julia Bartlett's gift had reached the heart. Emma Hopkins was also giving of herself to the Cause. Right after studying she had written: "I lay my whole life and all my talents, little or great, to this work."

One of Mrs. Hopkins' first contributions to the *Journal* had been entitled "God's Omnipresence" in which she praised the Truth in all places from the Buddhist Nirvana to the Zend-Avesta of the Persians. The danger that lay in this path, and in the path of all intellectual pursuits, was not yet seen, and Mrs. Hopkins was daily applying her many talents to Christian Science work. She wrote feelingly in the March *Journal:*

> Never but once in the history of man was persecution so malignant, and curses so causeless as those heaped against the scientists of today, who fain would ask for which of their good works the Boston clerical mob stoneth them.

As always the Leader was the one to meet the problem and lead the way. By March she had published two pamphlets for the protection of her babe and her cause. The *Historical* first was a booklet of twenty-one pages entitled *Sketch* *Historical Sketch of Metaphysical Healing* which February, 1885 sold for ten cents.

The second pamphlet, which also sold for ten cents or one dollar per dozen, was a reprint of an article in the March *Journal* by Mrs. Eddy entitled *DEFENCE OF* Defence of *CHRISTIAN SCIENCE Against Rev. Joseph* Christian Science *Cook and Dr. A. J. Gordon's Religious BAN.* March, 1885 One sentence from this sixteen page publication has solved many a problem for many of the Woman's children:

> A human sense of love sees no farther than to die for a

friend, but divine Love includes its enemies; and Love so great *destroys hate,* blessing itself in blessing its enemies.

In April the *Christian Science Journal,* with its changed name, had a new format. It was beginning its third year and it was growing up. In its new dress, it was still filled with refutations of false charges by pulpit and press including Mrs. Eddy's answer to Prof. Townsend and her brief speech at Tremont Temple. In another month she had risen above the storm clouds. The lead article in the May *Journal* was:

LOVE

By Mary Baker G. Eddy

What a word. I am in awe before it. Over what worlds of worlds it hath range and is sovereign...

Sometimes this gentle evangel comes to burst the pent-up storm of error with one mighty thunder-bolt, and clears the moral atmosphere, foul with human exhalations. It is a born blessing at all times, either as a rebuke or benediction.

The persecution though difficult had some beneficent effects. This letter from a stranger represented a portion of the public's reaction:

I had not known of the new metaphysical medical practice till I read of it in the interesting(?) letters of Prof. L. T. Townsend, published in *Zion's Herald* last winter. ...

I mean to try C. S. for my own infirmities, just from the information furnished by the contemptuous letters of Prof. T. Please send me some printed pamphlets or works on the subject, if there are any.

An article by a Boston reporter in the summer of 1885 also shed a ray of light. Lilian Whiting, of the *Traveller,* wrote:

Here in Boston...we are so accustomed to hearing of the marvels of the "mind cure" that we fail to really learn as much of its mysteries as people often do from a distance, and pondering all these things in my heart one day I resolved to go and see Mrs. Eddy...the originator...of "Christian Science" popularly known as "mind cure." Now of this I am

318

neither a disciple nor a scoffer, ...in view of what I am about to relate I beg to preface that I went to Mrs. Eddy with no positive feeling either way of either conviction or skepticism. ...I had never even seen a "mind curer," never heard one of their lectures, and had not read extensively of their...literature when I suddenly resolved to call upon Mrs. Eddy, if she would permit me to do so. My note of inquiry was met by a very courteous invitation to come to her at an hour named... and accordingly at 8 o'clock on that evening I rang the bell of the large and handsome residence on Columbus Avenue... known as the Metaphysical College. A maid ushered me

INTO A DAINTILY FURNISHED RECEPTION ROOM

where pictures and bric-a-brac indicated refinement and taste. Presently Mrs. Eddy came in and greeted me with a manner that while cordial and graceful, was also something more, and had in it an indefinable element of harmony and a peace that was not mere repose, but more like exaltation. It was subtle and indefinable, however, and I did not think of it especially at the time, although I felt it. ...

Mrs. Eddy impressed me as a woman who is—in the language of our Methodist friends—"filled with the spirit." It seems to be a merely natural gift with her. She is, by nature, a harmonizer. My own personal experience in that call was so singular that I will venture to relate it. I went, as I have already said, in a journalistic spirit. I had no belief or disbelief, and the idea of getting any personal benefit from the call, save matter for press use, never occurred to me. But I remembered afterward how extremely tired I was as I walked rather wearily and languidly up the steps to Mrs. Eddy's door. I came away, as a little child friend of mine expressively says, "skipping." I was at least a mile from the [Hotel] Vendome, and I walked home feeling as if I were treading on air. My sleep that night was the rest of elysium. If I had been caught up into paradise it could hardly have been a more wonderful renewal. All the next day this exalted state continued. I can hardly describe it; it was simply the most marvellous elasticity of mind and body. ...In the evening I had callers, and I told of my visit to Mrs. Eddy and later...chanced to allude to the unusual, and indeed,

utterly unprecedented buoyancy and energy I was feeling
"Why that's the result of your going to Mrs. Eddy," exclaimed
a friend. . . .I had not thought of it before, because you see I
went to have my mind stored, not cured, and in the journalistic sense, I forgot I was with the most famous "mind curer"
of the day. . . .

Miss Whiting had only one-half hour of the Woman's attention. The world had had her love and devotion for nearly twenty
years as she held uncomplaining guard for humanity, and the
effects were far reaching. As the Boston clergy raged against her
she had made it known that she would teach clergymen
gratuitously. Though her defamers scorned the munificent gift,
other clergymen did avail themselves of this opportunity of a
lifetime, nay, of an age, and the more spiritual among them
were greatly blessed and benefitted.

Even though the Woman was deeply wounded by clerical
attacks and hostile public opinion, she was never deceived as
to the real enemy. The real danger to her teaching was not the
open warfare, but the silent, secret attacks upon her students
to destroy her and her mission in their minds. In her *Historical
Sketch of Metaphysical Healing* she had written:

Thirteen years I have watched with critical acumen the
effects of the subversion of truth by a mental malpractice
. . .There is but one right way to deal with sin; namely, if you
cannot stop it, to expose it for the safety of others.

In the effort to protect her students she warned them of these
secret attacks and their effects, and she published this warning in her *Historical Sketch* for her students in time to come:

Duty demands a word of instruction from me on the unscrupulous methods of mental malpractice, to stay the
progress of those entering the path as metaphysical healers,
or Christian Scientists. . . .

If, as I understand it, my Father has shown me the way in
mental science, He has also shown me this awful abuse of it
that I may forewarn and forearm the age. . . .

The following is the mental *modus* of crime. To produce
physical sufferings, family discords, losses in business, inability to heal yourself and others, etc. If these tortures fail to

discourage the honest mental healers, the next attempt is to make them believe that mesmerism, *alias mental malpractice,* had nothing to do with their experience, and that Mrs. Eddy had scared them on this question to the result of producing it! If they can deceive you into believing this, it deprives you of understanding enough of the question for self-defence, and leaves you in their power, relieved of suffering and rejoicing in FREEDOM (?) If they cannot produce this blindness, their next step is to beg a quarrel between you and Mrs. Eddy; no matter how great your obligations or how highly you have had reason to respect her, you will hate her more or less. This abnormal effect is your proof that it is mesmerism, *alias* mental malpractice. Without cause you will then drop all intercourse with her, give her no opportunity to see you or to defend herself. Now you are ready for their next step,—to make you suffer over again, and believe that Mrs. Eddy or some of her students are causing it. This finishes the programme. They have covered their own crimes now, and you are in their power without knowing it, and cannot progress in metaphysical healing.

The *modus operandi* of malpractice against the Christian Scientist is not greatly different almost a century later:
(1) problems, and the inability to heal oneself and others which produces discouragement;
(2) the belief that malicous mental malpractice has nothing to do with these experiences and one need give it no thought at all, which produces a false sense of *freedom* which is *blindness* to malicious mind;
(3) the separation of Mrs. Eddy from her discovery and eventually from the student either consciously through rejection, or unconsciously through neglect, or most subtly of all, through denial of personality. If malicious mind can make the student see Mrs. Eddy as personality rather than as the Woman of the Apocalypse, that will choke out appreciation and gratitude, and will separate the Discoverer from her discovery in his consciousness;
(4) renewed suffering and inability to progress in metaphysical healing.
Under the Title "Malicious Mesmerism" the experience of

a student was published in the *Journal* for May, 1885:

> I had safely and delightedly closed a course of instruction under Mrs. Eddy at the Mass. Metaphysical College, Boston. All enthusiasm and hope, I set forth on my mission as a healer, but had hardly taken my first case when an unaccountable fear of my teacher took possession of me. Why was it? She had ever shown me the kindliest attentions, and certainly, no mother could have discovered the characteristics and capabilities of her child more correctly than she had mine, or more gently led her along an untried way than in her wisdom she endeavored to lead me. But all to no purpose, — the fear of her continued, and developed further, into a fear of everybody else; further still, — into fear of the very sunlight; for I dreaded each morning, bringing with it the memory that I was a "scientist."
>
> Over and over again the loving sisters of the "Association" advised me to hold possession of myself against this mesmeric effect,—as I had been instructed on the question of "malicious mesmerism." Nonsense, I said; it's my own self that is wrong; nobody can mesmerize *me!* Finally, one sister, in pure commiseration of my state...took it up for me, to set me free from the darkness and fear that seemed overpowering me. Suddenly, my heart lightened; life seemed again a pleasant thing, and hope dawned where despair had held sway.
>
> Since that effort was made in my behalf, and *on that ground,* I have never despaired, and my veneration and love for my teacher in divine science increase daily.

This student was saved. But the efforts of malicious mind to separate the students from the Revelator diversified and intensified; and to this day it has not stopped.

CHAPTER XLVII

CRITICISMS

Strangely enough, we ask for material theories in support of spiritual and eternal truths, when the two are so antagonistic that the material thought must become spiritualized before the spiritual fact is attained.

Mary Baker Eddy

1885

NINETEENTH century New England produced America's great literature. This era and locale also produced the literary scholar who filled a most important position in the best publishing houses,—that of proofreader. Authors of renown could frequently be found in the proofreader's office consulting with him on one point or another, asking and receiving advice.

Science and Health was brought forth with no such aid from the literary scholars. The proofreading for the first and second editions, if there had been any at all, was atrocious. Beginning with the third edition and Mrs. Eddy's association with John Wilson, typographical and orthographical errors were virtually eliminated; however, for lack of funds and time Mrs. Eddy had not been able to avail herself of any literary assistance whatsoever.

Early in 1885 her "book" was in its thirteenth edition, three of which had been revisions. Before its tenth anniversary in the fall she would have revised it once more. Her babe was performing its mission, blessing and healing mankind; but the Mother was ever improving and perfecting her work, and she could now afford the services of an English scholar.

Mrs. Eddy was wise enough to appreciate the talents of the thorough scholar, but the literary assistance was to her a secondary consideration. Students and patients who had experienced healing, accepted and embraced Science and Health joyously, but the author wanted a truly lucid textbook for the total stranger and for all time to come. Thus, when she employed James Henry Wiggin it was for the purpose of criticizing her new revision to help her in simplifying and clarifying her presentation.

At the time he started his task, Rev. Wiggin was not the only critical reader of Science and Health. A young woman from Nebraska, Miss C. Lulu Blackman, who was facing inevitable invalidism, had traveled to Chicago and been healed by Miss Ellen Brown. Some time later she applied to Mrs. Eddy for instruction in an abrupt letter in which she stated, "If it is necessary for me to be a dissatisfied and miserable Christian, I am not ready for this instruction." Mrs. Eddy answered simply, "Come and see." After the class the Teacher wrote to Miss Brown:

> Miss Blackman you had described to me briefly in a letter but I had forgotten your words until in the class I found myself beating furiously against certain traits, and in an instant recognized that they were the ones you alluded to with the hope that I should exterminate them. Well dear she went out very much advanced from what she came in.

Miss Blackman had been saved from the tempter,—the will power of the human mind,—in an interesting experience. Following the third lesson Mrs. Eddy had said, "Now go home and take your first patient." This student's first intent was to escape the assignment; which was followed by such temptation as she "had never before known." As she recalled:

> In my own estimation I was not ready to take a patient. ...It was a great relief to remember that I was a complete stranger in Boston and so could not possibly be called upon to give a treatment. Not willful disobedience but stress of circumstances would exempt me...When I opened the door of my rooming place a member of the family was found to be very ill...When he saw that I was making haste to escape to my room he called to me: "If you can do anything for me, why don't you do it?...

Suggestions taking form in words declared that I did not know enough of the Christian Science method to use it and declared that there was a power in my own mind that I could use instead. Error pleaded with me to substitute mortal mind for immortal Mind, arguing that mortal mind was my natural habitat, and that immortal Mind was too transcendental to avail.

I had been precipitated into a seeming mental realm where the supposititious forces of evil sought to establish the claim to equal or transcend the power of God. I realized that there was a greater question here than that of mere physical healing. The decision to rely upon divine Mind alone was made, and I answered the tempter, "I will not resort to will power, even if the young man dies." Then as a ministering angel this Scriptural verse came to me: "Put off thy shoes from off thy feet, for the place whereon thou standest is holy ground." I had forgotten the patient, but as I turned to leave the room I saw he was sleeping peacefully and that complete healing had taken place.

On the closing day of the class Mrs. Eddy spoke to each member individually as she bade him good-bye. Holding Miss Blackman's hand she looked directly into her eyes and said, "Thou art mine, saith the Lord, and none shall pluck you from out of my hand."

Not all the critical and skeptical members of that class were redeemed from the error that beset them. Mrs. Mary H. Plunkett from Detroit had written of her dramatic healing in Christian Science for the *Journal*. Shortly thereafter she applied to Mrs. Eddy for instruction, but she did not disclose the fact that she studied first with A. J. Swarts. "There is nothing hidden that shall not be revealed," and Mrs. Plunkett did not deceive Mrs. Eddy for long, if at all.

When the Teacher entered the classroom on opening day, September 14, all the members rose spontaneously. When she reached her slightly raised platform she turned and looked searchingly into the face of the first student in the first row. Speaking no word she proceeded to the next student silently knocking at the door of his consciousness, perceiving his response, and giving a benediction. After the individual mental examination of each member, she raised her eyes in prayer, and all repeated the Lord's Prayer with one accord. Then everyone was seated and the teaching commenced.

Before long Mrs. Plunkett's antagonism was brought to the surface, but she subtly endeavored to draw the members of the class away from Mrs. Eddy and to herself. She appealed particularly to a pretty woman from the midwest; but lovely, sweet Mrs. Laura Lathrop resisted these advances. Alas! however, another student fell victim to her wiles.

In the current issue of the *Journal* (September, 1885) Mrs. Hopkins had warned against false teachers, then added of those who were certificated:

> No student (I speak from knowledge of facts) has ever yet been qualified to teach Christian Science, except rudimentarily. . . . They are not to blame for this. They must wait and grow to their strength through suffering and watchful prayer. But she whose life of cleansing sorrow left her the fit transparency for revelations straight from the infinite Source, teaches the Science of God and His creations in all its divine completeness. No member of a class of the college ever left till he had ascended the full height of his understanding, borne thither by the strong pinions of our leader's inspiration.
>
> It rests then wholly with himself whether he keeps forever in view that revelation, and conscientiously strives to make it the end of all attainment. . . For this he alone is responsible. He cannot deny that he has caught the full meaning of prophecy and revelation, and been shown the way to God's saving presence. . . . How great then the folly of falling back to earthly ambitions and earthly ends, by claiming to work the same miracle—for the pottage reward of a little publicity and a few hundred dollars.

The heavens had opened unto Emma Hopkins and she had heard the voice from heaven saying, "This is my beloved Daughter in whom I am well pleased." And immediately she was led into the wilderness and tempted of the devil.

Mrs. Hopkins had not been in the class to see Mrs. Plunkett's open defiance of Mrs. Eddy before its close, but she was subjected to her subtle conversations; and she failed to resist the temptations the adversary placed before her. When Mrs. Eddy relieved her of the editorship in October, she proclaimed her loyalty, but her actions belied her words. Very soon she joined forces with Mrs. Plunkett and began the very type of teaching she had so recently condemned. Her criticisms of her beloved teacher were bitter as she assisted Mrs. Plunkett in endeavoring to usurp Mrs. Eddy's position.

It would appear that Mrs. Eddy had another Judas in the person of Mary Plunkett, who, it was later learned, was a cousin of Richard Kennedy. But she also had a reason for rejoicing, for in the same class she had found a Peter.

EMMA HOPKINS

CHAPTER XLVIII

ON THIS ROCK

Thou art Peter, and upon this rock I will build my church.

Jesus

1885

FOR nearly twenty years Mrs. Eddy had known her mission and been working tirelessly to fulfil it. Many earnest students had perceived that she was anointed of God above her fellows, but from Daniel Spofford to Emma Hopkins they had proved unable to sustain and maintain their own understanding when under fire from the enemy. Mr. and Mrs. Knapp had experienced the enemy's fire following their instruction the previous winter. Now they were overjoyed to be gaining new strength in this first class in the fall of 1885.

Before the term ended Mrs. Eddy explained the twelfth chapter of Revelation, which had not yet been included in Science and Health but would soon appear as "Apocalypse" in the new revision. Her explanation had profound meaning for one member of the class, for although she had made no reference to herself, Mr. Knapp exclaimed, "Thou art the Woman!" The Teacher turned to him. Had the thought behind his utterance been one of personal sense, he would have received a rebuke as had Daniel Spofford when she wrote, "the way you set me up for a Dagon is wrong and...I implore you to return forever from this error of *personality.*" But she gave Ira Knapp a sweet smile.

It had been more than three years that Mrs. Eddy had been aware of her own identity, longing for recognition in the eyes of just one student; but materiality and intellectualism blinded the eyes of her followers to her spirituality and her true identity. The humility of Ira Knapp had opened his eyes and awakened

328

his spiritual sense to behold God's messenger in her true being. Though she made no comment as she read his thought and answered with a silent smile, in her heart she responded, "Blessed art thou, Ira Oscar Knapp, for flesh and blood hath not revealed it unto thee, but my Mother which is in heaven. And I say unto thee, That thou art Peter, and upon this rock I will build my church; and the gates of hell shall not prevail against it."

The booklet, *THE LATTER DAYS: With Evidence from The Great Pyramid,* that had foretold the date of the Revelator's awareness of her own identity, had also stated that November 15, 1885, was an important date in English history. The event of the latter date had had its genesis in the classroom of the Metaphysical College in September or October. When the Knapps returned to their farm in New Hampshire, Ira's thought was no longer on farming or community affairs. Every day he was to be found pouring over his Bible and most especially the chapter of Revelation. In time he became known among his Scientist friends as "the Revelation man." By the fifteenth of November in 1885 the revelation that had come to him that day in the classroom was firmly grounded upon a rock. At last one student had beheld the Christ upon which she must build her Church.

CHAPTER XLIX

THE SIXTEENTH EDITION

*Those who have been disappointed in not earlier receiving
copies of Mrs. Eddy's New, Revised, and Enlarged edition
...should rejoice in the knowledge that the delay is for the
sake of making the book more perfect in every particular.*

Christian Science Journal, February, 1886

1885

I N the fall of 1885 the Christian Science church had grown
beyond the seating capacity of Hawthorne Hall. On the
Chickering   twenty-fifth of October all five hundred seats in
Hall   their new, larger quarters were filled when Mrs.
October, 1885   Eddy preached the first sermon in Chickering
Hall. The new revision of Science and Health was progressing
nicely. In addition to his suggestions and criticisms, Rev. Wig-
gin was preparing an index.

All the students, however, were not keeping pace with the
movement. The more intellectual seemed to have greater difficulty in pursuing the *straight* and *narrow* path. A few years
later Mrs. Eddy told a class:

> It is only by breaking the bottle that the fragments can in-
> flict wounds. The whole vessel cannot injure. There is some
> Truth in all creeds and ologies, but if you attempt to find the
> infinite in a fragment you will get hurt. Leave the fragments
> alone, and devote your time to the study of the *whole* Truth
> as revealed in the Bible and its key, Science and Health.

Arthur Buswell had found the demands of the *whole* Truth
too exacting and in December was dropped from the C.S.A.
Every student had his bout with animal magnetism and many

were defeated; but some came out victor and were stronger for the experience. Calvin Frye related an incident which was probably his own experience, for it was he who supervised the household, engaged the servants, paid the bills, etc. at the college. Regarding Mrs. Eddy's tenderness in assisting a student to do right he wrote:

> I knew a person who served her as steward in Boston. She knew that person was honest. He took the money from her with orders to pay the grocer and butcher monthly. After three months, neither one having received any payment. . . both made it known to Mrs. Eddy. She told them she had given the money monthly to her employee to pay them. The latter was then called to account. He said he had received the money from Mrs. Eddy, but knew not what had become of it. She then sadly recognized the cause, saw he was the victim of malicious mental malpractice, rebuked him sternly and pointed out the consequences of his yielding to this sin. The grocer and butcher advised Mrs. Eddy not to have too much charity: they thought it was unreasonable. She settled the matter by paying their bills, and nothing further was said on the subject. She believed that that student, left to himself, was strictly honest. He offered to refund the missing money to her, but her sympathy with his situation made her refuse it. It were needless to add this student was saved from becoming again the victim of this infernal spell.

Sometime after the fifteenth of November Mr. Wiggin and the printer of the new edition of Science and Health were beset with a problem, but it was not because of animal magnetism. It was, in fact, for a very opposite reason,—the Woman's overcoming of animal magnetism in the world. The chapter entitled "Demonology," which she had reduced in size for the previous revision, she had enlarged considerably and renamed "Animal Magnetism" for the forthcoming sixteenth edition. When her Peter appeared in the person of Ira Oscar Knapp, she could sound a new note and lead her students up higher. She could also cease the personal warfare with the Judases that hounded her footsteps,—Kennedy, Arens, Swarts, etc. At a later date she wrote in answer to the question, "How shall I treat malicious animal magnetism?":

The hour has passed for this evil to be treated personally, but it should have been so dealt with at the outset. . . . This growing sin must now be dealt with as evil, and not as an evil-doer or personality.

Mrs. Eddy always listened for God's voice. For thirteen years she had been directed to deal with the personality of the evil-doer and had followed that direction faithfully. A number of pages that were now in press were devoted to the exposure and denunciation of the malpractitioners. The new edition was not only in type, but cast, when Mind bade the Revelator to cease the personal warfare and turn her face in another direction. At this stage of production it was not an easy task to make changes, but Mrs. Eddy hesitated not to follow God's direction at any cost. So the new edition was stopped. Mr. Wiggin, under the nom-de-plume Phare Pleigh, later wrote of this period:

Whatever is to be Mrs. Eddy's future reputation, time will show. Little cares she, if only through her work the Truth may be glorified. More than once, in her earnestness, she has reached her bottom dollar, but the interest of the world to hear her word has always filled her coffers anew. Within a few months she has made sacrifices, from which most authors would have shrunk, to ensure the moral rightness of her book. . . . Day after day flew by, and weeks lengthened into months; from every quarter came important missives of inquiry and mercantile reproach; hundreds of dollars were sunk in a bottomless sea of corrections; yet not till the authoress was satisfied that her duty was wholly done, would she allow printer and binder to send forth her book to the world.

The new, revised edition in one volume was reviewed in the *Journal* for January, 1886, and an apology for its delay appeared in the February issue. When it finally came forth, the table of contents read in part:

The personal handling of animal magnetism had been de-
leted from that chapter and ten pages devoted to a new topic
under the title "Wayside Hints." The first hint was from
Jeremiah: "They shall ask the way to Zion, with their faces
thitherward." Mrs. Eddy had found one student who had
turned his face toward Zion, so now she could lead toward the
Holy City which lieth foursquare. "New Jerusalem" had always been in the Glossary, but after the inclusion of Wayside
Hints to the Holy City, another change was made in subsequent editions. The frontispiece, a picture of Jesus raising
Jairus' daughter, was changed to a portrait of Mary Baker
Eddy.

MARY BAKER EDDY
Frontispiece in Science and Health beginning with
the Twenty-First edition, Revised in 1886.

CHAPTER L

SHEPHERDING

Lovest thou me?...Feed my sheep.

Jesus

1886

IN the fall of 1885 an apostate student who professed to have "discovered an improvement on Christian Science" was bleating for "large flocks in mind-traffic, wandering about without a leader" to follow him into "a national convention." In the November *Journal* Mrs. Eddy labeled this man "a wolf in sheep's clothing." The true Leader was ever seeking methods to protect and defend her lambkins and her cause. In her words:

> For many successive years I have endeavored to find new ways and means for the promotion and expansion of scientific Mind-healing...and, if possible to build a hedge round about it that should shelter its perfections from the contaminating influences of those who have a small portion of its letter and less of its spirit.

The Christian Scientists' Association was restricted to graduates of the college. Many teachers now had associations National of their own, and Mrs. Eddy saw a need for uni-Association fication. In January she proposed the formation February, 1886 of a National Christian Scientist Association which would be open to all the students. An organizational meeting was held in New York City on the tenth of February, and the first annual meeting two months later in Boston, on the fourteenth of April.

The Leader also recommended that her students charter schools for teaching the rudiments of Christian Science. By mid-summer the California Metaphysical Institute was ad-

334

vertising in the columns of the *Journal,* followed by several
more in various locations.

From the editorship of the *Christian Science Journal,* Emma
Hopkins had gone to Chicago to edit Swarts' *Mind Cure* magazine, but Mrs. Eddy soon found an able replacement. The man
who had been highly recommended as a literary aid by her
printer, John Wilson, she had found to be exceptionally capable
and accurate. By the dawn of the new year she had engaged Mr.
Wiggin to edit the *Journal* while Sarah Crosse continued as
manager and publisher.

Rev. Wiggin had left the ministry several years earlier because of his disbelief in the Bible, and he now had the same
feeling toward Science and Health, although his academic
knowledge of that book far exceeded that of most students.
When a California clergyman attacked Mrs. Eddy and her work
with the venom that had shown itself in Boston a year earlier,
he came forth with a well-reasoned defence, Biblically re-
futing the clerical censure. Published as *Christian Science and
the Bible* by Phare Pleigh, this pamphlet found ready acceptance among Scientists.

Mrs. Eddy had a high regard for Wiggin's logic and fair-
mindedness, and invited him to join her next class which was
to convene March 29. That gentleman proposed to attend as an
observer, declining to become a student. He was perfectly
satisfied with his own philosophy, and his mind was closed to
the acceptance of the Truth of Christian Science. After meeting
this closed thought in the classroom the Teacher wrote him:

> You were wise in your conclusions about not entering the
> class at present as a student, and I will do as you sagely sug-
> gested, viz. pass you by with my questions and that will elicit
> no debate.

Though he refused to allow the Teacher to contend with his
opinions, he was not untouched by her ability. In the May
Journal, under the caption "In the Class-Room," he said:

> From hearing Mrs. Eddy preach, from reading her book
> (however carefully,) from talking with her, you do not get an
> adequate idea of her mental powers. Not only is she glowingly
> earnest in presenting her convictions, but her language and

illustrations are remarkably well drawn. She is quick in repartee, and keenly turns a jest upon her questioner, but not offensively or unkindly. She reads faces rapidly. A brief exposition of the Book of Job, which one day entered incidently into her statement of how God is to be found, would have done honor to any ecclesiastic. Critical listeners are often astonished at the strong hold she has upon her thought, and at the clearness of her statements, even when they cannot agree with her. While she is sharp to detect variations from her own views, and to expose the difference, she governs herself in the midst of discussion. In fact, Rev. M. B. G. Eddy is a natural class-leader, and three hours pass away in her lessons before you know it.

Despite the clerical attacks and her inability to reach Rev. Wiggin, Mrs. Eddy still had hopes that the clergy would accept Christian Science and become the leaders of the flock. Three clergymen, in addition to Wiggin, had accepted her generous offer of free tuition, and the Reverends Joseph Adams, George Day, and William Gill had attended the course eager to learn Christian Science.

Following the class Rev. Day returned to Chicago and began preaching for the infant church just organizing in that city. Mrs. Eddy invited Rev. Adams to preach to her church at Chickering Hall, but the members were dissatisfied with him as assistant pastor, and in June invited Rev. Gill to fill that position.

William I. Gill was a man of letters with several books to his credit. After attending the college course he had written Mrs. Eddy:

> I...find myself developing a strange intellectual affinity with you and your work. ...I now see that you are and will be one of the greatest benefactors of our time.

Gill was given increased opportunity for proving his sincerity and ability in August when Mrs. Eddy made him editor of the *Journal* which was growing steadily. Adams and Day were included in the next normal class in the fall.

Though she had fond hopes for clergymen and gave to them

lavishly and freely, all of her students underwent training and testing. The more capable the student, the more severe the test. Her "chosen disciple," Augusta Stetson, had had normal training in the spring. In the fall Mrs. Eddy sent a reluctant Augusta to New York City, but she was subjected to an unusual and rather severe test before that time. Mrs. Stetson had done a good deal of work in Reading, Massachusetts. One day Mrs. Eddy told her that if she could secure a hall and an audience including clergymen she would come there to speak. Mrs. Stetson wrote of this time:

> I immediately went to work and with the help of my patients engaged the Congregational Church. Four ministers were invited, and when the evening came the assembled audience occupied every seat. The four clergymen sat at the foot of the platform, but Mrs. Eddy was not there. I had gone to three trains in the afternoon to meet her and at last in despair I entered the church. I was in a dilemma. I was embarassed because Mrs. Eddy did not appear and I felt that I ought to apologize to the audience for her non-appearance. I had made no preparation to address this large assembly... and I had never lectured on Christian Science. I was desperate. I called on God to give me wisdom to know whether to apologize...or to do the best I could to give them some idea of the Science of being. Finally I decided that I must speak the Word. I addressed them for an hour and a half, prefacing my remarks with the statement that Mrs. Eddy must have been detained, but if they desired to hear me I would do the best I could...
>
> The next morning I went directly to Mrs. Eddy and told her that I thought it was most unkind for her to put me in that position. ...I asked, "Why did you not come?" She answered, "I was there."
>
> She smiled at my innocence and ignorance...She said, "But you stood, Augusta. You stood, you did not run."

CHAPTER LI

ANOTHER JUDAS

Human policy is a fool that saith in his heart, "No God"—
a caressing Judas that betrays you and commits suicide.

Mary Baker Eddy

1886

THE Christian Science movement was growing so rapidly that the Association had to hold its regular monthly meeting in the Odd Fellows Building in June of 1886. Of this meeting Josephine Woodbury wrote, paraphrasing the Leader's words:

> This Association...in the many upheavals of the last year ...has rid itself of some of the mere lookers-on...Every tidal wave which sweeps over this Association purges it. ...Its atmosphere, growing purer with years is not a comfortable inspiration to any but the lovers and correct followers of Truth.

Many of those who left went out to teach and to practise their own misinterpretations of Christian Science. Mrs. Eddy issued a notice in the *Journal* that only those who could show credentials to that effect were her students. This was followed a short time later by a notice to students that their certificates were invalid unless they bore upon the face the words *one year from date.* She also began conferring degrees upon her students to protect the correct teaching from the false. These were identified in the Journal:

Degrees from Metaphysical College

> C.S.B. Bachelor of Christian Science given to students who have taken the first course of instruction at the College.
> C.S.D. Doctor of Christian Science conferred on those who

take the Normal Course, if they have also practised accept-
ably three years in the Science and maintained a thoroughly
Christian character.

D.S.D. Doctor of Divine Science is given after the Course
in Theology, combined with three years of practice, to those
who have obtained a correct knowledge of the spiritual
signification of the Scriptures, and conformed their lives to
the teachings of Christ Jesus.

During the years that Mrs. Eddy taught at her college she
found not one student who was ready for the course in
Theology, so this course was never taught at 571 Columbus
Avenue although it continued to be advertised every month. In
all the years our Leader walked this planet the degree of D.S.D.
was conferred upon only one person.

After Rev. Gill's sermon on Sunday, July 4, Mrs. Eddy spoke
a few words including:

> The hour is come. The great battle of Armageddon is up-
> on us. The powers of evil are leagued together in secret con-
> spiracy against the Lord and against His Christ...Large
> numbers, in desperate malice, are engaged day and night in
> organizing action against us. ...Will you doff your lavender-
> kid zeal, and become real and consecrated warriors?

In July, Mary Plunkett and Emma Hopkins, as editor and
assistant editor respectively, began the publication of *International Magazine of Christian Science*, which was distributed by the Unity Publishing Company of which Mrs.
Plunkett was a partner. They, and many another disaffected
student, borrowed Mrs. Eddy's terminology, praised her when
it was to their advantage, and slandered her at other times.

Before the end of the year Mrs. Eddy revised her *Historical
Sketch*. This new edition, titled *Mind-Healing: Historical
Sketch*, contained the added information for her   Historical
students: Sketch
                                                      1886 edition

> If any honest Christian Scientist can be deceived into
> thinking that it is chance, not direction by malicious minds
> which are at work,—that ignorance instead of sin is what he
> has to meet at all times,—this error prevents him from un-

derstanding enough of the question to ensure his own defence, and leaves him in the power of Animal Magnetism,—perhaps temporarily relieved of his suffering, rejoicing in a hope of freedom which he afterwards finds to be vain.

Mrs. Eddy was a general directing the battle of Armageddon, appealing to her soldiers to doff their lavender-kid zeal and become consecrated warriors. The enemy was organizing action against her, and Mind was directing her to *organize* her defences. But her soldiers questioned her orders, and even, at times, her theology. The ministers, in whom she had hoped to find staunchest support, were often the most critical.

Rev. Gill was not reconciled to the fact that God knows not evil. It might have been for his benefit that she wrote "Origin of Evil" for the July *Journal*. The Truth was causing a chemicalization in that gentleman's thought while his wife was ever trying to pull him back to the orthodoxy he was outgrowing. After Thanksgiving dinner in Mrs. Eddy's home, Gill pursued the subject and seemed not to comprehend the Leader's answers. Mrs. Eddy finally stated, "Brother Gill, you will *never* understand these things until you heal the sick." He wrote her later that day and again the next morning, to which the Teacher responded:

> I trace a strong element of malicious mind acting on your morning thoughts. This to me is so very discouraging, for my morning thoughts always come clearer and are nearer His... You are a shining mark, you are in the open field, your bosom companion is dark as most all are on this question, the enemy are talking audibly and inaudibly to lead you astray.
>
> You see for a moment, in my atmosphere, the glimpse of this God-summit,... It is only a spiritual not an intellectual darkness that causes the human reason to reject this highest revelation of God.
>
> Your wife seeks to still the storm in your breast just when I should bid it rage, then it would vent itself and the sunshine of the above Truth would appear. I stand forever here. God put my feet on this Rock. ...
>
> You are not both mortal and immortal mind or body. The Ego, you, is *immortal only*. The mortal is the suggestive lie

calling itself you when it is not. . . . You are not two *opposites* but are one entity and individuality. The lying "you" is likened by Paul to that which was not him, "no longer *I* but sin."

Gill did not rise above the malicious mind acting on his thought, and by the end of the year Mrs. Eddy had to ask Mr. Wiggin to resume editorship of the *Journal*. The church had been less than satisfied with Gill's services and voted on the thirteenth of January that he was "not in any particular fulfilling the terms of our engagement with him." He proved unable to profit from the rebuke and resigned in a rage, following his resignation with attacks upon Christian Science and Mrs. Eddy. When the Association expelled him for his behaviour on the second of February, he went immediately to Arens. Gill's next article was a furiously violent attack against Mrs. Eddy published in *Religio-Philosophical Journal,* another Chicago mind-cure magazine. Mrs. Eddy wrote to her faithful student Ellen Brown, in Chicago: "It is the midnight of sin in Boston. The last Judas I hope has appeared."

JAMES HENRY WIGGIN

CHAPTER LII

LITERARY THIEVES

Thou shalt not steal.

Exodus

1887

S ARAH Crosse answered Gill's attack in the March *Journal* although a Chicago student had written to Mrs. Eddy, "Do not reply to it—he cannot hurt you or your cause by any such disjointed articles." The message of spiritual progress in March was a new hymn from Mrs. Eddy's pen:

"Feed My Sheep" March, 1887

FEED MY SHEEP

Shepherd, show us how to go
  O'er the hillside steep,
How to gather, how to sow,
  How to feed Thy sheep;
We will listen for Thy voice,
  Lest our footsteps stray,
We will follow and rejoice
  All the rugged way.

Thou wilt bind the stubborn will,
  Wound the callous breast,
Make self-righteousness be still,
  Break earth's stupid rest;
Strangers on a barren shore
  Lab'ring long and lone—
We would enter by the door,
  And Thou know'st Thine own;

So when day grows dark and cold
    Fear or triumph harms,
Lead Thy lambkins to the fold,
    Take us in Thine arms,
Feed the hungry, heal the heart,
    Till the morning's beam;
White as wool, ere we depart—
    Shepherd, wash us clean.

The lead article in the September *Journal* had been a revision of "An Allegory" by Mrs. Eddy which included this paragraph:

> The Stranger next enters a dark shabby dwelling, and he saith unto them, "Blessed are the poor in spirit, for theirs is the kingdom of heaven." But they understand not his saying. They have no conception of spiritual riches or immortal cravings, they are literary thieves, puffed up by stealing in the name of Truth, and they took the Stranger's pearls, and would kill him.

Twenty years earlier Mrs. Eddy had stood alone endeavoring to give the Science of man to a resisting world. At one time she had walked miles to a house where she had been told someone was interested in her message, only to have the door slammed in her face. Literally and figuratively doors had been slammed in her face from the outset, but she labored on, sustained by Love alone. By her incessant labors she had roused the world to interest in her message, and now on every side thieves were snatching her pearls and rushing off to sell them to a ready market.

Mind-cure publications were proliferating. Author after author was borrowing from her book without giving credit, else *explaining* Christian Science, or rewriting Science and Health, while teaching his own material misconceptions and calling it Christian Science. [Theosophy question October, 1886] A letter from one lost lamb was published in the *Journal* under "Questions Answered":

> Dear Mrs. Eddy: Not as an idle inquirer, but as an earnest,

343

sincere thinker after the *Truth,* do I address you; and I hope
you will, out of the goodness of your heart, answer me. I have
completed a course of Mental or Christian Science lectures.
My teacher is a practising metaphysician of Chicago. She is
also a "Theosophist," and during her lectures she introduced much of the Theosophic teachings and belief. When
we were through, she advised us to purchase Sinnett's works,
and several other books of like nature. I will say first, that I
have your book, and that, with my Bible, I study constantly.
After her suggestion I bought Sinnett's "Esoteric Buddhism,"
and have read it. I am now all confusion and mixed. I can
not reconcile it with the life and teachings of Jesus Christ. I
can not reconcile it with your teachings, consequently. Now,
will you help me? Are you a Theosophist? My teacher says:
"Theosophy is metaphysics (Christian Science), *only more
so."* Sinnett's book speaks of "the *necessity* of evil." Do "inanimate forms progress onward until a human Soul has been
formed"? Do you believe "in the certainty of some hundred
many-earth-lives to come,—the *repeated* in-carnations of a
Soul"? He says: "Our planet and ourselves are no more crea-
tions than an iceberg." He says: "The seventh principle of
man is *undefinable, incomprehensible,* and is the only God
recognized by esoteric knowledge." Does that agree with *your*
doctrine? He also says: "You can be immortal in good by
identifying oneself with God, or can be *immortal in evil* by
identifying oneself with Satan." He says there are *utterly
unspiritual Egos.* Do you believe in "the system of seven
worlds of man," and in the seven principles that the occult
science teaches men are composed of? Tell me, dear Mrs.
Eddy, can one be a thorough, consistent believer in the teachings of Theosophy and the occult sciences, and at the same
time a thorough, consistent believer in Christian Science,
and a successful *Healer?* I have studied in order that I may be
able to live the pure Christian life here, and *to do good;* oh, I
want to do *much* good, and I see daily where I can do it if I am
in the right path; and so it is for this I ask your help and advice, which I feel sure you'll not refuse to give me. If Divine
Spirit created man in his own image and likeness, how can
there "be unspiritual Egos"? or how can man be spiritually
evil and immortally evil?

Hoping anxiously for an early reply,
I am sincerely yours,
Mrs. H. D. Cope

Hopefully Mrs. Eddy's answer in the *Journal* helped the hundreds of others making similar inquiries:

Answer: Your interesting questions found ready response in my heart, and enlisted my interest in your situation, as hundreds of others are doing, but for lack of time remain unanswered. I can only touch briefly the borderland of comment on the vast questions proposed.

Just now, the darkest spot on the horizon of mortal mind that Christian Science can illumine is envy, and the strife for "who shall be greatest." It pushes Christianity aside to elbow in a crowd of robbers, that enter not in by the door, Truth, but would climb up some other way. Obscure, unlettered, unprincipled people are filling the field as Mind-Healers, who are mind-killers, building their only superstructure on false foundations—the power of evil and substance of matter. They are working out, through mortal mind, the claim of total depravity, in all its forms of animal magnetism. They rise on the merits of the true healer, to at length fall from their own demerits.

The above qualities, entering so largely into their work, engender the most difficult forms of disease.

Twenty years ago, when I first brought this subject to the consideration of the race, to be a Christian Science Mind-healer was no bid for respectability, popularity, wealth. It was a sharp appeal to conscience, spiritual growth, moral courage. The question then was, "Can you drink the cup?" On this basis there was no danger of injuring onesself or one's neighbor. The pioneer work has been done faithfully. Now comes the inquiry, Shall this work be overthrown by charlatans of the baser sort? Naught but the unselfish purpose, the higher understanding of God and the love of man, are incentives to real Mind-Healing. Once in this direction, and persecution, hardship, sacrifice, only "lead into green pastures, and beside the still waters."

Of "Esoteric Buddhism," its oriental necromancy, philosophy, or religion, I am happily ignorant. Such human philosophy may charm, allure, but it obscures the spiritual sense of Divine Science.

I recommend that you quit other reading and confine yourself for the present to the perusal of the Scriptures, and my work, Science and Health. This book has a Key to the Scriptures that never picks the lock, but opens the Word only as it turns in the grooves of God. This course pursued, and you will gain consolation and light. Theosophy is not allied to Christian Science: it misleads the understanding, whereas Christian Science enlightens it.

In good there is no necessity for evil. If evil has a necessity, it is to destroy itself.

The inanimate does not originate the animate. Intelligence never sprang from nonintelligence.

Soul is Spirit, infinite and eternal; hence Soul is neither sinful nor susceptible of growth—can neither sin nor die. "The wages of sin is death." Soul is immortal Spirit,—and is in nothing unlike Him. Mortals entertain a false conception of Soul, because the senses say God—Mind—is in matter. This *false view* of Life, substance and Intelligence is miscalled Soul. Flesh was never incarnated; God made manifest in the flesh is the divine outer action upon the inner vile affections of mortals. The influence from without cometh from Spirit. Whatever is from within is of the flesh.

It was a false teacher who told you that Christian Science and Theosophy are one.

Man is not as an iceberg; he is the image and likeness of his Maker; and the sunlight of Truth melts these frozen hypotheses of error with the warmth of divine Love.

Man has but one Principle, and that is God; and the Scripture saith: "Aquaint now thyself with God, and *be at peace.*"

Good is immortal, and evil is the opposite of good; hence evil is mortal.

The Ego is Spirit, and can be nothing else.

To your last touching enquiry, "Can one believe both Theosophy and Christian Science and be a successful healer?" I answer, No! "As well might a camel go through the eye of a needle." Christ is the Way, and the spiritual idea coincides at no point with the sensual or material.

Now dear friend, follow only the guidance of Truth and

Love; then you will be at peace, and heal the sick and sinner.

Yours tenderly,

Theosophists were not the only borrowers from Mrs. Eddy's Christian Science. Constant vigilance was necessary for the Mother to protect her child on every front. The previous summer she had published in the *Journal* that the book titled *Mind Cure on a Material Basis* was "shockingly unreliable, incorrect, and misleading on the subject of Christian Science," to which she added that "Such works as S. E. Titcomb's and Dr. W. F. Evans' are flooding the land, only to darken the light of Science."

On the eighth of February Julius Dresser delivered a lecture at the Church of the Divine Unity. This was a new organization which had been founded in Boston late in 1886 by another dissident student, Luther Marston, M.D. whom Mrs. Eddy had healed and taught two or three years earlier, and who had resided at her college for a time.

Dresser's lecture, which he entitled "The True History of Mental Science," was another attack upon Mrs. Eddy, attributing her great life work to Quimby, totally disregarding her years of unremitting toil,—of self-sacrificing labor. The literary thieves in this school of thought were stealing freely from Mrs. Eddy's published works excusing themselves by claiming that her Revelation from infinite Mind was not a revelation but a theft. The attack on this front could not be neglected. On the twenty-first of May Mrs. Eddy published the following notice in the Boston newspapers:

Offer to Quimby May, 1887

> To Whom it May Concern: Mr. George A. Quimby, son of the Late Phineas P. Quimby, over his own signature and before witness, stated in 1883 that he had in his possession at that time *all* the manuscripts that had been written by his father. And I hereby declare that, to expose the falsehood of parties publicly intimating that I have appropriated matter belonging to the aforesaid Quimby, I will pay the cost of printing and publishing the first edition of those manuscripts with the author's name attached.
>
> *Provided,* that I am allowed first to examine said manu-

347

scripts, and do find that they were his own compositions, and not mine, that were left with him many years ago, or that they have not since his death, in 1866, been stolen from my published works. Also that I am given the right to bring out this one edition under the copyright of the owner of said manuscripts, and all the money accruing from the sales of said book shall be paid to said owner. Some of his purported writings, quoted by Mr. Dresser, were my own words, as near as I can recollect them.

There is a great demand for my work *Science and Health with Key to the Scriptures;* hence Mr. Dresser's excuse for the delay to publish Quimby's manuscripts, namely, that this period is not sufficiently enlightened to be benefitted by them (?), is lost, for if I have copied from Quimby, and my book is accepted, it has created a demand for his.

Mary Baker G. Eddy

The offer was not accepted. Dishonesty cannot understand an honest heart nor an honest offer. But Dresser's lecture, which included Mary Patterson's praises of Quimby in the early sixties, was published in pamphlet form, necessitating an answer which Mrs. Eddy made in the June *Journal* under the title "Mind-Healing History":

In a peppery pamphlet Mr. Dresser delivers a stupendous eulogy over the late P. P. Quimby, as his healer, and exaggerates and fabricates in Quimby's behalf; but all that is kind, and I wish it was honest. ...

Did I write those articles in Mr. Dresser's pamphlet purporting to be mine? I might have written them twenty or thirty years ago, for I was under the mesmeric treatment of Dr. Quimby...I knew nothing then of the Science of Mind-healing; and I was as ignorant of mesmerism as Eve, before she was taught by the serpent. ...

It can be shown that Mr. Dresser tried Quimby's method, and relinquished it because he could not heal by it. I denounced it, after a few of my first students rubbed heads of their patients, and the immorality of one student opened my eyes to the horrors possible in Animal Magnetism. ...

His healing was never considered or called anything but Mesmerism. I tried to think better of it, and to procure him public favor. He was my doctor, and it wounded me to have him despised. The last time I saw him, he said, "You have made me all I am in Portland." In those days he needed friends. Why did not Dresser lecture then for Quimby, as he does now? He had no defender then but myself. I believed he was doing good; and even now, knowing as I do the harm in his practice, I would never revert to it, but for this public challenge. . . .

Is it love for our "mutual friend," or envy of the living, that would drag the silent departed so mercilessly before the people? I would touch tenderly his memory, speak reverently of his humane purpose, and name only his virtues, did not the man Dresser drive me, for conscience sake, to sketch the facts. I cannot defraud humanity of its claims, hide the true discovery, or close my eyes to usurpers, casting lots for Truth's seamless robe. Silencing my grief at treading less lightly on the ashes of the dead, I must write down Christian Science Mind-healing as the antipodes of Mr. Quimby's theory (if he had one!) and of his treatment of disease; . . .

It has always been my misfortune to think people better and bigger than they really are. My mistake is, to endow another person with my ideal, and then make him think it his own. . . . When I thought Mr. Quimby was doing good, it was natural for me to help him; and hundreds of others I have helped since then, sparing neither ease, time, nor money for this end.

The most unselfish motives evoke the most ingratitude; yet it is only by such motives that the best results are achieved. My final discovery of the Science of Mind-healing was the outgrowth of my motives and method. . . .

It was after the death of Mr. Quimby, and when I was apparently at the door of death, that I made this discovery in 1866. After that, it took about ten years of hard work for me to reach the standard of my first edition of Science and Health, published in 1875. . . .

Misinterpretations and misapplications of Truth constitute all error; and error can only be destroyed by the correct interpretation and application of Truth. The animal poison imparted through mortal mind, by false or incorrect mental physicians, is more destructive to health and morals than are the mineral and vegetable poisons prescribed by the matter physicians. This acknowledgement brings the wrath of mediums and mesmerists upon me, but never warps my purpose to enlighten mankind.

I discovered the Science of Mind-healing, and that was enough. It was the way Christ had pointed out: and that fact glorified it. My discovery promises nothing but blessings to every inhabitant of the globe. This glorious prospect seems to incense some degraded minds, and stimulate their unscrupulous efforts to thwart its benign influence and defeat its beneficence.

If ever Mr. Quimby's ominous manuscripts are brought to light, it will be when my copyrights have expired, and the dear-bought treasures of Truth are appropriated by both the evil and the good. Then, arm-in-arm, Mr. Dresser and his skeleton (like Dorcasina and her hero, in Female Quixotism) may enter the drawing rooms of Mind-healing Science. Stumbling up my stairs, they may fall unexpectedly into good company.

At the time of Dresser's attack in Boston and Gill's attack in a Chicago publication, Mrs. Eddy received an article from and by Joseph Adams which he was planning to republish in pamphlet form. It borrowed so heavily from her writings that she gave him a sharp rebuke for plagiarizing. He immediately left the Chicago Christian Science Institute where he was associated with Miss Ellen Brown and set up independently. By June he had launched his own publication called the *Chicago Christian Scientist,* and though he intended to remain a Christian Scientist and teach only from Science and Health, he did not differentiate between Mrs. Eddy's loyal students and those who mouthed her teachings while denying her leadership. When he applied to have his certificate renewed Mrs. Eddy wrote him:

> You have tried teaching Christian Science. Did you ever find a student who after taking twelve lessons was better able than you were to pioneer this cause? Then can you, only one year old in this knowledge know better than I who have worked it and earned my knowledge of it twenty-one years how to carry it out? After over ten years of experience and

success far beyond yours, I learned that nothing but organization would save this cause for mankind and protect it
from the devouring disorganizers. . . . You are commanded to
go to the lost sheep and gather them in: but you go to the
goats to gather them in.

The dissidents and literary thieves were legion, but they
were not the only problem the Leader had to meet.

MARY BAKER EDDY IN 1886
One of several photographs of Mrs. Eddy taken in
1886. Another in this series became the frontispiece
for Science and Health; still another the frontispiece
for *Miscellaneous Writings.*

CHAPTER LIII

DULL DISCIPLES

Only the devout Marys, and such as lived according to his precepts, understood the concrete character of him who taught—by the wayside, in humble homes, to itching ears and to dull disciples—the words of Life.

Mary Baker Eddy

1887

THE *Journal* began its fifth year in April of 1887 with a circulation of ten thousand. A short item in that issue has more import for serious students today than it had then:

FIRE, ELECTRICITY, AND DELAY

We owe our readers some explanation of our magazine's late appearance. ...a peculiar hindrance arose. This was in the electricity developed in the paper on which this Journal is printed. None of the printers...had ever known a case of such strong electric attraction. It seriously retarded the work, by causing the sheets to adhere tenaciously and annoyingly to each other.

A fire in the lower part of the building...also threatened disaster. ...the flames fortunately did not get under much headway before the engines had them under control.

The article did not quote the then current edition of Science and Health which stated, "Electricity is the essence of mortal mind, the counterfeit of the true essence of Eternal Mind;" nor did it note that with this issue the *Journal* was beginning a new department entitled "Animal Magnetism."

The National Christian Scientists' Association was to meet

at Tremont Temple in Boston on the thirteenth of April. Late in March Mrs. Eddy sent an urgent notice to her students to attend, saying in part: "I have gotten up this N.C.S.A. for you and the life of the cause. Address to N.C.S.A. April, 1887 I have something important to say to you, a message from God." Janet Colman, who was teaching a class at the time, had not planned to attend—until she received Mrs. Eddy's letter. Her word picture depicts the Leader's disappointment:

> She gave us a prayer, but we did not seem to have it to carry home with us, and no one else that we knew did either. Our Leader had us come to her house; did all that she could to have us wake up and hear. Just before I went back West to my class, I had to go back to get my certificate...so I went to the College to see Mr. Frye about it...I asked Mr. Frye if he thought that Mrs. Eddy would see me. ...She came into the back parlor and spoke to me. She rebuked us all for not listening to what God had for us, that we were so happy to see each other, that we made merry, and paid no heed to God's message...She turned from me and went down stairs to her supper. I burst into tears. I felt the rebuke so keenly; I felt she had told the truth. Soon I heard a step which I knew was hers, and I turned my face so as not to watch her go through the entry: the first thing I knew her dear arms were around me, and she kissed me and gave me a beautiful American Beauty Rose...This rebuke that she gave me went so deep that I never again felt the pleasures of the world the same. ...The sorrow over my thoughtlessness in not hearing "God's Message" to us did not leave me and later on...I heard a voice say, "I will bring all things to your remembrance" and then this prayer began to unfold: "Oh Lord, give me higher, purer, holier desires. Oh Lord, give me more self-abnegating desires. Oh Lord, give me a desire for more Love."

The students had planned and held a fund-raising concert after the meeting, and their social interests had taken precedence. Worldly activities dulled their ears to their Leader's spiritual call. They needed rebukes constantly to chasten their affections, but many reacted against God's messenger ("Thou art my battle-ax...saith the Lord.") rather than profiting as did Janet Colman.

Alternately praising and rebuking her students, repelling the attacks on every side, Mrs. Eddy was all the while at the helm steering the bark of Christian Science through the stormy seas and pointing the way her students should take. In a detailed article entitled "The Educational System of Christian Science Mind-Healing," she had recommended that qualified students establish institutions in good school buildings in the best portions of our cities. By April twenty academies and institutes from New York to San Francisco were advertising in the columns of the *Journal*. But the Leader's outline for individual progress was completely overlooked. The article also stated:

> To protect the public all my worthy students receive certificates of degrees, that are renewed annually, until they graduate with diplomas. . . .
>
> Until the students graduate, they are incapable of teaching more than the first lessons of the Science of Mind.

For more than a year the four college courses had been advertised every month. The *Journal* advertisement read:

> The Class in Theology completes the Collegiate course. This class includes six lectures on the Scriptures, and a summary of the Principle and practice of Christian Science. Tuition, $200. Students may graduate, who have passed through all the classes at this Institution satisfactorily.

No student ever graduated from the Massachusetts Metaphysical College!

While the Leader was eager for their spiritual progress, they were eager to build a church edifice. The *Journal* frequently
Strawberry   carried appeals for contributions, and the stu-
Festival   dents had held more than one fund-raising festi-
June, 1886   val. Mrs. Eddy had attended their Strawberry
Festival the previous summer, and though their social measures were destined for eventual failure, the words she spoke on that occasion are destined for fulfilment:

> After due justice had been done to the ices, berries and cake, Rev. Mary B. G. Eddy made an address from the por-

tico, to the effect that some day Christian Science will enable us to enjoy such a treat without raising the fruit, compounding the cake, freezing the cream, or buying the sugar; just as Jesus fed the multitude, without procuring the loaves and fishes through the usual channels of natural production and supply. She also narrated some incidents about the unusual and seemingly supernatural (but really natural) growth of apple-blossoms in icy winter, and of fresh shoots from dry stems in summer,—through the power of Mind. She argued that if belief produces disease, and its removal leaves health to have its perfect work, then false belief may also prevent the perfect fulfilment of Spirit in all our material surroundings, flowers and fruit not excepted.

Little note was taken of her words. The students were more often wandering in some by-way than *following* their Leader, though there were encouraging exceptions. Hanover P. Smith had written and published a tribute to his teacher entitled "The Writings and Genius of the Founder of Christian Science." One voice was raised in her behalf midst the tumult raised against her. By June the field showed sufficient advancement to allow Mrs. Eddy to teach her Metaphysical Obstetrics course for the first time. Hanover was one of the fourteen chosen students in that class.

Obstetrics class June, 1887

The healing was encouraging, and there was a great deal of it in the field. Much was faith healing, and all was attributable to Mrs. Eddy's teachings and writings; but there was some true scientific practice. Each month the *Journal* carried numerous testimonials. The January *Journal* had related the newspaper account of the introduction of Christian Science to Joseph Mann and his family. Joseph had been accidently shot in the heart. Three physicians, after examination, had pronounced the wound fatal. They had left the unconscious patient, when a visiting Christian Scientist, R. C. Hannon of Boston, entered the scene and healed the young man. The *Journal* adds:

> Mr. R. C. Hannon was for several years a sufferer from cancer in the stomach, which physicians failed to cure. Mrs. F. J. Stetson healed him in two treatments in Christian Science, and gave him a course of instruction, and bade him,

"Go into the world, preach the gospel, heal the sick."

The healings were carrying Christian Science far and wide, but news of another type was often reported in the *Journal*. That was the harassment of Christian Science practitioners, sometimes by legal action, imprisonment and fines, for spiritual healing. The persecutions were a trial for all Scientists, but perhaps the greatest trial for the Leader was not the persecution as much as the false claimants who, in the name of Christian Science, were adulterating her teaching. She wrote to Ellen Brown, "There are 20 false lecturers and teachers to one that is true."

JANET COLMAN

CHAPTER LIV

THE IMITATOR

For there shall arise false Christs, and false prophets, and shall shew great signs and wonders, insomuch that, if it were possible, they shall deceive the very elect.

Jesus

1887

OF all the false teachers, perhaps Mary Plunkett was the most offensive. She had scarcely completed the Primary class at the College when she was pouring out her scorn for Mrs. Eddy in a letter to her new friend, Emma Hopkins. No sooner had she returned to Detroit than she was telling the practitioner who had healed her, Mrs. Annie Knott, that she would take the Normal class and be head of the movement in all the territory west of Buffalo, else sweep Mrs. Eddy from the face of the earth.

After teaching Mary Plunkett, Mrs. Eddy added to the college advertisement:

> No invalids, and only persons of good moral character, are accepted as students. All students are subject to examination and rejection; and they are liable to leave the class, if found unfit to remain in it.

She had not issued a certificate to Mrs. Plunkett, but that woman was undeterred. She immediately set forth to outdistance the Leader. Mary Plunkett had the ability to match her audacity, and with her most important convert, Emma Hopkins, she soon had a magazine imitating the *Journal,* a college in Chicago, and classes and teachers spread broadcast. In all their work the two women appropriated the name Christian Science, causing a good deal of confusion in the public thought.

357

Mrs. Eddy's defence of Christian Science was unceasing, but her pamphlet by that name was out of print in August. Its place was filled, however, by a new publication from the Leader's pen entitled *Christian Science: No and Yes.* This pamphlet sold for twenty-five cents and was considered to be "just the thing to put into the hands of skeptical enquirers."

No and Yes published August, 1887

Mrs. Plunkett was bidding for those skeptical enquirers most aggressively. In August or September she journeyed to Boston to see Mrs. Eddy for the purpose of proposing that they divide the field by the Mississippi River,—the West to be her exclusive territory. If the following account was not of Mary Plunkett's visit, it was of the same character:

> A lady came to the door...with a box of American Beauty roses and begged Lydia to accept them and give them to Mrs. Eddy, and say that she would call in the afternoon to see Mrs. Eddy... [On seeing the bouquet] Mrs. Eddy said, Take them away; what a mockery!
>
> Lydia took them to the kitchen and all day long suffered severely. ...Mrs. Eddy finally said, "Lydia, ...What have you done with those roses?" "I took them to the kitchen, Mother." "Are they destroyed?" "No." "Go to the kitchen immediately and take the roses and put them in the fire." ...[Reluctantly] she complied...[and] immediately she was released from the pain and was her normal self again. ...About an hour later...Mrs. Eddy said to her, "You are free?" "Yes, Mother, I am." "Lydia, do you know what that means? That was theosophy. They believe that if they can get something into your hands they can use you as an avenue. Now be on your watch."

Shortly after Mrs. Plunkett's visit Mrs. Eddy received the following letter from a student in Chicago:

> I have this day heard a statement from Mrs. Plunkett to this effect; that she had recently called upon you; that she had found you sick, and unable to go on with your class; that you had invited her to return to the fold; and that she refused your invitation, because she could not agree with you about teaching. I did not credit her statements, and wish to

know the facts, over your own signature, that I may be able to deny these, and all such insinuations.

B. Sherman

Mrs. Eddy published both the letter and her response to it:

The woman referred to did call on me, about the first of September, and sent up my servant with her card and a bouquet of flowers. I was in good health and spirits; and the entire substance of my conversation with her was a calm and kind rebuke of any false position taken in the name of Christian Science. The substance of her talk was a timid attempt to raise herself in my estimation. After she had left me, I remarked to my clerk: "This call was made for the purpose of subsequently misrepresenting what I had said, and you ought to have heard our conversation."

Mrs. Mary H. Plunkett's report of our interview, as stated in the above letter, is an utter falsehood throughout. Nothing of the kind was said. It is not probable that I should ask a person to assist me in teaching Christian Science whom I regarded as too unsafe to be received into my Normal Class. Past experience had taught me her character; and I regret to add, that on the evening of her call I saw no improvement in her motives and aims.

She is reported as saying that she paid "three hundred dollars for her tuition at the Massachusetts Metaphysical College, and that I then required two hundred dollars more to grant her a certificate, which she refused to pay." These are the facts relative to our business transactions: When she entered the Primary Course she claimed not to have the money to pay for her tuition, and asked me to take some jewelry as part payment. I declined; but discounted one-third on her tuition, and she paid me just two hundred dollars. The only money I ever receive for certificates is twenty-five cents on each annually renewed certificate. I gave her no certificate, solely because she did not improve the opportunity she had in the class of receiving my instructions; and because I learned, with sad surprise, that only God's hand and lessons could so change her motives and morals as to make her receptive of Christian Science. My autumn term was referred to in our conversations: but I simply told her the Primary Class was postponed, to accommodate some members of the bar, who wished to enter my college, but were obliged also to attend the September term of court.

There are sometimes to be met certain adepts who compel honest people to besmirch their own pens, and to spend their time in correcting injurious falsehoods. If you converse with these masqueraders, however cautiously and kindly, they are sure to go away and belie you, and repeat (professedly) what they want people to think that you have said. This retards the cause of Christian Science. How shall we treat such defamers? If we refuse to meet them, we lose a possible chance of doing good to this class of creatures. Even if we do not grant them interviews, they will improve other chances to do us evil. Charity receives many blows; but uncharitableness in ourselves is more to be feared than the blows.

On the tenth of September Mrs. Eddy had a vision of what lay in store for the Children of Israel who disbelieved her sayings or refused to follow her lead. It caused her to give a resumé of her experience in learning that the basic evil to be overcome was not sickness, but sin:

Vision of September 10 1887

Step by step I began to learn that the remedy of sin must be searched out. ...The arguments to heal sickness caused by the fear of physical beliefs would not heal the sufferings caused by the fear of sin. ...

Here I find that I must learn through the Old Testament the way of sin and that the power of the Egyptian necromancy must be met over again with the power of Truth in divine Science, and that we must know how to conquer through Truth and Love the belief of hate and mediumship whereby Samuel was brought before Saul, or the mediums will use the power of their belief in spirits to produce diseases beyond any physical methods to do it. These beliefs produced through hate can only be met through Spirit. If the least animal magnetism or human belief is employed, it will prevent the recovery of the sick, and the mediums and mesmerists will kill all they undertake to kill.

When you think you have mastered disease on a physical

basis you are mistaken. You have got to learn that it must be
healed on the basis of sin causing it—not necessarily your
own sins but the sins of others, their hatred, envy and efforts
to kill you—just as you have had to heal disease on a physical
basis by taking up the minds that loved your patients and
were misleading their thought.

Now your teacher is learning her way in divine Science
through suffering, through the rule of sin...Twenty years ago
when she had mastered the physical cause of disease, no
circumstances material could produce a cold or catarrh upon
her. ...

Colds and catarrhs caused by the arguments and beliefs of
sin will reappear more sudden and inveterate than from
changes of the weather, exposures or contagion, when these
effects are caused by the faith of theosophy in empowering
evil spirits to do the work for them, as the witch of En-dor
brought up Samuel for Saul. That was a lie, but a larger and
more frightful lie, because it embraced a belief in the power
of the dead as well as the living to afflict the people.

All the beliefs of sin and their methods of destroying the
peace of mind, filling the body with disease, administering
poison through mind with more effect than the doctors could
administer it through matter, have to be met and overcome
through divine Science by every mortal here or hereafter.

The acknowledgement that sin was the basic cause of all
earth's problems was the stumbling-block for most of her students. They accepted eagerly all she said about good, but they
did not want to uncover evil; hence, for each one that followed
the Leader, there were twenty that practised mental healing in
their own way, closing their eyes to animal magnetism. From
this field it was not difficult for Mary Plunkett to gather quite
a following.

If Mrs. Eddy would not divide the seamless robe, Mrs. Plunkett intended to have all of it. The National Christian Scientist
Association had met in Boston in April. Mrs. Plunkett organized, from a convention of mental healers which met, also
in Boston, on the nineteenth of October, her organization
which she called the International Christian Scientist Association. In November Plunkett and Hopkins began a new monthly

journal called, *Truth, A Magazine of Christian Science.*

Her next move was to lay claim to all the eastern territory. Leaving Mrs. Hopkins to manage everything in the mid-west, she made her headquarters in New York City. Though there were two academies and several practitioners in that city listed in the *Journal*, the flamboyant Mrs. Plunkett took the town by storm and was soon referred to as the "high priestess" of Christian Science. Mrs. Eddy's sincere followers were practically inundated by the tidal wave she caused, but there was one student,—Mrs. Augusta Stetson,—who, more than all others, rose to the challenge. In later years Mrs. Eddy referred fondly to Mrs. Stetson as her "war-horse," but though Augusta was indispensable to the battle, staunch and faithful, the mockery of the imitator, the false leadership deceiving the public, could be overcome only by the true Leader.

CHICKERING HALL
Where Mrs. Eddy began preaching in October, 1885.

CHAPTER LV

MY SON, MY SON

SON. The Son of God, the Messiah or Christ. The son of man, the offspring of the flesh.

Mary Baker Eddy

1887

T HE Battle of Armageddon raged on, but few were aware of that fact. Though her enemies knew that Mrs. Eddy was a formidable foe, the world saw her as the capable, serene leader of a new movement which was spreading beyond national boundaries. How she needed help in her work! especially men to carry the weight. In her Primary class the previous May a man named Frank E. Mason had shown much promise. He had since written some fine articles for the *Journal,* and, tried in Mrs. Eddy's pulpit, had done very well. This new disciple had given encouragement to her weary hope, and by fall she had accepted him in her Normal class which began on the thirtieth of October.

To her students, new and old, Mrs. Eddy was the embodiment of strength; but she longed, at times, for just one to lean upon. Asa Gilbert had been that one for five short years. At his death she had turned to George Glover hoping he would leave prospecting and drinking to stand by her, but he would not; so she had given up any hope of assistance from her son.

The reverse, however, was not the case. In Lead City, Dakota, George began hearing reports of the spread of Christian Science, and his interest in his mother in-   Letter to
creased correspondingly. The leader of such a   George Glover
movement must be growing very wealthy. George   October, 1887
Glover is not the first son who desired to live in affluence at his mother's expense, but he is the first one who ever elected to do

363

so while his mother was fighting the Battle of Armageddon. His letter stating that he wanted to bring his family to Boston to be with her, prompted this response:

Boston, Oct. 31, 1887

Dear George: Yours received. I am surprised that you think of coming to visit me when I live in a schoolhouse and have no room that I can let even a boarder into.

I use the whole of my rooms and am at work in them more or less all the time.

Besides this I have all I can meet without receiving company. I must have quiet in my house, and it will not be pleasant for you in Boston. The Choates are doing all they can by falsehood, and public shames, such as advertising a college of her own within a few doors of mine when she is a disgraceful woman and known to be. I am going to give up my lease when this class is over, and cannot pay your board nor give you a single dollar now. I am alone, and you never would come to me when I called for you, and now I cannot have you come.

I want quiet and Christian life alone with God, when I can find intervals for a little rest. You are not what I had hoped to find you, and I am changed. The world, the flesh and evil I am at war with, and if any one comes to me it must be to help me and not to hinder me in this warfare. If you will stay away from me until I get through with my public labour then I will send for you and hope to then have a home to take you to.

As it now is, I have none, and you will injure me by coming to Boston at this time more than I have room to state in a letter. I asked you to come to me when my husband died and I so much needed some one to help me. You refused to come then in my great needs, and I then gave up ever thinking of you in that line. Now I have a clerk who is a pure-minded Christian, and two girls to assist me in the college. These are all that I can have under this roof.

If you come after getting this letter I shall feel you have no regard for my interest or feelings, which I hope not to be obliged to feel.

Boston is the last place in the world for you or your family. When I retire from business and into private life, then I can

receive you if you are reformed, but not otherwise. I say this
to you, not to any one else. I would not injure you any more
than myself.
                                    As ever sincerely,
                                    M. B. G. Eddy

Within days of the writing of this letter, a young doctor appeared at the door of the Metaphysical College who was about
George's age, and who embodied the qualities Mary longed to
see in her son. George was uneducated, loud, boisterous: Dr.
Foster was educated, quiet, refined. Foster, a practising homeopathic physician in Waterbury, Vermont, had witnessed healings of some of his own patients by Christian Science and had
come to investigate this new teaching. A Primary class was to
convene on the seventh of November, and Ebenezer J. Foster
became the second M.D. to enroll in that class.

Before the class ended the contrast between Foster and
George Glover was repeatedly emphasized, for George, undeterred by his mother's letter, arrived at her door with his wife
and family. The letter she had written him said, "if any one
comes to me it must be to help me and not to hinder me in this
warfare." A visiting family with three children was no help in
the battle, but George's uncouth appearance and behavior,
his illiterate complaining wife, and his desire to share in his
mother's fame and wealth were a great hindrance.

Mrs. Eddy made the best of an untenable situation and
took a house in Chelsea for the Glovers. She surprised her
church when she appeared on the platform of Chickering Hall
with three children and introduced her grandchildren to the
congregation. She gave them all the time she could, including
Thanksgiving Day, but while her opportunistic son was idling
about Boston, Dr. Foster was busily engaged back in Vermont
with his new-found knowledge. In his letters to his teacher he
addressed her as "Mother," referred to himself as "your child,"
and was genuinely eager to do all he could to assist her in her
work. He came much closer to fulfilling the term son than did
her own flesh and blood.

Who has not longed for human help and love? for the close-
ness of family? The Leader had many more experiences before
she added the word *Son* to the Glossary of Science and Health
and defined it "the Messiah or Christ."

CHAPTER LVI

METAPHYSICAL OBSTETRICS

*Scientific obstetrics: When this new birth takes place, the
Christian Science infant is born of the Spirit, born of God...*

Mary Baker Eddy

1887

DECEMBER was a busy month for the Christian Scientists in Boston. They were planning a Fair, a fund-raising event for their church building. They had been publicizing the event in the *Journal* for months and begging Scientists all over the country to donate funds and things, and also to attend on December 19, 20, and 21.

Mrs. Eddy took no part in this unscientific endeavor; neither did she endorse it. On the other hand, while she did not approve, she did not deter them, and she even attended on Tuesday evening with her son and his family. However, the "Extract from a letter" which appeared in the December *Journal* was probably published at Mrs. Eddy's request:

> True Christianity began to wane, as Truth became hid in churches and ritualistic forms; and just in proportion as you lay more stress on the formation of church-organizations... than you do on the work of healing, will your cause decline and eventually be lost. It is the practical work of doing good, so beautifully illustrated in Science and Health, that appeals so forcibly to others, and draws so many to you and the Cause.
>
> Not all your churches and preachers will do as much to win people to the Truth, as the few good healers, who are never heard of except in the homes of the people. ...Science and Health, [Mrs. Eddy's] masterpiece, is greater than any Church which she or her followers can establish. This book, or rather,

the truth therein, needs no church to proclaim it or bolster it. . .
The truths inculcated in her Science will outlive any
church or creed. While I condemn the mistaken policy of
embalming any truths,. . .so much grander than the lifeless
and idolatrous forms of a church, it does me good to hear how
much is being done by the patient, quiet mothers in behalf of
Truth, to make glad the homes of the people.

This letter departed not from the words of the author who
had written in her first edition of Science and Health, "We have
no need of creeds and church organizations to sustain or explain a demonstrable platform, that defines itself in healing
the sick and casting out error." No doubt that is why it was
published. But you cannot drive sheep: you can only lead
them. The "Letter Extract" pointed the way, but the Boston
Scientists and most of the field did not see it. They were far
more interested in the Church Fair and another event that occurred in December.

This second item of interest was the fact that Mrs. Eddy had
moved her place of residence. Though she could get her students
to repeat and to teach that *all* is Spirit, when   New home
they reported her move in the columns of the   in Boston
Journal they titled it "Change of Material Base":   December, 1887

At Christmastide Rev. Mary B. Glover Eddy began to oc-
cupy the new house which she has recently purchased on
Commonwealth Avenue, Number 385. The price is recorded
in the real-estate transactions. . .at forty thousand dollars.
It is a large house in the midst of a new block, and contains
twenty rooms. In front it overlooks the recently dedicated
statue of Leif Eriksson, the Norseman who discovered
America. . .five centuries before Columbus. . . .From the
rear windows there is a view of Charles River. . .The spot is
very beautiful, and the house has been finished and furnished
under the advice of a professional decorator.

All this activity was irrelevant to the cause. The real progress,
as always, was in Mrs. Eddy's activities. In November she had
published a twenty-seven page pamphlet entitled   *Rudiments*
Rudiments and Rules of Divine Science. She   published
also announced the preparation of a new volume   November, 1887

entitled *The Unity of Good and the Unreality of Evil* which should be forthcoming in December.

The previous June Mrs. Eddy had taught the first class in Metaphysical Obstetrics. On the fifth of December her second

Obstetrics
class
December, 1887

obstetric class convened. Metaphysical obstetrics bore little relationship to physical obstetrics, and the Wayshower was leading a few of her most experienced students into deeper waters than they had known before. It was the most challenging experience many of them had ever had. The Teacher wrote to a student after the June class that it was the class "best suited to the propulsion of the student." She wrote also that it was "the hardest and the best class I ever taught." Following the December class, Laura Lathrop said, in a letter to her teacher, that she had suffered no more in bearing her own two children than she had in admitting to herself the truth that would enable her to lift this burden for others.

The monthly advertisement for the Metaphysical Obstetrics class stated that it was "open only to students who have taken their Primary Course at this College," but most of the students had also taken the Normal Course and were tried and trusted practitioners.

Though women are generally more receptive of the spiritual idea, that only partially accounted for the fact that there were no men in the second class. The main reason was probably an unforeseen reaction by one of the men in the June class. John M. C. Murphy, who had been active since first studying with Mrs. Eddy in 1883, decided to learn material obstetrics after having been taught metaphysical obstetrics. He soon interested several others, who had not been among the chosen few for the advanced teaching, to accompany him to medical school. Though this was without Mrs. Eddy's sanction, once again she did not object. However, it proved to be the beginning of a very divisive influence in the Christian Scientist Association which took a heavy toll before another year had passed.

The advertisement for the College in the *Journal* continued to include the course in Metaphysical Obstetrics each month, but that advanced class was never again taught solely by Mrs. Eddy.

CHAPTER LVII

UNITY OF GOOD

Unity is the essential nature of Christian Science. Its Principle is One, and the demonstration of that One demands oneness of thought and action.

Mary Baker Eddy

1888

F OR months Mrs. Eddy had one obstacle after another thrown into her path, but her students seemed unaware of the problems and dangers. They were glamorized by her new home, the success of the Church Fair, and the general busy-ness. On the first day of the new year the Leader had a vision which, once again, involved the original malpractitioner:

Vision of
January 1
1888

> VISION OF JANUARY 1, 1888: I was in my own house. Richard Kennedy, the fiend, came in and was so pleasant and plausible. I began to rejoice, thinking he was being reclaimed. He said, "Come and see me rock my father." He sat in the chair to see if it would hold them and thought it would. He went for his father, when he jumped right up as sprightly as a young boy. The buildings seemed to be on fire. I tried to get there but everything seemed to obstruct. I got to where I could see it. Then tried to go back with the way hedged, I calling fire, fire. Kennedy seemed to have locked the door against me. Only one student realized there was a fire. I could not make them see it.

Mrs. Eddy was pushing on daily against obstructions which her students could not see, fighting the flames of the malpractitioners, while her students were fanning them. One early student recorded the Leader as often saying that "Evil fanned the flames, and the students blew the bellows."

January 30th saw the convening of a Normal class at the college. On the twenty-sixth of February Chickering Hall was *Christening* crowded "for a service which has long been *service* desired by many of the members of the church." *February, 1888* In a very impressive ceremony, without the use of water, Rev. Mrs. Eddy baptised twenty-nine children including her three grandchildren. Whether this was a concession or an experimental step, it was never repeated.

The next Primary class was scheduled to convene early in March. George Glover had no desire to learn Christian Science, but suggested that his wife be included in the class. The burden the Glover family imposed upon our Leader is revealed in this letter she wrote to George on the first of March:

> I want your children educated. No greater disgrace rests on my family name than the ignorance of the parents of these darling children.
>
> You could read in the Bible very well when you left your Mother long ago. It should be a shame to any one at any age not to be able to read. If I were fifty years old and could not read I would learn to do it then, even if I knew I should not live a year longer. ...
>
> If [your wife] will read to me a page of Science and Health wherever I open to it, I will then talk with you about her joining my next class.

During the month of March the little volume, *Unity of Good,* was published at last. Mrs. Eddy wrote to Ellen Brown (Now *Unity of Good* Mrs. John Linscott) regarding the new book that *published* it "was needed or it would never have taken *March, 1888* about six months to get published. The way is always blockaded in proportion to the weight of good that is to be carried over it."

On the fifth of March, Mr. and Mrs. Edward A. Kimball, of Chicago, were among the forty-seven pupils who assembled for the Primary class, following which they returned home to spend several years in quiet study and practice. During the course, Edward and Kate Kimball called on the Leader at her home on Commonwealth Avenue which visit Mrs. Kimball later recalled in these words:

We were taken up to her private sitting room which was on
the second floor, and she looked so different from her first appearance before us as a teacher when she rather loomed as a
tall woman and a manifestation of power. On this occasion
she sat curled up in an easy rocking chair, and looked rather
small and delicate, and she said she deeply wished sometimes that she could be a little old lady in a cap with nothing
much to do.

Much as she longed for rest, the battle was not over, and she
was almost the only one who even knew that there was a battle
going on. The students were involved with Shortened limbs
battling sickness; whereas the College advertise-   elongated
ment stated regularly: "N.B.—Mrs. Eddy de-   1888
clines to consult on disease." She declined consultation and did
not take patients, but she never ceased to heal. A workman
named Carter came to do some work at her new home. The
man wore a heavy iron shoe eight or nine inches high on one foot.
In later years Mr. Carter wrote:

> I was called to Mrs. Eddy's home on Commonwealth
> Avenue, in Boston. to do some light work. Mrs. Eddy came
> into the room where I was busy, and observing my condition,
> kindly remarked, "I suppose you expect to get out of this
> some time." I answered, "No; all that can be done for me
> has been done, and I can now manage to get around with a
> cane." Mrs. Eddy said, "Sit down and I will treat you." When
> she finished the treatment she said, "You go home and take off
> that iron shoe, and give your leg a chance to straighten out."
> I went home and did as I was told, and now I am so well that,
> so far as I know, one leg is as good as the other.

"Things to be Thought Of" by Mrs. Eddy was the lead article
in the March *Journal*. It included many points of resistance to
Unity of Good. Two paragraphs that were later eliminated, said:

> Because of the growing need of thoroughly qualified teach-
> ers, I am compelled to say that hereafter I shall receive only
> those students into the Normal Class whom I have prepared
> by a Primary Course.
> ...Let loyal Normal Class graduates from the Massa-

chusetts Metaphysical College organize a body to be called the Christian Science Union, and hold regular meetings at intervals of not over two weeks. The object of this Union should be mutual aid and improvement. ...it should be understood that no member is the leader of this body, though every member should strive to be the servant of God, and led by His Spirit.

The Leader felt the need for union, but once again her students were not following their Leader. "Vainglory" from Mrs. Eddy's pen the previous November had pointed to the pitfalls, but her admonition had gone unheeded.

MRS. EDDY'S HOME ON COMMONWEALTH AVENUE

CHAPTER LVIII

REBELLION

Error is foaming, and it hisses at the "still small voice of Truth," but it can neither silence nor disarm God's voice.

Mary Baker Eddy

1888

THE Boston Scientists should have been chagrined by the final result of their Church Fair. In June of 1886 the Church had bought a site in the Back Bay district of Boston. Instead of applying the metaphysics they had learned in order to meet the mortgage, they had resorted to the outgrown methods of their former churches. All were rejoicing in the tremendous success of the Fair when they were rudely awakened from their revels and their reversion to unscientific means. The treasurer absconded with all the money! Mrs. Eddy said, "He was an honest man."

Those who learned from this lesson renewed their efforts to *follow* their leader and her teachings. For six months Mrs. Eddy had been meeting much mental resistance to *unity of good* which had forced her into more spiritual latitudes. Once again her students were being sifted as to who could follow into these deeper waters. In this trial many succumbed to the malicious suggestions which came to their consciousness criticizing and condemning the Leader.

Frank Mason, now assistant pastor living and working at the college, wrote a timely article entitled "The Pearl of Loyalty." It was the leader in the May *Journal,* but before that issue appeared an incident occurred which brought the growing rebellion to the surface. A member of the Association, Mrs. Abby H. Corner of West Medford, Massachusetts, was indicted for manslaughter. She had attended her daughter in a child-

birth which had been fatal to both mother and child. The newspapers pounced on the story with malice and denunciations
of Christian Science.

Mrs. Eddy responded with an article for the Committee on
Publication to send to the Boston *Herald:*

> The lamentable case reported from West Medford of the
> death of a mother and her infant at childbirth should for-
> ever put a stop to quackery. There has been but one side of
> this case presented by the newspapers. We wait to hear from
> the other side, trusting that attenuating circumstances will
> be brought to light. Mrs. Abby H. Corner never entered
> the obstetrics class at the Massachusetts Metaphysical
> College. She was not fitted at this institute for an accoucheur,
> had attended but one term, and four terms, including three
> years of successful practice by the student, are required to
> complete the college course.
>
> The West Medford case, so far as is known, is the first in-
> stance of death at childbirth in the practice of Christian
> Science. This fact is of vital importance when compared with
> the daily statistics of death on such occasions caused by the
> use of drugs and instruments. Does medical malpractice and
> the mortality that ensues go unnoticed because of their
> frequency?
>
> Committee on Publication
> Christian Scientists' Association

Every word she wrote was the truth. Mrs. Corner's side of
the case had not been presented, so Mrs. Eddy's reference to
quackery was not aimed at her student but at the malpractice
which was overlooked in the "regular" schools. The main issue
was the attack on Christian Science, on her college, and her
teaching; but the rebellious students did not so see it. Their
indignation which had been aroused by the unjust press
coverage, was turned with fury against their teacher.

Sarah Crosse had objected as a member of the Committee
on Publication to Mrs. Eddy's response, but the other two
members had submitted it anyway. Mrs. Crosse, together with
Mr. Murphy, the leader of the medical faction, became
aggressive in their intent to oust Mrs. Eddy from her Association. Though the Corner case was the exciting cause, the re-

mote cause was the intent of malicious mind to separate the Discoverer from her discovery.

A special meeting of the C.S.A. was held on the second of June ostensibly on Mrs. Corner's behalf. This and the regular meeting on June 6 became very stormy indeed, causing the secretary to resign. The dissenters endeavored to elect Murphy to the position, but failed. William B. Johnson was elected to fill the vacant post.

Mr. Murphy moved that the Association contribute two hundred dollars toward Mrs. Corner's legal expenses, but this was voted down; for Mrs. Eddy, though absent, had requested that the students aid Mrs. Corner by individual subscriptions. One hundred seventy dollars was pledged, but the dissidents contributed nothing.

Mrs. Eddy herself offered to pay to have a medical expert brought in to give evidence, but Mrs. Corner's counsel assured her that it was not necessary, as indeed it was not. The Leader also wrote an article for the June *Journal* entitled "Malicious Newspaper Reports" which included the following:

> ...when the press assumes the liberty to lie, it discounts clemency, mocks morality, outrages humanity, breaks common law, gives impulse to violence, envy, and hate...
>
> In times like these it were well to lift the veil on the sackcloth of home, where weepeth the faithful but stricken mother, and the bruised father bendeth his aching head, where the bereft husband, silent and alone, gazes in dull despair at the vacant seat, and the motherless little ones, wondering, huddle together, and repeat with quivering lips words of strange import.

Sad to say, the stricken mother did not remain faithful.

Calvin Frye and William B. Johnson did their best to keep order at the Association meeting, but it was next to impossible. Two days later Mrs. Eddy sent Mr. Johnson to Chicago to apprise her leading students in that city of the situation in Boston, for the National Christian Scientist Association was to meet in the Windy City the following Wednesday. Mr. Johnson carried this letter with him:

Boston, June 8, 1888
My dear Student.

Listen to this faithful student. Our vice-president in Boston is heading a new faction. Ask Mr. Johnson about it who bears this letter.

As ever your faithful Teacher,
M. B. G. Eddy

Mr. Johnson was sent to the pastor of the Chicago church, Rev. George B. Day; to the heads of the Chicago Christian Science institutes: Mrs. Elizabeth Webster and Mrs. G. W. Adams—Union Park Institute; Mr. and Mrs. Noyes—Illinois Institute; Mrs. Larminie and Mrs. Bell—Hyde Park Institute; Mr. and Mrs. Linscott—Chicago Institute; plus Mr. and Mrs. Bradford Sherman.

In a history of the Christian Science movement, Mr. Johnson's son wrote:

> That the revolutionists might obtain the needed power to force their issue, they conceived a plot to get control of the books of the secretary. . . . while father was in Chicago. . . one of the dissenters called at our home, engaged my mother in pleasant conversation and suggested that, as my father was away and there was to be another meeting, it was necessary that they have the records. It was all done in such a natural way that mother had no suspicion and gave them up.

On the twelfth of June, when many of the faithful were in Chicago for the annual meeting of the National Association, another meeting was called at which Mrs. Crosse led a violent attack against Mrs. Eddy. Failing to control the meeting completely, she and thirty-five other members resigned. Newer members were intimidated, for the dissenters included several of the most prominent Boston Scientists. One is reminded of Jesus' experience:

> From that time many of his disciples went back, and walked no more with him. Then said Jesus unto the twelve, Will ye also go away?

CHAPTER LIX

MEET IN CHICAGO

For Christ's and for humanity's sake, gather together...
Mary Baker Eddy

1888

THE April *Journal* had announced that it had "been recommended that the Annual Meeting of the National Christian Scientist Association be held in Chicago on the second Wednesday in June, instead of May." The May *Journal* urged all to attend, but it also carried "A Word from the Teacher" saying that she would not be there. She said further:

> I warn those who are halting or getting blind, neither to stop and rest on my personality for all they achieve, nor to abuse it;...

But this warning was not heeded by those who were "halting or getting blind."

Just before the June *Journal* went to press Mrs. Eddy inserted another appeal for unity of good in a call to her students:

> Christian Scientists: For Christ's and for humanity's sake, gather together, meet *en masse*, at the annual session of the National Christian Scientist Association. Be "of one mind, in one place," and God will pour you out a blessing such as you never before received. He who dwelleth in eternal light is bigger than the shadow, and will guard and guide His own.
>
> Let no consideration bend or outweigh your purpose to be in Chicago on June 13. Firm in your allegiance to the reign of universal harmony, go to its rescue. In God's hour the powers of earth and hell are proven powerless. The reeling ranks of pill-drivers, with poisons, nostrums, and knives, are impotent

when at war with the Omnipotent! Like Elijah, look up, and behold; "they that be for us are more than they that be against us."

Error is foaming, and it hisses at the "still small voice of Truth," but it can neither silence nor disarm God's voice. Spiritual wickedness is standing in high places; but, blind to its own fate, it will tumble into the bottomless pit.

Christians, and all *true* Scientists, marching under whatsoever ensign, come into our ranks! Again, I repeat: person is not in the question of Christian Science. Principle, instead of person, is next to our hearts, on our lips, and in our lives. Our watchwords are Truth and Love; and as we abide in these, they will abound in us, and we shall be one in heart, one in motive, purpose, pursuit. Abiding in these, not one of you can be separated from me, and the sweet sense of journeying on. "Doing unto others as ye would they should do unto you," conquers all opposition, surmounts all obstacles, and secures success. If you falter, or fail to fulfill this Golden Rule, though you should build to the heavens, you would still build on sand.

Is it a cross to give one week's time and expense to the Jubilee of Spirit? Then take this cross, and the crown will come with it. Sending forth currents of Truth, God's methods and means of healing, and so spreading the Gospel of Love, is in itself an eternity of joy that outweighs an hour. Add one more noble offering to the unity of Good, and so cement the bonds of Love.

Mrs. Eddy will herself attend the convention.

The regular meeting of the C.S.A. on the sixth of June was an open battle for supremacy,—to oust the Leader and control the college Association. Shortly after this chaotic meeting Mrs. Eddy, who had not been present, called a few trusted students to meet at her house on Commonwealth Avenue. She had sent William B. Johnson to Chicago to contact the faithful leaders there. A few days later, in the company of Calvin Frye, Captain and Mrs. Eastaman, and Dr. E. J. Foster, the Leader departed for the Convention.

Four years earlier Mrs. Eddy's companion on this same route had been Mrs. Sarah Crosse who was even now heading a movement against her teacher. In 1884 the Leader's arrival in Chicago had gone practically unnoticed, but the seeds of Truth she had sown in that city had flourished and were bearing fruit. Eight hundred delegates assembled at the First Methodist Church on Wednesday afternoon for the first business meeting. After opening exercises and election of officers:

> It was voted to waive further business till the following day: whereupon...Rev. George B. Day introduced the President to the audience. From the depths of her personal experience, and out [of] a heart yearning to bestow its priceless treasures upon those who listened, the revered Teacher, Mrs. Eddy, spoke. Those who understand her best said...that never before had she so sternly, yet tenderly, shown the demands upon her students. For them she rent the veil of personal sense; to them she showed the hidden workings of Animal Magnetism, in its latest and subtlest intrigues. She warned those who would pass through this wonderful epoch in the history of Christian Science to watch and pray without ceasing. This duty done, she turned, with that mighty power which she possesses to the God whom she obeys and reflects, and away, apart from a sense of sin or consciousness of individual ambition, pride, hope, or fear, she centered the gaze upon the Shekinah, and led willing ears to listen to the oracles of Good—and, listening, to obey.

Before the second business meeting the next afternoon, a public meeting had been planned at the Central Music Hall. The delegates were to be the speakers, and Mrs. Eddy had consented to attend and sit on the platform.

On the morning of June 14 nearly four thousand people filled the auditorium of the Central Music Hall. As Rev. Day was escorting Mrs. Eddy to the stage entrance she was seen to shake her head and protest with an outward sweep of her hand. He had just informed her that she had been advertised in all the papers as the speaker for the day. With no topic and no preparation, she hesitated at the door, then lifted her eyes for inspiration and guidance. As the Leader walked onto the stage, the whole vast audience rose to its feet and welcomed her.

CHAPTER LX

SCIENCE AND THE SENSES

*I have not spoken of myself; but the Father which sent me,
he gave me a commandment, what I should say, and what I
should speak.*

Jesus

June 14, 1888

AFTER being introduced the Leader recited the first verse
of the ninety-first Psalm. Her voice filled the auditorium
in the address which followed so that she was heard distinctly
in the remotest corner. A shorthand reporter in the audience
recorded her words as follows:

I will take for a topic, although my remarks must be wholly
impromptu, "Science and the Senses."

The National Christian Science Association brings us here
to minister to and to be ministered unto; to aid one another
and to help the whole human family; to quicken and extend
the interest already felt in advance of medicine; to watch
with great joy the growth and progress of Christian Science in
this miracle of the Occident, Chicago; to perpetuate and
strengthen our institutions and organizations, that we may
learn that in union there is strength; to build up through
God's right hand that pure and undefiled religion whose
Science demonstrates God and the perfectibility of man.

This "consummation devoutly to be wished," must begin
with individual growth. The lives of true reformers must at-
test the fitness of their mission. They must be true themselves
if they the truth would teach, they must overflow—for it
needs an overflow of heart—to give the lips full speech.

Science is absolute and is in its very nature revolutionary.

380

It upsets all that is not upright. It destroys all false evidence. It says to the five personal senses, "Having eyes ye see not, and ears ye hear not; neither can you understand." What did Science cost Galileo? An awful price: the temporary loss of his own self-respect. Even that at last succumbed to his fear—fear, that awful weapon in the hands of tyrants with which to subjugate their fellow-mortals.

In no one thing seems Jesus of Nazareth more divine than in his simple faith in the immortality of Truth. He said, "Heaven and earth shall pass away, but my words shall not pass away;" and they have not. In the mighty sweep of more than nineteen centuries these words still live and speak louder than ever. They are as the voice of one crying in the wilderness, "Make straight his path"—make holiness universal! This voice is being heard. The grandeur of its power, and the glory of its presence is being seen and felt as of old, healing the sick and casting out evils. This is Science.

Jesus articulated his words in a decaying language and committed them to the providence of God. He did it by the wayside, in humble homes—to idle listeners, itching ears and dull disciples. But he taught them the spirit and the word.

This labor of love was *not* lost; but it must be interpreted through Science. Why? Because the human conceptions are incapable of interpreting Science, that which must speak for its divine Principle, God. Hence Christian Science must interpret his words, and to that end some one must be raised up "to whom the arm of the Lord is revealed," to interpret wonderful words again, words of Truth, Love, Life, omnipotence, omnipresence and omniscience, Soul and Substance.

Who is sufficient for these things? Nothing but divine utterance can give human lips expression to interpret God. And as we kneel in our weakness before Him, His strength will be made perfect in our weakness. Shall we for a moment consider these words and their meaning, which in times past, in the present and in the future will and must still speak to the sinner, so long as there remains a single error for Truth to deny or destroy?

Science and the senses are at war and it is a revolutionary struggle. We have had two already on this continent and each has begun and finished on a metaphysical basis—a struggle for freedom and liberty of our being. In this struggle we are fettered and imprisoned by the *senses*, and we must make no compromise whatever.

Now, let us begin and look over our program of battle. First, are we right on the personality of God? The senses say No!, because they derive their idea of personality from finite form, limited mind, mortality and erring thought. Is that a basis on which we should form an idea of personality? Then listen to the demands of this Mind, the unerring and loving Father and Mother of us, and it said, "Be ye also perfect." There we have a commandment in the Fatherliness and Motherliness of our God to arrive at the fulness of the stature of man in Christ.

In this direction we must commence to-day upon the basis of Jesus Christ's demonstration; namely, he annulled the laws material, he walked over every demand, and placed them under his feet. He spoke in all that he said only the words of Truth. He rebuked sin, sickness and death, and demonstrated his ability to destroy them.

On that demonstration a premise and its conclusion rests— the antipodes of the evidence of the senses and their testimony. Now, he inaugurated this battle, not I. I should fight as having no leader did I not know that God with one makes a majority. Let us take his line of battle, and speak as having him alone as our authority.

What is God's personality? If we judge it from the personality defined by our lexicons, doctrines and theories, we should conclude an unlimited mind must have started from a limited body. Let us rather start with God, not as a man, but with man made in the image and likeness of God. Then our result in premise and conclusions must be a man like God, and not a God like man. Let us base our evidence upon the infinite to whom all things are possible.

God is individual beyond what we can conceive. In this individuality I recognize a loving Father, an ever-present Mind, that Love which is divine Love, not human love— divine pity, not human pity. That love is expressed in the divine sense in just what these senses would declare hate. If we do not accept the definition from Science instead of the senses, would it not follow that this individuality of God and His knowledge of us as His children would acquaint Him with sin, sickness and death? If it would, let us reason together and see if it is so.

We learn from the Scriptures, "The Lord, He is God, and there is none beside Him." Then what is there that would testify of sin, sickness and death? Is it God? That which is unlike Him cannot represent Him. Now we come to a tight place. How does God pity me and my infirmities if He knows nothing about them? I answer you in this simple simile of a woman's thought: If I can heal them twice as well if I know nothing about what they believe is the matter with them, hence my conclusion that we may consider the love and pity so much error; because it knows nothing *to* pity, and as love has an infinite source, it cannot bring itself into sympathy with error and so removes it.

If light brought with it a spot of darkness, it would retain that darkness, but it destroys that darkness. The "darkness comprehendeth it not," to be sure, but when light comes, it disappears.

That is God's pity and sympathy. Although we draw in a measure our sense of Deity from the personal sense, Divine Science alone must interpret God. If there is no sin, why one thought of it?

Many times we bow our heads in despair, saying, When shall I be like unto Him? There is so much on all sides to meet—pride to be eradicated, jealousies to be displaced, envy to be destroyed, evil speaking to be done away with, and all that is unlike Him to be utterly extinguished. Who shall deliver me from the body?

Thanks be to Him who giveth us the victory. Divine Science comes to us here. God who is the divine Principle speaks through His servant, "Though your sins be as scarlet, they shall be like wool." Did God say "sin?" No, human thought interpreted that. He said, All things are possible to God. Is not that a remedy for sin? It is only when you believe God is not All-in-all that you are a sinner. Whenever you come to hate sin and find no pleasure in it because you see its nonentity and nothingness, and your heart thirsteth after God, then you will see that "God is all and there is none beside Him." Truth is all, error is not. Love is universal and eternal.

I love every mortal who claims the right of Mind. I love them and will love them, and the more they hate me, the more I will love them. I will get the balance on my side, and the balance will be on the side of God.

What did Christ come to save if there is no sin? He came to save the sense of sin from its fallen sense. This sense of sin he did not entertain. He could not feel a sense of that which was absent from him. And yet he spoke as one having authority, "You are nothing!"

He cast out and trampled under foot the sense of human blindness, when he knew that Mind saw. He spat upon the ground and treated with contempt the clay, for the moment *that* was gone, the blindness was gone, and even the eye! Why? Because we see with Mind, and the man is right who says "I see!" when he understands.

Why did he come? I ask the question in Divine Science, in conflict with the senses. Remember Science and the senses are at war on every point we have tested; and they are more at war on this one—as to what God is and what He does—than others. Hence I say, What came God for to the senses? To our concept and demand he came as an infant, as a child, subject to the law and demands of infancy. Did Christ as God appear then in Science? Could he have done it? Can infinity become finite? Then this coming was a mortal concept. Before Abraham was he existed. He returned to that understanding of himself. He appeared only to our senses.

When you talk to a child you bring your conversation down to the child's apprehension. He came thus to us, not that he left his own state with the Father as the eternal high image and likeness of God, but to our concept he interpreted this wonderful God. I regard his coming with all the sacredness that I ever did when I kneeled at my mother's knee, but I have so changed in the growth of my life that I trust that the human concept of the creature has developed into a sense of the infinite. The senses say he came: Jesus said, "I am in heaven." The senses say, Mary must be purified after the birth of the highest idea of man, Life, Truth, and Love. Science says that the mother was purified to give birth to this

Jesus of Nazareth. The senses say this coming was to the human race. Science says that God is eternal Truth and Love, and Divine Science is the interpreter of this God.

There never was a coming or a going. It is our blindness that obscures our sense of his presence. Remove that blindness and he comes to us. He is ever here. This is the fact in Science and cannot be changed by our human reasoning on the evidence of the personal senses. I speak briefly on this subject for I have not the time.

Are sin, sickness and death facts to which our Lord and Master ministered as facts? No, Jesus came from God to manifest the action of Truth, Life and Love. These are declaratory of God, and therefore he was no authority for that which he came to destroy. It would be self-contradictory. It would be a kingdom divided against itself. Therefore, he stands firm in the conviction of their nothingness and proves that nothingness by their destruction. God destroys all that seems unlike Him.

Now it seems to me that the summary of these remarks rests upon this basis: What is the advantage of this contradiction of the senses? or what is the advantage of retaining the evidences of the senses by which to arrive at God? Let me illustrate: Here is a friend in great grief and you go to this friend, grieving yourself over this same sorrow. You find yourself inadequate to remove that grief. You will only assist it and add sorrow to sorrow. You declare it is sympathy on your part, and kind. It is a mistaken kindness. Shall not a tree be known by its fruits? If another comes without that sorrow and says there is really no occasion for it, that one will bring relief.

Now here are the words of God. Science says, Come without sin, sickness and death in your thoughts with all holiness. Do not come in His name without His spirit. Come with the character of divine Love and the power of Spirit that casts out all that is unlike it, and then go back, if you please, from the senses that contradict Science and say, "Like cures like."

I dislike that in homeopathy but I like the attenuation of drugs, for it gives more power to mind and less to matter.

If you tell the truth to error, whether it be sin, sickness or death, you have brought that which will destroy it, because truth is a divine verity.

Then say to me, if you will, has not a patentee a right to place his invention where it can best be seen? Take the words of our Master, "Judge me not but by my fruits." Whoever is imbued with the principles of Christian Science is alone, more alone than the north star in this world, because that is distinct, if it is distant; it is clear, if it seems cold. But let us come in contact with the evidence of the personal senses and lay [the axe] at the root of the tree and cut down all that you love, and you will not handle that individual as kindly as the North Star. They must be alone: they cannot be understood.

Remember the stranger within your gates, and that stranger will be better able to execute his divine mission in meeting your thought and ministering to it, healing your sick and speaking words of Truth that will destroy error.

Christian Scientists have a history and if I were to be allowed a poor parody on the beautiful verse of Tennyson it would read thus:

> Traitors to right of them,
> M.D.'s to left of them,
> Priestcraft in front of them,
>   Volleyed and thundered!
> Into the jaws of hate,
> Out through the door of Love,
> On, to the blest above,
>   Marched the one hundred.

CAPTAIN JOSEPH S. EASTAMAN

CHAPTER LXI

AFTERMATH

The multitude throng thee and press thee.

Luke

How long wilt thou go about, O thou backsliding daughter?
for the Lord hath created a new thing in the earth...

Jeremiah

June 14, 1888

MRS. Eddy had been totally unprepared to speak to the surprisingly large audience at Central Music Hall, but *no one* was prepared for that which transpired when she finished. A newspaper account reads:

> The scenes that followed when she had ceased speaking will long be remembered by those who witnessed them. The people were in the presence of the woman whose book had healed them, and they knew it. Up they came in crowds to her side, begging for one hand clasp, one look, one memorial from her, whose name was a power and a sacred thing in their homes. Those whom she had never seen before—invalids raised up by her book, Science and Health,—attempted to hurriedly tell the wonderful story.
>
> A mother who failed to get near her, held high her babe, to look on their helper. Others touched the dress of their bene-factor, not so much as asking for more.
>
> An aged woman trembling with palsy, lifted her shaking hands at Mrs. Eddy's feet, crying, "Help, help!" and the cry was answered. Many such people were known to go away healed. Strong men turned aside to hide their tears, as the

people thronged about Mrs. Eddy with blessings and thanks.

Meekly, and almost silently, she received all this homage from the multitude, until she was led away from the place, the throng blocking her passage from the door to the carriage.

A reception at the Palmer House where Mrs. Eddy was staying had been planned for the evening. As the hour approached, the parlors, corridors, and stairways were crowded with the wealthy and fashionable alongside the humblest workingmen. When Mrs. Eddy came from her private suite to the drawing-room, the situation was almost a repetition of the morning scene.

Some who were present were aware that Mary Plunkett quickly got in line to shake the Leader's hand that her students might construe this as an endorsement. As the line moved forward, Mrs. Eddy suddenly wheeled about, ignoring Mrs. Plunkett completely, passing her by to shake hands with the next person.

The multitude thronged her, so she greeted her followers for only a short time. Calvin Frye and, most likely, Dr. Foster and Captain Eastaman came to her rescue and helped her to withdraw by a side door. The newspapers hailed her public appearances as a great triumph, but Mrs. Eddy said to those nearest her that this was not the way to further Christian Science.

There was no criticism of the affair, however, in her article "To Loyal Christian Scientists" in the July *Journal*. There was praise for the National Association and much that pointed to the treachery in the college Association in Boston:

> Pen can never portray the satisfaction that you afforded me at the grand meeting in Chicago of the National Christian Scientist Association. . . .
>
> The reception in the spacious rooms of the Palmer House, was like all else, purely Western in its cordiality and largeness. . . .
>
> In Christian Science the midnight hour will always be the bridal hour, until "no night is there." . . .
>
> Out of the gloom comes the glory of our Lord, and His divine Love is seen in affliction. When a false sense suffers, the truer sense comes out, and the bridegroom appears. We

are then wedded to a purer, higher affection and ideal.

I would that all my students had their lamps trimmed and burning at the noon of night, that not one of them was borrowing oil, and seeking light from matter instead of Spirit, or at work erroneously, thus shutting out spiritual light. Error giveth no light, and it closes the door on Truth. ...

Falsehood is on the wings of the winds,...Error is walking to and fro in the earth, trying to be heard above Truth. ...Whosoever proclaims Truth loudest becomes the mark for error's shaft. The archers aim at Truth's mouthpiece...

The stake and scaffold have never silenced the messages of the Most High. Then can the present mode of attempting this—namely, by slanderous falsehoods, and a secret mind-method, through which to effect the purposes of envy and malice—silence Truth? Never. ...

No evidence before the material senses can close my eyes to the Scientific proof that God, Good, is supreme. Though clouds are round about Him, the divine justice and judgment are enthroned. Love is especially near in times of hate, and never so near as when one can be just amid lawlessness, and render good for evil. ...

Error will hate more as it realizes more the presence of its tormentor. I shall fulfil my mission, fight the good fight, and keep the faith.

There is great joy in this consciousness, that throughout my labors, and in my history as connected with the cause of Christian Science, it can be proven that I have never given occasion for a single censure, when my motives and acts are understood and seen as my Father seeth them. ...

Those only who are tried in the furnace reflect the image of their Father. ...

For two years I have been gradually withdrawing from active membership in the Christian Scientist Association. This has developed higher energies on the part of true followers, and led to some startling departures on the other hand. "Offences must come, but woe to him through whom they come."

Mrs. Eddy's yearning for unity had brought much error to the surface,—error which was still foaming and frothing in the

C.S.A. back in Boston. She had called for unity in the National Association, and to material sense that call was answered. But material sense makes no progress. All progress is spiritual, and the Leader was alone meeting the demands of the hour.

Little did the students understand her words about "the midnight hour" and being "tried in the furnace." The Leader *alone* met the trials and demands, and pioneered the way of spiritual (the only true) progress while her students were rejoicing in the false sense of triumph. All Chicago was hailing this triumph unaware of the real issue. At a later date Mrs. Eddy said to a student, Miss Robertson:

> Do you know when I had most evil in my life to meet? It was when I spoke in Chicago on *Science and the Senses*. The newspapers said it was a triumph for the Cause. For me it was a trial and tribulation. I, and I alone, had to carry the whole burden. All the Christian Scientists were happy, but I fought with animal magnetism all night after that talk.

One spiritually sensitive student had a glimpse of the import of Mrs. Eddy's trial and triumph on the night of June 14. Janet Colman had a vision just before retiring. She wrote in her reminiscences:

> That night as I was getting into bed, had not laid down, when at the foot of the bed I saw Jesus' form rise up in white, then our Leader in white rose up beside Him. She put out her arms and embraced Him. He melted into her, then she rose up beyond my gaze. ... [After telling Mrs. Eddy] she told me not to speak of it to any one, not even to her students; it was too far beyond the age at that time. When *Christ and Christmas* came out, the picture CHRISTIAN UNITY expressed more what I saw at Chicago. God has been so good to me to let me see our Leader in her right light.

Though the age was not prepared for it, June 14, 1888 saw the fulfilment of the prophecy of Jeremiah, "the Lord hath created a new thing in the earth, A woman shall compass a man."

CHRISTIAN UNITY
The ninth picture in *Christ and Christmas.*

INDEX

221, 231, 239

Barbour, Rev. Charles, 272

Barry, George W., 113, 120,
128, 134-136, 142, 145,
153-155, 160, 168, 173-174,
176-177, 179, 202

Bartlett, John H., 25, 27

Bartlett, Julia S., 210-211,
217-219, 226, 235, 237,
240, 242, 244, 248,
251-252, 255, 265-267,
273-275, 285, 298-305,
314-317

Bell, Mrs. 376

Ben (family dog), 5

Berry, Gov., 48, 59

Billings, Mary Baker
Glover, 208

Blackman, Miss C. Lulu,
324-325

Blavatsky, Helen, 311

Blish, Prof. George, 305

Brown, Miss Ellen, 294, 324,
341, 350, 356

Brown, George T., 313

Brown, Miss Lucretia, 168,
170, 172, 179-181

Brown, W.F. and Co., 182

Buswell, Arthur True,
198-199, 201-203, 225, 240,
250-251, 264-265, 268, 273,
283, 285, 298-299, 304, 330

Butler, Gen. Benjamin F.,
47

Byrd, Admiral Richard E.,
77

Carpenter, Dr., 258, 311

Carter, Mr., 371

Carter, Mrs. Mary Esther,
93

Chadwell, Mrs., 126

Chard, Mrs. Sarah G., 42

Charles, Mr. George B., 287,
293

Cheney, Miss Florence, 145

Cheney, Mahala Sanborn,
29

Cheney, Russell, 39-40, 48

Chicago, 293, 295-297, 380,
390

Chickering Hall, 330, 336,
365, 370

Choate, Clara, 175-176, 178,
194, 198, 200-201, 208-209,
215, 220, 228, 239,
245-246, 248-249, 256,
265-268, 272, 285, 293-295,
297, 302, 364

Choate, George, 178,
208-209, 249, 272, 278, 364

Choate, Warren, 268

Christ and Christmas, 8, 12

Christian Science Journal,
283, 289-290, 295, 299

Christian Science
Publishing Company, 153

Christian Scientist
Association, 157-158, 178,
197-198, 213, 217, 231, 239-
240, 253, 272, 279, 285, 334,
338, 368, 374-375, 378,
389-390

Clark, Mrs., 82, 85-86,
128-129

Clark, Mrs. Ellen, 218, 220

Clark, George, 85-86, 129

Clement, Sarah, 32-33

Collier, George, 195-196

Colman, Janet, 273, 279,
285, 313, 353-354, 390

Conwell, Col. Russell, 190,

BIBLIOGRAPHY: *Author Title Publisher Copyright #vol # pages Edition*

Armstrong, Joseph The Mother Church Christian Science Publishing Society 1897 103 second

Baker, Alfred E., M.D., C.S.D. Instruction in Metaphysics Carpenter, Gilbert C., Jr., C.S.B. 45 first

Bancroft, Samuel Putnam Mrs. Eddy As I Knew Her In 1870 Longyear Foundation 1923 127 first

Bates, Edward P. Reminiscences... Construction of The Mother Church ... The Gethsemane Foundation, St. Maries, Idaho pub.-1989 40 second

Bates, Ernest Sutherland, P.H.D. & John V. Dittemore Mary Baker Eddy, The Truth and the Tradition Alfred A. Knopf 1932 512 first

Beals, Ann Crisis in the Christian Science Church Ann Beals, P.O. Box 801143, Santa Clarita, California 91380 1978 145 first

Beasley, Norman, The Continuing SPIRIT, Duell, Sloan&Pierce, N.Y.1956 403 1st

Beasley, Norman The Cross and The Crown Duell, Sloan & Pierce, N.Y. and Little, Brown & Co., Boston 1952 664 first

Beasley, Norman , (© by Meredith Publishing Co.) Mary Baker Eddy Duell, Sloan & Pierce, N.Y. 1963 371 first

Braden, Charles S. Christian Science Today; Power, Policy, Practice Southern Methodist University Press, Dallas 1958 SMU 432 first

Brisbane, Arthur Mary B. G. Eddy, The Ball Publishing Co., Boston 1908 64 first

Brisbane, Arthur What Mrs. Eddy Said to Arthur Brisbane M. E. Paige, Publisher, 33 W. 42nd St., NewYork 1930 64

Brosang, Ernest J. , A Christian Science Library, Ernest J. Brosang 1990 214 first

Byrum, E. E. Miracles and Healing Gospel Trumpet Company 1919 302 first

Caldwell, Sallie Bowman Mary Baker Eddy Christian Science Publishing Society 1936, 1942 20 first

Canham, Erwin D. The Christian Science Monitor: To injure no man, but to bless all mankind. The Newcomen Society in North America, 1954 28 first

Carpenter, Gilbert C., C.S.B., & GCC, Jr., C.S.B. Mary Baker Eddy, Her Spiritual Footsteps Carpenter, Gilbert C., Jr., C.S.B. 1934 432 first

Carpenter, Gilbert C., Jr., C.S.B. On the First Evening in February of 1866 ...The Carpenter Foundation 2 first

Carpenter, Gilbert C., Jr., C.S.B., COP-Rhode Island Questions and Answers on Christian Science, Newport County Sentinel, Tiverton, R.I. 1932 128 first

Carpenter, Gilbert Congdon, C.S.B., G. C. C., Jr., C.S.B. Poems of Spiritual Thought Gilbert C. Carpenter, Jr., C.S.B. 1933 30 first

Carpenter, Jr., Gilbert C., C.S.B. 500 Watching Points for advancing students of Christian Science Gilbert C. Carpenter, Jr., C.S.B. 1942 317 first

Carpenter, Jr., Gilbert C., C.S.B. Address on Christian Science The Newport County Sentinel, Tiverton, Rhode Island 1932 32 first

Chanfrau, Henrietta Remin. of Mary Baker Eddy The Gethsemane Found., St. Maries, Idaho 1994 12, second

Christian Science Publishing Society Editorial Comments on the Life and Work of Mary Baker Eddy CSPS 1911 132 first

Christian Science Publishing Society Landmarks from Bow to Boston Christian Science Publishing Society 1948 N.P. fourth+

Christian Science Publishing Society Mary Baker Eddy Mentioned Them Christian Science Publishing Society 1961 239 first

Christian Science Publishing Society Permanancy of The Mother Church and Its Manual-Revised Edition CSPS 1954 28 Revised

Christian Science Publishing Society   We Knew Mary Baker Eddy-Volume I
Christian Science Publishing Society   1943 1/4 87 first

Christian Science Publishing Society   We Knew Mary Baker Eddy-Volume II
Christian Science Publishing Society   1950 2/4 75 first

Christian Science Publishing Society   We Knew Mary Baker Eddy-Volume III
Christian Science Publishing Society   1953 3/4 96 first

Christian Science Publishing Society   We Knew Mary Baker Eddy-Volume IV
Christian Science Publishing Society   1972 4/4 110 first

Christian Science Publishing Society - 12 authors Mary Baker Eddy, A centennial
appreciation Christian Science Publishing Society 1965 115 first

Compilation from Ladies Home Jour. & C.S. Monitor America's Twelve Great
Women Leaders during the Last ... Associated Authors Service, 222 West Adams
St., Chicago, IL 1933 55 Century of Prog.

Covington, Benjamin N. A Clarion Call Benjamin N. Covington, Atlanta, Georgia
1985 53 first

d'Humy, Fernand E. Mary Baker Eddy Fulills Prophecy Library Publishers, New
York 1953 217 first

d'Humy, Fernand E. Mary Baker Eddy, in a new light Library Publishers, New
York 1952 181 first

Dakin, Edwin Franden MRS. EDDY, The Biography of a Virginal Mind Charles
Scribner's Sons, N.Y., London 1929 553 first

Dickey, Adam H., C.S.D. Memoirs of Mary Baker Eddy, Lillian S. Dickey, C.S.B.,
Brookline, Mass. 1927 141 first

Eddy, Mary Baker, Collectanea of Items by and about Mary Baker Eddy Carpenter,
Gilbert C., Jr., C.S.B. 193 248 first

Eddy, Mary Baker Essays on Christian Science ascribed to Mary Baker Eddy
Carpenter, Gilbert C., Jr. C.S.B.   158 first

Eddy, Mary Baker First Church of Christ, Scientist and Miscellany Allison V.
Stewart, Boston, Mass. 1913 364

Eddy, Mary Baker Footprints Fadeless Joseph Armstrong, 95 Falmouth St. (orig.),
GCC, Jr. 1902 67 First

Eddy, Mary Baker Fragments Gathered From Unpublished Items Gilbert C.
Carpenter, Jr., C.S.B. 1947 208 first

Eddy, Mary Baker Instruction in Metaphysics, Gilbert C. Carpenter, Jr., C.S.B. 45

Eddy, Mary Baker Items by and about Mary Baker Eddy culled from the press
Carpenter, Gilbert C., Jr. C.S.B. 1961   116+40 first

Eddy, Mary Baker Notes on the Course in Divinity recorded by Lida Fitzpatrick,
1903,4,7 Carpenter, Gilbert C., Jr. C.S.B. 60 second

Eddy, Mary Baker, Poems, Mary Baker Eddy (priv. printed) 1910 79 Presentation

Eddy, Mary Baker Repaid Pages, Mary Baker Eddy, Concord, N.H. , 1896 First

Eddy, Mary Baker Retrospection and Introspection Trustees under the Will of Mary
Baker Eddy 1891, 1892 95

Eddy, Mary Baker Rudimental Divine Science/No and Yes Trustees under the Will
of Mary Baker Eddy 1891, 1908   46

Eddy, Mary Baker Science and Health 124th

Eddy, Mary Baker, Science and Health with Key to the Scriptures, Eric William
Winston Taylor 1906 700

Eddy, Mary Baker Science and Health with Key to the Scriptures, Allison V.
Stewart, Falmouth and St. Paul Streets, Boston, Mass. 1875, 1906 700 1910

Eddy, Mary Baker Stetson Letters Ann Beals, The Bookmark

Eddy, Mary Baker, Unity of Good, Tstees of Will of Mary Baker Eddy 1908 64

Eddy, Mary Baker   Visions of Mary Baker Eddy as recorded by her secretary, Calvin A. Frye, Carpenter, Gilbert C., Jr., C.S.B. 1935 89 second

Eddy, Mary Baker   What is Nearest and Dearest to My Heart The Harmony Shop, 38 West St., Boston 1907 1 first

Eddy, Mary Baker (many authors about MBE) Misc. Documents relating to Christian Science & Mary Baker Eddy, Carpenter, Gilbert C., Jr. C.S.B. 232 first

Eddy, Mary Baker as prepared by Alfred E. Baker, Notes on Metaphysical Obstetrics, Obstetrics Class of June, 1900, Carpenter, G. C., Jr., C.S.B. 1930 41 first

Eddy, Mary Baker G. Historical Sketch of Metaphysical Healing. Eddy, Mary Baker G. 1885 1 21 first

Eddy, Mary Baker G., Mind-Healing: Historical Sketch. Eddy, Mary Baker G. 1886 1 24 first

Eddy, Mary Baker G. Miscellaneous Writings 1883-1896 Trustees under the Will of Mary Baker Eddy 1896 471

Eddy, Mary Baker G. Retrospection and Introspection Joseph Armstrong, 250, Huntington Ave., Boston, Mass., 1907 1891, 1892 130

Eddy, Mary Baker G. Rudimental Divine Science Joseph Armstrong, CSD, 95 Falmouth St., Boston, Mass., 1897 1891 35 tenth

Eddy, Mary Baker with commentary by GCC, Sr., & Jr. Mary Baker Eddy, Her Spiritual Precepts, volumes I-V Gilbert C. Carpenter, C.S.B., & Gilbert C. Carpenter, Jr., C.S.B. 1942 5 np first

Eddy, Mary Baker, compiled by G. C. Carpenter, Jr. Fragments Gathered from Unpub. Items ascribed to Mrs. Eddy, Carpenter, G. C., Jr., C.S.B. 1947 208 first

Eddy, Mary Baker, compiled by G. C. Carpenter, Jr. Watches • Prayers • Arguments Carpenter, Gilbert C., Jr., C.S.B. 1950 114 final

Eddy, Mary Baker-©James Neal & Thomas Hatten Church Manual of The First Church of Christ, Scientist, in Boston, MA Christian Science Publishing Society, 95 Falmouth St., Boston, Mass. 1897 76

Eddy, Rev. Mary Baker, Christ and Christmas, Mary Baker Eddy 1897 53 third

Eddy, Rev. Mary Baker, Pulpit and Press Mary Baker Eddy 1895 131 first

Ernest Sutherland Bates, Mrs. Eddy's Right-Hand Man, Harper & Bros 1931 162 12

F. A. Moore, ed. Gems for You William H. Fisk, Manchester, NH 1850 312 first

F. E. H. The Latter Days with Evidence from The Great Pyramid London: Robert Banks & Son, Racquet Court, Fleet Street, E.C. 1895 40 first

Fisher, H. A. L. Our New Religion, Jonathan Cape & Harrison Smith, New York 1930 201 first

Flower, B. O. Christian Science as a Religious Belief and a Therapeutic Agent 20th Century Company 1909 158 first

Fosbery, Arthur F., C.S. Healings Done by Mrs. Eddy, Arthur F. Fosbury, C.S.

Frye, Calvin A. Diary Calvin A. Frye n/a n.p. photost

Gilman, James F. Recollections of Mary Baker Eddy Gilbert C. Carpenter, Jr., C.S.B. 1937? 92 second

Glover, Mary Baker, Science and Health, Christian Scientist Pub. Co. 1875 456 first

Glover, Mary Baker   Science and Health Asa G. Eddy, Lynn, No. 8 Broad Street 1876 2nd 167 second

Glover, Mary Baker   Science and Health 19th

Glover, Mary Baker The Science of Man by which the sick are healed embracing Q's & A's . . . Mary Baker Glover 1870 22 second

Glover, Mary Baker (Mary Baker Eddy) Science and Health Winifred W. Gatling, Mizpah, Jaffa Road, Jerusalem, Israel 1874   456 first

Grekel, Doris Principle and Practice, Science in Education, 1980 353 first
Grekel, Doris The Individual Christian Scientist-vol. 4, no. 4 661 first
Hanna, Septimus J. Christian Science History CSPS 1899 44 first
Hanna, Septimus J. The Christian Science Case Ernest J. Brosang, 4 Glen Rd.,
    Bound Brook, NJ (republished) 21
Hanna, Septimus J.-orig. published by CSPS Healing through Christian Science.
    Discourses & Editorials, Ernest J. Brosang, Bound Brook, NJ 1902 36
Harper's Magazine vol. 162, 2/31
Hartsook, Andrew Christian Science after 1910 Andrew Hartsook, Zanesville, Ohio
    1993 215 first
Hay, Ella H. A Child's Life of Mary Baker Eddy Christian Science Publishing
    Society, One Norway Street, Boston, Mass. 1942 120
Henry, Edward L. The Birthplace of Mary Baker Eddy-Bow, New Hampshire The
    Woodbury E. Hunt Company, Concord, New Hampshire 1914 np(12) first
Henty, Doris Dufour, C.S. Addresses and Other Writings on Christian Science,
    Mulberry Press, Box 461, Carmel, Calif. 93921 1990 346 first
Houpt, Charles Theodore Bliss Knapp, Christian Scientist Charles Theodore Houpt
    1976, 1979 417 first
Hufford, Kenneth Mary Baker Eddy: The Stoughton Years Longyear Foundation,
    120 Seaver St., Brookline, MA 1963 41+2 first
Irving C. Tomlinson, M.A., C.S.B. Twelve Years with Mary Baker Eddy;
    Recollections and Experiences CSPS, Boston, Mass., USA 1945 227
Johnson, William Lyman From Hawthorne Hall The Homewood Press,
    (Dorchester) Boston, Mass. 1922 421
Johnson, William Lyman The History of the Christian Science Movement The Zion
    Research Foundation 1926 2 958 first
Johnston, Julia Michael Mary Baker Eddy: Her mission and Triumph Christian
    Science Publishing Society 1946, 1974 195 ?
Jones, Elizabeth Earl Reminiscences of Mary Baker Eddy Elizabeth Earl Jones
Joseph S. Robinson Waymarks . . in the life of Mary Baker Eddy The Pond-Ekberg
    Company, Springfield, Mass. 1942 108 LimitedDe Luxe
Kathrens, R. D., (compiler) Sidelights on Mary Baker Eddy-Glover-Science Church
    Trustees Controversy Kathrens, R. D. 1907 88 first
Keene, John Henry Christian Science and its Enemies. W. E. C. Harrison & Sons,
    Baltimore 1902 49 first
Kimball, Edward A. Lectures and Articles on Christian Science Edna Kimball
    Wait, Chesterton, Indiana 1921 486 first
Kimball, Edward A.-edited by Frank Baker Smith, Teaching and Addresses of
    Edward A. Kimball, C.S.D., Metaphysical Science Assoc., Los Angeles, CA 1917
    382
Knapp, Bliss Ira Oscar Knapp and Flavia Stickney Knapp: A Biographical Sketch
    Plimpton Press 1925
Knapp, Bliss The Destiny of The Mother Church Bliss Knapp 1947 234 first
Kratzer, Rev. G.A., Dominion Within, Kratzer, Rev. G.A. 1913 224 first
Kratzer, Rev. G.A. Revelation Interpreted The Central Christian Science Institute,
    Chicago 1915 396 first
Lambert, Rev. L. A. Christian Science • Before the Bar of Reason Christian Press
    Association Publishing Company 1908 212
Longyear, Mary Beecher The Genealogy and Life of Asa Gilbert Eddy Mary
    Beecher Longyear 1922 140 first

Longyear, Mary Beecher The History of a House • Its Founder, Family and Guests
The Zion Research Foundation, Brookline, Mass. 1925 69 first

Lord, Myra B. Mary Baker Eddy Davis & Bond, Boston 1918 62 first

Meehan, Michael Mrs. Eddy and the Late Suit in Equity Meehan, Michael 1908
371 Authorized

Milmine, Georgine Mary Baker G. Eddy; The story of her life & the history of C.S.,
S. S. McClure Co. (and originalholder of copyright) 1906 4

Milmine, Georgine , The Life of Mary Baker G. Eddy and The History of Christian
Science, Doubleday, Page & Company, New York 1907 495 first

Norton, Carol The Christian Science Church; Its Organization and Polity Christian
Science Publishing Society 1904 38 first

Norton, Carol, NCSA copyright holder The New World Christian Science
Publishing Society 1894 np second

Norwood, Edward Everett Remin. of Mary Baker Eddy, Edward Everett Norwood

Nowell, Ames, C.S.B., D.D., Th.D. Mary Baker Eddy, Her Revelation of Divine
Egoism Veritas Institute, Inc., New York 1963, 1965 264 first

Oakes, Richard F., C.S., Discerning the Rights of Man, Richard F. Oakes, 1971 42

Oakes, Richard, C.S., compiler Divinity Course and General Collectanea of Items
By & About MBE Rare Book Company, 286 second

Oakes, Richard, C.S., compiler Essays and other Footprints, Rare Book Co. 280

Oakes, Richard, C.S., compiler Mary Baker Eddy's Lessons of The Seventh Day
Christian Science Research Library, Christian Science Found., 1989 377

Oakes, Richard, C.S., compiler, Mary Baker Eddy's Published Writings-(other than
Prose) 1895-1910, Christian Science Research Library, C.S. Found. 1987 535

Oakes, Richard, C.S., compiler Mary Baker Eddy's Six Days of Revelation Christian
Science Research Library 1981 561

Oakes, Richard, C.S., compiler The Story of The Chicago Addresses of Mary Baker
Eddy Richard Oakes 1988 70 Revised

Orcutt, William Dana Mary Baker Eddy and her books Christian Science
Publishing Society 1950 198 first

Orgain, Alice Distinguishing Characteristics of MBE's Progressive Revisions of S &
H, Rare Book Company, 99 Nassau Street, New York, NY 1933 80

Orgain, Alice Story of the Christian Science Manual • Proving its immortality Rare
Book Company 1934 331 first

Orgain, Alice L. The Detached Branch, The Olive Branch of Peace The Detached
Branch, 1931 503 first

Orgain, Alice L., A Loyal Christian Scientist, As It Is, A. L. Orgain, 1929 949 first

Peel, Robert Mary Baker Eddy, The Years of Authority, 1892-1910 Holt, Rhinehart
and Winston of Canada 1977 3/3 528 first

Peel, Robert Mary Baker Eddy, The Years of Discovery, 1821-1875 Holt,
Rhinehart and Winston of Canada 1966 1/3 370 first

Peel, Robert Mary Baker Eddy: The Years of Trial, 1876-1891 Holt, Rhinehart and
Winston of Canada 1971 2/3 391 first

Powell, Lyman P. Mary Baker Eddy: A Life Size Portrait The MacMillan
Company, New York, 1930 1930 364 first

Quimby, Phineas P./ ed. by Horatio W. Dresser The Quimby Manuscripts Thomas
Y. Crowell Company, New York 1921 462 first

Ramsay, E. Mary Christian Science and its Discoverer Christian Science
Publishing Society 1923, 1935cs 118 second

Richard Southall Grant Landmarks for Christian Scientists from Bow to Boston
Rand Avery Co., Boston, Mass. 1937 174 third

Salchow, John G. Souvenir Album of the Home of Rev. Mary Baker Eddy, Chestnut Hill,... John G. Salchow 1911 np first

Sargent, Laura and Victoria Reminiscences of Mary Baker Eddy

Sass, Karin with illustrations by Christa Kieffer Mary Baker Eddy: A Special Friend Christian Science Publishing Society 1983 np second

Seal, Frances Thurber Christian Science in Germany Longyear Historical Society, 120 Seaver St., Brookline, MA 02146 1931 83 third

Searle, George M. The Truth about Christian Science Paulist Press, NY 1916 305

Shannon, Clara M. Sainsbury, C.S.D. Golden Memories The Gethsemane Foundation, St. Maries, Idaho pub.-1990 36 second

Shannon, Clara M. Sainsbury, C.S.D. In the Service of Mary Baker Eddy-Remin. by Clara M. Shannon, Longyear Foundation, Brookline, Mass. 1958

Simonsen, Reverend Severin E. From The Methodist Pulpit into Christian Science & How I Demonstrated ... M. Simonsen, Fair Oaks, CA 1928 294 ninth

Smaus, Jewel Spangler Mary Baker Eddy, The Golden Days Christian Science Publishing Society 1966 CSPS 193 first

Smillie, Paul R. Loving Our Leader The Gethsemane Foundation, St. Maries, Idaho 1988 52 first

Smillie, Paul R. Mary Baker Eddy: The Prophetic and Historical Perspective-Vol. I The Gethsemane Foundation, St. Maries, Idaho 1979 333 second

Smillie, Paul R. Our Leader's Demonstration of Generic Man The Gethsemane Foundation, St. Maries, Idaho 1987 12 first

Smith, Clifford P. Historical and Biographical Papers; First Series Christian Science Publishing Society 1934 1/2 103 first

Smith, Clifford P. Historical and Biographical Papers; Second Series Christian Science Publishing Society 1934 268

Smith, Judge Clifford P. Christian Science and Legislation Christian Science Publishing Society 1905,1909 128 second

Smith, Judge Clifford P. Christian Science: Its Legal Status, A Defence of Human Rights, Christian Science Publishing Society 1914 127 first

Smith, Judge Clifford P. Historical and Biographical Papers Christian Science Publishing Society 1934 127 first

Smith, Karl N., and Walter H. Wilson Support for the Christian Science Board of Directors Plainfield Community Church, Plainfield, NJ 1945 np.

Smith, Louise A. Mary Baker Eddy: Discoverer and Founder of Christian Science, Christian Science Publishing Society 1990 198 20th century

Spencer, Ralph B. The Overwhelming Evidence Concerning Spiritual Healings thru MBE Ralph B. Spencer, Seekonk, Mass. 02771 1963, 1976 68 Fourth

Springer, Fleta Campbell According to the Flesh; a biography of Mary Baker Eddy Coward-McCann, Inc., New York 1930 CMcC 497 first

Stetson, Augusta E., C.S.D. Reminiscences, Sermons and Correspondence / 1884-1913 G. P. Putnam's Sons, New York and London 1913 1200 first

Stetson, Augusta E., C.S.D., Sermons Which Spiritually Interpret the Scriptures and Other Writings G. P. Putnam's Sons, New York and London 1924 1277 first

Stewart, Myrtle The 1910 Coup Stewart, Myrtle 1972 58 first

Still, M. Adelaide, Reminiscences of Mary Baker Eddy M. Adelaide Still

Studdert Kennedy, Hugh A. (Anketell) Mrs. Eddy As I Knew Her The Farallon Press, 58 Sutter St., San Francisco, CA 1931 118

Studdert Kennedy, Hugh A. (Anketell) Christian Science and Organized Religion The Farallon Press 1930 335 first

Studdert Kennedy, Hugh A. (Anketell) Mrs. Eddy The Farallon Press, San Francisco 1947 507 first

Swain, Richard L. The Real Key to Christian Science Fleming H. Revell Company 1917 95 fifth

Tomlinson, Rev. Irving C. , M.A., C.S.B. Twelve Years with Mary Baker Eddy: Recollections and Experiences ©1945,1966,renewed 1973, CSPS 227 first

Twain, Mark Christian Science with notes containing corrections to date Harper & Brothers Publishers, New York & London 1899 362

Walter, William W., The Unfoldment William W. Walter 1921 206 first

Wilbur, Sibyl, Cradled Obscurity or The Finding of the Christ,The Bookmark 11

Wilbur, Sibyl The Life of Mary Baker Eddy Christian Science Publishing Society 1907 384 first

Williamson, Margaret The Mother Church Extension Christian Science Publishing Society 1939, 1968 2/2 109

Wright, Helen Mary Baker Eddy: God's Great Scientist-Volume I Helen Wright 1984 1/3 255 first

Wright, Helen Mary Baker Eddy: God's Great Scientist-Volume II Helen Wright 1984 2/3 133 first

Wright, Helen Mary Baker Eddy: God's Great Scientist-Volume III Helen Wright 1987 3/3 265 first

Wright, Helen M. If Mary Baker Eddy's Manual were Obeyed-Enlarged Edition Helen Wright 1986 231 Second, enlarged

Wright, Helen M. Mary Baker Eddy Reveals Your Divinity Hearthstone Book 1991 271 first

Wright, Helen M., Humanity's Divinity, HM Wright Publishing 1994 331 first

Wright, Helen M. Made Whole Through Our Marriage To God HM Wright Publishing 1996 346 first

Wright, Helen M. Mary Baker Eddy's Church Manual and Church Universal Triumphant Helen Wright 1981 319 first

Young, Alan MBE-Her Pleasant View and Infinite Vision The Bookmark 9

To Obtain Additional Books
In this Trilogy by Doris Grekel

Please contact your local bookstore for the following titles:

The Discovery of the Science of Man (Volume I)
The Life of Mary Baker Eddy (1821-1888) 412pp
ISBN: 1-893107-23-X   Paperback $16.95

The Founding of Christian Science (Volume II)
The Life of Mary Baker Eddy (1888-1900) 538pp
ISBN: 1-893107-24-8   Paperback $18.95

The Forever Leader (Volume III)
The Life of Mary Baker Eddy (1901-1910) 673pp
ISBN: 0-9645803-8-1   Paperback $22.95

If your local bookstore does not have them in stock, you can order these titles from your bookstore through "Books in Print" or you may contact the publisher, Healing Unlimited, at (800) 962-1464.